AF361566

Praise for *The Fall of Kentucky's Rock*

"Western Kentucky, once the 'Gibraltar of Democracy,' is one of the most crimson corners of Republican red Kentucky. But in his engaging and well-researched book, George Humphreys highlights facts probably not well known in Kentucky: 'starting in 1931 and continuing to 1979, the region was home to a host of [Democratic] governors, state legislative, and administration leaders, not duplicated in the history of Kentucky politics.' Hence, his book is a worthy addition to Bluegrass state historiography."—Berry Craig, author of *Kentuckians and Pearl Harbor: Stories from the Day of Infamy*

"This book adds a much needed chapter to the political history of western Kentucky."—Bill Cunningham, former justice of the Kentucky Supreme Court and author of *On Bended Knees: The Night Rider Story*

"George Humphreys' timely and important study of western Kentucky politics from 1931–1979 chronicles the rise and decline of regional Democratic Party dominance. The author examines the physiographic features, historical, social and religious forces that helped to form and define the region's culture and politics. His thoroughly researched work adds significantly to understanding the period's influential leaders, its issues, factions and movements while examining reasons for the Party's wane and the Republican ascent."—Jody Richards, Speaker of the Kentucky House of Representatives, 1994–2008

"From Alben Barkley to Earle Clements to Wendell Ford and beyond, western Kentucky has produced key state and national leaders. But to a more recent generation, those names mean little. Once the Gibraltar of Kentucky Democracy, that rock has so splintered that the area is solidly Republican, and the names of many of those important leaders have been almost forgotten by new voters. George Humphreys' *The Fall of Kentucky's Rock* provides readers a fresh and important chronicle of an oft-forgotten region of the commonwealth. In this work, his excellent research, clear and compelling prose, and sound conclusions give readers a penetrating look at the politics, and the leaders who won—and lost—elections there."—James C. Klotter

"As a western Kentuckian myself, I found Humphreys' detailed account of a colorful period in Kentucky's political history both interesting and entertaining."—Steve Beshear, Governor of Kentucky, 2007–2015 and author of *People Over Politics*

"Humphreys superbly describes the complex heritage that shaped Kentucky's Gibraltar of Democracy."—Bobbie Smith Bryant, author of *Farming in the Black Patch*

"From McConnell's 1984 upset to the 1994 Gingrich Revolution turning congressional seats red, this seminal study of "'how the west was won'" is valuable context and perspective. Having depended on big margins in the west for my statewide wins, just as my grandfather, Governor Keen Johnson had done, Humphreys' excellent writing is required reading to see how things changed, where politics stand, what comes next."—Bob Babbage, Secretary of State, 1992–1996

THE FALL OF KENTUCKY'S ROCK

THE FALL OF KENTUCKY'S ROCK

WESTERN KENTUCKY DEMOCRATIC POLITICS SINCE THE NEW DEAL

GEORGE G. HUMPHREYS

UNIVERSITY PRESS OF KENTUCKY

Scholarly publisher for the Commonwealth,
serving Bellarmine University, Berea College, Centre
College of Kentucky, Eastern Kentucky University,
The Filson Historical Society, Georgetown College,
Kentucky Historical Society, Kentucky State University,
Morehead State University, Murray State University,
Northern Kentucky University, Transylvania University,
University of Kentucky, University of Louisville,
and Western Kentucky University.

Editorial and Sales Offices: The University Press of Kentucky
663 South Limestone Street, Lexington, Kentucky 40508-4008
www.kentuckypress.com

Library of Congress Cataloging-in-Publication Data

Names: Humphreys, George G., 1949- author.
Title: The fall of Kentucky's rock : western Kentucky Democratic politics since
   the New Deal / George G. Humphreys.
Other titles: Topics in Kentucky history.
Description: Lexington, Kentucky : University Press of Kentucky, [2021] |
Series: Topics in Kentucky history | Includes bibliographical references and index.
Identifiers: LCCN 2021039349 | ISBN 9780813182339 (hardcover) |
   ISBN 9780813182346 (pdf) | ISBN 9780813182353 (epub)
Subjects: LCSH: Democratic Party (Ky.)—History. | Kentucky—Politics and
   government—1865-1950. | Kentucky—Politics and government—1951-
Classification: LCC F456 .H86 2021 | DDC 976.9/041--dc23

This book is printed on acid-free paper meeting
the requirements of the American National Standard
for Permanence in Paper for Printed Library Materials.

Manufactured in the United States of America

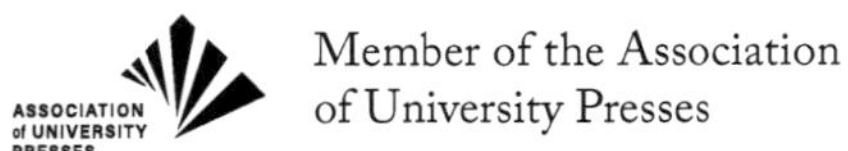

Member of the Association
of University Presses

Contents

Illustrations follow page 132

Abbreviations

AAA	Agricultural Adjustment Administration
AFL	American Federation of Labor
CCC	Civilian Conservation Corps
CIO	Congress of Industrial Organizations
CWA	Civil Works Administration
ERA	Equal Rights Amendment
FBI	Federal Bureau of Investigation
FERA	Federal Emergency Relief Act
GRVCL	Green River Valley Citizens League
KEA	Kentucky Education Association
KERA	Kentucky Education Reform Act
KFBA	Kentucky Free Bridge Association
KOW	Kentucky Ordnance Works
KPPL	Kentucky Public Power League
KU	Kentucky Utilities
LBL	Land between the Lakes
LCVA	Lower Cumberland Valley Association
LTVA	Lower Tennessee Valley Association
NAACP	National Association for the Advancement of Colored Persons
NLRB	National Labor Relations Board
NRA	National Recovery Administration
PSC	Public Services Commission

PWA	Public Works Administration
RA	Resettlement Administration
REC	rural electric cooperative
REA	Rural Electrification Authority
RTC	rural telephone cooperative
STOP	Stop Taking Our Privileges
TVA	Tennessee Valley Authority
UMWA	United Mine Workers of America
WKIC	West Kentucky Industrial College
WPA	Works Progress Administration

Preface

My interest in writing this history of western Kentucky politics began several years prior to completing in 2004 my career as a staff director in the Oklahoma legislature. While there, I completed several writing projects focused on that state's politics and started to give serious consideration to a project focusing on my native state. As my wife and I settled in her hometown of Drakesboro in Muhlenberg County, I became seriously interested in writing a history of western Kentucky politics since the New Deal. During that period, the region, which has had relatively scant historical treatment, produced seven Democratic governors, beginning with Madisonville's Ruby Laffoon in 1931, including Albert Benjamin "Happy" Chandler's two terms, and ending in 1979 with the five-year administration of Julian Carroll, the only governor from the Jackson Purchase area of far west Kentucky. With the long federal career of Paducah's Alben W. Barkley, which included nine years as majority leader in the US Senate during the Great Depression and World War II and one term as President Harry S. Truman's vice president following their tremendous upset election victory in 1948, and the dependable large Democratic majorities that earned the region the reputation as the Gibraltar of Kentucky Democracy, I was convinced that a history of western Kentucky deserved to be written.

Western Kentucky, I came to learn, has been too often lost in histories of Kentucky. This is something I might have picked up in graduate school at Murray State University five decades ago from colleague Berry Craig, whose recently published work on the Civil War in the Jackson Purchase conclusively demonstrates that far western Kentucky, secessionist from the war's outset and Confederate into the twentieth century, did not fit the pattern of neutral Kentucky's conversion to the Lost Cause long after it was lost. Moreover, western Kentucky's history is underappreciated in Kentucky historiography, which draws heavily on events and people in central and eastern Kentucky. This calls for a more inclusive telling of the commonwealth's history, one fitting to a state where the role of counties and regions is so impactful.[1]

Considerable attention to politics, which drew me to this project at the start, is contained in the pages that follow. Although I was born in the Jackson Purchase, I have lived the majority of my life elsewhere, much of it in Oklahoma. As a result, I take issue with other authors whose views on the political history of the commonwealth either explicitly or implicitly accept the view of poet James H. Mulligan that Kentucky politics are "the damnedest." Written in 1902, two years after the assassination of Governor William Goebel, the only such event in American history, Mulligan's observation is clearly understandable. Nevertheless, it seems questionable for it to be repeated down through the years given that there is no acceptable measure to back it up and that politics in many other states, such as Louisiana, New York, Illinois, and Oklahoma—where two governors were removed through the impeachment process in its short history—might make rival claims. Certainly, Kentucky politics has been colorful and has added spice to the arcane process of electing public officials and lawmaking, but we do a disservice to the state's politics, in my opinion, by not looking deeper at where it has enriched our lives or in other cases where it has fallen short.[2]

Projects such as this one require the contributions and support of many persons knowledgeable of the topic at hand. First of all, I thank Al Cross, the former Russellville newsman and political columnist at the *Louisville Courier-Journal* and the current director of the Institute for Rural Journalism at the University of Kentucky, who provided initial encouragement and numerous comments on the final chapter, for which I am deeply indebted to him, and James C. Klotter, the Kentucky historian and professor emeritus of history at Georgetown College and the most prominent Kentucky historian of our generation. Dr. Klotter, in addition to including this title in the Topics in Kentucky History series at the University Press of Kentucky, generously opened doors for me to meet with Terry Birdwhistell, Kentucky oral historian and former dean of libraries at the University of Kentucky, and Al Smith, the former Logan County newspaper editor and longtime host of KET's *Comment on Kentucky* series. With their assistance, I compiled a list of individuals for oral interviews, which are now archived as part of the West Kentucky Politics and Kentucky Legislature Oral History Projects at the Louie B. Nunn Oral History Center at the University of Kentucky.

Kentucky is truly fortunate to have a wealth of oral histories, many of them accessible online. Those at the Nunn Center and the Forrest C. Pogue Library at Murray State University were critical to my work. The special-collections facilities at the University of Kentucky provided additional assistance by allowing access to the excellent set of papers located there and permission to use photographs included in this book. Other university special collections that proved useful are those at the Kentucky Building at Western Kentucky University and the Pogue Library at Murray State University.

Local librarians and museum staff in western Kentucky were most cooperative in my search efforts, particularly at the Hopkins County Historical Society, where I was allowed access to the archives of Governor Ruby Laffoon. Among the many western Kentucky local libraries that assisted in this project are those in Logan, Hopkins, Christian, Daviess, and McCracken Counties. I owe a special thanks to the librarians at Madisonville Community College and the Muhlenberg County Public Library for filling numerous interlibrary-loan requests. I was delighted midway through my research to learn about newspapers.com, which enabled me to access during the recent pandemic not only the *Louisville Courier-Journal* but also regional newspapers from Owensboro, Paducah, Madisonville, Hopkinsville, and Russellville.

State agencies also were supportive by responding to my many requests for information. They include the Kentucky Legislative Research Commission library, the State Board of Elections, the Kentucky Department of Financial Institutions, the Kentucky Department of Tourism and Travel, and the Kentucky Transportation Cabinet. The Kentucky Association of Electric Cooperatives directed me to resources on electrification in

Kentucky and gave me several leads on people in the power industry of western Kentucky whom I might want to interview.

Federal agencies were also quite willing to assist on matters related to western Kentucky politics at the national level. Donald A. Ritchie, historian emeritus in the US Senate Historical Office, shared his research on Senator Alben W. Barkley and answered several questions about the service of other western Kentuckians who served in the Senate. Randy Sowell at the Harry S. Truman Library provided very useful information about the relationship between Barkley and Harry S. Truman. The Lyndon B. Johnson Presidential Library sent a copy of the LBJ and Earle C. Clements correspondence. My understanding of the intergovernmental relationships in the evolution of the highway system expanded from the insights provided by Richard Weingroff in the Office of Infrastructure at the US Department of Transportation, who also sent me a digitized copy of the Kentucky road map from 1931 reproduced in chapter 1.

Madisonville Community College helped with the costs for the maps and photographs presented in this history through two professional-development grants. Dr. Richard Dodds, a photographer from Earlington, used his talents to bring the photographs to the standards required by the University Press of Kentucky. University of Kentucky cartographer Dick Gilbreath did an excellent job with the maps.

I shared at an early stage of my work aspects of it to various groups, including the Jackson Purchase Historical Society, the Hopkins County Historical Society, and faculty and staff at Madisonville Community College. I thank Thomas Kiffmeyer, David C. Turpie, and Robert S. Weise for including my article on western Kentucky in the spring–summer 2015 issue of the *Register of the Kentucky Historical Society* focused on twentieth-century Kentucky.

I owe a great debt of gratitude to the University Press of Kentucky, which agreed to publish this work, and to its partners, which sustained the press after it lost its state appropriation in 2018. The press is essential to preserving the cultural legacy of the commonwealth. Ashley Runyon, now the director of the press, was very kind in the early stages of my work. Patrick O'Dowd assumed her editorial duties and was instrumental in spurring me on to complete this project. Sarah Olson and Annie Barva guided me through the final writing stages. I appreciated Annie's thorough efforts in the copyediting, during which she not only helped with making the manuscript more readable but also caught numerous errors. I appreciated their enthusiasm and commitment to this project. Comments from an early reader led me to add material more focused on local developments that I think greatly improved the final manuscript. The two final readers prevented numerous errors or suggested appropriate revisions in my interpretations. They also encouraged the inclusion of more humor, which I trust readers will appreciate as a change of pace from my more sober writing style. The press's marketing team has been extremely helpful in directing my thoughts to presenting my research to the public.

My greatest appreciation goes to my wife, Rebecca Hope Neathamer, who encouraged and prodded me to complete this book. For someone who took pride in always meeting deadlines before retirement, her efforts in the past several years were too often necessary.

Western Kentucky

A Geographical, Economic, and Historical Introduction

"United we stand, divided we fall," Kentucky's aspirational state motto, perhaps ironically foretells a history of the commonwealth that has been marked by division, not the least of which has been between regions. Jesse Stuart, one of Kentucky's foremost literary figures of the twentieth century, whose roots were solidly planted in the soil of his native Appalachian mountains but came to know well western Kentucky through his series of summer writer workshops at Murray State University, highlighted in his volume *My World* (1975) in the Kentucky Bicentennial Bookshelf series that Kentucky was actually six "worlds," including in the western part of Kentucky the Jackson Purchase, a portion of the Pennyroyal or Pennyrile, and the Western Kentucky Coal Field regions. The validity of taking into account the influence of local populations in Kentucky has been upheld in a variety of contexts, including the classic study of the impact of the state's counties by Robert Ireland, who refers to them as "little kingdoms," and Penny Miller's identification of regionalism as a divisive or "centripetal" force in the commonwealth's politics. The Kentucky historian James Klotter emphasizes the need for more regional histories in a survey of the state's historiography published in 1982, but few regions have received the interest they deserve, with the exception of the Appalachian region in eastern Kentucky, which has inspired extensive interest over the past 150 years.[1]

The state's historiography, as Patricia Anne Hoskins has pointed out in her dissertation on the Civil War in the Jackson Purchase, demonstrates a lack of understanding or interest in western Kentucky. For example, there is an extensive literature stemming back to E. Merton Coulter's *The Civil War and Reconstruction in Kentucky* (1926) that emphasizes the transition from Kentucky's neutrality during the war to its embrace of the South and "the Lost Cause" after the war was lost. However, this was certainly not the case for western Kentucky (or for the Upper Cumberland area of eastern Kentucky, regarding which Al Cross and David Cross recently asserted that no Southern realignment took place after the Civil War), where, as Berry Craig's *Kentucky Confederates* (2014) documents, the far western Jackson Purchase, called at the time the "South Carolina of Kentucky," and other portions of western Kentucky aligned themselves solidly with secession after Ft. Sumter and suffered under federal martial law for a large portion of the war. Patricia Hoskins shares Craig's perspective by rejecting what the historian Anne Marshall terms the "great paradox" of Kentucky history in *Creating a Confederate Kentucky* (2013): immediate support for secession and rejection of neutrality and the overwhelming numbers of enlistments to the Southern forces compared to those in blue was proof of that part of western Kentucky's fidelity to the Confederacy. This overgeneralization of Kentucky's postwar embrace of the Lost Cause appears in recent publications, such as Maryjean Wall's *How Kentucky Became Southern* (2012) and Marshall's *Creating a Confederate Kentucky* (Marshall does make it clear that she considers Kentucky southern before the Civil War, but it became "more southern" after the war).[2]

The reductionist tendency in Kentucky histories appears in other disciplines. In an otherwise fine examination of Kentucky's tobacco experience in *Burley: Kentucky Tobacco in a New Century* (2013), the ethnologist Ann K. Ferrell also overlooks the important contribution of dark tobacco, commonly raised in the "black patch" of western Kentucky. Despite tobacco farmers' struggle to survive economically after the connection was made between nicotine and cancer at the end of the twentieth century, dark tobacco remains important in a large part of western Kentucky and a significant part of the region's history, in particular the Black Patch Tobacco War of the early twentieth century. Bobbie Smith Bryant's recent work on tobacco farming today in western Kentucky is a useful complement to Ferrell's work.[3]

If there is a general consensus that regionalism persists in Kentucky, there is not one on the shape of those regions. From the physical sciences, there is agreement that there are five geographic regions, three of which—the Jackson Purchase, the Western Kentucky Coal Field, and the Pennyroyal (a.k.a. the Pennyrile)—are totally or partially in western Kentucky. However, there is no similar agreement among historians and social scientists on cultural or political regions. This absence of consensus can lead to a significant lack of clarity in discussing the state, such as when the "Golden Triangle region" was defined in the past half century to include that part of the state centered around the more prosperous Louisville, Lexington, and northern Kentucky cities, but the rest of the state was lumped together as "agrarian Kentucky," which included much of Kentucky, east and west, with agrarian economies based on subsistence farming into the twentieth century and with most inhabitants subsisting "in a state of chronic social and economic 'arrest,'" according to Thomas Clark. The historian William Ellis interestingly echoes Clark in identifying the regions lying outside the Golden Triangle as "the problem crescent." Penny Miller also recognizes the duality of contemporary Kentucky in which the "other Kentucky" (outside the Golden Triangle), encompassing western Kentucky, which she fails to define, is characterized for its adherence to the traditional rural values.[4]

In truth, all of these Kentucky scholars would admit that more precision is needed in defining the commonwealth's regions. Clark, for example, divides the commonwealth into five regions: eastern or mountainous Kentucky; the Bluegrass; the Western Kentucky Coal Field or Pennyroyal region; the Jackson Purchase in the extreme west; and northern Kentucky. Miller tends to follow Clark's outline of regionalism, but she appears to grant the existence of a geographically undefined western Kentucky, which one presumes would encompass the Jackson Purchase, the Western Kentucky Coal Field, and a portion of the Pennyroyal. What unites western Kentuckians, she states, is a strong feeling for the "virtue of the rural life." Other scholars have made the issue of discussing regionalism in Kentucky even more problematic. The Kentucky historians James Klotter and Freda Klotter, authors of *A Concise History of Kentucky* (2008), split the commonwealth into seven "human or cultural regions." Included are the Jackson Purchase and "West Kentucky," divided by the strip of land that once lay between the Cumberland and Tennessee Rivers and was once known as "Between the Rivers" before the rivers' impoundment to create Lake Barkley and Kentucky Lake but is now uninhabited and called the "Land between the Lakes." Western Kentucky is said to be west of I-65, but the Klotters exclude Warren County and Bowling Green (home to Western Kentucky University), which is part of south-central Kentucky. I-65 as the eastern edge of western Kentucky has been recognized in the Kentucky General Assembly, where the Western Kentucky Legislative Caucus, encompassing all lawmakers west of that interstate, stretching from Louisville to Franklin south of Bowling Green, has functioned for nearly half a century. This caucus questionably attempts to coordinate interests representing Elizabethtown, a city that is one hour's drive from Louisville and nearly three hours from Paducah to the west. To the human or cultural regions, the Kentucky Long-Term Policy Research Center, a defunct entity attached to the Kentucky General Assembly, adds an economic-development regional scheme that splits the commonwealth into four quadrants, one of which is "west Kentucky," combining the three westernmost area-development districts; however, it sends Ohio, Logan, Warren, and Simpson Counties to the central policy region. Outside sources only add confusion to this matter of regionalism. For example, John H. Fenton's study of the Ohio River valley border states breaks Kentucky into ten regions, creating four sections in the west: the Jackson Purchase; an Owensboro–Henderson region encompassing Daviess, Henderson, Union, Webster, and McLean Counties; the Western Kentucky Coal Field; and the western portion of the Pennyroyal (Breckinridge, Meade, Edmondson, Grayson, and Hart Counties). Finally, a recent road map of western Kentucky pushes its eastern border to include Breckinridge, Grayson, and Edmondson Counties.[5]

There is no intention here to launch deeper into the thorny issue of regionalism in Kentucky. Rather, the task at hand is to put forward a working definition for the reader of what western Kentucky, depicted in map 1, should be considered for this work. That task was complicated by those living on the eastern edge of the region, especially in Bowling Green in

Warren County, who increasingly identify with what they consider south-central Kentucky, and by persons in the Jackson Purchase, who see the Purchase, or far west Kentucky, including Paducah, as separate from western Kentucky east of the Land between the Lakes. Some suggest that the eastern border of the region should be the Green River, a major river that flows northward into the Western Kentucky Coal Field through Butler, bisecting Muhlenberg and McLean Counties before joining the Ohio River near Henderson. This study defines Western Kentucky as all counties west of a line connecting the eastern borders of Hancock, Ohio, Butler, Warren, and Simpson Counties. The remaining borders are the Ohio River on the north, the Mississippi River to the west, and the Tennessee state line on the south. Western Kentucky, encompassing 11,130 square miles and twenty-eight counties, represents 28 percent of the state's land mass. The entire Jackson Purchase and the Western Kentucky Coal Field geographic regions as well as much of the middle and the western portion of the Pennyroyal region are part of western Kentucky.

The area is blessed with five major rivers; in addition to the Ohio and Mississippi Rivers, there are the Green, the Cumberland, and the Tennessee Rivers, all of which drain western Kentucky and empty into the Ohio River. The rivers were highly significant to the regional economy historically by providing perhaps the easiest method for settlers to travel in the eighteenth and nineteenth centuries and for transporting goods, especially tobacco, to market in New Orleans. These rivers—along with the Bayou De Chien, Obion Creek, and Clarks River in the Jackson Purchase; the Rough, Barren, and Mud Rivers, which are Green River tributaries; and the Tradewater River, which drains a significant portion of the Western Kentucky Coal Field—contribute substantially to one of the richest agricultural regions of the state. Large portions of the Jackson Purchase, the land south of US 68 to the Tennessee state line from Bowling Green to the Cumberland River, and a rich corn belt covering much of Union, Webster, Henderson, Daviess, and McLean Counties along the Green and Ohio Rivers are among the state's best farm land.[6]

Tobacco, especially the heavy, dark-fired variety used for chewing and cigars, was and remains a very important part of western Kentucky life. Many western Kentucky towns developed around the tobacco industry. Prior to the explosion in the demand for light burley associated with cigarettes during the First World War, the dark tobacco of

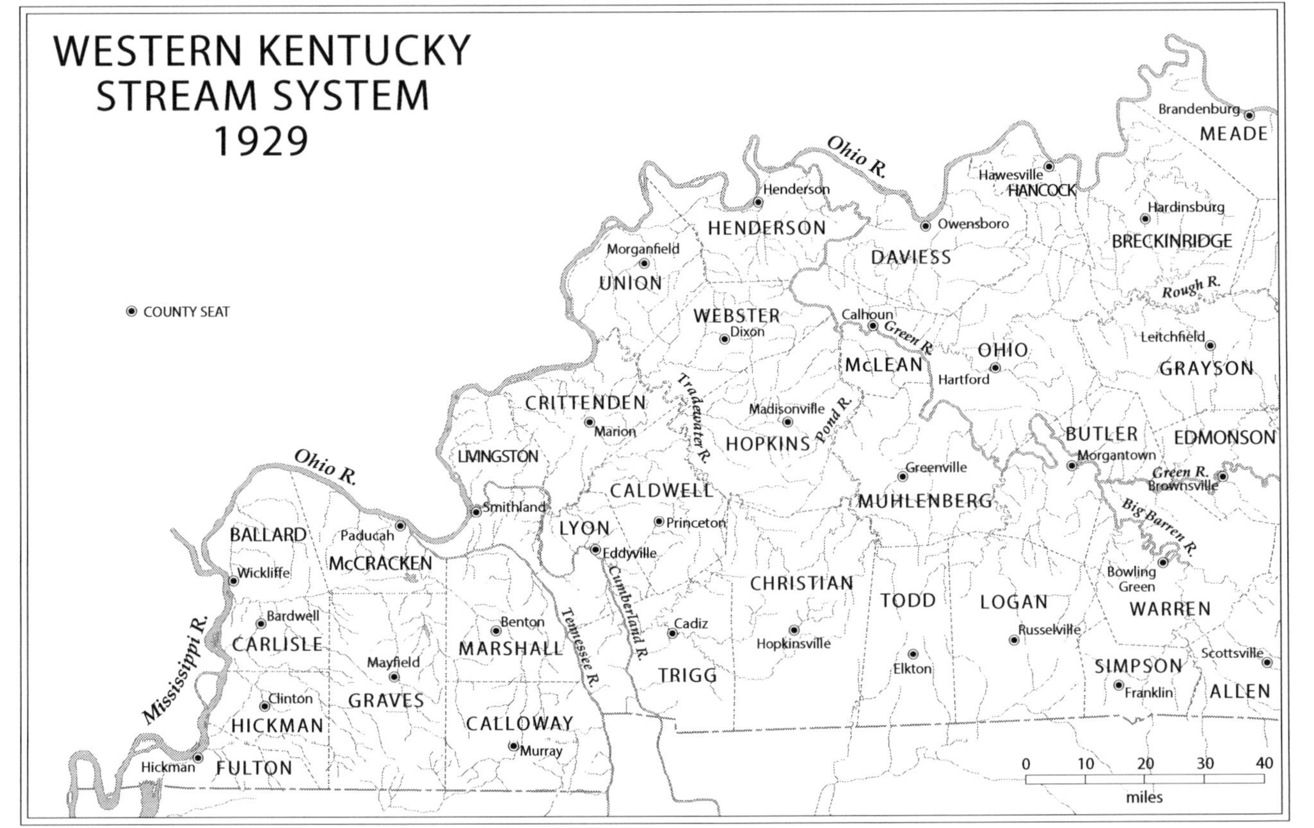

Western Kentucky stream system, 1929. *Source:* Map created by Dick Gilbreath based on Kentucky Geological Survey, *Geographic Map of Kentucky* (Frankfort: Kentucky Geological Survey, 1929).

western Kentucky was in high demand for chewing tobacco and snuff, the most common uses of tobacco. By the Civil War, millions of pounds of tobacco packed in large hogsheads were shipped to towns such as Mayfield, Paducah, Owensboro, and Hopkinsville for processing locally or sent downstream by barge on the many western Kentucky rivers to New Orleans. At the start of the Civil War, Christian County led the state in tobacco production at 11.5 million pounds per year; Daviess, Todd, Graves, Trigg, Logan, Hopkins, and Caldwell Counties were producing more than 2 million pounds each per year. The war, which brought great setbacks to tobacco production in Virginia and North Carolina, proved a boon to the tobacco industry in western Kentucky. In 1890, W. F. Axton noted in his history of Kentucky tobacco that the "Giants of the West" (Christian, Daviess, Graves, Henderson, Logan, Todd, and Webster Counties) were each producing between 7 and 11 million pounds of dark-fired or dark air-cured leaf per year. With the demand for tobacco in all forms ever expanding, regional farms of all sizes were engaged in growing tobacco, and the countryside was dotted by barns where the tobacco was cured, often by means of the dark-firing process, with controlled fires using sawdust and oak or hickory slabs.[7]

It is well to keep in mind that the realities of western Kentucky agricultural life in the early twentieth century fell far short of the bucolic image of an independent, prosperous yeoman farmer. Farm census records from 1925 suggest that approximately one-fourth of farmers did not own the land they farmed and were considered either sharecroppers or tenant farmers. Fulton County was at the higher end of the spectrum for the proportion of tenant farmers (62 percent). The harshness of their lives is captured by Edna Humphreys (1907–1991, the author's paternal grandmother), whose father was a sharecropper in Hickman County and who recalled that her family moved every two years, normally around Christmas, when the landowner searched for a more beneficial arrangement. According to her, "We hauled our belongings in a wagon with a cow plodding along behind." Rural families, with few exceptions, enjoyed few modern conveniences such as electricity, indoor plumbing, and ownership of cars or tractors.[8]

Well into the twentieth century, western Kentucky was an isolated, rural area in a rural state, despite being home to five of the commonwealth's ten largest cities in 1910, Paducah (sixth), Owensboro (seventh), Henderson (eighth), Hopkinsville (ninth), and Bowling Green (tenth). Geography certainly contributed to the sense of isolation. For example, Paducah, the largest city in the Jackson Purchase and located on the Ohio River, is nearly 140 miles from Bowling Green, now the largest city in western Kentucky, located along the Tennessee line. Paducah is 220 miles from Louisville, approximately 250 miles from the state capital, Frankfort, and more than 400 miles from Pikeville near the West Virginia line in eastern Kentucky. Travel from western Kentucky to these cities, although still time-consuming, would have been much more daunting before the advent of automobiles, the construction of bridges that replaced the many river ferries used for crossing the region's major rivers, and the later construction of high-speed, limited-access highways in Kentucky after 1950. Even today, western Kentuckians, depending on where they live, are closer to St. Louis, Memphis, and Nashville, where they take advantage of shopping, entertainment, and medical facilities, than to Louisville or Lexington.[9]

The isolation, particularly that experienced by many small farmers, a sizable number of whom did not own their land and worked as tenant farmers or sharecroppers, made for a bleak life in the nineteenth century. The historian Thomas Clark offers the starkest view of what he calls "agrarian Kentucky," where those caught up in it grew up, lived, and died "in a chronic social and economic 'arrest.'" This view, suggests James Klotter, more accurately depicts parts of eastern Kentucky than western Kentucky, where those writing about growing up on a farm vividly remember the hard work and lack of modern conveniences enjoyed by town folks but also tell of working together with kinfolk and neighbors, church socials, county fairs, mule or court days in nearby towns where people gathered to sell or trade items, shop, and trade gossip at a nearby country store, and, if one lived near a navigable river, steamboats or packet boats bringing a variety of entertainment opportunities well into the twentieth century and allowing for passenger travel on the rivers or to the outside world.[10]

The region's isolation was exacerbated by its great rivers, which carve it into three peninsulas sharing the Ohio River as a northern border: the Between the Rivers area (now known as the Land between the Lakes), bordered by the Ohio, Tennessee, and Cumberland Rivers; the Jackson Purchase, lying between the Mississippi and Tennessee Rivers;

and the area between the Cumberland and Green Rivers to the east. Prior to the construction of a number of bridges designed to carry automobile traffic after World War I, crossing the rivers was accomplished by a considerable number of crude ferries operating privately with tolls or by way of passenger or freight railroads that traversed several railroad bridges. Frequent floods made use of the ferries even more dangerous. The Mississippi River Great Flood of 1927, for example, caused flooding along the Cumberland, Tennessee, and Mississippi Rivers, resulting in tremendous property damage in numerous area cities. The river breached the city of Hickman's flood wall, and flooded its streets for months.[11]

Traveling western Kentucky by road before the 1930s, even after automobile travel became widespread, was a significant challenge due to the poor condition of the highways. The best roads at the turn of the century were operated by private interests, who charged travelers tolls in return for maintaining the roads, but these interests fell victim to the ire of locals during the "tollgate wars" at the end of the nineteenth century which resulted in the roads' acquisition by local governments in the region. Greater federal and state responsibility for road construction and maintenance started after World War I, but, as reflected in map 2, roads in western Kentucky, including US highways, were in 1931 largely dirt or gravel affairs—extremely dusty during hot summers, mud bogs during the winter and spring months, and subject to deep pot holes that often made travel an arduous task.

Women, certainly, felt the isolation most intensely. Without modern conveniences and indoor plumbing, routine household chores such as cooking, cleaning, washing, ironing, and tending to the children relied on drawing water from a stream or a well, a heavy chore. With good reason, they complained about the heavy "sad irons" that had to be heated on the stove. Farm women were also expected to raise vegetables for the family table and help the men when they were needed. Opportunities for socializing were more limited than for the males, in part due to social conventions. The primitive road conditions prevented even the most adventurous women from venturing on their own to town or to visit neighbors. Childbearing started early, and farm families tended to be larger than those in town. James Klotter offers a glimpse of gender relations in the early twentieth century in which women, even after

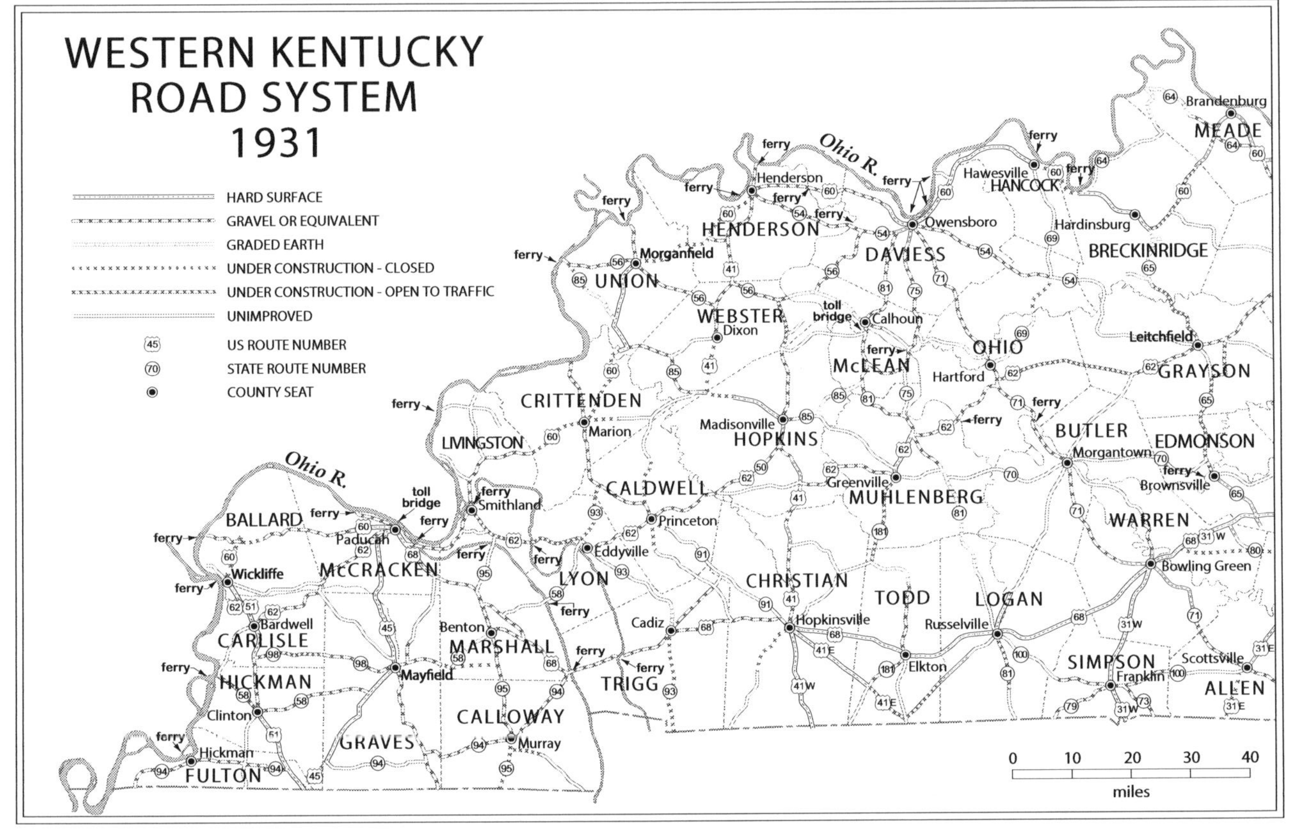

Western Kentucky road system, 1931. *Source:* Map created by Dick Gilbreath based on Kentucky State Highway Commission, *Official Road Map of Kentucky* (Frankfort: Kentucky State Highway Commission, 1931).

securing the right to vote in 1920, were "subservient" to men throughout the commonwealth. Women, despite a growing number finding opportunities outside the home between the two world wars, "existed as a helpmate, chiefly as a quiet appendage to the household." Suzanne Hall, writing of turn-of-the-century black-patch farm culture in the early decades of the twentieth century, concludes that even though women shouldered their share of the family workload, "the society, culture, and religion defined a woman's sphere as home, family, and church, and her task [as one] of nurturance, even at the cost of self-sacrifice."[12]

The history of western Kentucky women has yet to be written, but what has been written testifies to the difficulties they faced in the opening decades of the twentieth century. Governor Albert B. Chandler, who was raised at the turn of the century by his father after his mother abandoned the family in the small western Kentucky rural community of Corydon near Henderson, sympathized later in life with his mother's decision to escape the harsh life of raising two young boys on a fifty-acre farm with no modern conveniences and little in the way of future prospects. Looking back, Chandler understood that for a "vivacious, energetic and pretty" young woman, the choice was to leave or accept the "unending slave work in house and field until, washed-out and sickly, she would wearily sink into an early grave like many near-poor women of her time." However, most women remained at home and endured, but often at a cost. The novelist Bobbie Ann Mason, who grew up outside of Mayfield just after World War II, would recognize Chandler's mother in her own mother and paternal grandmothers. In her autobiography, Mason tells her readers of a grandmother who after decades of "mind-numbing, back-breaking labor and crippling social isolation" on the farm was depressed to the point that she had to be institutionalized for a period at Western State Hospital in Hopkinsville.[13]

However, women did have collective outlets to shape their environment despite not being allowed to vote until the ratification of the Nineteenth Amendment in 1920. In a recent history of the suffrage movement in Kentucky, Melanie Goan recalls significant optimism in the Kentucky Equal Rights Association that western Kentucky might play an important part in marshalling support for women's suffrage. Susan B. Anthony visited Owensboro, Hopkinsville, and Bowling Green in 1879 to raise interest in the issue, and Frances Woods, a paid recruiter, was later dispatched to organize local chapters in western Kentucky at the turn of the century, but her efforts met with mixed success. Hopkinsville, she concluded, might be organized by the right person, but only "very gradually in a number of years." Paducah foundered as suffrage raised fears that it was "one of the forerunners of race-equality." Other efforts in Princeton, Henderson, and Hawesville in Hancock County failed to generate enough interest to form chapters, but Woods did identify local contacts. Madisonville was a different story. Through the energetic efforts of Virginia Franceway and her connections to the local Women's Christian Temperance Association chapter, fifteen dues-paying members, each pledging to recruit five additional members, formed a Hopkins County Kentucky Equal Rights Association chapter. Laura Clay, the state's suffrage leader, planned to hold the association's annual meeting in Madisonville in 1907, hoping to enhance the suffrage influence in the region. However, those plans fell apart following the death of Franceway's daughter in childbirth.[14]

Goan uncovers suffrage stirrings elsewhere arising from the efforts of noteworthy women such as Sallie McConnell Hubbard, president of the seven-member Fulton County Kentucky Equal Rights Association chapter, who made a critical $1,000 contribution to the state chapter, and Josephine Fowler Post from Paducah, who was active in the suffrage movement at the local, state, and national levels and lobbied for ratification of the Nineteenth Amendment in Frankfort. In the years leading up to ratification, local chapters were also established or revitalized in Russellville, Hopkinsville, Bowling Green, Owensboro, Henderson, and Hawesville.[15]

Lee A. Dew and Aloma W. Dew, authors of an excellent history of Owensboro, cast light on the suffragette movement in that western Kentucky city. Owensboro had established a suffrage organization, the Political Equality Club, in 1895 when Susan B. Anthony visited the state again, accompanied by Carrie Chapman Catt, Anthony's replacement as president of the National American Woman Suffrage Association, but the club closed several years later. Nevertheless, interest in the issue would not die in the years leading up to World War I. Owensboro state representative Elmer L. Brown opposed women's suffrage in the 1914 session of the General Assembly after claiming he was unable to discern an interest among the women in his home district. However, the Dews note that Mary Fitts, in a high school graduation speech, supported women's suffrage, and Pearl Ferguson gave a number of speeches locally in favor of it. Owensboro, home to some 200 members of the Daviess County Woman's Suffrage Association, hosted the state Kentucky Equal Rights Association convention in November 1914. During the convention, Josephine Fowler Post of Paducah, Katherine Rudy of Owensboro, and Mrs. W. T. Fowler of Hopkinsville from western Kentucky were named part of the state's eleven-member delegation to the next national convention. Membership in the organized suffragette movement in Owensboro more than doubled by the time the suffrage amendment was ratified, and women soon joined several new organizations, such as the Woman's Citizen League under the direction of Nannie Sutton Conant and the Suffrage Association, to better prepare for their responsibilities as voters.[16]

These efforts had only mixed results, however, in convincing western Kentucky lawmakers to support the Nineteenth Amendment. First Congressional District congressman Alben W. Barkley voted for it; however, the region lagged well behind the state's overwhelming approval of the amendment when it was ratified in January 1920. The regional vote supported ratification 7–3 in the Senate and 13–10 in the House.[17]

Religion today has a strong influence in western Kentucky, but that was not always so. In the period following statehood in 1792, western Kentucky was considered part of the frontier, where lawlessness often prevailed. John Breckinridge, US senator for Kentucky and attorney general in President Thomas Jefferson's cabinet, was so alarmed about settlement in western Kentucky that he said it was "filled with nothing but hunters, horse-thieves, & savages, . . . where wretchedness, poverty & sickness will always reign." Peter Cartwright, a Methodist circuit rider in Logan County at the time who later moved to Illinois and became a political rival of Abraham Lincoln, believed the area to be a "Rogues' Harbor," home to every brand of sin, including gambling and horse racing. However, it was in western Kentucky that the Great Revival, the manifestation in Kentucky and other southern states, of American's early nineteenth-century Great Awakening, began. The Great Revival was marked by rapturous revivals attended by large crowds that could go on for days. The movement started from a series of mass meetings of the Muddy River, Red River, and Gaspar River Presbyterian churches in the Russellville area and soon spread widely in Kentucky and other parts of the south to establish a brand of evangelical Protestantism that prevails in western Kentucky to this day. John Boles, a historian of the Great Revival in Kentucky, writes that contemporary observers were left with the sense that "against the backdrop of recent deism, materialism, and widespread indifference to religion, these gigantic revival meetings with thousands in attendance, multitudes falling to the ground wailing and shouting, and reports of the miraculous transformations of entire communities, seemed all the more stupendous." Lest the recent converts revert to their previous religious laxity, many feared that the enormity of the massive New Madrid earthquake in December 1811 and its series of aftershocks centered in western Kentucky and Tennessee foretold events leading up to Jesus's return.[18]

The legacy of the Great Revival survives in the proliferation of Baptist, Cumberland Presbyterian, Methodist, Church of Christ, and Pentecostal denominations that dot the western Kentucky countryside with their revival traditions, leaving, according to Boles, a uniquely southern and "peculiar cast of mind" that is "highly individualist, localistic, and conversion-oriented," supported by a fundamentalist, literal acceptance of the Bible, the same literality used to support slavery in the antebellum era. The emphasis on biblical authority, interpreted literally, has supported many western Kentuckians' opposition against evolution, women's rights, and gay rights in recent decades.[19]

Western Kentucky, many would suggest, especially in the case of the Jackson Purchase, was the area most sympathetic with the Confederate South and later the "Lost Cause." In the case of the Purchase, as the historian Hughie Lawson suggests, ties to the South had crystallized because of family connections stemming from the unusually high percentage of settlers from Virginia, North Carolina, and Tennessee, strong allegiances to western Tennessee churches, and decades of commercial interaction that began with shipping tobacco by river to New Orleans, which was reinforced by construction of the New Orleans & Ohio Railroad to Paducah and the Mobile & Ohio Railroad to Columbus on the Mississippi River before the Civil War. Support for slavery in the Jackson Purchase in the years before the Civil War was on an upswing because, as the historian Patricia Hoskins contends, white yeomen farmers hoped to capitalize on use of bond slaves for tobacco production. The pro-Confederate sentiment was more muted in other parts of western Kentucky, such as the Green River Valley from Bowling Green northward to the Ohio River. The Green River historian Helen Crocker unveils a stronger commitment to a policy of neutrality or continuation of the union but with protections for slavery, exemplified by former governor and current US senator John J. Crittenden, a former Whig supporter of Henry Clay from Russellville, who in the months following secession unsuccessfully searched for a compromise to avoid civil war. She also notes the number of slaveholders who harbored emancipation sympathies and demonstrated those sympathies by the provisions they made to free their slaves. Even in the Green River Valley, though, the harshness of Union occupation ultimately turned many residents—other than in Ohio and Butler Counties, where slavery was never a strong force and became solidly Republican after the Civil War — against the Union, reinforced Confederate loyalties, and ratcheted up local hatreds. In perhaps the best county history in western Kentucky, Otto Rothbert asserts strong Union support in Muhlenberg County located in the Western Kentucky Coal Field, where more than 900 men enlisted in the Northern army compared to the less than 150 who enlisted in the rebel forces.[20]

The Purchase joined with other western Kentucky counties in rejecting Republican and native Kentuckian Abraham Lincoln's presidential election effort in 1860, which they viewed as a threat to the continuation of slavery and the union. After the Democratic Party split into southern and northern wings, five of the seven Jackson Purchase counties (Carlisle County was created in 1886 by dividing up Ballard County) voted for John C. Breckinridge, the former vice president from Kentucky and future Confederacy secretary of war, whose supporters were generally considered prepared to support secession in the event of a Lincoln presidency. The Jackson Purchase was not alone in its Southern sympathies; Livingston, Lyon, Caldwell, Trigg, Webster, and Hancock Counties also voted for Breckinridge. Constitutional Union candidate John Bell from Tennessee, running on a platform of remaining in the union *and* continuing slavery as part of the compromise written at the constitutional convention that left the matter of slavery to the states, carried the remaining counties in the region. Lincoln failed to poll more than single digits in any western Kentucky county and received no votes in

Calloway, Franklin, Fulton, Graves, Livingston, Lyon, Marshall, McLean, Simpson, Union, and Webster Counties.[21]

In the months between Lincoln's election and the beginning of hostilities at Fort Sumter, Kentucky's political leaders struggled to arrive at a compromise with those southern states that had seceded to form the Confederacy, but much of western Kentucky, in particular the Jackson Purchase, agitated during a series of county meetings in January 1861 to join with Kentucky's southern neighbors. These meetings were followed later by a secession convention in May (the only such effort of its kind in a loyalist state) held in Mayfield to separate the First Congressional District from Kentucky and the Union and a statewide convention that met in November 1861 at Russellville that declared for the Confederacy and established a provisional government at Bowling Green, which Northern forces would quickly disperse. The divided Southern sympathies in the region were also characterized by the numbers of men mustered into the Union and Confederate armies. As one would expect, the enlistments into the Confederate armies were heaviest in the Jackson Purchase. Berry Craig, the authority on the Civil War in the Jackson Purchase, has found that it was notable for the overwhelming percentage of its soldiers who fought in the Southern armies (Fulton County provided only one soldier to the North, and Hickman only sixteen, five of whom were black). Other western Kentucky counties that experienced significantly more enlistments to the South were Trigg, Lyon, Caldwell, Livingston, Union, Webster, and Henderson Counties.[22]

The Lost Cause continued to stir the hearts and minds of western Kentuckians long after the Civil War. For politicians running for office in the years following the war, participation in the Confederate army was a definite political asset, even more so if they showed signs of wounds suffered in battle. Memorials related to the Civil War in western Kentucky were principally to honor Confederate soldiers. Anne Marshall lists twenty-eight Civil War monuments erected in Kentucky between 1895 and 1930, half of them located in western Kentucky. Of those, all but one are Confederate monuments; the outlier recognizes the dead of both sides and is located on the Butler County courthouse grounds in Morgantown on the eastern edge of the region, where sectional feeling during the war was divided and Republican political influence has flourished. The largest Civil War monument in Kentucky is dedicated to Jefferson Davis located in Fairview, the birthplace of the Confederate president, east of Hopkinsville in Todd County. The 351-foot-high obelisk, the fourth-tallest monument in the country, was completed in 1924 with monies donated by several groups supportive of the Lost Cause and deeded over to the commonwealth. It was Kentucky's second state park and called, in the words of a Paducah newspaper, a "sacred trust." Nearly lost to history is the Blue and Gray State Park, located north of Elkton in Todd County, which was the product of a local association that donated the land in hopes that the park would be a benefit to the local economy and was one of the state's earliest resort parks. Located near the Jefferson Davis Memorial State Park on what at the time was called the Jefferson Davis Highway (a transcontinental highway that bisected western Kentucky east to west from Bowling Green through Hopkinsville and is now designated US 68), the park was dedicated in 1929 "to recognize Kentucky's divided Civil War past," to memorialize soldiers on both sides, and to provide a respite at the hotel located on the grounds for travelers wishing to visit the two Civil War presidents' Kentucky birthplaces. The park, which opened after securing a state appropriation, was a popular gathering place for locals but failed to attract outside visitors. Governor Ruby Laffoon from Madisonville closed the park in 1933 due to its failure to sustain itself financially, and it transitioned to a Works Progress Administration transient camp during the New Deal and was later sold by the state.[23]

Not all segments of western Kentucky shared the pro-Confederate sympathies of perhaps a majority of the populace in the decades following the end of hostilities. That would have been the case with the region's sizable black population. When much of the slave population in the Confederate states was freed by the Emancipation Proclamation in 1863, Kentucky, as a neutral state, waited to free its slaves until ratification of the Thirteenth Amendment in 1865 after the war's end, with the notable exception of the many slaves in the region who earned freedom for themselves and their families by enlisting in the Union army at recruitment camps, including those at Paducah and Owensboro. Resentment among whites in the region, reinforced by the presence of the Freedmen's Bureau, which was set up to assist the freed slaves, helped inflame the racial violence against freedmen that has been well documented by George C. Wright, historian of racial violence in Kentucky, and by Patricia Hoskins with a focus on uncontrolled violence against blacks in the Jackson Purchase at war's end. Wright's research sheds light on racial violence against blacks after 1865 and concludes that western Kentucky's record was among the worst in the commonwealth. He documents the lynching of forty-four blacks in the Jackson Purchase and another eighty-one in other parts of the region during the two decades following the Civil War. Fulton County—a relatively small county in terms of population in the extreme southwest corner of Kentucky, where there were a large percentage of blacks and slavery had been well established to work the cotton and tobacco fields—led Kentucky with twenty lynchings, followed by its neighbor Graves County with thirteen. According to Wright, "Afro-Americans were lynched for getting 'out of the place' assigned them by white society." This "transgression" of assigned place in the Jim Crow conditions of post-Civil War status in western Kentucky was associated with blacks engaging in violent acts, very often to defend themselves against threatening whites; with allegations of immoral behaviors most commonly involving what were perceived as affronts against the dignity of white women; and with economic success "above their assigned station in life."[24]

This pattern continued through the Black Patch War at the beginning of the twentieth century. Numerous black farmers lost their lives at the hands of white-capped forces fighting the influence of the tobacco trusts, and others were forced to flee their tobacco farms after being threatened by the night riders. Special targets were the Between the Rivers community of Golden Pond and Birmingham (which was eventually destroyed by the impoundment of the Tennessee River to create Kentucky Lake), located on the Tennessee River in Marshall County. So thorough was the harassment of blacks in these towns that Marshall County became known as a "sundown county" in which blacks were not safe to be out in public after sunset. The county's black population from that time to the present has been negligible. However, several historians—including Bill Cunningham, who writes that those charging night riders with virulent racism have given them "simply a bum rap"—have raised questions regarding the characterization of Kentucky's night riders as virulently racist, noting the especially heinous murders of David Walker and his family near Hickman in October 1908 by white cappers from the Reelfoot Lake area across the nearby Tennessee state line. Nevertheless, the evidence points to the fact that many black families in the Black Patch decided to leave western Kentucky in an ever-growing stream as part of the general black exodus out of the South. In 1910, western Kentucky black farmers numbered nearly 5,400, but in 1950 there were less than 2,000, a nearly two-thirds reduction.[25]

These violent acts often drew wide community support. The western Kentucky historian and former Kentucky Supreme Court justice Bill Cunningham describes in considerable detail the case of a black man, Lube Martin, who killed a Murray lawman in 1916 for his harassment of Martin's wife. Following Martin's arrest, a crowd of approximately 1,000 locals threatened not only to lynch Martin but also to kill the circuit court judge and the commonwealth attorney if they did not turn him over to the crowd—a threat that was blocked only by the resolute intervention of Governor A. O. Stanley, a Democrat from Henderson, who rushed by train to the Jackson Purchase scene, where he defused the situation. Though Martin was saved from lynching by the mob, justice was hardly served by the quick trial and speedy execution that followed, typical of the "legal lynchings" that blacks in western Kentucky at the time too often experienced. "Community justice" applied to blacks in western Kentucky, as the historian Christopher Waldrep depicts it, was a mockery of the "separate but equal" legal standard promised them in the era of Jim Crow.[26]

Certainly, a number of black farmers—notably those living near Birmingham in Trigg County and Marshall County in the Jackson Purchase, which listed no black farmers in the 1954 US census—left the region due to threats levied by night riders during the Black Patch Wars, who ranged over the countryside, as Wright notes, committing acts of violence against blacks, often with the goal of forcing them to flee their land.[27]

Area blacks would not soon forget these depredations, including Rufus Atwood, the longtime president of what is today Kentucky State University, the state's public historically black institution of higher education. Atwood grew up in Hickman before World War I. As a student attending the Riverview School, a two-room Jim Crow facility in Hickman, he was well aware of the night riders' heinous murder of David Walker. Atwood left Hickman to start college at Fisk in Nashville, but he answered his country's call during World War I and was mustered out as a sergeant first class. He left the Jackson Purchase for good after a returning black soldier was lynched in Hickman in December 1918, a sign that local law enforcement officers would not tolerate returning black soldiers getting out of line. In the most extensive study of race relations in western Kentucky, Jack Glazier offers the example of lesser-known figures in Hopkinsville, such as Prentice Nance, who fled the region in the 1930s for "breaching racial etiquette" in their interactions with whites after the war.[28]

Among the talented blacks who left western Kentucky to make their mark in the world were Alice Allison Dunnigan from Russellville, who, after several teaching positions in segregated Logan and Todd County schools, moved to the nation's capital in 1942 and worked in several federal agencies and then became a full-time journalist and a pioneering journalist for her race and gender at the White House and congress, and Ted Poston, a black journalist from Hopkinsville. Raised in an educated family, Poston in 1935 became the first black full-time journalist of a major white daily and represented his race on various matters in President Franklin D. Roosevelt's administration. The feminist intellectual Gloria Jean Watkins, writing under the pen name "bell hooks," was born in Hopkinsville in 1952, attended segregated schools there, but graduated from the integrated Hopkinsville High School. After leaving Kentucky and establishing an international reputation, she returned to the commonwealth, where she is now associated with the bell hooks Institute at Berea College.[29]

The brutality of race relations in the southern-style Jim Crow separation of the races in many spheres of public life was in fact sanctioned by both Kentucky state law and the US Supreme Court decision in *Plessy v. Ferguson* (163 US 537 [1896]), which upheld the suspect notion of separate-and-equal public accommodations and was met with great satisfaction by many western Kentucky Democrats, who dominated the political scene in the postbellum period. Once the Union military left the South, the Democratic Party, which had dominated western Kentucky politically since the days of Andrew Jackson, easily emerged as the victor over the Republican Party (GOP) in the presidential election of 1868. Butler, a coal field county lying on the eastern edge of the region, was alone in voting for Ulysses S. Grant, the GOP victor; eight counties voted Democratic in majorities at a rate greater than 90 percent. Fulton County gave an anemic six votes for Grant. The strength of

Table 1
Western Kentucky Gubernatorial Voting, 1927–1959

Year	Region's Democratic Majority	State Democratic Majority	Region's % of Democratic Majority	Winner
1927	26,968	–	–	Flem Sampson (R)
1931	52,870	71,531	71.0	Ruby Laffoon*
1935	53,576	95,158	56.3	Albert "Happy" Chandler**
1939	49,650	106,130	46.8	Keen Johnson**
1943	20,019	–	–	Simeon Willis (R)
1947	46,403	100,039	46.4	Earle Clements*
1951	38,167	58,331	65.4	Lawrence Wetherby
1955	60,012	128,976	46.5	Albert "Happy" Chandler**
1959	74,680	180,093	41.5	Bert Combs

* Raised in western Kentucky.
** Raised in western Kentucky but entered politics and had professional career elsewhere.

Source: Data compiled from Malcolm E. Jewell, *Kentucky Votes,* vol. 2: *Gubernatorial and Primary Elections, 1923–1959* (Lexington: University Press of Kentucky, 1963).

the Democratic Party in western Kentucky was appropriately captured in 1917 by the novelist and wit Irvin S. Cobb, Paducah's version of Will Rogers, as the "Democratic Rock of Ages." And former Democratic vice president from Kentucky John C. Breckinridge was reported to have said of the party's support in the First Congressional District that it was "solid as Gibraltar." For our purposes, the "Gibraltar of Kentucky Democracy" can be expanded to include all of western Kentucky, as it proved to be for more than half a century, starting with the Great Depression—a predictably Democratic stronghold with majorities approaching 50,000 in most elections (see table 1), which helped the party maintain political control in the commonwealth.[30]

Local Democrats drew support from many of the newspapers that before television carried considerable influence among readers and were aligned mostly with the ruling party in western Kentucky. George Goodman, the new owner of the *Paducah News-Democrat,* assured his readers in 1922 that his paper "is Democratic politically by heredity, birth and belief." Goodman followed in the footsteps of Urey Woodson, publisher and owner of the *Owensboro Messenger,* who was a delegate to every Democratic National Party Convention from 1880 to 1932 and was state party secretary from 1904 to 1912. Welcoming a gathering of western Kentucky newspaper leaders to Paducah in 1923, one Paducah editorial writer speaking for the group praised the work of his colleagues yet felt they had been on the whole "overlooked and discounted" in Frankfort. The writer further complained that "in politics, in patronage, in notice from the rest of the state, where dwell mainly, the great chiefs who pull around them the mantle of high office, West Kentucky gives most and gets the least." That earlier generation of Democratic print partisans paved the way for a later generation, including Democrats Harry Lee Waterfield from Clinton and Henry Ward from Paducah, elected officials who made major contributions to the commonwealth's political history, along with others, such as Lawrence Hager, whom Woodson encouraged to take over the *Owensboro Inquirer* at his retirement to form the *Messenger-Inquirer,* Edwin J. Paxton, owner of the *Paducah Sun,* who bought Goodman's paper in 1929 to form the *Paducah Sun-Democrat,* and Al Smith, the publisher of the *Russellville News-Democrat,* all of whom shunned electoral politics even as they embraced their roles as Democratic partisans. Since getting their start in Paducah newspapers in the late nineteenth century, the Paxton family oversaw a Democratic editorial page until E. J. "Jack" Paxton assumed the reins of the *Paducah Sun-Democrat* in the late twentieth century, when he and subsequent Paxtons began holding to a very conservative and Republican editorial line at the family's flagship *Paducah Sun* (although they have allowed a greater degree of editorial independence to the other major regional newspapers, the *Madisonville Messenger* and *Owensboro Messenger-Inquirer,* that the Paxton Group has acquired in recent years).[31]

The emphasis on western Kentucky as the Gibraltar of Kentucky Democracy does not mean to overlook those areas of the region that were solidly Republican over the decades, however. On the eastern edge, Butler and Ohio Counties generally voted Republican, as did Crittenden County just east of the Western Kentucky Coal Field. Butler County was home to William S. Taylor, Kentucky's second GOP governor and the only one from western Kentucky. His tenure was cut to less than two months after the Democratic Kentucky General Assembly laid much of the blame on him for the assassination of William

Goebel just before Democratic lawmakers swore him in as Taylor's successor. Counties with significant black populations, such as Christian and McCracken, periodically voted Republican until President Franklin Roosevelt brought a significant percentage of black voters into the New Deal Coalition. Other counties, notably Muhlenberg and Caldwell, were competitive counties that shifted from one party to the other.[32]

Coal lagged behind tobacco in terms of its importance in the western Kentucky economy. The mines in eastern Kentucky are part of the Appalachian coal field, and the Western Kentucky Coal Field, on much flatter land than in eastern Kentucky, is part of a larger field that extends into Illinois, Indiana, Missouri, and Iowa. The Cincinnati Arch, a large uplift dating back more than 200 million years ago, splits the two fields. Mining on a relatively small scale in western Kentucky started to take place in the 1820s, but coal soon began to be sent by river as far as New Orleans. Before the Civil War, the Edgefield & Kentucky Railroad line, built between Guthrie in Todd County and Nashville, expanded the demand for western Kentucky coal. In the decades following the war, the commonwealth was under the spell of a "railroad 'mania,'" according to two Kentucky historians of the period, and western Kentucky experienced a burst of railroad construction, with the Louisville & Nashville Railroad dominant in the coal field and Pennyrile areas and the Illinois Central the strongest carrier in the Jackson Purchase. In some cases, adverse consequences arose from this frenzy, such as the boondoggle in Muhlenberg County, where, after a hotly contested vote in 1868, the county issued $400,000 in bonds for rail construction between Elizabethtown and Paducah, but that construction was never completed, and the bonds left the county staggering "under a financial and political burden that greatly depreciated values, delayed industrial development, and harassed officials and taxpayers with most distressing legal uncertainties."[33]

Despite setbacks, western Kentucky by the turn of the century had an extensive rail network that contributed to the development of the region's coal industry and brought passenger rail service for those who could afford the fare. Production in the Western Kentucky Coal Field soared from approximately 200,000 tons in 1870 to more than 3 million tons per year at the start of the twentieth century as the railroads fed coal to markets in Nashville, Memphis, and Evansville. By the 1920s, according to the Kentucky historian Duane Bolin, there were approximately 10,500 miners in the western field, most working in mining towns such as Providence in Webster County; Madisonville and Earlington in Hopkins County; Sturgis in Union County; and Greenville, Central City, and Drakesboro in Muhlenberg County, where there were fifty-three active mines. Muhlenberg and Hopkins Counties were for many years by far the largest coal producers in the region. For many years, Earlington, at one time with a population of 4,000, was home to the Henderson subdivision of the Louisville & Nashville Railroad. In Muhlenberg County, Central City took advantage of its position at the juncture of the Owensboro & Nashville (later part of the Louisville & Nashville) and the Illinois Central lines to build an economy based on mines and the railroads. Dawson Springs, located on the Hopkins–Caldwell County line, took advantage of both its waters, which drew visitors, including the Pittsburg Pirates baseball team for its spring training in 1915, to its estimated fifty hotels, and the ten passenger trains that stopped daily, so that it soon became a prosperous resort town.[34]

In the half century following the Civil War, the pace of change quickened in western Kentucky as the outside world became relatively less distant with the advent of the railroads, telegraph, and later the telephone. These technological advances would be especially noticeable in the region's larger towns but barely so on the farms, where life in most regards remained unchanged well into the twentieth century. Nevertheless, western Kentucky's leaders emerged from World War I ready to lead the region forward as it endeavored to exert itself more vigorously in the national economic stage.

Owensboro, for example, was served by a local subscription telephone exchange in 1880 that expanded quickly from 10 to 150 subscribers within a year and boasted contacts with seventy-one cities, including nearby towns in the Western Kentucky Coal Field, Louisville, and Evansville, Indiana. The primitive state of the industry can be judged when, after a rival Harrison Telephone Company was established in 1895, Owensboro businesses needed separate telephones to talk to customers subscribing to one exchange or the other. In Hickman County, a rural part of the Jackson Purchase, local telephone systems arrived at the turn of the century. The few subscribers were responsible for their own telephone lines, and service was extremely limited. Those who had a line were frequently called upon by neighbors to make an essential call to a doctor or a local business. Alben Barkley, western Kentucky's most prominent political figure who climbed the political ranks to become Harry S. Truman's vice president in 1948, lived in Clinton at the time. He was seventeen when, while he was with his father "in a dry-goods store, making our purchases after disposing of a load of wheat, and, while seated near the old drumhead heating stove, sucking on the stick of candy which the storekeeper had given me, I noticed a man talking into some queer-looking black instrument with a little crank that was hanging on the wall." Hickman County soon was home to telephone exchanges at Oakton, Beulah, and Columbus in addition to the Hickman County Telephone Company; these exchanges were later consolidated first by Cumberland Telephone and Telegraph Company and then in 1930 by the Bell system. Nevertheless, even up to 1954 the majority of farm households in western Kentucky, according to agricultural census reports for that year, did not have telephone service.[35]

By the end of the nineteenth century, municipal utilities made life in western Kentucky cities and towns more bearable by providing businesses and residents with running water and electricity. These services aided considerably in the establishment of several large local industries, such as the Owensboro Wagon Company, which started slowly by producing approximately 300 wagons bearing the "OwensborO" logo in 1883 but grew to one of the country's largest concerns of its type, producing 30,000 wagons and 10,000 buggies in 1910 and employing 3,500 people. To the west, the Illinois Central undertook a massive expansion of its repair shops. The shops opened in the fall of 1927 with twenty-three buildings and more than 450 workers on hand, which increased to 2,100 by 1930. They were considered among the largest, most modern in its industry. Industrial development was not limited to large urban areas. Elsewhere in the Jackson Purchase, there were other large manufacturers. Mayfield was a hub for clothing concerns. The Mayfield Woolen Mills started small in 1860, but by the 1920s it was the nation's largest pants manufacturer with more than 5 million square feet of space and approximately 1,000 workers. Merit Clothing Company was a later arrival, but it grew into the town's largest clothing manufacturer, growing by the

1930s to a labor force approaching 800 workers. The Louisville-based Mengel Box Company opened a factory on the Mississippi River town of Hickman in 1901, attracted by the abundance of lumber in the region and river access, and employed as many as 600 before fire destroyed it in 1942. However, without a profit incentive to extend these services to sparsely populated rural areas or public programs, such industrial improvements were consigned to cities and towns.[36]

From early settlement of western Kentucky, regional leaders cooperated to improve transportation to the outside world. That was certainly the case with the development of the Green River, as the historian Helen Crocker sets forth in her brief history of the river, especially the lower Green River between Henderson and its junction with the Barren River and Bowling Green, approximately 175 miles. In fact, in the mid-1830s, based on the enthusiastic promises coming from business leaders in the Green River Valley, the Kentucky General Assembly, inspired by hopes that the Green River would attract steamboat traffic, approved the construction of a series of locks and dams as one of the young state's earliest publicly financed river projects. Though the costs and time needed to bring about the promised improvements were much greater than the initial estimates, the *Governor Breathitt* docked at Bowling Green in December 1842 to pick up a commercial load bound for New Orleans. The value of this river traffic proved somewhat disappointing, however, and was disrupted by the Civil War as both sides inflicted damages on the river's navigation infrastructure. Traffic improved after war's end when the state in 1868 chartered the Green and Barren River Navigation Company, a consortium of business and political interests along the lower Green River that some referred to as the "Monarchs of Green River," to manage river traffic. As complaints about that management mounted, oversight responsibilities passed to the US Army Corps of Engineers in 1888. Crocker gives the corps high marks for its management of river traffic operations up to the Great Depression, encouraging greater competition among the riverboats and facilitated the widespread local interest in logging along the Green River and its tributaries. Loggers at the turn of the century floated hardwood trees downriver to Evansville in huge "rafts," and Evansville became a noted lumbering center. However, Crocker connects the collapse of the river trade with the Great Depression and the burning of the steamboat *Evansville* shortly after completing its landing at Bowling Green in 1931. Further commercial use of the Green River would be delayed to the second half of the twentieth century.[37]

Of greater interest to the majority of those residing in western Kentucky was the development of roads. Without a federal or state system of highway transportation in the nineteenth century, the building and maintenance of roads in the region were left to counties and private entrepreneurs. Corporations, with the General Assembly's approval, sold bonds to investors for road construction and maintenance, and the bond payments were made with tolls collected at tollhouses typically set up at five-mile intervals. The toll roads, most of them gravel, were considered the best-maintained roads in the state; other roads were maintained by nearby residents, who were pressed by law to work the roads annually. Western Kentucky had few hard-surface roads until well into the twentieth century; until then, travelers frequently complained that the roads were impassable due to the mud caused by rain storms and intolerably dusty when dry. Anger boiled over at the turn of the century when travelers, who resented the tolls and the toll-road operators' failure to fully maintain the roads, engaged in what came to be known at the time as the "toll-gate war" by avoiding toll payments through the use of "shungates" designed to bypass the tollhouses. In some cases, resistance, greatest in central Kentucky, became violent with the destruction of tollhouses. In Daviess County, there were nearly two dozen toll roads at the time, many of which, according to the county attorney, failed to meet the standards set by the authorizing charters, were, as an *Owensboro Messenger* editorial expressed, barriers to local growth, and hurt farmers, who depended on the roads to get their goods to market. Local meetings were held to protest the toll roads, and a fence that one of the companies put up to prevent access to a shungate on a road operated by the Owensboro and Henderson Gravel Road Company was removed by angry farmers at least eight times. County authorities sided with "free-road" advocates and by 1903 took advantage of a state law to purchase the toll roads. Other counties' turnpike contests were less contentious, as in the cases of McCracken County, one of the first counties to eliminate its toll roads in 1897, and Christian County, which purchased fifty-five miles of toll roads in 1900.[38]

Once the toll roads were put out of business, a vacuum in the state's transportation policy was created as local property owners in western Kentucky were not willing to accept higher taxes to finance this new obligation. The accepted practice in the commonwealth was to press local men for maintenance of local roads. Although the historical record of this "forced labor system," which was a legacy of English and Virginia antecedents, is scant, Alben Barkley recalled it in his boyhood days as a "wonderful experience, a sort of jubilee, or get-together for the men" notable for the "swapping of stories" that took place.[39]

At the same time, the region would be caught up in the nationwide enthusiasm for "good roads" that was driven by bicycle enthusiasts, who were soon joined by the flood of automobile owners and local farmers wanting "to get out of the mud" and looking to the federal and state governments for solutions to the sorry shape of the nation's highways. In western Kentucky, the business community organized well-publicized multicounty assemblies at Owensboro and Hopkinsville in July 1901 that attracted thousands of western Kentuckians to listen to good-roads boosters and to view advancements in road construction and maintenance. However, the enthusiasm quickly gave way to division over the particulars of financing the improved roads. Who would be responsible for the funding: federal, state, or county government? Conservative western Kentucky farmers were unlikely to favor funding mechanisms dependent on raising property taxes. A resolution issued at the Owensboro city assembly stressed the need for leadership from the federal government, but it failed to call for specific remedies from Kentucky state and local governments.[40]

Regional voters' reluctance to back plans calling on them to help finance improved roads nearly led to the defeat in November 1909 of a state good-roads constitutional amendment to allow county voters to approve road-construction bonds for up to 2 percent of a county's assessed property valuation. Although the local press generally endorsed the proposal, the voters in Graves, Daviess, Henderson, Crittenden, Simpson, Muhlenberg, Ohio, McLean, Webster, Calloway, and Warren Counties voted it down. Nevertheless, counties in the region used the new amendment: Daviess County, for example, approved a $600,000 road bond issue in 1915 after federal postal officials threatened to stop rural free deliveries there due to the poor condition of its roads.[41]

The Good Roads Movement generated a great deal of interest in western Kentucky when proposals were made to bring several interstate roads through the region. Among the planned roads that ultimately were built through the region (see map 2) were the transcontinental Jefferson Davis Highway, sponsored by the United Daughters of the Confederacy and running from Arlington, Virginia, to San Diego through Bowling Green, past Jefferson Davis's birthplace in Todd County to Paducah; a western branch of the Dixie Highway called the Lincoln Jackson Way, starting in Chicago and passing through Louisville past Lincoln's birthplace, Mammoth Cave, Bowling Green, and Russellville before entering Tennessee north of Springfield, Tennessee, and extending to Nashville and ultimately Jacksonville, Florida; and the Dixie Bee Line, designed to shorten the travel between Chicago and Florida), which essentially followed the route of today's US 41 from Henderson past Madisonville and Hopkinsville to Nashville. These roads, touted as superhighways in their days, fell far short of today's high-speed highways. In an initial test of the Lincoln Jackson Way in 1915, its board of directors averaged twenty miles per hour on the Nashville to Bowling Green stretch. The road's rough condition in the Mammoth Cave area earned the state a black eye when the *Chicago Tribune* ran a story in October 1920 designating it "the World's Worst Road." This would hardly be the last blast from out-of-state critics aimed at Kentucky's roads. Road construction was topping the commonwealth's agenda before the country's entry into World War I as the legislature put $1.7 million into a road fund that most western Kentucky counties hoped to match their own funds for the good-roads program or the new state road system aimed at linking county seats.[42]

With the war over and the creation of the Kentucky Highways Department, interest in highway construction was restored. Ben Weille, a Paducah resident whose family owned Weille's, one of Paducah's leading clothing stores for more than a century, was a major figure in the development of Jackson Purchase highways at the time and a leader in the creation of the Jefferson Davis Highway Association. By the time association members met at a large gathering in Memphis in February 1916, Weille had already laid out the road's ninety-mile stretch from Paducah through Benton, Hopkinsville, and Fairview. Like most highways in the commonwealth at the time, the Jefferson Davis Highway lacked a hard surface and was especially treacherous through the Between the Rivers area and from the Tennessee River to the McCracken County line. Road conditions were hardly better on the Dixie Bee Line Highway, which opened in late 1926, swinging west in Webster County through Clay and Poole to connect to Henderson and Dixon, both county seats, rather than taking the shorter "bee line" through Slaughters and Sebree to Madisonville. Much of the Dixie Highway was dirt, so that it was hardly passable during extremely cold weather even with a forty-mile-per-hour state speed limit. Those gathered for the official opening were embarrassed when the state engineer's vehicle became stuck while traveling the road south of Earlington in Hopkins County to meet Governor William J. Fields for the ceremony in Hopkinsville.[43]

The dynamics of highway construction in western Kentucky changed dramatically with the establishment of state and federal highway authorities at the end of World War I. With considerable new revenue sources and greater authority over the construction of roads as part of the state and federal highway systems, the region was soon able to reach out to other sections of the state and nation. The experience gained through the Good Roads Movement was rewarded when the western branch of the Dixie Highway, the Dixie Bee Line, and the Jefferson Davis Highway were designated in the original federal highway system as US highways 31W, 41, and 68, respectively. Additional western Kentucky federal highways named were the Ohio River road, Highway 60, running east to west through Hawesville in Hancock County, Owensboro, Henderson, Morganfield in Union County, Paducah, and finally Wickliffe near the junction of the Ohio and Mississippi Rivers; Highway 62, running through Beaver Dam in Ohio County, Central City and Greenville in Muhlenberg County, Princeton in Caldwell County, to Paducah; Highway 45, running south from Paducah through Mayfield to Fulton on the Tennessee border; and US 51, also running north and south from Wickliffe to Fulton.

However, the early benefits western Kentucky received from the recognition of it as part of the federal highway system suffered due to the poor condition overall of the state's roads and the outside labeling of Kentucky as a "detour state." A principal drawback of western Kentucky's roads at the time was the absence of bridges over its numerous large rivers, forcing the use of ferries, many of which were still in use in 1931, as indicated in map 2, and operated privately. Travelers resented the tolls and the resulting significant delays. For this reason and the generally poor surface conditions of roads in the commonwealth, automobile clubs in other states advised their members to avoid Kentucky roads.[44]

To address this situation, existing civic organizations or newly created local associations, frequently soliciting cooperation from neighboring communities, were formed to promote the completion of the major highways. The Dixie Bee Line Association, for example, promoted improvements on what ultimately became US 41, and the West Kentucky Good Roads Association promoted highway improvements in the region in general and for US 60, the Ohio River road, in particular. Paducah, with the leadership of Citizens Bank president Richard Rudy and the Paducah Board of Trade, made a giant leap forward in 1927 by putting together the plans and private financing for the Paducah–Brookport bridge (later known as the Irvin S. Cobb Bridge, which is still in use), and it opened in 1929 as the first vehicular bridge over the Ohio River in western Kentucky.[45]

Passage of a new bridge law, popularly called the Murphy Act, in the 1928 legislation session promised an extensive $10 million bridge program and offered western Kentucky an opportunity to reduce a major hindrance in its highways. The program allowed the Highway Commission to authorize the construction or purchase of traffic bridges by the sale of bonds to be retired by tolls collected on the bridges. In an editorial, the *Paducah News-Democrat* considered that the commission's plans—which included western Kentucky, where the need for bridges was the greatest—would go far in reducing the sense of isolation in the region and "promote progress faster in the next few decades . . . than we have progressed at any other stage in our history."[46]

The Highway Commission soon approved construction of a series of vehicular intrastate bridges in western Kentucky: Tennessee River bridges at the Clark's River juncture south of Paducah, and the Eggner's Ferry Bridge on US 68; a bridge over the Cumberland River at Smithland in Livingston County on US 60 and the Canton Ferry Bridge on US 68; and a bridge over the Green River at Spottsville between Owensboro and Henderson. The package also included an Ohio River bridge for US 41 between Henderson and Evansville to be built jointly by Kentucky and

Indiana. A short time later, the commission also approved three Green River projects that resulted in the purchase of a private toll bridge between Rumsey and Calhoun over the Green River and new bridges at Rockport in Muhlenberg County on US 62 and at Livermore, which also crossed the Rough River. These projects were immensely important in reducing the isolation of western Kentuckians from the rest of the commonwealth and in nurturing tourism in the region.[47]

The establishment of public institutions in western Kentucky began as early as 1854 when Western State Hospital in Hopkinsville opened its doors for treatment of mental patients. In its first year, the hospital had 113 patients, but by 1919 that number rose to more than 1,200. A second institution, Kentucky State Penitentiary, was located on the banks of the Cumberland in Eddyville, which had been chosen over Bowling Green for the ample lands on which inmates could raise crops and the access to coal for heating purposes (also perhaps because of the influence of former Confederate general Hylan B. Lyon, an Eddyville resident and member of the board making the location decision). Funding difficulties caused construction of the prison to be delayed, but the "Castle on the Cumberland" (the historian Bill Cunningham's description likens the prison to a "large medieval fortress") opened in December 1889 at a cost of $275,000. The federal government built Outwood Veterans Hospital near Dawson Springs, which President Woodrow Wilson approved in 1919 as a tuberculosis sanitarium for veterans. In February 1922, an estimated crowd of 15,000, many of them arriving by train, heard speeches from Governor Edwin P. Morrow and other political luminaries at a dedication of the hospital, which had a capacity for nearly 500 residents in nearly thirty buildings.[48]

Additional public institutions were also established in western Kentucky in the early decades of the twentieth century to satisfy the rapidly increasing demand for trained public-school teachers. Many western Kentucky communities were home to private colleges, poorly financed and with undifferentiated academic programs often equivalent to what might today be considered a high-school curriculum. There were very fine graduates from these institutions, however. Future vice president Alben W. Barkley, for example, graduated with a bachelor's degree from Marvin College, one of two colleges in Clinton, the county seat of Hickman County. After graduation, he attended Emory College in Oxford, Georgia, which put him in sophomore college classes. Other colleges in the region included Ogden College and Potter College in Bowling Green, which eventually were absorbed into what is today Western Kentucky University; Logan Female College and Bethel College in Russellville; and Bethel College for Females in Hopkinsville, a school for young women that later became a coeducational junior college before closing in 1964.[49]

A major new direction was taken by the Kentucky General Assembly in 1906 when it agreed to establish two state-funded teacher-training colleges, one in the eastern part and the other in the western part of the state. Henry Hardin Cherry, the president of Southern Normal School in Bowling Green, lobbied aggressively for the western school, spending more than two months in Frankfort talking to lawmakers and then defeating other western Kentucky towns in securing the location of Western Kentucky State Normal School at Bowling Green. Cherry continued to lobby in Frankfort for his school, which exceeded Eastern Kentucky State Normal School in both enrollment and state appropriations. It was eventually upgraded to Western Kentucky Normal School and Teachers College but failed to meet the demand for college-trained public-school teachers in western Kentucky. State legislators sought to remedy that problem in 1922 by authorizing an additional school in both the eastern and the western sections of the state. This decision provoked intense competition among the Jackson Purchase towns of Benton, Clinton, Mayfield, Paducah, and Murray as well as among Hopkinsville, Henderson, Morganfield, Owensboro, and Princeton east of the Cumberland River. Murray ultimately prevailed behind the strong backing of the politically influential Rainey T. Wells, veteran member of the Kentucky Tax Commission, who helped raise local funds for the Murray site. Each town was visited by the selection committee and made presentations on its plans to raise funds for the college's initial building. Fortunately for Murray, its presentation was the last, and it was the only one that had already raised money for the building and land, so it won the selection contest by a unanimous vote. Murray State Normal School opened in the fall of 1923; it initially drew half of its students from Calloway County in particular and 90 percent from the Jackson Purchase overall. Enrollment increased and included more students east of the

Jackson Purchase after bridges crossing the Tennessee and Cumberland Rivers were constructed. The college's title was upgraded to Murray State Normal School and Teachers College in 1926.[50]

However, the new public colleges were prohibited by state law from enrolling black students and thus were unable to satisfy teacher-training needs in the black community. Funding from northern philanthropic organizations such as the Julius Rosenwald Fund significantly improved the physical conditions of schools for black children. Rosenwald, whose fortune came from Sears Roebuck, aligned his interest in black educational uplift with the philosophy of Booker T. Washington, the most influential voice on education for blacks at the beginning of the twentieth century. One or more Rosenwald schools, many of them with one or two classrooms, were established in a majority of western Kentucky counties between World War I and the Great Depression; on the larger side, Rosenwald High School in Madisonville opened in 1931 with ten classrooms.[51]

To respond to the needs for improved teacher training and in trades considered appropriate for the Jim Crow segregated conditions for blacks in western Kentucky, D. H. Anderson, a black educator in Paducah, made it his life's mission to establish a college based on the Booker T. Washington "Tuskegee philosophy" that black higher-education training in the South should focus on those careers, including teaching, open to blacks in the Jim Crow conditions prevailing in western Kentucky in the 1910s. Determined to succeed, he started fund-raising for and construction of the college in 1911, but he soon determined that the long-term success of his venture depended on state support, which he finally received in 1918 when the Kentucky General Assembly appropriated $8,000 to West Kentucky Industrial College, which joined what is today Kentucky State University in Frankfort as the second black public college in the commonwealth and second public college in western Kentucky. The school, soon recognized as a junior college, with dormitories for men and women, provided training in a variety of trades and teaching and established itself as a vital part of the black social and educational experience in western Kentucky into the mid-1930s, with Anderson as president the driving force behind it.[52]

2

The New Deal and Western Kentucky

An estimated crowd of 50,000 was on hand for the inauguration of sixty-two-year-old Democrat Ruby Laffoon as governor of Kentucky in December 1931. The crowd included 125 from Madisonville arriving on the Louisville & Nashville Laffoon Inauguration Special; additional western Kentucky political luminaries boarded the train in Owensboro, notably the venerable newspaper publisher Urey Woodson, who was part of the Laffoon escort, and Ernest M. Ford, newly elected state representative and father of future governor Wendell Ford. Laffoon's thirty-three-year-old running mate, Albert Benjamin "Happy" Chandler, who grew up in the western Kentucky community of Corydon near Henderson before entering into a legal and political career in the bluegrass city of Versailles, was to be inaugurated as lieutenant governor. The two were among the seven men from western Kentucky who served as governor from 1931 to 1979 (Chandler served two terms). The influence of the Gibraltar of Kentucky Democracy was never greater than during that timeframe. However, the two men honored that day were central figures in the coming deep factional split that dominated Kentucky Democratic politics for the next four decades, which on a number of occasions offered Republicans, a distinct minority in terms of registration, electoral victories.[1]

Laffoon was politically ambitious, but he was not, in sharp contrast to the athletic, energetic Chandler, an imposing candidate physically. From childhood injuries he sustained while working on the farm that left one leg shorter than the other, Laffoon walked with a pronounced limp. The Laffoons were a political family; Uncle Polk Laffoon Sr. had represented Kentucky's Second Congressional District for two terms, during which the future governor was a congressional aide. After studying law, Ruby Laffoon entered state and local political races with mixed success. His initial efforts to win statewide office were thwarted, but he was later elected to the circuit court for Hopkins County twice. Polk Laffoon Jr. was active in the Jockey Club in northern Kentucky and part of the bipartisan combine representing the state's dominant economic interests. The same political machine had paved the way for election of GOP governor Flem Sampson in the election of 1927, but Republican chances in 1931 were diminished by the political scandals during his administration and the economic depression that many Kentucky voters attributed to the Republican president Herbert Hoover. With young Polk's backing, Ruby Laffoon was the favorite going into the Democratic state convention in 1931, the last one Democrats held to pick the party's gubernatorial candidate; he won the nomination on the first ballot, defeating, among others, Lieutenant Governor James Breathitt from Hopkinsville and Murray State president Rainey T. Wells. There was considerably more controversy over Chandler's nomination as the powerful eastern Kentucky politician Fred Vinson, a future US cabinet officer and Supreme Court chief justice, fought hard on the convention floor for his candidate as the rightful pick. Laffoon supporters long believed his retelling of the story of an eager Chandler on bended knee promising loyalty—short-lived, as it would turn out—to the future governor at the convention. Chandler also had strong backing from leaders in the bipartisan combine who carried the day.[2]

In the general election, Republican candidate William B. Harrison, former mayor of Louisville, tried to make the race competitive by suggesting that the elderly Laffoon would die in office and that he would be controlled by the political bosses in the bipartisan combine. Laffoon mounted a vigorous campaign, making the normally Democratic *Louisville Courier-Journal,* which had opposed the Democratic convention and backed Harrison's candidacy, a foil for the ruling political and economic interests in Frankfort and Washington responsible for the economic woes associated with the Great Depression. Laffoon told a western Kentucky crowd in Princeton at the end of the campaign, "I don't want to raise prejudice against any sector of the state . . . , but they [people in Louisville] seem not to have realized that Kentucky extends west of the Salt River." His message resonated in western Kentucky, excited about the prospect of electing the first governor from the region since A. O. Stanley of Henderson in 1915. The major western Kentucky newspapers swung their support behind Laffoon. Urey Woodson's editorial in the *Owensboro Messenger* slapped back at the *Courier-Journal,* stating that "the Democratic country press of Kentucky will redouble its effort for the success of the Democratic state ticket." Indeed, the region's press aided Laffoon's campaign by helping to turn out enthusiastic crowds in his final campaign swing through the First Congressional District. Laffoon was joined by popular native son US senator Alben W. Barkley in his hometown of Paducah, where a large and exuberant crowd listened as Barkley attacked what he considered were the ineffective economic promises of Hoover and Sampson and promised that a Laffoon administration meant that western Kentucky would no longer be neglected in dividing the state's highway expenditures. Laffoon delighted those attending with a little gallows humor in responding to a question about how he was getting along with the "Hoover prosperity": he was doing well "now that I was eating one meal a day, and not buying much, because I didn't have anything to buy with." Not surprisingly, with Senator Barkley's endorsement, the *Paducah Sun-Democrat* strongly backed Laffoon's election "because we of western Kentucky have always been at the short end of the horn." Laffoon's hometown paper, the *Madisonville Messenger,* condemned the *Courier-Journal* for its support of Harrison, called for an end to highway-spending favoritism toward the Bluegrass and eastern Kentucky regions, and eagerly anticipated that favor shifting to western Kentucky and especially Hopkins County.[3]

Laffoon's 72,000-vote victory margin was one of the largest in state history to that time and was made possible by the nearly 50,000-vote edge given to him in the Gibraltar of Kentucky Democracy. He carried 81 of the state's 120 counties, notably losing in Jefferson and Fayette Counties, but he swept western Kentucky except for the traditionally Republican Butler, Crittenden, and Ohio Counties, which Harrison carried by very slim majorities. Laffoon took Ballard, Calloway, Carlisle, Fulton, Graves, Hickman, Hopkins (his home county), Logan, Marshall, McLean, Simpson, Todd, Trigg, and Union Counties by better than two-to-one margins over Harrison.[4]

Laffoon's administration is remembered today principally for his unsuccessful efforts to implement the general sales tax in Kentucky. John Ed Pearce, a former political columnist for the *Louisville Courier-Journal,* calls the Laffoon administration "just short of a fiasco"; another historian suggests that Laffoon was simply "unlucky and made his situation worse." However, proper recognition has not been made of the very difficult economic straits in the Kentucky economy that he inherited and the powerful opposition that he faced in trying to push his program through the legislature. His standing among the commonwealth's governors would be much higher had the candidate he chose to replace himself had not lost in one of state's most bitterly contested gubernatorial primaries.[5]

After a decade of economic expansion following World War I, the collapse of financial markets in late October 1929 marked the beginning of the nation's Great Depression. However, for many western Kentuckians, the go-go days of the Roaring Twenties had not been so spectacular. This was particularly true for the region's farmers, who did well during the war but were hurting after the war because farm prices, in part due to overproduction, turned downward. In many regards, much of rural western Kentucky had so far remained untouched by the technological improvements of the twentieth century, and federal and state policy makers preferred to rely on "the hidden hand" of market forces rather than initiate programs and policies designed to improve rural conditions. Rural electrification was in its infancy; of the more than 61,000 farms in western Kentucky, less than 2 percent were on the electrical grid, according to 1930 US census data (Ballard, Butler, Carlisle, Hickman, Lyon, Marshall and Trigg Counties each reported ten or fewer farms with electricity). Fewer than 3 percent of the reporting farms had indoor plumbing, but more than one-fourth did have telephone access. Most farms in the region—indeed, an overwhelming percentage—were located on dirt roads, much of which were unimproved and so became impassable in bad weather. The Kentucky Progress Commission, created by GOP governor Flem Sampson to survey the impact of the Depression, concluded that the commonwealth's farm families had realized little in the way of progress during the 1920s and that for most "the situation is becoming worse every year." Severe drought in 1930 devastated crops in the Jackson Purchase. County extension agents reported to Frankfort heavy losses in corn and tobacco crops, and dairy cattle and other livestock in Fulton and Graves Counties were sold for whatever farmers could get due to a lack of feed. Overproduction of the tobacco crop in 1931 and a sharp reduction in prices caused concern that violence such as had taken place during the Black Patch Wars might return. To cool tempers, tobacco sales throughout the region were delayed.[6]

Urban areas were perhaps somewhat at first shielded from the hard times. According to historians Lee Dew and Aloma Dew, Owensboro's economy had been hurt when Prohibition forced the shutdown of local distilleries, but the city's diverse industrial base and growth in key industries kept that city's economy from collapse in the first years of the Great Depression—for example, Ken-Rad was a major producer of vacuum tubes for a rapidly expanding radio industry. A survey of American cities in 1930 ranked Owensboro in the top-fifteen cities with an economy in "fair to good" shape. However, western Kentucky could not long escape the impact of the national banking collapse. In Paducah, the suicides of the presidents of First National Bank and City National Bank shook depositor confidence. These desperate acts were accompanied by the collapse of the Bank of Kentucky, the state's largest financial institution, in November 1930, which also severely rattled the city's banks, several of them surviving only following mergers. Among the region's banks that closed were the Hopkins County Bank, Bank of Arlington in Carlisle County, Cadiz Bank & Trust in Trigg County, McElwain-Megular Bank & Trust in Franklin in Simpson County (brought down by the closing of the Bank of Kentucky), Webster County Bank in Clay, Farmers Bank of Hickman in Fulton County, Bank of Russellville in Logan County, Bank of Sturgis in Union County, Farmers State Bank (taken over by First National Bank of Greenville) in Muhlenberg County, Henderson County Savings Bank (consolidated with the Ohio Valley Banking & Trust), First State Bank in Livingston County, Central Trust Bank in Owensboro, and Farmers Bank of West Louisville in Daviess County. In addition, the Kevil Bank and Bank of Barlow in Ballard County, Citizens

Bank of Drakesboro in Muhlenberg County, and Farmers & Merchant Bank of Slaughters closed, but authorities allowed them to reopen after their reorganization. Fear and panic abounded in the region as depositors and local businesses worried over the viability of banking institutions. Local authorities' sensitivity to rumors that could result in a bank panic caused the arrest of a Madisonville coal miner in late 1930 for negative comments about the conditions of local banks.[7]

There was no escaping the social costs of the downwardly spiraling economy. Jobless men in Paducah marched downtown in November 1930 asking for work rather than charity. In the region's coal fields, the industry struggled through the 1920s as the price dropped from more than $4 per ton during the war to $2.06 in 1926 before plummeting to $1.31 in 1932. Mines collapsed, and miners were idled. The United Mine Workers of America (UMWA) union saw membership gains during the war wiped away in the Western Kentucky Coal Field before the New Deal despite determined efforts to organize the field. As Ruby Laffoon prepared to give his inaugural address, reports to Frankfort from his home area projected 1,000 unemployed miners in Hopkins County and an additional 1,500 in Muhlenberg County. Without effective federal or state relief organizations, the Red Cross secured assistance from Quakers for food to provide free school lunches to the miners' children in the two counties. The "alarming and distressing" plight of the destitute did not go unnoticed. In Hopkins County, Mayor B.N. Gordon of Madisonville coordinated a countywide effort to call on those with jobs to donate one day of pay monthly and on farmers to donate surplus foods from their crops for what was expected to be short-term relief. More effective was Governor Laffoon's plan to accelerate the hiring of highway workers, at that time the nearest alternative to a government unemployment program.[8]

The 1932 legislative session proved to be very disappointing for Governor Laffoon, though. Soon after taking office, he chafed as the political bosses who had helped put him in office now sought to call the shots. Notable among these leaders in the bipartisan combine holding government posts were Ben Johnson, the powerful chairman of the state Highway Department who had lost that post during the Sampson administration, although only until a "ripper bill" designed to reduce the governor's powers enabled his return to that post, and who was now a fixture in the Highway Department; Johnson's son-in-law, state auditor Dan Talbott; and state senator Allie Young from Morehead. Lieutenant Governor Happy Chandler, who had apparently quickly forgotten his earlier professed loyalty to the new governor, was aligned closely with the political bosses. When Laffoon attempted to tap his own man as House Speaker, the political bosses succeeded in imposing on him their choice, John Y. Brown, who was raised near Sturgis in Union County before moving to Lexington to practice law and who was also father of future governor John Y. Brown Jr. Altogether, western Kentucky was well represented in the legislative leadership with Brown, Lieutenant Governor Chandler from Henderson County as Senate president, and Charles G. Franklin, Laffoon's campaign manager from Madisonville, as Senate president pro tempore.

The battle that session was fought over the budget and Laffoon's call for passage of a general sales tax to offset declining state finances, which, unless a tax plan could be developed, would call for steep budget cuts. His sales tax proposal drew strong opposition in state government from what was becoming an anti-Laffoon faction led by Ben Johnson, Dan Talbott, and Happy Chandler and from outside state government by the Kentucky Retail Association, the Kentucky Merchants' Association, and the Kentucky Commercial Executives' Association, which could muster grassroots opposition to the Laffoon plan. The governor delayed presenting his spending plan until mid-February, when before a joint legislative session he called for a three-cent sales tax, which he quickly reduced by a penny to quell a groundswell against his program. The retailers wasted no time in organizing local opposition by encouraging stores to close the following Saturday so that legislators could gauge district opposition. In Laffoon's home county, approximately 100 merchants sent telegrams to Senator Charles G. Franklin and Representative Fred Beshear asking them to oppose the sales tax. Regional newspapers reported that western Kentucky was united in opposing the tax. Merchant groups from western Kentucky communities such as Benton, Bowling Green, Calhoun, Franklin, Hawesville, Hickman, Mayfield, Owensboro, Paducah, Princeton, and Wickliffe adopted resolutions in protest. The opposition was strongest in communities along the Ohio River and Tennessee state line, where businesses believed they would lose trade to nearby states that did not have the tax. Some local merchants joined a throng of 700 merchants at the Capital Hotel in Frankfort in late February in what the *Louisville Courier-Journal* termed a "violent meeting" in advance of legislators' return to work to take up the sales tax. The opposition was dealt a setback when in a bipartisan vote the House passed the sales tax, although reduced to one cent. A tearing Speaker John Y. Brown Sr., not required to vote, was among the thirty-one votes against the bill. James D. Via, a Hickman County Democrat who had lost to Brown in the Speaker's race, told House members that "as long as Ruby Laffoon wants it [the tax] I am going to stand for it."[9]

When the bill arrived in the Kentucky Senate, Happy Chandler, who profited over the course of his long political career from his anti–sales tax stance, stood in the way. First, he announced that the Senate, unlike the House, would hold a hearing on the sales tax, thus giving the retailers time to marshal their opposition. An Owensboro delegation was on hand to deliver a resolution from local merchants demanding that Senator Gates Young oppose the sales tax. Fifty rode the train from Paducah; among them was *Paducah Sun-Democrat* editor Elliott C. Mitchell, who at the hearing told lawmakers that western Kentucky was united in disapproving the plan. Nobody at the hearing spoke in favor of the Laffoon proposal. As many as 10,000 opponents were on hand to fight against the sales tax, some of whom later became unruly. An estimated 100 or more protestors forced their way into the governor's mansion, where they caused minor damage. The Laffoon family was not present, but the governor termed the crowd's action "a disgrace and an outrage."[10]

Happy Chandler exercised considerable power in determining the fate of the sales tax legislation. Following the public hearing, the Rules Committee killed the bill, and Chandler, insisting that it would take a two-thirds majority for a discharge motion to enable a floor vote, forced Laffoon to concede defeat, marking the first time in nearly three decades that a governor had not prevailed in getting his program through in his first session. However, the two leaders would reengage over the sales tax over the next four years, but the stakes would be higher as the unrolling of New Deal relief programs in the commonwealth called on state leaders to come up with significant state revenues to match federal expenditures.[11]

Western Kentucky's most powerful Democratic leaders, Governor Laffoon and US senator Alben W. Barkley from Paducah, jumped on the bandwagon early in support of Democrat Franklin D. Roosevelt's presidential candidacy in 1932. Barkley, first elected to Congress from the First Congressional District in 1912 at the start of Woodrow Wilson's administration, had earned considerable credit from Democratic leaders in his unsuccessful gubernatorial race in 1923, which helped catapult him to the US Senate in 1926. Considered one of his party's strongest orators, he was picked to deliver the keynote address for the first but not the last time at the Democratic National Convention to be held in Chicago in 1932. Humorist Will Rogers took exception to the speech as a simple "note" because it took nearly two hours to deliver, interrupted by several demonstrations of approval by the assembled delegates. Barkley's message was that of a partisan calling on fellow Democrats to "remove from the body of our nation the dead flesh and decayed bones resulting from twelve years of Republican quackery." The speech was also notable, given his long support for Prohibition, for conceding that the Eighteenth Amendment had failed in its aim to staunch the flow of alcohol and suggesting consideration of a referendum for the states to repeal it. Barkley's hometown paper predicted that a vice presidency was likely and swelled that he had already demonstrated that "he is the greatest keynoter in the history of the party."[12]

The November election was as much a vote against Hoover and the Republican Party, whom many voters blamed for the Depression, as a vote for Roosevelt. The margin for Roosevelt in western Kentucky, which had voted Democratic by a mere 6,000 votes in Al Smith's 1928 presidential run, exceeded 60,000, with the Democratic Party picking up toss-up counties such as Caldwell and Christian but losing in Republican-leaning Crittenden, Butler, Ohio, and Hancock Counties (Butler and Ohio Counties gave Hoover wins by less than 100 votes each). Earle C. Clements, a Union County official at the time and future Kentucky governor, later recalled that he sensed that the years of unemployment and widespread hunger had engendered in the people at the time a spirit of despair and a desire for revolutionary change. There was also a sense of optimism present in the change of administrations in Washington that promised something Roosevelt called a "new deal," which neither he nor those who voted him to office understood in terms of specific policies.[13]

The first order of business for Roosevelt after taking office in March 1933 was to address the crisis in the nation's banking sector after an early panic in Michigan forced the governor there to declare a banking holiday, which was followed soon by holidays in California, Tennessee, and several other states. In Kentucky, Governor Laffoon requested banks to close on March 1. Western Kentucky banks responded in several ways to the governor's request. Daviess County and Owensboro banks closed as directed and planned once they reopened to prevent potential runs by restricting customers' withdrawals to 5 percent on existing assets per day. In sharp contrast, Jackson Purchase banks conducted business as usual, with a few exceptions that chose to follow the governor's edict. Ed Gardner, the respected president of the First National Bank of Mayfield, assured his customers that Laffoon's order, although needed in eastern and northern Kentucky to prevent panic, was unnecessary in the Purchase. A *Paducah Sun-Democrat* editorial followed Gardner's lead in lampooning Laffoon's "jackass holiday," which it said was necessary in nearby counties only if their citizens proved to have "longer ears than the ordinary donkey."[14]

There was no such equivocation when FDR, following his inauguration, directed all banks to close their doors starting March 4 until Congress had time to enact emergency legislation, which would be passed on March 9. In the first of a series of radio fireside chats with the American people, Roosevelt soothed widespread anxieties in telling listeners that the only thing they need fear "is fear itself" as banking authorities systematically authorized banks, provided they could prove their solvency, to reopen. His message was well received in western Kentucky. Readers of the *Paducah Sun-Democrat* were told that the message was delivered "in language anyone can understand" and that "all sound banks will be reopened, and kept sound, and that unsound banks will stay closed until they reorganize their affairs into soundness." The president's efforts had the desired effect in western Kentucky: banks were soon cleared to reopen, and depositors' confidence was restored, as evidenced by brisk deposit activities. Depositor anxieties were further reduced later that spring by the passage of the landmark Glass-Steagall Banking Act, which created the Federal Deposit Insurance Corporation, insuring all deposits up to $2,500.[15]

The direction of the New Deal came during Roosevelt's first one hundred days. Among the highest priorities was putting people to work. To that end, young men were enrolled in the Civilian Conservation Corps (CCC), a favorite program of the president created by executive order, and sent to military-style camps set up in forests throughout the country. There they performed a variety of conservation and public-work projects for lodging, meals, and $1 per day, most of which was sent home to their families. Western Kentucky was allotted more than 1,100 spots in the initial CCC recruitment, including more than 90 for Daviess and McCracken Counties. One of the earliest camps was located near Benton in Marshall County, where 170 young men, including two dozen from the county, were engaged in erosion-remediation efforts in the Jackson Purchase. Reception of the CCC in the region was very positive as it was seen as a step toward helping, in the words of a *Paducah Sun-Democrat* editorial, "the industrious and energetic citizen who is unemployed through no fault of his own" in contrast to "the loafer, the gimme-a-dime-please-mister-drifter" who preferred to "remain at his warm flop-house."[16]

The CCC, which ended with America's entry into World War II, opened camps with an average 200 enrollees in Paducah, Hartford, Morganfield, Clinton, Benton, Columbus, Henderson, Marion, Dixon, Cadiz, Murray, Madisonville, Mayfield, Dawson Springs, Central City, Owensboro, and Sebree. In keeping with the Roosevelt administration's reluctance to challenge deeply held sentiments against racial integration in the South, separate camps for blacks were provided in Russellville and Morganfield, concentrating on soil conservation. Local communities were eager to secure a CCC camp because of the additional revenues they received from the purchase of supplies, jobs created, and projects undertaken.[17]

Though many CCC camps focused on conservation measures, such as the Marion camp that planted tens of thousands black locust trees and black walnut seedlings on Crittenden County farms during the two years it was active, others concentrated on public projects. Most notably, the CCC was critical in establishing state parks in western Kentucky. Emma Guy Cromwell, director of state parks during the Laffoon administration, stated: "There is no arithmetic adequate . . . to calculate the immense amount of good accomplished by this agency [the CCC]." At Columbus in Fulton County, a CCC camp restored the trenches and fortifications of the Columbus–Belmont Civil War battlefield on the

Mississippi River, where Confederates had sought to deny passage downriver to Union gunboats in one of the earliest significant engagements of the war in Kentucky. The battlefield's origins as a state park had come in 1928 with a $5,000 state appropriation and promises that local backers, organized the following year as the Columbus-Belmont Park Association, could secure land for the park. Glenn W. Lane, the local state representative, worked closely with Cromwell to secure a CCC camp in Columbus for laying out the state park, and the Columbus-Belmont State Park was dedicated on July 4, 1935. On a more modest scale, the Dawson Springs camp worked on what was then called Dawson Springs State Park, near the once thriving tourist community there. This park suffered over the years from competition with the much larger Pennyrile State Forest and eventually was removed from the state park system; today it is a 4-H camp operated under the auspices of the University of Kentucky.[18]

Perhaps the most important CCC work on the region's state parks was at John James Audubon State Park in Henderson. The renowned nineteenth-century ornithologist, naturalist, and painter James Audubon (1785–1851) had spent about ten years in Henderson during his early career. The local librarian in the first few decades of the twentieth century, Susan Towles, whose grandfather had befriended Audubon during his Henderson days, was passionate about her vision to establish Henderson as a center for celebrating Audubon's career. The retired Kentucky Supreme Court chief justice John Palmore, also from Henderson, knew Towles and her two unmarried sisters in the 1930s as elderly women, strong Democrats, and "unreconstructed Confederates." She borrowed $1,000 to purchase an important collection of Audubon's work from a Boston bookstore in 1913 and added to that the long-term loan of another important collection. The federal government approved the Audubon CCC project and listed the park in the National Park Service. On several hundred acres of land donated by locals, CCC enrollees and later Works Progress Administration (WPA) workers laid out the park with hiking paths and roads; clearing underbrush; putting in water and sewage systems; constructing a light plant; establishing both a small lake for birds visiting the area as part of the Great Mississippi Flyway and a larger recreation lake; and constructing the existing Tea House and the marvelous museum notable for its French Provincial architecture.

The museum, opened in July 1938, housed a significant collection of paintings by Audubon and his sons as well as many items associated with the painter.[19]

New Deal relief programs took a variety of forms, including direct payments to the destitute, commonly referred to, often with disdain, as the "dole," and public-work projects that put the unemployed to work. Roosevelt inherited from the Hoover administration the Federal Emergency Relief Act (FERA) of 1932, which funneled money to localities for putting men back to work. In Kentucky, Governor Laffoon appointed Harper Gatton, the school superintendent from Madisonville and Laffoon's friend, to administer the program. Although federal authorities distrusted Gatton's heavy-handed administration and questionable reports on the needs of Kentucky's poverty-stricken people, they nevertheless responded with a $672,000 loan issued in September 1932 for forty-one counties where sufficient documentation of need was presented. Among the original counties funded in western Kentucky were Hopkins, Webster, Henderson, Union, Caldwell, Lyon, McCracken, and Fulton. Future loans extended the program to additional counties in the region, including Butler, Calloway, Crittenden, Daviess, Livingston, Logan, McLean, and Todd. Workers earned $1.50 per day, distributed pursuant to orders from Gatton in script to assure that wages would go to family necessities. The program got off to a fast start with an estimated 8,100 workers in twenty-seven counties and relief provided to an estimated 50,000 families. McCracken County received the greatest funding in the Jackson Purchase area, approximately $20,000. By the following June, more than 160,000 persons in western Kentucky were enrolled, working mostly in a variety of temporary public-works jobs. Of this total, an estimated one-third came from the especially distressed Western Kentucky Coal Field.[20]

The Civil Works Administration (CWA) was created by an FDR executive order to replace FERA and placed under the national direction of Harry Hopkins, who was building a deserved reputation for achieving quick results from the relief programs he directed. The CWA's goal was to put 4 million unskilled and semiskilled unemployed men in useful public-work projects to offset what proved be the very cold winter of 1933–1934. Joseph E. Brent's study of the CWA in the Jackson Purchase, where

6,500 individuals found work before the program ended in April 1934, gives high marks for its effectiveness and popular support. When accusations of favoritism in Ballard and Lyon Counties were leveled against local program administrators, and when protests sparked by the Unemployed Welfare Association of Paducah and McCracken County led to meetings in December attended by an estimated crowd of 700 against the lack of sufficient CWA projects to meet the local need, state and federal authorities responded promptly by insisting that selection of workers needed to be fair and by adding additional work projects in McCracken County. In its short period of operation, the CWA concentrated its efforts on a wide variety of useful projects, including road improvements, recreational fields, and drainage works. As the CWA wound down its mission, a Mayfield grocer wrote enthusiastically of its work: "We hardily commend C. W. A. as the only plan yet devised that really puts money into circulation through the right channels."[21]

In contrast to the FERA and CWA missions, which were designed to put large amounts of public dollars to work to ameliorate poverty either through employment on public jobs or through direct subsidies, Congress created in Roosevelt's first 100 days the Public Works Administration (PWA), which focused on more large-scale public-construction projects. The historian George Blakey underscores the bureaucratic unwieldiness of the program with the example of the construction of Cherry Hall on the campus of Western Kentucky State Teachers College. The administration there insisted on the use of local stones for the building, but the PWA delayed construction by insisting that cheaper limestone should be used. The dispute ended when Harold Ickes, the federal administrator of the PWA, indicated a willingness to go along with the college provided that the college absorb the additional $21,000 in cost. The offer was refused, and construction went forward with the less-expensive Indiana stone, but Blakey suggests that if the project had been one under Harry Hopkins, the college would have gotten its way, and the federal government would have absorbed the difference. Nevertheless, the PWA legacy in western Kentucky includes new courthouses in Hopkins, McCracken, Ohio, and Webster Counties; a large addition to the Union County courthouse; and new post offices in Owensboro and Mayfield. Owensboro benefited from a number of PWA projects, none of which was as important as the construction of the Glover H.

Cary toll bridge over the Ohio River, which opened in July 1940, for which the PWA provided 45 percent of the funding.[22]

The New Deal programs came with considerable financial and political costs to the commonwealth and its governor, though. Required state matches caused significant political tensions with federal authorities that dogged Ruby Laffoon throughout the remainder of his administration and forced a showdown with anti-Laffoon Democrats, who persisted in opposing him in passing the state sales tax necessary to pay the state's share of New Deal relief programs. Laffoon's relationship with federal relief authorities started on the wrong foot when, citing unemployment and hunger in the coal fields and underresourced institutions caring for children and persons with tuberculosis, he requested a $15 million loan for Kentucky's FERA program late in the Hoover administration, a sum that Kentucky relief officials thought was grossly exaggerated.[23]

By the summer of 1933, the federal government was prepared to provide Kentucky with $9 million in FERA relief, provided that the state could come up with a $3 million match, which it clearly did not have. Harry Hopkins, the trusted FDR welfare adviser, made it clear that federal relief funding would terminate on August 15 unless a matching plan were in place. To that end, Laffoon called the legislature into special session, with the shutdown in the relief program putting pressure on lawmakers to act. Prospects for success were not high given the mixed results in the recently held primary election, which were marked by high emotions among the antagonistic Democratic factions. Neither side appeared to have gained great advantage, but Laffoon endured embarrassment by the defeat of Fred Beshear, great uncle of future governor Steve Beshear, in the state representative race for Hopkins County, the governor's home county. Given high turnover, Laffoon could hope to attract support to his side; he now also had a constituency for the sales tax that he had lacked in the 1932 regular session: the thousands of Kentuckians benefiting from federal relief programs to oppose the merchants prepared to rally to the Johnson-Chandler-Talbott anti-Laffoon forces. The Muhlenberg County fiscal court in the heart of the Western Kentucky Coal Field, for example, adopted a resolution before the special session supporting the $3 million match, and an *Owensboro Messenger* editorial termed the legislature's failure to raise taxes "too ghastly to contemplate" as "starvation will stalk through the Commonwealth." Legislators needed to understand that "hunger provokes riot, theft and disorder." In fact, the jobless did march on Frankfort during the special session. Munnell Wilson, a colorful one-term state representative elected in 1905 from Hopkins County and popularly dubbed the "walking munn" after he walked to Frankfort to take his oath of office, promised to recruit 5,000 unemployed miners from the Western Kentucky Coal Field. Although he fell significantly short of his goal, leading only a handful of Muhlenberg unemployed coal miners to Frankfort, they were joined by 300 to 500 pro–sales tax marchers from northern and central Kentucky. Tyler Munford received a petition from 3,500 of his Union County constituents urging his support of Laffoon and the sales tax, which caused Munford to reconsider his opposition to the measure and to make the vital motion to suspend House rules in order to revitalize the sales tax bill. A report in late September from Central City in Muhlenberg County that merchants were forced to feed more than fifty families to avoid widespread looting was followed by a telegram to the governor from ministers in Central City warning him that "if relief doesn't come immediately only God knows what will happen."[24]

As the session got under way in late August, Laffoon's influence in the House improved with the departure of Speaker John Y. Brown Sr. to the US Congress. Frank Lebus moved up from majority floor leader to that vacant seat, and Clarence E. Evans from Simpson County took the floor leader position. The two leaders were considered acceptable to both Democratic factions. Harry Hopkins appeared before a legislative joint session on August 22 to tell the assembled solons that the White House was indifferent as to the nature of the tax that would be passed, but the restoration of federal relief funding, which had been withdrawn in mid-August, was contingent on finding the $3 million match. Hopkins did not make a favorable impression; many members reportedly felt they were being "blackmailed" by the Roosevelt administration, given its decision to take away funding for Kentucky. Henry Ward, a young news writer on the *Paducah Sun-Democrat* who had earlier in the month been elected as state representative from Paducah, said that tempers in the special session were higher than they had been in the previous year's regular session. A month passed before the House cobbled together its tax plan, with increases in beer and whiskey taxes and a penny sales tax (now called a "consumers tax"). The bipartisan 56–38 vote in favor of the plan included twelve critical Republicans, whose votes were essential to passing the bill. Denny Smith from Hopkinsville, who had been a vocal opponent, announced that he still opposed the sales tax in principle, but with the gallery filled by the unemployed from western and northern Kentucky, he conceded that the "public welfare" now demanded the bill. Clarence E. Evans, the House majority leader from Franklin, voted against it.[25]

With Lieutenant Governor Chandler and his allies once again in control of the Senate, however, the House bill was dead on arrival there despite protestations from Senator Carl Franklin, the Senate president pro tempore from Madisonville. Chandler quickly announced his opposition to the Senate's measure, and the sales tax failed once more. In its place, the Senate put together a package of tax increases on beer and liquor for relief funding, which proponents insisted would be sufficient to resolve the pending crisis given their belief that Laffoon exaggerated the amount needed.[26]

Skeptics of the Chandler plan were correct, though: in rejecting the sales tax, Chandler and his allies failed to provide adequate tax revenues to meet the state's match for the relief program. With considerable difficulties, Laffoon secured a bond in October for that month's $250,000 state match of federal relief funds, but future prospects for finding matching funds were bleak. He despondently notified Washington on November 6 that Kentucky, unable to make its required state portion of relief funding, was forced to abdicate to the federal government the state's responsibility for funding and administering the program. Bitterly, he stated that "it is a measly outrage that Kentucky has fallen down in her duty." Harry Hopkins appointed Thornton Wilcox to replace Harper Gatton, who had returned earlier to his post as Madisonville school superintendent, but the struggles between Washington and Frankfort would continue.[27]

Laffoon now recognized it was necessary to develop a strategy to take control of state government if he wanted any chance to redeem his term in office. To that end, before the start of the 1934 session, he surrounded himself with his "brain trust" (a name used in imitation of what President Roosevelt called his New Deal advisers). The trust included from western Kentucky Thomas Rhea of Russellville, the wily and experienced politico and member of the Highway Commission; Rhea's young protégé Emerson "Doc" Beauchamp, also from Russellville; controversial former lieutenant governor and current adjutant general Henry H. Denhardt from Bowling Green; and former Owensboro senator Gates Young. The group's task was to come up with a series of knockout blows to the opposing Democratic faction. In contrast to the 1932 session, Laffoon, with assistance from Rhea, succeeded in organizing the legislative leadership for the 1934 regular session, with the exception of the anti–sales tax Senator Robert Humphreys from Mayfield, who was elected Senate president pro tempore. Todd County's Woodfin E. Rogers, a Laffoon supporter, was chosen as House Speaker. During Democratic caucus proceedings, the attorney general blocked Happy Chandler from presiding, a prelude of what was in store for him. With a degree of concealed pride, the governor said he had not sought to get as involved as he did, but once the opposition contended that it would pick the leaders, he had no choice, and he "would not gloat over it."[28]

In fact, Laffoon had further designs for securing control in the General Assembly as it organized. With the bipartisan combine backing that Laffoon used in electing Senate leadership, Happy Chandler was "ripped" of his Senate powers in rules adopted for the session by transferring responsibilities for creating committees, assigning bills, and other matters to a five-member committee, including Lee Gibson from Owensboro, supportive of Laffoon. In addition, the new rules substituted a simple majority for the two-thirds requirement for discharging bills from committee that Chandler had used to thwart Laffoon efforts to pull sales tax measures from Senate committees. After seven hours of intense debate, the changes passed by a substantial 22–14 vote that split the western Kentucky delegation. The changes were opposed by Senate president pro tem Robert Humphreys from Mayfield, who would become one of Chandler's closest political allies over his long political career, and by James Breathitt, the former lieutenant governor from Hopkinsville whose nephew would later defeat Chandler in a tough gubernatorial primary in 1963. Among the ten Republican senators voting for the ripper measure was Thomas J. Edge from Muhlenberg County. Trying to make light of what took place, Chandler explained that "a minority of Democrats and a majority of Republicans succeeded in overcoming the will of a majority of Democrats and a minority of Republicans." New House member Henry Ward wrote in his *Paducah Sun-Democrat* column, perhaps too quickly, that Chandler would become one of the "forgotten men."[29]

The higher-priority target for Laffoon's revenge, however, was Ben Johnson, the chair of the Highway Commission and leader of the anti-Laffoon forces. The governor made clear his mistrust of Johnson, perhaps the commonwealth's strongest political boss, by demanding in May 1933 that all highway contracts and purchases be approved through the governor's office. A defiant Johnson complied but deluged Laffoon's office with thousands of pages of documents. A reorganization bill passed in the 1934 session contained broad authority for Laffoon to remove his appointees and was recognized by many lawmakers as a weapon that the governor could wield to eliminate Johnson. Johnson fought in the courts for six months to keep his post before Laffoon finally fired him in January 1935 and appointed Thomas Rhea to replace him as chair of the Highway Commission. Western Kentucky legislators were largely not sad to see Johnson leave. Benton senator Ray Smith, speaking for most of the Jackson Purchase delegation at a Paducah Lions Club meeting in November 1933, charged that Ben Johnson was a "menace to the state" for ruining the administrations of four governors.[30]

Federal takeover of relief programs in the commonwealth was not accompanied by a release from the required matching state funds. Threats to shut down the programs in March 1934 forced the governor to send Washington $300,000 from liquor revenues to avoid a disruption in benefits. The recurring tensions also forced him to call lawmakers, who had been assured that they would not be asked to take up the sales tax during the regular session, to return to Frankfort for a special session in May for that purpose. Federal authorities, convinced that Laffoon was sincere in plans to address the state match and optimistic that he would succeed in convincing lawmakers to act, delayed cuts that would have been devastating to an estimated 130,000 Kentucky families and would jeopardize $3 million a month for unemployed workers participating in public-works projects.[31]

Despite the governor's recent steps to weaken his opposition, the anti–sales tax forces were unwilling to concede defeat. In western Kentucky, retailers, who had several influential voices in the General Assembly, held several rallies before the session got under way. Senator Breathitt was on hand for a rally in Princeton organized by Rumsey Taylor, a young Princeton businessman who would later exercise strong political influence locally and statewide, and drafted the anti–sales tax resolution sent to Frankfort. In Paducah, Happy Chandler and Senator Robert Humphreys were featured anti–sales tax speakers before a large audience of merchants and other local listeners at a rally hosted by the local women's club. The resolution adopted by those present opposed the sales tax while supporting additional taxes to meet the needs of state government and public schools. An alternative pro–sales tax resolution to meet pressing relief needs was offered by the Paducah and McCracken County Reemployment League, but no vote on it was allowed.[32]

However, the governor's position was strengthened by a special joint legislative committee's report warning that without immediate enactment of a three-cent sales tax and a state income tax, vital state services would have to be cut, and public schools would be able to open for only two months in the coming year. The Kentucky Education Association supported the sales tax, as did the powerful Kentucky Farm Bureau, whose members wished to protect previously passed property-tax cuts. Laffoon was gratified by the groundswell of sales tax supporters, some arriving on special trains from the college towns of Bowling Green and Murray, who demonstrated for the tax in Frankfort. A twelve-car caravan of farmers from Hopkins County responded to the Farm Bureau's call for counties to send delegates. Black students from West Kentucky Industrial College in Paducah joined a crowd estimated at 10,000 at a rally where President Henry H. Cherry of Western Kentucky State College and President John Wesley Carr of Murray State College spoke. Laffoon said that the rally and his inauguration were the two happiest days of his term in office: "You cannot imagine how it makes a governor's heart throb in love for his people when he sees them leave their homes and places of business to let the governor know they endorse his program."[33]

At first, opposition forces appeared to be in control, as the sales tax was defeated in the House by significant margins. Nevertheless,

Laffoon supporters, notably Russellville's Sam Milam, House manager of the bill, saw opportunities to reverse some of the votes against the package. Fulton County representative Glenn W. Lane, although initially pledged to retailers from his district, which nudges the Tennessee state line, to vote against the measure, admitted that he was personally in favor of it. William J. Garnett from Christian County was considered an opponent of the sales tax, but he made clear that he would vote for it if the anti–sales tax forces could not come up with a viable alternative. Henry Ward, who considered himself a legislative independent on the sales tax, took the lead on the second vote to cut out the penny from the sales tax earmarked for counties in order to gain support from local officials, before once again voting against the bill. In fact, Lane, Garnett, and Ward were part of the razor-thin majority that passed the bill on its third effort.[34]

Administration forces exerted themselves in ultimately passing on a third vote the three-cent sales estimated to bring in $11 million annually, with help from seventeen House GOP members, but only by the thinnest of margins. The final vote needed on a tax measure was cast by Speaker Woodfin Rogers from Guthrie (House Speakers in Kentucky customarily don't vote). In doing so, Rogers took a swipe at retailers who had persisted in their opposition to the tax when he announced, "I now vote aye." Marion McCarthy from Webster County, a Laffoon supporter on many matters, opposed him this time and issued prophetically this jeremiad: "The people of Kentucky will rise up in their power and if necessary burn this capitol to see that the sales tax is repealed." Senate majority leader James H. Thompson, after the House vote, suggested that the bill's passage in the Senate was now a "cinch."[35]

Following the House vote, both sides projected they would ultimately win in the Senate. In fact, the bill moved fairly quickly through the Senate to its final vote on June 15, again with the barest of constitutional margins, on a bipartisan vote and with a majority of Democrats opposed. Western Kentucky split as Thomas J. Edge, a Republican senator from Muhlenberg County, Democrats James Breathitt, Robert Humphreys, and Lee Gibson from Owensboro, and Thomas O. Turner from Calloway County voted against the sales tax. A chastened Happy Chandler left the capitol before the bill was enrolled so that he would not have to sign it, leaving that to Humphreys, who called the bill a

"Republican job." With supporters surrounding him, Governor Laffoon signed the bill as soon as it reached his desk that evening.[36]

An Associated Press writer noted in December 1934 the remarkable turnaround in Laffoon's political fortunes, from their low ebb in his first two years in office to the "almost dictatorial" powers he now held, unlike any recent Kentucky governors. Tensions remained with the federal government over relief programs, but they had eased considerably by the appointment, supported by Senator Barkley, of George H. Goodman, the former editor and owner of the *Paducah News-Democrat*, in late October 1934 as the federal administrator of relief programs in Kentucky. The *Owensboro Messenger-Inquirer* proclaimed him "admirably fitted for the important position" and capable of ending "for all time the friction that had existed in relief work in Kentucky." Indeed, he proved to be an effective administrator who worked well with authorities in Frankfort and Washington until he moved to administer the federal Office of Price Administration at the start of World War II. All that remained for Laffoon to do to secure his legacy as a first-rate governor was to make certain his pick to replace him prevailed in the next year's gubernatorial election.[37]

It is important not to overlook the importance of the federal relief programs in local economies. From the start of the New Deal in 1933 through December 1935, the federal government sent $57 million to Kentucky to help the despondent. In the hard-hit western coal fields, Hopkins and Muhlenberg Counties received approximately $2 million.[38]

The relief programs previously discussed were just a few of the New Deal programs that, taken together, represented a fundamental change in the role of the federal government in the lives of western Kentuckians, who would increasingly look to Washington rather than to Frankfort for solutions to the many problems that they could not solve on their own. For example, new federal programs designed to slow down the alarming foreclosures on farms and homes were created soon after Roosevelt took office. The Home Owners Loan Corporation's office in Paducah, which opened in January 1934, quickly had more than 1,100 loan applications from western Kentuckians requesting loans to put off "greedy mortgagees" on the verge of foreclosing on homeowners. The shift in political leadership to the federal government was especially true in the case of agriculture and mining, both of which were profoundly important in the western Kentucky economy.[39]

Among the spate of sweeping reforms associated with the New Deal passed in 1933 was the creation of the Agricultural Adjustment Administration (AAA), giving federal agricultural planners authority to redress the depressed economic conditions on the nation's farms. In response to projected surpluses and low prices for cotton and hogs, both important in western Kentucky, emergency programs sought to convince producers to cut production in those commodities that summer. For participating farmers, subsidies were provided from taxes on processors, with an expected added benefit from higher prices for what they did take to market. Many regional farmers, with help from county extension agents who explained the benefits of enrolling in the program, joined. Eighty-seven cotton growers in Fulton and Calloway Counties plowed up approximately 20 percent of their crop in return for more than $40,000 in federal subsidies. Hickman County farmers at first resisted, but after the enactment of a new federal law that made the cotton program "semi-compulsory" in 1934, approximately 2,000 Jackson Purchase growers signed contracts for the 1935 crop.[40]

Along with plowing up crops, which may have seemed radical and wasteful to the sensibilities of the time, federal farmers, with input from producers, also decided that the impending glut of hogs going to market necessitated the slaughter and disposal of an estimated 4 million hogs that summer. To those outside the farming community who were shocked or amused by the program, the *Paducah Sun-Democrat* responded that "it is straight business." More than 3,000 farmers in the eleven most western counties and 500 from Daviess County were among the many who enrolled in the program. The 600 enrolled hog farmers in Hickman County received $75,000 in subsidies. Given the speed with which the program was rolled out, there were those, in particular small growers, who did not get contracts; others struggled to arrange to deliver their hogs to the Eckert packinghouse in Evansville, and then the packinghouse was unprepared for the large number of hogs at first, or the farmers had difficulties locating other packinghouses that would take their hogs. In the future, these logistical difficulties would be sorted out by establishing quotas, which also eliminated the necessity of slaughtering the hogs.[41]

Commodity programs were established for other crops, the most important of which for western Kentucky farmers was the one dealing with tobacco. For many farmers, tobacco was their largest and perhaps only cash crop at the time. However, hard times had beset tobacco growers as the cash value for the crop harvested in 1932 was less than half the value of crops harvested before the Great Depression. Murray native John B. Hutson, who had a doctorate in agriculture from the University of Kentucky, proved to be a capable manager of the tobacco program in the commonwealth who worked with growers, buyers, and politicians to substantially reduce tobacco acreage for the tobacco auction in 1934 on the model that had worked previously for cotton. Hutson as well as Kentucky congressmen Fred Vinson and Virgil Chapman developed a program that called for a 50 percent reduction in tobacco acreage, for which farmers were given $20 per acre, but panic ensued with the auctioning of the bumper crop of 1933, which at first promised such meager sale returns that Governor Laffoon proclaimed a "holiday," similar to the holiday called for banks earlier in the year, which checked the fall in prices and encouraged growers and buyers to accept the quota plan. The new curtailment program worked well as state farmers increased their income by $7 million as production was cut 28 percent.[42]

There would be disruptions in the commodity programs, notably after the US Supreme Court struck down the AAA in 1935. There followed an interlude before passage of the Soil Conservation and Allotment Act in 1936, which tied subsidies and curtailments to soil conservation and adoption of modern agricultural methods. However, farmers were partial to the AAA commodity programs, which ultimately resurfaced in legislation in 1938 that disposed of the tax on processors that the Supreme Court had rejected. The historian George Blakey offers that with these programs Kentucky farmers stepped beyond the Jeffersonian defense of the yeoman farmer upheld in *I'll Take My Stand: The South and the Agrarian Tradition* (1930) by the Vanderbilt agrarians (including Todd County native Robert Penn Warren) and replaced it with a "revolutionary" accommodation with "urban amenities, technological innovation and dependence on federal assistance."[43]

Rational planning, a central impetus behind the initial New Deal programs, underlaid the creation of the National Recovery Administration (NRA) in 1933, which affected western Kentucky in many ways. The idea of the NRA, perhaps the most important legislation to the early New Deal reformers, was that all Americans should be called upon to do their part to end the Great Depression. Operating under industry-wide codes, businesses would be expected to raise worker wages, cut workers' hours, hire more employees, and end child-labor practices. In return, firms that complied would be recognized with the Blue Eagle emblem, and consumers would be encouraged to trade only with those concerns showing the Blue Eagle. Enthusiasm for the NRA was initially high in western Kentucky. The *Owensboro Messenger-Inquirer* boosted the NRA, suggesting that "the program cannot fail because the country cannot afford to have it fail." In Owensboro, an estimated 20,000, including several bands and marchers representing local fraternal organizations and a black section, were on hand for an NRA parade on August 31 that stretched more than five miles. The city's largest employer, Ken-Rad, gave its 1,700 workers engaged in the production of radio tubes a 20 percent wage hike. Paducah's organizational drive was on a smaller scale, with an estimated 600 volunteers, but supporters in both cities combed the neighborhoods to obtain signatures of locals promising to trade only with stores displaying the Blue Eagle. Merchants in Madisonville agreed to set their business hours from 8:00 a.m. to 5:00 p.m. Monday through Saturday, with an option of staying open to 9:00 p.m. on Saturday, and hairdressers in Mayfield standardized their prices and hours of business from 8:00 a.m. to 6:00 p.m. The local NRA committee in Bowling Green encouraged residents to report businesses that might be displaying emblems but not living up to the ideals.[44]

Enthusiasm for the NRA and the Blue Eagle could not sustain itself, however. In a rural area such as western Kentucky, there developed hostilities as area businesses came to believe the NRA and its industry codes favored large businesses and urban areas. By 1935, stories appeared in regional papers questioning, as the Great Depression lingered, the impact of the NRA in restoring prosperity. In the courts, Kentucky mine operators fiercely and successfully fought the code governing their industry. The demise of the NRA and the Blue Eagle was hardly mourned when the US Supreme Court declared it unconstitutional in the spring of 1935. The lasting impact on western Kentucky, especially in its coal counties, came from a small provision, Section 7a, in the NRA legislation, giving labor unions for the first time federal support to organize collectively.[45]

The story of labor organization in the western Kentucky mines during the 1930s has not received the attention it deserves, in part due to the emphasis on developments in eastern Kentucky and "Bloody Harlan." Duane Bolin provides glimpses into the labor tensions in western Kentucky mines between World War I and the New Deal when efforts to organize the coal field by the UMWA came to nothing at the hands of coal operators determined to stand against the union and the two sides engaged in considerable violence. However, colorful UMWA president John L. Lewis was rewarded for his strong support of the 1932 Roosevelt presidential campaign by the collective-bargaining protections in the National Industrial Recovery Act of 1933, considered the "Magna Carta" of the American labor movement. Lewis and the UMWA now had the leverage with which to undertake a new campaign to organize the western Kentucky mines. The campaign would be a long one, with only a partial victory for the UMWA.[46]

It is useful to keep in mind that mining was a very dangerous endeavor at the time. Since 1920, four mine disasters in the western field had claimed twenty-seven miners' lives. The writer Bobby Anderson lists sixty-four other miners who died in separate incidents in Muhlenberg County mines. All of this happened at a time when federal and state mine-safety protections were virtually nonexistent. As an industry, coal operators were resistant to government intervention, evidenced by their difficult talks with NRA regulators and union representatives during the Blue Eagle campaign. When John L. Lewis staked out his position on wage and hours in favor of $5 per day for a thirty-hour week, western Kentucky coal operators walked away from the table complaining that they could not survive on what they anticipated coming from the discussions. Back home, operators in Hopkins, Christian, and Webster Counties, as members of the Operators Association of West Kentucky, issued a manifesto announcing opposition to any form of negotiation rights for the UMWA based on its past "lawless acts." Instead, the association recognized a "company union," the Independent Miners Union, with headquarters in Madisonville, which complied with the new federal collective-bargaining law. The operators' attitude, which they declared was "unalterable," remained strong in the western half of the coal field for years. To them, any concessions to the UMWA in the Western Kentucky Coal Field would mean "death to the industry," and "no power exists anywhere to compel us to change [our view]."[47]

Industrial war in the western coal field, with most of the action taking place in Hopkins County, the largest coal producer in the western field and home to District 23 of the UMWA, had been declared. UMWA representatives were on hand in July for a meeting in Madisonville aimed at organizing the field. In a resolution issued, operators in Muhlenberg and Ohio Counties were recognized for the "manly way" in which they had received UMWA representatives, a sharp contrast to the reception by the operators to the east. Mass meetings in September were held in Beech Creek in Muhlenberg County, Earlington, and Providence to encourage interest in the union. By the end of the year, the UMWA had organized nine mines in Henderson County with an estimated 1,200 workforce. Working to establish the union's presence, UMWA picketers were present at numerous mines, provoking clashes with forces employed by the mine operators. A federal labor relations agent gauging labor unrest in Hopkins County in August 1933 heard reports that several miners at the West Kentucky Coal Company's Fox Run Mine were forced to join the company union but were fired after joining the UMWA. Later in August, nearly 400 miners supporting the UMWA went on strike at the Hart and Sixth Vein Mines when several miners who had joined their brothers were fired, allegedly for their union membership. Reports of gunfire and dynamite explosions circulated. Numerous UMWA supporters, including the union's district president, were arrested for conspiring to intimidate non-UMWA members.[48]

Western Kentucky coal operators not only had to respond to the UMWA insurgency but also had to resist the wage-and-hour provisions imposed on them by the NRA industry code. After reluctantly accepting the initial $4 per day and forty-hour work week provisions developed in NRA negotiations in the summer of 1933, a new coal code adopted in the spring of 1934 called for a $5 daily wage for a seven-hour work day. Operators sharply reduced mining activity until they could obtain relief and sent a delegation to Washington to plead that the new scale would cost 10,000 jobs in the Western Kentucky Coal Field, but 1,200 UMWA miners strongly supported the change at a rally in Central City and signaled that they would picket mines that refused to pay the new wages. Operators filed suit, and Judge Charles I. Dawson, born in the small community of Pineville in Logan County, where he once practiced law and would be the GOP gubernatorial candidate in 1947, agreed with the coal operators. According to Dawson, "I don't have the slightest doubt about the unconstitutionality of this act as it affects the administration of local business." Miners working in non-UMWA operations quickly went back to work under a new contract based on the previous $4 per day wage, but operators also conceded to the seven-hour shift. UMWA mines soon followed.[49]

Though it appeared that the union had been dealt a significant setback, UMWA membership had risen by the end of 1934 to roughly 5,000 of the estimated 11,400 miners working in the Western Kentucky Coal Field. Most miners who were not members of the UMWA nevertheless belonged to company unions, such as the Mutual Benefit Association, which organized the workers of the West Kentucky Coal Company's mines, the largest coal operator in the region, with ten mines in the western counties. The UMWA made the West Kentucky Coal Company its special target in the coming years by filing unfair-labor complaints against it with the National Labor Relations Board (NLRB). The NLRB found the UMWA complaints credible and ruled in 1938 that the company had to sever its relationship with the company union and pay workers back for previous union dues. The company sought to overturn the NLRB ruling in the courts, but a UMWA strike against mines in eight Appalachian states, including the Western Kentucky Coal Field, intervened. The settlement with the operators gave the UMWA sole responsibility for organizing the Western Kentucky Coal Field. However, operators were not compelled to recognize the union, and the UMWA lost two critical votes held for miners at the West Kentucky Coal Company in 1942 that left the Western Kentucky Coal Field divided equally between union and nonunion mines into the post–World War II period.[50]

As Governor Laffoon looked in early 1935 to his political prospects for the upcoming gubernatorial campaign, he had every reason to be confident. Because Kentucky governors were precluded from running for consecutive terms, a law that stayed in place until 1992, he had close at hand a candidate whom he completely trusted to succeed him, Thomas Rhea, the "sage of Russellville" or the "Gray Fox," as he was known. Rhea was the unquestioned political boss of Logan County in western Kentucky and one of the Democratic "kingmakers" who had been actively involved in the selection of Kentucky's governors and US senators since the turn of the century. Rhea was perhaps Laffoon's most trusted adviser and replaced Ben Johnson as chairman of the Highway Commission in January 1935. With Johnson's departure, Laffoon had a free hand over the state workforce and had workers' pay assessments to the Kentucky Democratic Party at his disposal to back Rhea's campaign. Rhea was a wily political strategist, although not the most gifted campaigner, but that would not be a concern once the decision was made again to settle the Democratic Party's candidate for the general election by a convention. After all, that was how Laffoon, with the backing of the bipartisan combine, had been nominated. This time, he anticipated that he would control the convention. And given the poor standing of the Republican Party in Kentucky, Rhea's election would be an almost certainty.

Though the governor's plan was adopted by the Democratic State Central Committee, there was a sharp reaction from those who thought the decision should be given to Democratic voters in a primary. Senator Alben Barkley and even President Roosevelt, who feared that the convention could have an adverse impact in the state on Roosevelt's reelection campaign in 1936, supported a primary. Throughout the state, there was considerable adverse public reaction to the convention, which the *Louisville Courier-Journal* captured in the early months of 1935. It printed the many editorials opposing the convention from local papers. Within the Democratic Party, calls for a primary were voiced by a large number of county Democratic committees. A *Courier-Journal* reporter on assignment to gauge public opinion in western Kentucky found very strong sentiment for the primary, suggesting that in several counties "opposition to a convention is militant and bitter and threatening." The *Hickman Courier* called the convention decision "tragic" and a "betrayal of the Democratic voters of Kentucky," and the *Hopkinsville New Era* charged that a convention was "not only a slap to the face to the Democratic voters of Kentucky but an open affront to President Roosevelt." The *Owensboro Messenger-Inquirer* straddled the fence by suggesting that a judgment as to the wisdom of a convention would have to wait until

November for voters to decide if the convention's candidate should be entrusted with the task of replacing Laffoon. A straw poll of county Democratic Party committee members conducted by the *Courier-Journal* before the Kentucky Democratic State Central Committee vote demonstrated strong opposition to the convention in all western Kentucky counties.[51]

Laffoon did not reverse himself in wake of the criticism, but Happy Chandler soon threw a monkey wrench into the governor's plans when Rhea and the governor traveled to Washington, DC, on February 6. Once they crossed the state border, Chandler as acting governor sprang into action by calling the General Assembly into special session to pass legislation requiring a primary. This was a high-risk maneuver given the uncertainty whether the lieutenant governor had the power to call a special session or whether Laffoon, upon his return, could cancel it. Chandler later claimed that the reason for his action was not a self-serving one as he supported the candidacy of former governor J. C. W. Beckham. In any case, Chandler's political fortunes unquestionably would improve if an anti-Laffoon Democratic nominee would be picked by primary voters. But first he had to await the results of the governor's challenge in the Kentucky courts, even while the called special session got under way. Many of the pro-Laffoon lawmakers chose not to attend the session until the legality of Chandler's call was confirmed. Even if Chandler won the court battle and lawmakers met in special session, Laffoon had considerable strength in the legislature stemming from his patronage powers; six of the ten state representatives in the First Congressional District had state jobs that gave the governor considerable leverage over their votes. Others, however, such as the plucky Henry Ward from Paducah, voiced support for a compulsory primary without fear of the consequences.[52]

The Kentucky Court of Appeals, the commonwealth's highest court at the time, acted quickly given the significance of the controversy and gave Chandler the win he desperately needed by deciding that Chandler had the legal authority to call the special session. Laffoon, temporarily on the defensive and perhaps sharing the assumption that the lieutenant governor was acting on the behalf of the aging Beckham, soon reversed course to support a primary; he went further by supporting a run-off primary if no candidate could win a majority in the initial primary. The run-off, the governor hoped, could dissuade the aging Beckham from running or give Rhea a decisive advantage with all the resources that Laffoon could direct to the campaign. The run-off idea proved to be a fatal mistake for Laffoon and Rhea. Beckham decided not to throw his hat in the ring, but Rhea faced a crowded field, including the energetic Happy Chandler for an early August initial primary and a mid-September run-off if necessary.[53]

It appeared at the time that Rhea, with the political influence that the governor could assert in his behalf and Rhea's own exceptional skill as a political organizer (President Roosevelt had picked Rhea as one of his five floor managers at the Democratic Convention in 1932), would have a clear advantage over Chandler, who many considered a political lightweight. As the head of the Highway Commission, Rhea had an opportunity to build connections with the county courthouse rings that could benefit his campaign. However, he clearly lacked the youth, the dynamism, and oratorical skills that Chandler had in abundance.[54]

Happy Chandler, whose father was a poor farmer from Corydon outside the city of Henderson, could not claim a family political heritage upon which to base his campaign. He was a young man on the make with enough personal force and bombast to make the primary a close one regardless of the many advantages Rhea held. Certainly, he could count on the anti-Laffoon faction, uniting the *Courier-Journal*, Ben Johnson, Dan Talbott, and J. C. W. Beckham. One factor of enormous importance was that he was the candidate who had done his utmost to stop the sales tax and would repeal it upon being elected. He would use that history to great advantage, and his campaign style caught voters' attention and made them loyal Happy followers. In his autobiography, Chandler would recall that "I took to campaigning like a June bug to a duck's back." In 1935, Chandler campaigned in all Kentucky counties, pulling into towns at the head of a motorcade to speak to a crowd alerted that he would be there to speak. He made greater use of sound trucks and microphones than any previous Kentucky politician. Always dressed in a white suit, frequently dampened with perspiration caused by the heat of Kentucky in the late spring and summer months, he entertained the crowds with songs; favorites were "There's a Gold Mine in the Sky," "Sonny Boy," "Happy Days Are Here Again," and, of course "My Old

Kentucky Home." He spoke with few notes, but he had a great gift for recalling the names and circumstances of people whom he met on the campaign trail, which he could use to great effect in his speeches.[55]

The August Democratic primary results hardly surprised anyone. Rhea finished first among the five who had filed, but he failed by a 5 percent margin to avoid a run-off to win a majority against Chandler who only trailed Rhea by three percent. In western Kentucky, Rhea won the majority of counties, with the notable exceptions of Hickman, McCracken, Marshall and Graves Counties in the Jackson Purchase; Henderson County, Chandler's home county (Where Chandler was aided by the influence of his campaign manager, Robert Humphreys); and Warren County went to Chandler. Rhea's chances in the run-off suffered when the two strongest candidates not making the run-off threw their support to Chandler. Nevertheless, Rhea got a boost from endorsements in western Kentucky's largest newspapers. In endorsing him, the *Paducah Sun-Democrat*, referring to its mission as "first, last and all the time West Kentuckian," disparaged Chandler, who was raised in Henderson County, as "the sing-song boy" and touted Rhea as the life-long western Kentuckian who would support the region's goals to take tolls off the bridges and secure its fair share of highway funding. Laffoon's Madisonville hometown newspaper strongly endorsed Rhea, playing on sectional competitiveness by publishing a telegram from Lexington political boss Billy Klair that urged voters to support Chandler and stated that "WESTERN KENTUCKY now has the present governor and two senators" (US senators Alben Barkley and Marvel M. Logan from Bowling Green). The *Madisonville Messenger* also warned that the region stood to be "stripped bare" by a Chandler administration. However, Chandler finished the campaign strong, edging Rhea out by a 53–47 margin. Part of the turnaround came in western Kentucky, where Chandler held onto the counties he had previously won but where he also went on to win Daviess County by one vote, and to add Christian Calloway, Marshall, McLean, Ohio, Simpson, Union (where rising political star and Rhea campaign manager Earle C. Clements was the county judge), and Warren Counties to help carry him into the general election.[56]

The run-off so embittered Laffoon and Rhea to Chandler's general-election campaign that they rebuffed President Roosevelt's efforts to reconcile the two Kentucky Democratic Party factions. This level of rancorous discourse among the Democrats often opened the door for Republicans in Kentucky, but not this time because voter antipathy toward the GOP for perceived failures to respond appropriately to the Great Depression was still present. In the general election, Chandler's 95,000-vote margin, 53,000 of those votes from western Kentucky, over GOP candidate King Swope was nearly 24,000 votes better than Laffoon's win in 1931. Democrats swept the other statewide offices, including lieutenant governor, which went to Keen Johnson, who had been born in Lyon County and raised as a preacher's son in western Kentucky, and agriculture commissioner, which went to Garth K. Ferguson, who was a newspaper publisher from Bardwell in Carlisle County. Both Johnson and Ferguson had originally been slated with Rhea.[57]

The thirty-seven-year-old Albert Benjamin "Happy" Chandler, son of a tenant farmer from Henderson County, took the reins of Kentucky state government as the second straight chief executive from western Kentucky. In response to the many who had not taken Chandler seriously in the past, he proved to be energetic, ambitious, and confident in his abilities. Before the start of the 1936 legislative session, he removed, using the ouster powers Ruby Laffoon had wrested from the General Assembly, nearly 3,500 state employees, including many supporters of Thomas Rhea, in part to reduce the state budget. All the other Democratic statewide constitutional officers elected in November had been slated with Rhea, but Chandler proved early on that he would not tolerate disloyalty. Lieutenant Governor Keen Johnson, publisher of a newspaper in Richmond, demonstrated more loyalty to Chandler than he had to Ruby Laffoon. However, Agriculture Commissioner Garth K. Ferguson, a native of Ballard County in western Kentucky and also a newspaper publisher, demonstrated more independence, which Chandler met by firing the members of the State Fair Board after they reappointed the former secretary of the board, Eugene Flowers, the outgoing agriculture commissioner and Rhea supporter from Russellville. Other western Kentuckians also felt Chandler's wrath. Tom Logan, warden at the Kentucky State Penitentiary in Eddyville, was among those fired in Chandler's postinauguration purge; Emerson "Doc" Beauchamp, a young man from Russellville with ambitions to move up in Kentucky politics, resigned his position as tax commissioner rather than be fired. Perhaps one of Chandler's most remembered actions midway during his first term as governor came after the death of Henry H. Cherry, the respected first president of Western State Teachers College in Bowling Green, in September 1937. The college alumni were already upset by Governor Chandler's recent decision to move the college's graduate teacher program to the University of Kentucky, but the anger of student, faculty, and alumni was redoubled by his insensitive decision to bring to Cherry's funeral Paul Garrett, the superintendent of Woodford County schools who had given young Chandler a coaching job and now was expected to be installed as Cherry's successor without consulting with the college's regents. The decision was delayed a few days, but the regents bent to Chandler's will. The editorial writers for the *Owensboro Messenger* wrote at the time that "one thing is certain, the governor again demonstrated that he is a determined young man, more determined that his will be done than almost anything else."[58]

Chandler quickly organized his leadership team to prepare for the approaching 1936 session. There was a considerable western Kentucky presence on that team, starting with Lieutenant Governor Keen Johnson, who as the presiding officer in the Senate stood in sharp contrast to Chandler when he had held that office. Former Mayfield senator and Chandler campaign chairman Robert Humphreys was installed as Senate clerk, and John Kirtley, campaign chief fund-raiser and a businessman from Island in McLean County, was elected House Speaker.[59]

When the legislature convened in January, Governor Chandler presented a bold agenda, featuring a short regular session that would begin with the repeal of the sales tax (which was scheduled to expire in July) and then a series of special sessions, the first for government reorganization, followed by sessions to write the state budget and to provide tax revenues to balance the budget. With Democratic majorities of 66–34 in the House and 26–12 in the Senate, it was reasonable to expect that Chandler had workable majorities. Most legislators considered repeal of the sales tax (that would take place upon its signing), given the emphasis that Chandler put on it during the campaign, a popular mandate. In the end, only Sam Milam, House author of Laffoon's sales tax from Thomas Rhea's hometown of Russellville, was the only vote cast against repeal, which sailed through both chambers. Chandler signed the repeal with a statewide radio audience listening in on January 15, 1936. Repeal left not only Ruby Laffoon's legacy tattered but also a $3 million hole in the state budget that would need to be addressed later either by significant cuts in services or by additional taxes.[60]

A second measure of significance to western Kentucky passed during the regular session was the creation of the state's county road program, for which Chandler is due considerable credit. He withstood pressure from county officials who sought to send the $2 million from the state gasoline tax to the county fiscal courts rather than to the Highway Commission. Chandler shrugged off local officials who objected to state control of the road program by telling them that "they might as well make up your mind to it." Its enactment resulted in the transfer of many farm-to-market roads across the commonwealth to the Highway Commission. The program, in Chandler's mind, would make considerable strides in satisfying the long cry from farmers to "get them out of the mud" and, through use of convict labor, ease the overcrowding in the state's prisons. Estimates at the start of the program indicated that as many as fifteen inmates per county could be dedicated to the program, with each convict responsible for thirty-nine miles of road maintenance. This aspect of the program was soon dropped, however, due to local public opinion that supported more jobs for "drought stricken farmers" desperately in need of the thirty cents per hour pay. In addition, the additional patronage and road contracts were the coin of the realm for local politicians.[61]

Reorganization, taken up in the first special session, drew considerably more opposition than had sales tax repeal. The plan, based on reports by efficiency experts at Griffenhagen & Associates, was the work of a task force appointed by Chandler and chaired by former governor J. C. W. Beckham. The principle aims of the bill, which at least one historian considered the most important bill passed during the first Chandler term, were to reduce the number of state agencies and commissions and to strengthen the power of the Kentucky governor. Opponents pointed to changes in the Highway Commission, which, with Laffoon's reorganization, operated with nine voting commissioners, each representing a congressional district and one of whom was designated to oversee agency operations. Chandler's plan, which was passed into law, made the nine members advisers to a commissioner (originally Ben Johnson, who returned to power with Chandler's election) who would be appointed by the governor and would be responsible for all agency operations. Others, including several elected constitutional officers, rallied behind Agriculture Commissioner Garth K. Ferguson, who believed the reorganization ripped his powers. Passage of the bill without the loss of significant Democratic votes required considerable effort from Chandler, who negotiated a series of amendments, including reversing himself on the ripper provisions aimed at Ferguson. Ruby Laffoon had made significant steps toward establishing a strong-governor form of government in Kentucky, but Chandler draws most of the credit in this area by establishing, as historian James Klotter notes, "the basic structure of state government for over three decades, *and* he received more political power as well."[62]

As legislators returned to Frankfort for a second special session starting in mid-March 1936 to write the state's new biennial budget, Chandler reminded lawmakers they would be called into another special session again to address the anticipated $12 to $15 million shortfall (equivalent to $225–280 million today). Working through a joint legislative committee, lawmakers, with Chandler's approval, developed prior to the session a general budget outline for slightly more than $23 million for each of the next two fiscal years. Pleased with the committee's work, Chandler announced that lawmakers should proceed immediately with passage of the budget with no changes. However, while the governor and Speaker Kirtley were out of town, the budget bill ran into bipartisan objections, resulting in the bill being sent back to committee. Garth Ferguson, Railroad Commissioner Robert E. Webb of Mayfield, and Attorney General Bev Vincent, leaders of a group of state officials objecting to provisions in the bill that they claimed they had not seen, primarily attacked Chandler allies Dan Talbott and Ben Johnson for accumulating far too much power in one family. However, Ferguson, still nursing his grievances against Chandler's interference in staffing at the State Fair Board, including the recent firing of seven employees, charged that the budget and reorganization plan "give the people of Kentucky a government of vengeance, by vengeance, for vengeance, where arbitrary tyranny would usurp the place of government in the management of affairs of state." The squabble did not garner much support back home, however, as evidenced by the editorial writers of the *Paducah Sun-Democrat*, who charged that the rebels were "common spoilists." Upon his return, the governor succeeded in passing the budget bill through both chambers with only three votes against it, including Russellville Democrat Sam Milan, whose floor remarks echoed Ferguson's.[63]

A final, much longer, and more contentious special session focused on tax increases to replace the repealed sales tax and to fund the state's $3 million share of the new old-age pension program arising from federal social security legislation of 1935, which Chandler had agreed to during the campaign. Returning to his preference for piecemeal taxes that he had demonstrated while lieutenant governor, Chandler, hoping to raise $12 million to balance the already approved state budget, asked the General Assembly to establish personal and corporate income taxes and to raise taxes on beer and alcohol, automobiles, cigarettes, utilities, and nonessential items (including ice cream and soft drinks). The taxes on various industries drew considerable opposition, however. The Kentucky Farm Bureau, backed by county chapters in western Kentucky, coordinated with Louisville cigarette factories to pack the capitol with 3,000 protestors for the defeat of the tobacco tax in the House while the governor was out of Frankfort. Upon his return and after the governor made a statewide radio address denouncing the tobacco interests and the "mob" that had gathered to fight his bill, the House and Senate proceeded to pass the tobacco tax. The pattern was repeated on other tax matters; opposition efforts would be made until the governor interceded to push his program forward. The administration and legislators floundered for more than a month as they sought consensus. Key western Kentucky lawmakers, such as Sam Milam from Russellville and Tyler Munford from Morganfield, still loyal to Ruby Laffoon and Tom Rhea, and young, nonaligned Henry Ward from Paducah refused to help Chandler, but they could not stop him from passing the $12 million annual tax increase in the six-week special session, which gave him most of what he asked of the legislature, including a personal and corporate income tax.[64]

With the conclusion of the tax special session, Chandler had placed Kentucky on a much more secure fiscal footing with regards to New Deal obligations than Governor Laffoon had. Chandler had profited politically during his campaign by aligning himself with Roosevelt and the New Deal, and he followed through on promises to provide old-age pensions, although at substantially lower amounts than many states offered. Nevertheless, as the New Deal historian George Blakey argues, the governor was philosophically closer to conservative southern Democrats, such as US senator Harry Byrd of Virginia, than to FDR. He was more committed to paying off the state debt, for example, than to taking on additional revenue obligations associated with New Deal initiatives. John Ed Pearce judges Chandler "was strictly a 'pay as you go' man and deplored the Roosevelt spending." It was nearly inevitable that there would be tensions between him and Washington during his term in office.[65]

Social security was the product of a new burst of federal energy in 1935 that constituted what the historian David Kennedy terms a "second New Deal." Among the many programs established that year was the Works Progress Administration, a replacement for previous relief programs and the most recognizable of all New Deal programs administered by Harry Hopkins. George Goodman, the Paducah WPA administrator, continued as director over the commonwealth's program. Madisonville, one of six district headquarters for the WPA, was headquarters for the thirty-one-county western Kentucky region, with twelve subdistricts. The first approved WPA project in western Kentucky, a transportation project involving 125 workers doing shoulder work on highways in Muhlenberg County, did not start until mid-August 1935. Nevertheless, by the winter of 1936, the WPA was fulfilling its pump-priming task with an estimated 68,000 unemployed on WPA projects statewide.[66]

Critics of the WPA unfairly called its workers "leaf rakers" engaged in projects that were purely "boondoggles," but George Goodman reported after the program's first year that nearly 50 percent of the approximately $16 million spent in Kentucky went to highway projects, the rest going to projects associated with public buildings, parks and recreation, and infrastructure. Nearly $3 million was spent creating useful sewing projects that engaged women in virtually all western Kentucky counties to sew for the needy.[67]

Blakey credits the WPA for 14,000 miles of road construction; 73,000 bridges, culverts, and viaducts; 900 public buildings; and 65,000 outdoor toilets in the commonwealth in a time when such facilities generally lacked the comforts of running water. Owensboro was one of several western Kentucky towns that wisely used WPA assistance for municipal improvements. According to city historians, the WPA helped nearly double the number of hard-surface streets in the city, built the Owensboro-Daviess County Hospital, and built the Owensboro Technical High School. In Paducah, Stewart Nelson Park, sponsored by the Colored Civic League at a cost of $32,000, was located on a fifty-two-acre plot to provide recreation for local blacks. More than $1.7 million in early WPA funding was spent in the region to reduce the incidence of malaria and other serious illnesses related to unsanitary conditions. Through improved drainage ditches and elimination of mosquito breeding grounds, public-health officials soon noted significant improvements in the fight against malaria, or "yellow jack," which had been endemic in the region in the past.[68]

Other programs created during the second New Deal affecting western Kentucky were more reflective of the prevailing interest in directing federal funds to improve conditions for the rural poor. The South, including western Kentucky, was a special concern to New Deal planners, who desired to check what one historian of the New Deal calls "an economically and socially backward rural culture tied to sharecropping agriculture." Considerable efforts were made to move farmers off marginal lands marked by large-scale soil erosion. This was the task of the Resettlement Administration (RA), created in 1935 (then redesignated the Farm Security Administration in 1937), which encouraged farmers to relocate on better land but also undertook numerous large-scale projects, several of which were established in western Kentucky. The RA announced plans to spend approximately $600,000 on approximately 50,000 acres where the soil was severely eroded in the Between the Rivers area (now Land between the Lakes), which became Coalins Forest and Game Reservation (*coalins* was the colloquial term applied to strips of land that had been harvested as charcoal from the area's forestry for a long-dead local iron industry). More than seventy-five families were removed in this instance. Plans called for the reforestation of the area with millions of seedlings and the prevention of further soil erosion with the erection of tens of thousands of check dams. Harvesting of the Coalins timber was expected to start in approximately fifteen years. A substantial benefit to local residents was the hiring of up to 1,000 men to implement federal plans. A second project involved the relocation of families living on 15,000 acres of what was considered substandard land in northwest Christian County, which became the Princeton Game Refuge and later Pennyrile Forest State Park Resort. In explaining the reason behind the project, RA director Rex Tugwell explained that "help has been sought and is being given to those victims of circumstances who have no hope for the future." Reporters at the time described the area involved as so depleted that the impoverished locals had to get by largely on raising sorghum and Indian corn, making what they could from wildcat coal mines on the edge of the Western Kentucky Coal Field, and selling moonshine to surrounding cities.[69]

To assist in relocating some of those whose land was taken for these forest projects, the RA established the Christian-Trigg Farms relocation project southwest of Hopkinsville near Julien. From an office in Hopkinsville, a staff of approximately forty engaged in the purchase of bankrupt plantations and available farms totaling 8,300 acres, from which individual farm tracts could be carved out in relatively small parcels for the estimated 106 families, most of them former tenant farmers handpicked by social workers from the nearby Princeton Game Refuge and Coalins projects. Unlike most other resettlement communities, Christian-Trigg Farms was spread out with the expectation that the families would become part of the surrounding communities. The project left behind little that would recall that the area had been part of a New Deal experiment.[70]

High on the agenda for the rural South was extending the benefits of affordable electricity to the vast majority of rural residents without access. Efforts prior to the New Deal had not been very successful. Luther Draffen, a businessman from Calvert City in Marshall County and a zealous advocate for rural electrification in the Jackson Purchase, made numerous trips to the state offices of Kentucky Utilities in the 1920s in a futile effort to persuade it to step up its efforts to bring services to western Kentucky. Jackson Purchase residents grew excited in the mid-1920s over the prospect of private construction of a sixty-foot hydroelectric dam on the Tennessee River on the border of Trigg and Calloway Counties that would secure a nine-foot, year-round navigation channel from the river's mouth to Pickwick Landing, south of Shiloh

Battlefield in Tennessee, and provide electricity to nearby counties. Several applications by private concerns to build a dam at the sight were awarded for an Aurora dam, but no construction resulted.[71]

The direction of western Kentucky rural-electrification advocates dramatically shifted with Congress's creation of the Tennessee Valley Authority (TVA) in 1933, which writer Neal Peirce in 1975 labeled "the greatest single American invention of this century" and certainly the most expansive effort toward comprehensive regional planning attempted by New Deal reformers. Although initial projects focused on the upper Tennessee Valley, industry and political leaders in the lower Tennessee Valley, including a large portion of the Jackson Purchase, quickly voiced their interest in development in their area. By the end of the year, the Lower Tennessee Valley Association (LTVA) was established to coordinate efforts for the many county Aurora Dam Clubs in Kentucky and Tennessee. Kentucky state senator Thomas O. Turner from Murray was elected the original LTVA president. By this time, TVA authorities assured locals of their interest in the Aurora Dam project but made it clear that it must be a TVA project, a demand that the LTVA accepted. Expectations for an early start on the project were high in the LTVA. Its publicist, the *Paducah Sun-Democrat* editor Elliott C. Mitchell, explained to locals in advocating for the Aurora dam that "this section of the country has always been discriminated against from the beginning of time," and now "the people of this district have declared themselves as demanding their rights."[72]

The fight to secure a TVA dam on the lower Tennessee River was a long, difficult one. Early conversations with TVA suggested it supported a series of low dams, including one at Aurora, but locals, led by Luther Draffen from Calvert City with backing from Murray congressman Voris Gregory and Senator Barkley, held out for a high dam that would generate the electricity needed for the region and secure a year-round navigation channel on the Tennessee River. TVA gave tentative approval for future construction of hydroelectric low dam at Aurora in mid-December 1933, and President Roosevelt pledged support for the project contingent upon a $30 million appropriation in the 1934 congressional session, but progress was delayed as prior private claims on the site needed to be resolved. Resolving these claims before the Federal Power

Commission took time, but the real issue was the lobbying by railroad, coal, and private utility interests, all of which backed eastern Kentucky congressman Andrew May in strongly opposing the project at every step. He was among those who condemned TVA in principle as "socialistic." Dam supporters from the Jackson Purchase and western Tennessee would not be deterred; they submitted a petition signed by 30,000 locals to Washington in May 1935. The diligent work of Congressmen Voris Gregory, the First District US congressman from Mayfield, and then of his brother Noble following Voris's death in 1936, however, could not overcome May's opposition and TVA's delays. Frustrations by Aurora Dam supporters mounted as TVA seemed in no hurry to get started with construction. Further progress would be delayed until natural events intervened in 1937.[73]

In the meantime, rural electrification in western Kentucky made slow progress under the Rural Electrification Authority (REA), created in 1935 by Congress, and the Kentucky Rural Cooperative Corporation Act of 1936, which gave rural areas authority to enter into rural electric cooperatives (RECs) in order to distribute power to isolated rural households willing to pay a small amount to be wired for the electricity. The need for electrical power had been clear since World War I to planners at the US Department of Agriculture, who estimated rural households spent long hours pumping and carrying water, worked as many as twenty days more per year than urban households in washing clothes, and were unable to enjoy modern food preservation and preparation. Many believed that the lack of electricity was a major reason why many rural residents left the country for towns nearby or joined the exodus from the South to what they thought were greater opportunities offered by factory jobs in the North.[74]

The REA took hold in western Kentucky thanks to the work of the Kentucky Farm Bureau and the agriculture extension agents who worked closely with local leaders to generate interest in establishing RECs. The Henderson County REC was the first in Kentucky to deliver electric service in 1937 using a low-interest federal REA loan of $190,000 to run 153 miles of electrical lines. The Henderson REC was followed in short order by the Jackson Purchase Rural Electric Cooperative, providing service to 770 homes by late 1937, and the Hickman–Fulton Counties REC was preparing to begin operations in the near future. By 1941, according to the Kentucky historian Thomas D. Clark, who sees rural electrification as one of the most significant social events of the twentieth century, it dramatically cut back on the "stoop and lift" chores associated with farm life and opened the rural population to the outside world through the wonder of the radio. Electric service to farm households increased statewide from 3 percent at the start of the New Deal to nearly 17 percent at the start of World War II in large part due to the work of the RECs.[75]

Judging the popularity of the New Deal in western Kentucky, given the primitive nature of consumer polling in the day, is difficult. The *Literary Digest* did poll a large number of Americans in 1934 and 1935, which helps shed some light on the matter. In the poll taken in 1934, Kentucky joined, with a nearly two-to-one margin of respondents, forty-seven other states indicating approval of the early New Deal programs. In the following *Digest* poll, though, FDR's and the New Deal's popularity declined sharply, with twenty-three states registering disapproval, but Kentucky was not among them. The poll in 1935 provided more information about western Kentucky: 55 percent of respondents from Madisonville, 69 percent from Bowling Green and Henderson, 73 percent from Hopkinsville, 67 percent from Mayfield, 58 percent from Owensboro, and 59 percent from Paducah supported the New Deal. These polls, however, had an inherent problem in that results came from published sources such as phone directories that resulted in respondents likely to be more affluent than the public at large.[76]

A better measure of FDR's popularity could be found in the election cycle of 1936. US senators Marvel M. Logan from Bowling Green and Alben W. Barkley from Paducah were regarded as New Deal supporters, as were Congressmen Voris Gregory and Glover Cary, representing the First and Second Congressional Districts, respectively. The president's regard for Barkley was reflected in his selection of Barkley once more to deliver the keynote address at the Democratic National Convention in Philadelphia that year. Barkley praised FDR and the New Deal for recognizing the "infinite complexities" of modern life and developing programs that enabled the nation to pick itself up and reorder American society so that "the weak may be protected from the strong and rapacious and the approximation of justice among all classes may be secured." The enthusiasm for his performance led his hometown paper to proclaim, "We now 'seize the future by the forelock,' and now nominate him for the presidency in 1940."[77]

Marvel Logan, who had slid through a congested Democratic primary that summer against strong opponents John Y. Brown Sr., raised near Sturgis in Union County, and former governor J. C. W. Beckham in his last campaign, fared very well in western Kentucky, where he defeated his GOP rival by more than 30,000 votes in both the First and Second Congressional Districts. FDR's vote total slid slightly in the First District, where only McCracken County increased its support for the president; nevertheless, he carried the district by a healthy 36,000 votes, slightly more than the victory total for Noble Gregory, who ran to replace his late brother Voris.[78]

However, one western Kentuckian, US Supreme Court justice James C. McReynolds from Elkton in Todd County, despised Roosevelt and was in a position to do him and his programs considerable harm. McReynolds had graduated from Vanderbilt and had earned a law degree from the University of Virginia before returning to Nashville to practice law and teach at Vanderbilt. He earned a reputation for his antitrust work against the tobacco trust at the turn of the century, for which he was made an assistant US attorney general by President Theodore Roosevelt in 1903. President Woodrow Wilson appointed McReynolds attorney general in March 1913, but Wilson biographer A. Scott Berg concludes of McReynolds's time on the Wilson cabinet that "a repugnant personality and name-calling racism" undermined his effectiveness, and Wilson appointed him to the Supreme Court the following year. Contemporary opinions tend to reinforce Berg's characterization; former secretary of state Dean Acheson, who was on friendly terms with McReynolds after World War I, said of him that his "views were rigid and ultra-conservative, his temperament was passionate." In a portrait of the justice in *Time* in 1939, he was described as "intolerably rude, anti-Semitic, savagely sarcastic, incredibly reactionary, puritanical, prejudiced." It was widely reported that he went out of his way to demonstrate his lack of respect for Louis Brandeis and Benjamin Cardozo, the two Jewish justices with whom he served during his years on the bench. His hatred for FDR and the New Deal was no secret; he was the only justice to rule against all thirteen key New Deal pieces of legislation that came before the Court. Jeff Shesol, writing on the clashes between the White House and the Supreme Court, concludes that McReynolds stood out among the anti–New Deal justices, known as the "Four Horsemen," for his personal dislike for FDR and reported determination not to retire so long as Roosevelt was president.[79]

Official Washington gathered on January 20, 1936, for FDR's second inauguration. With a second landslide victory, he appeared to be in complete control over the executive and legislative branches; many present expected him to give a hint that he was ready to launch his assault on the Supreme Court, which had handed down rulings that ripped apart major planks in the New Deal. On that, they were disappointed. All in all, the crowd was somewhat eager to escape the downpour that drenched Washington that day. It also rained throughout the Ohio River Valley, as it had for the previous several weeks, where the water levels of the river and its many tributaries quickly rose above flood stage.

3

From the Ohio River Great Flood to the Atomic Age

The heavy downpour on the inaugural events for President Franklin D. Roosevelt in January 1937 dwarfed in comparison with what was unfolding in the Ohio River Valley, where weeks of heavy rains threatened flooding of the river over its 980-mile course. In Louisville, the river was predicted to crest at thirty-eight feet, well above than the twenty-eight-foot flood level. Downriver, in western Kentucky, folks were well aware of the rising waters, but they took assurance that the flooding could not be any worse than that of the previous year and certainly not more than the flood of 1913, which did not result in great losses in life or property. They certainly could not fathom that the coming days, as rain that month exceeded twenty-five inches, as ice and sleet complicated rescue efforts in flooded areas, would bring forth the greatest twentieth-century natural disaster experienced in western Kentucky and what was considered a thousand-year flood of the Ohio River.[1]

Their confidence soon proved undeserved, but by the time that realization took hold on inauguration day, residents in many areas of western Kentucky were marooned by the deadly waters of not only the Ohio River but also the Green, Tennessee, and Cumberland Rivers. Flooding on the Green River stranded an Illinois Central passenger train for several days in Central City, which had become an island.

Flooding at Rumsey and Calhoun caused large numbers of residents to be evacuated. A Hopkins County National Guardsman drowned on the Pond River near Slaughters in Webster County when the outboard motor on his rescue craft fell off; a family of eight in Uniontown in Henderson County also drowned as the raging Ohio River swept their house away. A number of communities, such as Hawesville in Hancock County, ran short of food and had to be supplied by barge from Owensboro. River levels on the Green and Ohio Rivers reached record highs. Along the Mississippi River, locals feared a repeat of the Great Mississippi Flood of 1927, but federal efforts to bolster flood control paid dividends in 1937. Nevertheless, many from the river counties took refuge on higher ground as cresting of the Mississippi River came within inches of lapping over the flood wall built in Hickman, the seat of Fulton County. Several hundred CCC enrollees from Clarksville, Tennessee and WPA workers sandbagged the levee to keep the town dry, and it held, so the only flooding occurred with a break in the levee near the Mengel Box Company, which was severely damaged. Highways throughout western Kentucky were often impassable and dangerous. Rail, ferry, auto, and bus service to and from Owensboro and Paducah ceased in the last week of January, leaving western Kentucky isolated until the flood waters receded.[2]

Owensboro coped with the disaster comparatively well. The Red Cross was on hand and started mapping emergency procedures. Only 1,000 citizens were forced to seek shelter after their homes flooded. To assist with communications, Ken-Rad, the local radio vacuum tube manufacturer, set up a short-wave radio station; all liquor stores closed their doors in an effort to tamp down on those who would take advantage of the emergency by looting. The experience in Paducah was incomparably worse.[3]

The Paducah area was hit by a strong wind-and-ice storm in early January that downed tree limbs and power lines as the Ohio River started its rise. The flood threat was even more serious there compared to the upriver cities such as Owensboro as the flooded Green, Tennessee, and Cumberland Rivers fed the rushing Ohio River waters headed for Paducah. As days went by, predictions regarding how high the river would rise continued to increase, and then on the evening of January 21 the Red Cross local director received the telegram to "prepare for the worst flood in the history of the lower valley." Indeed, like Owensboro, Paducah was soon marooned as all transportation to the outside ground to a halt, and basic services started to break down. Boats were the only mode of transportation, but they were hindered by stalled automobiles left on the roads and plunging temperatures that covered the water with ice. An estimated 30,000 residents became refugees to nearby cities in western Kentucky and western Tennessee after officials first recommended and later ordered evacuation of the city. Mayfield, Murray, and Fulton each housed several thousand refugees.[4]

Civilian authority in Paducah temporarily broke down. David Welky, author of the most comprehensive history of the flood of 1937, says of Paducah: "Confusion reigned as city, county, and private organizations floundered through the unanticipated emergency." The vacuum was filled by two attorneys and a preacher, who stepped up to oversee the evacuation. They were aided by short-wave radio operators who provided much-needed communications assistance after the radio station WPAD temporarily went silent. The Red Cross provided very valuable effort in the emergency relief, but the federal government was critical to the emergency response. CCC enrollees and WPA workers spent countless hours in the massive cleanup. The TVA sent boats and workers to assist in evacuating people trapped by the flood waters until dozens of Coast Guard cutters arrived to help. Army and National Guard soldiers were also on hand to help. It was a rather dejected *Paducah Sun-Democrat* editorial writer who observed on February 1, nearly two weeks after the beginning of the evacuations, that "the second industrial city of Kentucky is no longer a city, but a complicated arrangement of little islands formed of homes, stores, churches and office buildings protruding pitifully along the edge of endless miles of turbid brown water."[5]

Paducah, once the waters started to recede, undertook a massive recovery effort and began consideration of steps that would prevent another flood of similar scope. President Roosevelt sent a team into the disaster area, led by WPA director Harry Hopkins, including an inspection visit to Paducah in early February. Hopkins described this city, with its estimated property damage pegged at more than $27 million ($464 million in today's dollars), "the hardest hit city they have viewed thus far on their trip" and promised federal assistance with the cleanup. Indeed, an estimated 1,200 WPA workers were engaged in the cleanup work for more than a month. The difficulty of the cleanup effort can somewhat be gauged by the location of the final two drowning victims, two elderly sisters (one of whom had been a defendant in the dynamite killing of a woman carrying an unborn child some years earlier) in their home nearly two months after the flooding began. Far more difficult for the city was the recognition that there were no easy fixes to prevent future devastating floods, but until something was done, Paducah's future would be hampered because business interests would be reluctant to take a risk in a flood-prone community. City leaders looked to Washington to take a major role in this effort.[6]

Paducah had close at hand a powerful voice in Washington in the person of Senator Alben Barkley, who had made his home there since finishing college. His attentions were then focused on the Supreme Court crisis that President Roosevelt had provoked soon after his inauguration by calling on Congress to pass legislation that would expand the size of the Court to offset the influence of its conservatives, such as Justice James C. McReynolds from Todd County, Kentucky. Ironically, the court-packing plan that the president pressed forward was inspired by McReynolds, who while US attorney general early in the presidency of Woodrow Wilson had considered reforms that would have allowed presidents to add judges to the superannuated judiciary of his day. Roosevelt's plan, if enacted by the Congress, would add six seats to the Supreme Court, sufficient to assure FDR the liberal justices he wanted to sustain his New Deal programs.[7]

With strong majorities in both congressional chambers and a landslide victory in November, FDR felt confident that he could prevail in the fight that began in the Senate. Although much of the responsibility for passing the court-packing plan fell to Majority Leader Joseph T. Robinson, an Arkansas conservative who badly wanted the Supreme Court seat Roosevelt hinted might be offered him, Barkley, as assistant majority leader, was also part of the president's Senate team. Opposition to the plan was strong in the Senate, beginning with Hatton Sumners, the Texas chairman of the Judiciary Committee. Kentucky's junior senator, Marvel M. Logan from Bowling Green, was in the committee minority on the matter. His initial reluctance to embrace the president's plan gave way to the view that it was now necessary in order to preserve the Constitution and the Supreme Court because "the United States of America cannot live unless we find some way to enact such laws as will bring protection, peace and happiness to all the people of the nation."[8]

The Supreme Court fought back. Tension on both sides, including Chief Justice Charles Evans Hughes, was intense, but after months of reflection and conversation with Justice Owen Roberts, who had joined with Hughes and the ultraconservative "Four Horsemen" (including McReynolds) earlier to form an anti–New Deal majority on a number of past rulings against Roosevelt's programs, Hughes joined with liberal justices in a surprise opinion in March 1937 on *West Coast Hotel Co. v. Parrish* (300 US 379), upholding a Washington State minimum-wage act by a 5–4 vote. That opinion, tabbed as "the switch in time that saved nine," was followed by a series of White House wins in the Supreme Court and the retirement of conservative justice Willis Van Devanter shortly thereafter, which offered FDR an opportunity to declare victory and drop his reform demand. However, Roosevelt would not concede. Robinson continued to press for court reform, perhaps counting on the summer heat of Washington, DC, in the days before air-conditioning to aid in his efforts. Instead, the stress and extreme heat resulted in the Senate majority leader's death in mid-July due to a heart attack suffered at his apartment.[9]

With Robinson's funeral and subsequent contest to fill his position as Senate majority leader, deliberations on the Supreme Court were temporarily placed on the back burner. Barkley and Senator Pat Harrison of Mississippi, the chair of the powerful Finance Committee and favorite of the conservative Democrats, were the two likely contestants. When apprised by Barkley and others that Harrison, the least committed to the New Deal, had a very strong chance of beating Barkley, Roosevelt issued a letter addressed to "My dear Alben," praising the work done by Barkley and fellow Kentucky senator Marvel M. Logan on the court-packing bill, which was considered a clear signal that the president preferred Barkley as Robinson's replacement. Though FDR told Harrison that he had no intention to intervene in the race, New Deal advocates close to the president campaigned behind the scenes. There is little doubt that the president's support was the deciding factor in Barkley's 38–37 win in a secret ballot, not determined until the last ballot, which Barkley said later looked "as big as a bedquilt," was counted.

Barkley remained majority leader through Roosevelt's presidency and finally relinquished the post following the GOP electoral victory in 1946. It would take years to shed the impression left by the "dear Alben" letter that he was, as the Senate historian Donald Ritchie termed him, "the president's man." Nevertheless, Barkley held the highest political position ever held by anybody from the Jackson Purchase to that time and one that would be beneficial to western Kentucky in the coming years.[10]

The court-packing legislation fell on Barkley's shoulders once he was elected majority leader. James Libbey, Barkley's biographer, asserts that the senator had long been distressed by the Court's rulings that declared New Deal agricultural programs unconstitutional. At the Democratic National Convention in 1936, he voiced his concern that to abdicate to the present Court on the great issues of the day meant that "the people will have ceased to be their own rulers, having to that extent practically resigned their Government into the hands of that eminent tribunal." At an evening rally at the Chicago Stadium in mid-April 1937, he told the audience that enactment of judiciary reform would secure "the new economic bill of rights of the toiling masses." In his speech at the Jefferson Day Dinner in Owensboro, he said the recent changing of votes on the Court could not be trusted to continue and that he was unwilling to be "subject to the whims of one member of the supreme court [*sic*]"—a slap at McReynolds to which Barkley added: "What chance . . . has a government got with an old codger who declares he will not resign as long as a certain man is president of the United States?" Nevertheless, Barkley soon recognized that the chances of passing court-packing legislation were hopeless, and so he worked closely with Vice President John Nance Garner in convincing FDR to accept the will of the Senate. Marvel Logan played a lead role in working up a face-saving substitute bill of little consequence. On balance, FDR had prevailed because the Court's center abandoned the Four Horsemen, and with Justice Van Devanter's retirement, FDR made one of his eight appointments—which later included a replacement for McReynolds, who remained on the bench until 1941—during his four terms as president to fashion the Supreme Court that he wanted. However, there was a price to be paid. Although Pat Harrison moved in the Senate to make Barkley's position as majority leader unanimous, days later he gave his first anti–New Deal floor speech.

The check on the court-packing plan strengthened the hand of the anti–New Dealers in the Senate and slowed down new domestic reform programs.[11]

The highest priority for western Kentuckians following the flood of 1937 was to take measures to prevent its repeat. In the Jackson Purchase, a consensus formed to back construction of a floodwall in Paducah and construction of the TVA dam on the lower Tennessee River that had stalled up in Washington. In early March 1937, the Paducah Flood Control Committee, chaired by civic leader Con Craig, who had been active in the Paducah-Brookport Bridge project (now the Irvin S. Cobb Bridge), formed to bring federal and local officials together behind an estimated $5.3 million floodwall project. Federal support developed quickly when General Edward M. Markham, chief of the US Army Corps of Engineers, and Senator Barkley viewed the scene. Markham recognized that the solution was not to be found in upriver projects because the existing Ohio River dams had done little to stop the onrushing waters of the recent flood. For his part, Barkley pledged his support for full federal assumption of flood-control efforts in Paducah and the more than 150 other communities lying on the Ohio River subject to severe flooding. According to him, "Uncle Sam is willing to protect his people and will protect them."[12]

Barkley inserted an amendment to the flood-control bill of 1937 that was consistent with his pledge to Paducah in providing up to $2 million for the flood wall and exempting the city from the normal requirement to acquire rights-of-way, but amendments in the House left city leaders responsibility for rights-of-way that would cost as much as $1 million. Raising that sum, a despondent editorial writer at the *Paducah Sun-Democrat* wrote, "just can't be done." Without cooperation from local landholders to significantly reduce the right-of-way costs, "we might as well kiss goodbye the idea of flood protection." Civic leaders did not give up, though. A meeting of the Manufacturers and Wholesalers Association in October came to a consensus that "Paducah can choose between building a flood wall, or losing some of its chief manufacturing institutions, and bidding good bye, for all times, to the hopes of securing new factories." The Paducah Flood Control Committee worked to reduce the expected right-of-way costs to $200,000 through land donations, negotiations with landowners, and, as a last resort, condemnation. City voters in November 1937 approved a bond issue for that amount in a 7–1 landslide. Completion of the project was expected to take two to four years, but difficulties in obtaining the right-of-way acquisitions and the oncoming world war delayed completion until July 1949. When the Army Corps of Engineers attempted to turn over maintenance to the city, the city balked due to a lack of expertise and money. Passage of a city payroll tax removed the impasse, and the flood wall proved its worth when Paducah remained dry in 1950 while rampaging waters inundated Eddyville and Kuttawa on the Cumberland River as well as nearby Smithland at the mouth of the Tennessee River.[13]

The more comprehensive flood-control effort calling for construction of a TVA dam on the lower Tennessee River remained bottled up in 1937 by Congressman Andrew May from eastern Kentucky with support from railroad, coal, and public-utility interests. Barkley, Senator Kenneth McKellar of Tennessee, and area congressmen from Kentucky and Tennessee, now including Noble Gregory from Murray, also had to contend with TVA chairman Arthur Morgan's proposed $300 million, five-mile-wide "superdam" across the Tennessee and Cumberland near Gilbertsville, which would have inundated the Between the Rivers area. Morgan's departure from the TVA due to conflicts with the other two directors was fortuitous for supporters of the lower Tennessee River Valley dam. Nevertheless, the historian B. Anthony Gannon, who has written extensively on the construction of what is today Kentucky Dam, rightly hails the race entered into by dam supporters in the late 1930s as one that ended in a "photo finish" between them and the conservative anti–New Deal bloc seeking to rein in spending for expensive new projects such as the dam.[14]

Interest in the Aurora site gave way due to engineering concerns and local insistence voiced by the Lower Tennessee Valley Association that a high dam near Gilbertsville, rather than the low dam previously considered upriver at Aurora, would benefit locals with more hydroelectric power and the nine-foot year-round channel on the Tennessee River promised by creation of the TVA. The TVA began preliminary work at Gilbertsville in late 1937, but construction could not proceed until Congress appropriated sufficient money for the estimated $112 million project that would encourage TVA to begin construction. Dam supporters counted on a $2.9 million appropriation in 1938 for that purpose, but there was once again stiff resistance in Congress, reflected in the failure to secure the necessary appropriations for the Gilbertsville Dam in two conference committees, a failure that Barkley and Noble Gregory attributed to conflict among TVA directors. That problem was alleviated by Roosevelt's dismissal of Morgan, but success still involved an unusual move in the House. The House manager of the bill undertook what Gannon calls a "sneak attack" in which the House "instructed" its conferees to adopt the Senate language on the dam that was passed by seven votes in the House. An exuberant *Paducah Sun-Democrat* proclaimed that the news that the dam's appropriation would be approved "was the best news this section of Kentucky had received in many months."[15]

Momentum was now on the side of those supporting the dam project, but there would be rough patches along the way. One was encountered when the fight was joined over a $12 million appropriation for the project in 1939. Congressman May was once more leading the opposition, but in a rather odd development his efforts were supported by Mayor Edgar T. Washburn of Paducah, who sent the congressman a note to complain about the TVA failing to give downriver communities adequate notice before releasing waters from the Tennessee River at the Pickwick Landing Dam near the Shiloh Battlefield. However, the letter went on to grossly inflate the numbers of families who would be uprooted by completion of the Gilbertsville Dam. This complaint embarrassed congressional supporters of the dam and led to the Paducah City Council's repudiation of the mayor's imprudent letter. The letter probably had little impact on the heated debate that took place on the US House floor. May railed that the TVA was "a socialistic endeavor that would have a disastrous effect on the [coal] industry," and Democrat George Johnson of West Virginia followed in a similar vein, saying, "There is not a single man here who has coal fields in his district . . . who can afford to vote for the Gilbertsville Dam, because that is entering a wedge which will destroy the value of your coal fields." Republican Everett Dirksen of Illinois tried to rally House members in opposition to the dam by asking if they preferred "to surrender to the Senate or are we going to reaffirm the independence and dignity of the House?" The dam opposition proved its strength by reversing the Appropriations Committee's recommendation with an amendment that called for a stop in construction. Yet once again, the Senate voted approval of the dam appropriations, and in the final showdown the House ultimately approved the construction funding by a close 184–175 vote.[16]

Construction began that summer on the Gilbertsville Dam (now Kentucky Dam), the largest of all TVA dams at more than 8,000 feet long and more than 200 feet high. Its construction required the relocation of more than 2,600 families and inundation of the small communities of Birmingham in Marshall County area as well as Johnsonville and Springville in Tennessee. Up to 5,000 badly needed jobs were created during its construction. When completed, it impounded more than 160,000 acres to form Kentucky Lake, the largest manmade lake in the eastern United States, and was of tremendous importance for flood control and navigation purposes as well as for recreation and power generation. Five generators would provide 160 kilowatts when the dam was completed in September 1944. Kentucky Dam and the TVA would be a source of considerable change in western Kentucky in the decades to come.[17]

Meanwhile, in Kentucky politics Governor Happy Chandler met with some resistance in establishing political control in western Kentucky. Although he was raised in the region, he had moved east for college and had settled in the Bluegrass. Thomas Rhea had a stronger claim on western Kentucky Democratic voters in the gubernatorial primaries. Democratic Party leaders in the district checked the governor's efforts to impose Hubert Meredith, an attorney from Greenville in Muhlenberg County who had campaigned vigorously for Chandler, as the party's nominee for the early election in 1937 to replace recently deceased Second Congressional District congressman Glover Cary. Instead, they chose Attorney General Bev Vincent, one of Chandler's critics. But the colorful Meredith was rewarded anyway when the governor appointed him to fill the vacant attorney general office following Vincent's victory in the special congressional election.[18]

Of more consequence was Chandler's appointment of Robert Humphreys, the former Mayfield senator and Chandler campaign manager, as the head of the Highway Department after Chandler ousted Ben Johnson in July 1936. Not only could Highway Commissioner

Humphreys be expected to give more attention to road needs in western Kentucky than had Ben Johnson, but he could prove to be an ally in the free-bridge movement launched by Henry Ward and the *Paducah Sun-Democrat* at the start of the legislative session. No region had more toll bridges than western Kentucky, which included intrastate bridges over the Tennessee, Cumberland, and Green Rivers as well as the Ohio River bridges at Wickliffe, Paducah and Henderson (the Owensboro bridge opened in 1940). On the editorial pages of the *Paducah Sun-Democrat,* the Highway Commission was praised for its purchase of the Paducah-Brookport Bridge in May 1935, which had run into financial difficulties under private management, but the writer complained that "Western Kentucky is being retarded in its development by these toll bridges," which "constitute barriers to the well-being of the entire state." An underlying belief was that once again the region suffered from state policy makers' favoritism toward Appalachia and central Kentucky, which financed those regions' highways with tax revenues, while western Kentucky motorists were forced to pay bridge tolls on theirs. Complaints were loudest in the Jackson Purchase, but the issue extended farther east, where subscribers of the *Owensboro Messenger-Inquirer* told their readers of the state's failure to provide an Owensboro highway bridge over the Ohio River, and local motorists paid high tolls for bridges on US 60 for travel to Henderson and Paducah as well as for bridges south of the city at Livermore and Rumsey-Calhoun.[19]

The driving force behind the free-bridge movement was the brash, energetic state representative Henry Ward from Paducah. His column in the *Paducah Sun-Democrat,* "Seen While Roaming," and the daily reminder on the editorial page of the paper's support for removing tolls on Kentucky bridges led to the creation of the Kentucky Free Bridge Association (KFBA) in February 1936 by Paducah civic and business leaders. Hopes for success were initially raised in March by Ben Johnson at a Highway Commission meeting when he said that "the main ambition I now have is to see Kentucky's toll bridges free." There was an expectation that the bridge issue could be part of a fourth special session that Chandler never called in 1936. Progress floundered on the prevailing assumption that any money spent on paying off toll bridge bonds would result in less money to spend on highways. With the legislature not scheduled to convene again until January 1938, Ward and the KFBA met with leaders throughout western Kentucky and all sections of the commonwealth to promote their message that elimination of bridge tolls would encourage motorist traffic, which would increase gasoline purchases, from which bridge bonds could be paid off and encourage the state's travel industry, hurt by out-of-state motorist associations' suggestion that their members bypass Kentucky in part because of the tolls. Ward spent two months before the 1938 session in meetings throughout Kentucky, landing support from the Kentucky Farm Bureau and the mayor of Louisville, who hoped the bridge campaign would result in the removal of the tolls on the city's Ohio River bridge. Ward's meetings with the governor and legislative leaders in preparation for the 1938 session failed to dissuade Governor Chandler that the free-bridge campaign's goal was a $3.5 million appropriation. In the annual State of the Commonwealth speech to a joint legislative session, Chandler dismissed the campaign as a facade to promote Ward's political future.[20]

The antitoll forces, disappointed that their legislative program failed to advance, found opportunities at the Highway Commission, where a committee tasked to examine the toll bridge issue filed a report in January 1938 with Robert Humphreys that supported the KFBA position that the tolls hindered tourism and should be removed. Humphreys visited Paducah in early March for a speech to local leaders, including members of the KFBA, where he announced "that the time has come when general reductions on bridge toll charges are feasible." His plan was to start with an experiment to determine if reducing tolls from fifty to twenty-five cents on the Paducah-Brookport Bridge over the Ohio River would be offset, as the free-bridge advocates believed, by increased vehicular traffic. With the encouragement produced by this experiment, tolls were reduced on the Canton and Eggner's Ferry bridges, where traffic increases did result in more revenue. In celebration of these advances on the toll program, Paducah leaders announced that the city would host a West Kentucky Day celebration in late August. Approximately 300 Paducahans fanned out throughout western Kentucky and southern Illinois promoting the event and the importance of regional cooperation that had made this victory possible and would help in future endeavors. However, other priorities for the region and nation now intervened so that the issue of free bridges, still posted daily on the *Paducah Sun-Democrat* editorial page, remained at a standstill through the war years when the bonds were retired. Finally, on August 25, 1945, Governor Simeon Willis welcomed several thousands gathered at the Eggner's Ferry Bridge over the Tennessee River at Aurora to celebrate the removal of the bridge tolls, and others gathered at bridges to listen to the governor's broadcasted speech. When remaining tolls were taken off the Livermore Bridge over the Green and Rough Rivers, the Rockport Bridge over the Green River, and the Ohio River bridge at Owensboro, the long struggle of the free-bridge movement, which had begun a decade earlier, was over.[21]

Governor Chandler's administration brought the curtain down on West Kentucky Industrial College (WKIC), a public two-year college for blacks in Paducah and the long dream of its founding president D. H. Anderson to provide western Kentucky blacks a higher education consistent with the teachings of the Tuskegee philosophy of Booker T. Washington. Efficiency reports examining state services had criticized the college to governors and lawmakers. WKIC, reported to be the third-largest black junior college in the United States, escaped a deep budget cut during the 1936 session recommended by Chandler's Government Reorganization Commission, but state senators Ray Smith from Benton and Franklin Rives of Hopkinsville took up WKIC's cause. In a significant turnaround, the college's funding was restored, and additional money was provided to support plans for WKIC to become a four-year institution.[22]

WKIC's reprieve proved to be brief as turmoil surrounding Anderson's administration forced him out as president in March 1937 and Governor Chandler took steps to close WKIC and consolidate public higher education programs at Kentucky State. Plans for four-year status at WKIC ground to a halt in the weeks before the 1938 session, and Henry Ward attempted to rally the college's supporters in a desperate attempt to save it. Charles Anderson, the first black state representative, organized a meeting that pulled together leaders from the state's black churches and the Kentucky Negro Educational Association, at which they learned Chandler planned to provide more funding for Kentucky State and to convert the Paducah campus into an institution for "feeble-minded" young black men. A clergyman in the audience, speaking for many in the gathering, argued that young black students in western

Kentucky would be placed at a severe disadvantage if they were forced to travel to Frankfort for their higher education. Chandler, who was making preparations for his US Senate race, could ill afford this controversy to linger. He moved quickly to secure a commitment from the National Youth Administration, a New Deal program, to fund a technical school for blacks with a complete high school curriculum. By mid-January, after a meeting between Paducah leaders and the governor, Henry Ward concluded that "any efforts to prevent abandonment of West Kentucky Industrial College appear doomed to failure." D. H. Anderson, who had been relegated to the status of "president emeritus" in 1937, was given the nondescript title of "field operative" in the new West Kentucky Vocational School for Negroes and died in financially straightened circumstances in 1952. The loss to the black community resulting from the closing of WKIC cannot be overlooked. That sense of loss is present in the alumni oral histories on file at Murray State University.[23]

Kentucky voters in 1938 witnessed one of the state's greatest political clashes as two of the commonwealth's political giants, both with strong western Kentucky roots, tilted for the Democratic US Senate nomination. For both Senate majority leader Alben Barkley and Governor Happy Chandler, there was a great deal riding on the outcome. Barkley was considered to be on the short list of FDR successors in 1940; Chandler, blocked by the Kentucky Constitution from running for a second term as governor and with the next US Senate opening scheduled for 1942, saw that his own presidential aspirations for 1940 would suffer greatly if he did not throw his hat into the ring in 1938. Though both men ran pro-Roosevelt campaigns, FDR clearly backed Barkley for his solid embrace of the president's political agenda, as reflected in a speech to a large crowd at an early July Woodmen of the World picnic in Owensboro: "I am a New Dealer. I am a Roosevelt man." In contrast, Chandler was politically more influenced by Senator Harry F. Byrd, the conservative former governor of Virginia who was part of the anti–New Deal coalition that FDR set out to break by taking the unusual step of participating in the primary campaigns, including Kentucky, to shore up political support for the New Deal. John Ed Pearce, a contemporary political observer of the Kentucky scene, later wrote that Chandler was "a southern conservative, a Republican who found himself in the

Democratic camp mainly through the accident of birth and geography." Chandler conveyed his independence from the White House from the start of the campaign by snubbing a Louisville dinner honoring Barkley in January 1938, to which Roosevelt made a point of sending emissaries to lavish praise on the majority floor leader, and by participating in an event held the same day, where the governor told supporters that if he were to run, "I would not call upon any Senators or any other fellows from the North to come help me."[24]

Indeed, Chandler had considerable assets going into the campaign, including his youth and political energy, which made his speeches events that drew large crowds, as they had in the gubernatorial primary in 1935, where, as Pearce recalls, Chandler had employed "name-calling, ridiculing, promising, sweating, hugging, kissing, . . . breaking into a rendition of 'Sonny Boy' at any or no provocation." As governor, he also had access to a large patronage network of state employees and the traditional political slush fund from the assessments into which state employees paid from their paychecks. Barkley, now sixty-one, had not had a demanding political race since his election to the Senate in 1926, giving Chandler hopes that the senator was out of touch with the voters. He certainly discounted Barkley's national stature built on his keynote speeches and leadership position, telling an Owensboro crowd in late July that the senator was "swelled up like a poisoned pup." Holding himself up as a contrast, Chandler boasted in Barkley's hometown of Paducah, "Why I know more people in this county by accident than Barkley does on purpose."[25]

The campaign delivered memorable moments of political theater, the first of which came on July 8 when President Roosevelt, who had great concerns that the election of Chandler would be construed as a Roosevelt defeat and send to the Senate another demagogue like Louisiana's Huey Long, made several appearances in the state on a campaign swing to support his preferences in several Democratic senate primaries. At the Latonia Race Track in northern Kentucky, Chandler, unwilling to concede to FDR's approval of Barkley, leaped between Roosevelt and the senator in the backseat of an open-air car, providing a photo opportunity for himself. Chandler made great use of that image in his campaign and a portion of the president's comments suggesting that Chandler would make a "good senator from Kentucky," which distorted FDR's actual summation of the two candidates. What the president really said was that Chandler, as "a very junior member of the Senate[,] . . . would take . . . many, many years to match the National knowledge, the experience and the acknowledged leadership on the affairs of the Nation of that son of Kentucky, of whom the whole Nation is proud, Alben W. Barkley." Chandler then left the Barkley procession, which took FDR and Barkley to additional campaign stops in Louisville, Bowling Green, and Russellville, where Chandler's candidacy was ignored and where Ruby Laffoon and Thomas Rhea were on hand to be recognized by the president during the only presidential visit ever to that town.[26]

There was considerable mudslinging during the campaign, including an accusation that the Roosevelt administration was encouraging federal relief workers to support the Barkley campaign. Although Harry Hopkins and George Goodman denied it, the national press descended on the state to investigate. The Scripps-Howard reporter Thomas Stokes's Pulitzer-prize winning coverage of the campaign looked into Chandler's use of patronage during the campaign but saw nothing amiss in state workers, but he raised serious allegations about New Deal programs being used to support Barkley. His coverage caused congressional investigators to review the allegations, ultimately encouraging Congress to enact the Hatch Act in 1940, which limited political activities of federal employees. Senator Barkley managed, with the evidence of Chandler's political exploitation of state employees, to extend those restrictions to state employees funded by federal dollars.[27]

Chandler and Barkley, who had earned the nickname "Iron Man" from his energetic gubernatorial campaign of 1923, were among the most energetic Kentucky campaigners of the twentieth century, but the governor must have thought his youth would favor him in the end. Two weeks before the election, however, Chandler became seriously ill with a stomach disorder that he was convinced was caused by poison added to his ice water. He blamed the Barkley campaign, but police investigators considered the poisoning a "political bedtime story." While Chandler was on his sickbed, Kentucky House Speaker John Kirtley from McLean County and Bowling Green state representative Rodes K. Myers joined Mrs. Chandler to fill Chandler's campaign engagements. Barkley made light of the whole matter by claiming that he had added an "ice water guard" to the campaign, and, as he wrote later, when someone poured him a glass of water during his speeches, "I would hold it up and look quizzically at the crowd," who would yell that "it may be poisoned," causing him to "shudder fearfully and put it down."[28]

Barkley sought an advantage by turning the campaign into a referendum on the president and the New Deal. In a speech at Hopkinsville, he claimed that Chandler was a pawn of Wall Street "who has willingly placed himself in a position of being against the President" and who "has won many friends among the Tories of Wall Street and among the Republican politicians of Kentucky and of the nation who desire the destruction of the President's program." In his customary "Barkley tour" of western Kentucky at the campaign's closing, he said to a Mayfield crowd that a Chandler victory would be a "stab in the back" to FDR and reminded the farmers that "because we've given the farmer credit and a market, because we have put government in partnership with farmers so they can make an honest, profitable living, the farmers of Kentucky voted to reelect Roosevelt in 1936 and are going to vote to reelect me." When Chandler said that as a result of his stewardship the state budget had eliminated a $30 million debt, and Kentucky was now in the position to raise the old-age assistance from $20 to $30 per month, Barkley scoffed that "the reason why the budget of Kentucky is balanced and the budget in Washington is unbalanced is because we have done our duty to the people in Washington and they have not done it in Frankfort." Back on the campaign trail, Chandler sought to cut into the senator's votes in western Kentucky before the election during campaign stops in Bowling Green, Mayfield, and Madisonville. In Bowling Green, he outlined his program for the country: "I want to get you a house and a few acres of ground with 15 or 20 years to pay it for it . . . so if you get out of work you can go there, raise cows, ducks, chickens, and children and have more fun than anybody ever saw." Barkley, participating at the "political speaking" at the Fancy Farm Picnic, sponsored by St. Jerome's Catholic Church in Graves County and only a few miles from his birthplace in Lowes, which Chandler did not attend, appeared confident in a victory called on voters to send him back to Washington with the largest vote margin in Kentucky history.[29]

In the end, Barkley won with a very comfortable 70,872 edge, carrying seven of nine congressional districts, including the two in western Kentucky. One historian looking back on the race in 1938 correctly concluded that Barkley had an advantage over Chandler by never making strong political enemies. In contrast, Chandler had to overcome Democrats loyal to Ruby Laffoon and Thomas Rhea as well as former friends such as John Y. Brown Sr., the Union County native and former ally during the Laffoon administration who had turned against Chandler for failing to honor a commitment to support Brown in the US Senate race in 1936. Brown campaigned for Barkley statewide, including in western Kentucky. The size of Barkley's victory in the First Congressional District, where Chandler lost every county, underscores that Chandler hurt himself to a large degree by his own actions. He hoped to cut into Barkley's advantage in McCracken County by tapping Brady M. Stewart, county judge from Barkley's home, as campaign chair, but Barkley crushed the governor there because Chandler had alienated both Henry Ward, who handled communications for the Barkley campaign, failed to support the free bridge issue, and alienated blacks in closing the WKIC. Agriculture Commissioner Garth Ferguson from Ballard County and Ferguson's son-in-law Harry Lee Waterfield, a first-term state representative from Hickman County whom Chandler tried to defeat, aided Barkley's strong performance in the far west. Old scores with Ruby Laffoon and Thomas Rhea cost Chandler in Logan and Hopkins Counties; he even lost in his home Henderson County thanks to the work of state representative George Clay, another lawmaker whom the governor had failed to oust. Chandler outpolled Barkley in only two western Kentucky counties, Butler and Warren, where Rodes K. Myers and Paul Garrett, the new president whom the governor had forced upon Western State College, enabled Chandler to eke out a close win. Alben Barkley proceeded to win reelection in the general election in November by a very large margin.[30]

Happy Chandler's defeat in his run for the US Senate left him with an uncertain political future. Because he was not be allowed by state election law to run for the governorship again, his immediate task was selection of a suitable candidate who could win in the fast-approaching gubernatorial race and secure for Chandler a strong voice in the Kentucky delegation to the 1940 Democratic National Convention. He did not have to look far: Lieutenant Governor Keen Johnson, who in 1935 had run on the Rhea slate but had proved in office to be loyal to Chandler, fit the bill.

Johnson's ties to the Laffoon–Rhea faction appeared an asset, offering an opportunity to broaden Johnson's support. His experience as a newspaper publisher and former president of the Kentucky Press Association meant that he could expect warm support from the commonwealth's newspapers. First, though, he had to defeat the fervently anti-Chandler John Y. Brown Sr. in the Democratic primary.[31]

Brown was by this point an experienced statewide campaigner. After the Kentucky congressional plan had been thrown out by the courts, he had won his seat in Congress in a statewide race in 1932, but he had lost his US Senate primary in 1936 to Marvel M. Logan. Johnson had several decided advantages in the manpower and financial resources that Governor Chandler put into the race. The campaign was, like the recent US Senate primary, an ugly one. Brown attempted to follow Barkley in making the race a referendum on FDR and the New Deal. Johnson responded with attacks focusing on his opponent's ties to unpopular labor organizations. At an Owensboro rally, Johnson vigorously attacked his opponent, charging that Brown had close ties to organized labor and was the "man Friday" of John L. Lewis, president of the Congress of Industrial Organizations (CIO) and the UMWA, who had reportedly announced his intention take political control of Kentucky in order to win his position on closed union shops. Speaking at a picnic at Kuttawa Mineral Springs Park in his home Lyon County, Johnson, while proudly telling listeners of his backing from the American Federation of Labor (AFL), asserted that the CIO was controlled by foreigners and Communists.[32]

Results at the polls gave Keen Johnson a respectable 30,000-vote edge over Brown, but they split western Kentucky. Brown won nineteen counties there, including large counties such as Henderson, Hopkins, and McCracken. Tyler Munford, Keen Johnson's campaign publicity chief, helped deliver Union County for Johnson. Senator Marvel Logan's unexpected death on October 3 put Johnson into the governor's mansion when Chandler and he agreed that Chandler would resign as governor if Johnson would send him to fill Logan's vacated senatorial seat. Now Governor Johnson, the third consecutive western Kentuckian to hold the spot, defeated the GOP candidate King Swope in November by a landslide 106,000 votes, nearly 50,000 of which came from western Kentucky. Other Democratic western Kentucky candidates also fared well in the general election of 1939: Greenville's Hubert Meredith, the incumbent state attorney general, now won a full term, and Rodes K. Myers, the former state representative from Bowling Green, was elected lieutenant general.[33]

Keen Johnson, the eldest child of a Methodist preacher, was born in the small community of Brandon's Chapel located in the Between the Rivers region bounded by the Tennessee and Cumberland Rivers in Lyon County. His father, as Methodist ministers did in those days, moved often, serving a number of communities throughout the state. Young Keen lived in Eddyville and Kuttawa in Lyon County as well as in the small Ohio River community of Tolu in Crittenden County. He completed high school at the Vanderbilt Training School, a Methodist preparatory school, in the Todd County community of Elkton. World War I interrupted his college studies, but he graduated from the University of Kentucky after the war with a journalism degree. Beginning in 1925, he was the editor and copublisher of the *Richmond Daily Examiner*, and he took an active role in state press and Democratic activities.[34]

War clouds were on the horizon as Keen Johnson took the reins of power in Kentucky in 1939. Much of his administration's energies would be directed to following President Roosevelt's lead first in preparing America to assume its role as the "arsenal of democracy," a nonbelligerent providing economic assistance to the Allied powers against their fascist enemies, and then, after Pearl Harbor, as in FDR's words, in fully replacing Dr. New Deal with Dr. Win the War. In these circumstances, state politics took second place in the minds of Kentuckians. The governor offered a steady hand by paying off what was left of the state debt, honoring Chandler's promise to increase old-age pensions, and leaving office with $10 million in reserve.[35]

Keen Johnson's administration was pivotal for the role it played in the clash between public and private power over TVA energy from construction of Kentucky Dam (formerly Gilbertsville Dam) that, unless public-power forces prevailed, threatened to block progress in western Kentucky. A Kentucky Court of Appeals opinion in December 1940 invalidated a contract, similar to those TVA used in other states, between the southeastern Kentucky town of Middlesboro and TVA on grounds that the contract would surrender regulatory authority over the town's electrical utility to a federal entity. It fell to the Kentucky General Assembly to intercede if cities in the vicinity of Kentucky Dam would be allowed to light their homes and businesses with cheap power from Kentucky Dam. Henry Ward, Paducah's state representative, had become a leading advocate for public power in his work on REC legislation and his legislation in 1940, of which the *Paducah Sun-Democrat* noted, "It is no exaggeration to say that upon the success of the pending Ward bill . . . to bring cheap electricity to the state depends the future prosperity or retardation of Kentucky and, in particular, of Western Kentucky." But without support from Governor Keen Johnson and with strong opposition from private utilities, especially R. M. Watt, the president of Kentucky Utilities (KU), Ward's bill failed. It became clear that there would be a showdown in the 1942 legislative session, and the outcome depended on which side Governor Johnson would take. The Kentucky Municipal League rallied to the side of public power by calling on the cities and towns to organize. The Kentucky Public Power League (KPPL), chaired by Mayor Pierce E. Lackey of Murray, was established following a meeting in Murray in February 1941 attended by the mayors of Paducah, Mayfield, Murray, and Benton. Ward, who by now was one of the more experienced Kentucky House members and had made an effort to establish a good working relationship with Governor Johnson, also attended the meeting and worked with the various interested parties on a bill that he intended to file in the coming session. He also quickly secured the governor's pledge to work on legislation to help the KPPL's program. Lined up on the other side were the powerful KU and other private utilities as well as their railroad and coal allies, all of whom feared the impact of public hydroelectric power on their industries.[36]

Caught in the middle was the Kentucky Public Services Commission (PSC), chaired by John Kirtley, the two-term former Kentucky House Speaker during the Chandler administration from Island in McLean County, whom Governor Johnson tasked to develop the required legislation for the 1942 legislative session to enable Kentucky cities and towns to purchase TVA power. The PSC's draft caused an uproar among the commonwealth's cities and towns, whose municipally operated utilities, as outlined in the draft, would come under the PSC's oversight. TVA attorneys confirmed Ward's concerns about Kirtley in saying that the bill draft at that time had many "joker" provisions that would prevent TVA from selling its power in Kentucky. At a mid-January meeting of the Kentucky Public Power League at Mayfield, mayors from Benton, Clinton, Hickman, Calvert City, Paducah, Bardwell, Fulton, Mayfield, and Murray went on record to support Ward's TVA legislation. On the editorial page of the *Paducah Sun-Democrat*, the writer unloaded on the anti-public-power forces led by KU and Kirtley. On Kirtley, the editorial stated that he "has indicated a far greater concern on its part for protecting the private power interests—including their profits and privileges—than for serving the public."[37]

KU initiated a determined attack against the TVA bill, suggesting to lawmakers that there was no need to rush the legislation given that Kentucky Dam would not be completed until 1944 and especially that Ward's bill would give TVA special privileges by allowing municipalities to enter into contracts directly with TVA, a federal entity, without any role for the PSC and thus undermine the state's rights. Tempers erupted at the public hearing on the bill on February 3, 1942, held before the House Public Utilities Committee. Weeks spent to work out differences between all the interested parties had failed to achieve a compromise. KU president R. M. Watt charged that Ward's bill would destroy private-power companies in Kentucky. After one House member on the committee scolded Ward, who was acting House majority leader for the 1942 session, for his "stupid insolence," chairman Lee Allen Rhoads from Henderson had to separate the two men before words turned to blows. More serious was the confrontation between Ward and John Kirtley, who testified the following day. Amid his heavy questioning of Kirtley, Ward said the PSC chairman needed to file as a lobbyist against the bill, which provoked Kirtley to shout back that "no sane or sensible man would be for this bill." The bill's fate now depended on Governor Johnson, with whom Ward had kept in close touch during the negotiations but who also was considered a personal friend of Kirtley. In the end, Johnson publicly repudiated Kirtley's stance in saying that the only comment in Kirtley's committee testimony with which he found no disagreement was that the PSC chair did not speak for the governor.[38]

After the private-power forces launched a public campaign against the bill, Johnson demonstrated his full support for the public-power bill in a speech before a joint legislative session broadcast statewide by radio. He deemed the legislation vital to the future development of the commonwealth as "the first and most essential step toward providing cheap, ample power for industry" that would save consumers $7 million ($110 million in 2020) annually. Although the governor never mentioned Kirtley by name, he resigned his office "because I don't have to stand insults from everybody." In the end, Kirtley took some satisfaction when Ward amended the bill to address a number of Kirtley's concerns. The amended bill passed the House, with Governor Johnson on hand, by a one-sided 85–10 vote. The vote showed strong support from western Kentucky lawmakers, except for Byron Royster from Sebree, Faust Y. Simpson of Morganfield, and Republican W. H. Hunt from Central City, all of whom represented the Western Kentucky Coal Field. Passage in the Senate was less contentious.[39]

The legislation provided the green light for municipalities to go ahead with plans to contract with TVA for their power needs. There would be later unsuccessful yet closely fought battles in the upcoming legislative sessions to pass the "Moss Bill" (the bill's author was the Senate's Republican minority leader Ray Moss from Pineville in eastern Kentucky), which sought to greatly increase the costs for municipalities to convert to public power. Despite this attempt at obstruction, contracts were concluded for TVA power by the western Kentucky towns of Hopkinsville, Murray, Mayfield, Russellville, Bowling Green, and Franklin. Several of these communities went on TVA's grid before Kentucky Dam was completed when TVA purchased the Kentucky-Tennessee Light and Power Company in order to provide power to western Kentucky. A number of other Jackson Purchase towns, such as Barlow, La Center, Kevil, and Bandana, ran into complications, though, because KU provided not only electricity but also water and ice, and KU insisted that they reimburse it for all utilities before switching to TVA, causing the switch to be delayed for decades.[40]

The Johnson administration was also important for western Kentucky in its effort to address glaring inequities in legislative district populations. Without federal compulsion to provide equal representation, like what the US Supreme Court would later impose on legislatures in 1962, but in light of the General Assembly's decades of failure to address population inequities, the governor called a special session to redistrict the two legislative chambers. Matters were made worse in western Kentucky by its stagnating population, which also put its political representation on the line. In the House, where the average district size was a population of 38,652, McLean, Simpson, Trigg, Webster, and Ohio were among nineteen single-representative-member counties with populations less than 19,000; McLean and Simpson were among the smallest House districts, each with fewer than 12,000 residents. Earle Clements's Senate district, which included Crittenden, Union, and Webster Counties, had only 38,653 people (the ideal district size was approximately 74,500) and thus was among the smallest Senate districts.[41]

Hopes for a short session in early 1942 were not realized as strong opposition to redistricting developed in the House, including Harry Lee Waterfield, the son-in-law of Garth Ferguson and antiadministration leader from Hickman County. The task of shepherding redistricting in the House fell to Majority Leader Henry Ward. Tempers flared early on by the charge in a joint session that the opposition members were "saboteurs" in trying to preserve the existing districts, which were a "mockery of democracy." In the end, administration forces took control in pushing the legislature to pass the redistricting legislation that took away two of western Kentucky's eleven state Senate seats and reduced the number of its House seats from thirty-seven to twenty-four by (1) eliminating single-county districts for Trigg, Caldwell, Webster, McLean, Simpson, and Allen Counties and (2) eliminating one of the two Warren County districts. But the Paducah area gained by adding a second McCracken County district. Later redistricting plans reduced the state representatives in the region to nineteen following the 1990 US census.[42]

The bombing of Pearl Harbor on December 7, 1941, and America's entry into World War II on the side of the Allies brought an end to the Great Depression and the New Deal. While many men and women enlisted in the armed services, all Kentuckians were called upon to do their part in the war effort. Richard Holl, historian of the Kentucky home front, notes the contribution of Kentucky agriculture to the Food for Freedom initiative aimed at increasing production. In Fulton County, one of the few commonwealth counties involved in this initiative, the value of its cotton output increased from approximately $600,000 in

1939 to more than $1 million in 1945; overall, the county's agriculture output, with much larger corn and sweet potato crops, more than doubled. Muhlenberg County, located in the middle of the Western Kentucky Coal Field, also increased the value of its agriculture production. Tobacco, in great demand by the armed forces, increased sharply both in the amount produced and in value during the war. Farmers also upped production in corn and livestock.[43]

In western Kentucky, several large concerns quickly altered their operations to assist in the war effort, notably the Modern Welding Machinery company (which received a navy contract to build buoys months before war was declared), Ken-Rad Corporation, Glenmore Distillery in Owensboro, and Merit Clothing Company in Mayfield. Ken-Rad, with a peacetime workforce of approximately 2,000 producing radio tubes, was a vital war concern in that it converted tubes designed to receive radio signals to tubes transmitting them for the armed services. General Jimmy Doolittle, after his daring bombing of the Japanese mainland, sent a note to Bendix radio, which used Ken-Rad tubes, that "now it can be told officially: Radios you helped build aided us to bomb Tokio [*sic*]." Glenmore Distillery, the largest Kentucky producer of spirits with a workforce of about 350, engaged in the production of industrial alcohol for smokeless gunpowder and had contracts with several large munitions firms. Merit Clothing, one of several large clothing factories in Mayfield, secured contracts in the first months of the war to produce 35,000 pants and 25,000 overcoats for the army.[44]

Because of the immense need for explosives, three new factories of considerable size were built in the region. Near Henderson and close to the Western Kentucky Coal Field, the Ohio River Ordnance Works, with approximately 500 employees, was in the planning stages before Pearl Harbor. The plant converted gaseous coke to anhydrous ammonia, which would be delivered to munitions factories to be converted to nitric acid. Leaders in the Jackson Purchase also eagerly sought to land explosives operations. After losing out on an aluminum-smelting plant near Paducah allegedly due to insufficient energy sources, leaders in the Jackson Purchase formed the Kentucky Defense Council to work with area congressmen in persuading decision makers in Washington to locate war installations in the area. Their efforts were quickly rewarded by announcements in February 1942 that the Kentucky Ordnance

Works (KOW), operated by Atlas Powder Company, would be located outside Paducah and that a National Fireworks factory would be located near Viola, a small hamlet in northwest Graves County. KOW, built to manufacture TNT, involved nearly 6,000 workers in the construction phase for a plant that employed approximately 1,000. The Viola site, located on 1,500 leased acres with a $4 million construction cost, had a workforce of 3,000, the majority of whom were local women, and was engaged in artillery loading for the navy. The two Jackson Purchase munitions factories were closed after hostilities ended; the Henderson plant was later purchased by the Spencer Chemical Company and continued to be engaged in production of anhydrous ammonia.[45]

Western Kentucky also sought its share of military training facilities starting in the months prior to the nation's becoming a formal belligerent. Owensboro quickly landed in March 1942 a Coast Guard training station for 200–250 trainees, which replaced the CCC camp located there. Two larger bases were landed near Hopkinsville and Morganfield. Starting in the summer of 1940, the Hopkinsville Chamber of Commerce aimed to secure a base on the grounds of the Pennyrile State Forest, but military authorities determined that the forest was too small and had rougher terrain than what they had in mind. Instead, their attention was drawn to the rolling terrain along the state border between Hopkinsville, Kentucky, and Clarksville, Tennessee. With a large labor pool drawn from both Hopkinsville and Clarksville, location of a base there would gain favor with two powerful US senators, Alben Barkley from Kentucky and Kenneth McKellar from Tennessee. In early 1942, the army acquired more than 100,000 acres for an armored training base soon to be known as Camp Campbell, named after William Bowen Campbell, a former governor of Tennessee who fought in several nineteenth-century wars and for one year was a brigadier general on the Union side during the Civil War. (For the base's name, several alternatives with Confederate ties were given consideration, including Jefferson Davis, whose birthplace was nearby.) Construction of Camp Campbell was completed by a workforce of 10,000 in time for the arrival of the first trainees in September 1942. A third camp, Camp Breckinridge (named in honor of the former US vice president from Kentucky and the last Confederate secretary of war) was constructed near Morganfield on approximately 30,000 acres. After being announced in spring 1942, training there began later that fall; the camp employed more than 1,000 civilian workers and brought with them considerable commercial traffic to nearby Sturgis and Morganfield.[46]

Initial postwar plans called for a considerable downsizing of the military and munition works, but as the historian Richard Holl details in his study of the war on the commonwealth's home front, there would not be any replication of the "return to normalcy" that occurred following World War I. Although the new war plants in Paducah and Viola closed, and plans called for the decommissioning of the Owensboro Coast Guard training installation, Camp Campbell, and Camp Breckinridge, Cold War conditions returned the nation to a wartime readiness. Holl notes that this state of affairs sidetracked the notion to deactivate Camp Campbell, which by the end of 1945 had taken on a deserted appearance. It was soon designated to house atomic bombs and was assigned several airborne army units; permanent status came in 1950 with the base's upgrade to Ft. Campbell. Holl overlooks, however, the similar evolution of Camp Breckinridge, which was closed in 1946 but reopened in 1950 as a training camp for an estimated 25,000 troops to serve in the Korean War. The camp closed in 1959 and became the home for the Breckinridge Job Corps Center in 1965 as part of the War on Poverty program.[47]

War did not entirely sidetrack labor conflict in western Kentucky, even though organized labor was under strong pressure to avoid conflict as the nation's energies were focused on defeat of the enemy. However, in the case of Ken-Rad, headquartered in Owensboro and with satellites in Bowling Green and Rockport, Kentucky, as well as Tell City, Indiana, dissatisfaction with management boiled over as its more than 3,000 workers, a majority of whom were women who took jobs previously held by men, went on strike in 1943. Prior to the war, Ken-Rad was nonunion, but the United Auto Workers organized floor workers in August 1942. Dissatisfaction that low wages were causing a drop off in production led more than 100 women to walk out briefly in early 1942. The local paper criticized the striking women as "hurting the lads in the armed forces." The union's wage concerns were submitted to the federal War Labor Board, which initially chose to intervene, but complaints did not stop. The War Labor Board eventually urged the owner, Ray Burlew, to raise wages and provide for a minimum fifty-cent hourly wage, but he refused. Matters got out of hand, and President Roosevelt ordered the military to take control of the headquarters in Owensboro and then eventually all of the satellite sites in April 1944 until the union and Burlew finally negotiated a settlement the following month.[48]

Labor unrest was the dominant theme in the Western Kentucky Coal Field in 1943 as UMWA president John L. Lewis chose to challenge President Roosevelt, whom Lewis had opposed in the presidential race in 1940, and to ignore wartime no-strike and no-wage-hikes regulations in place. The existing mine labor agreement was to expire at the end of March, and Lewis made it clear that he wanted to include in a new agreement a $2 per day increase to $7 for his members and that he was prepared to strike until he got it. Coal operators complained that the increase was prohibitive. The Roosevelt administration tried to hold the line because the unions in other industries would want the increase miners received for their workers, too; FDR had a weak hand to play, though, as coal was essential to the massive military buildup under way. From April through December 1943, the western Kentucky UMWA coal workers went through a series of short strikes and contract extensions, punctuated by President Roosevelt's decision to take military control of the nation's coal mines in early May after negotiations failed to resolve the wage issue. Mines in Muhlenberg and Ohio Counties, where the UMWA represented the vast majority of miners, were idled for the strikes. Those in the western counties were generally spared because the largest coal operator, the West Kentucky Coal Company, was nonunion, and mines organized by the Progressive Mine Workers, an AFL union with nearly 4,000 members working under a contract that did not expire until mid-1944, were unaffected by the UMWA strikes.[49]

Lewis's tactics, although applauded by his membership, made him one of the most unpopular men in the country. Servicemen overseas considered the strikes, which depleted the nation's coal reserves to a dangerous level, a stab in the back. An editorial in the *Owensboro Messenger-Inquirer* backed FDR's decision to take over the operation of the mines, stating that miners were "soldiers no less than the men on the fighting front" and that "the miner who lays down his tools at this juncture is guilty of deserting his post of duty." Months of negotiations ended when the Roosevelt administration receded from its position to stand firm against wage hikes, and the union and industry negotiated a new contract very close to Lewis's initial $2 per day increase by adding an additional hour daily for a forty-eight-hour work week and by cutting breaks. New contracts in the Western Kentucky Coal Field were signed with the Tri-County Coal Operators and the West Kentucky Coal Operations by the end of 1943. The UMWA presence in the region was further enhanced after Lewis began negotiations to rejoin the AFL. In the bargain, the Progressive Mine Workers closed operations, and many of its 4,000 members in the western coal field would vote to have the UMWA represent them by the end of the war.[50]

In 1943, Kentucky elections took place in an atmosphere charged by concerns over wartime inflation and rationing, labor disruptions in the coal fields, and four years of scandals surrounding state purchasing practices stirred by Democrat Hubert Meredith, the attorney general from Muhlenberg County. After all the ballots were counted in November, Kentucky voters elected its first Republican governor since 1927 and the only governor not from western Kentucky since 1931. Simeon Willis won by less than 9,000 votes; with no western Kentuckian on the Democratic slate after Henry Ward and Rodes K. Myers lost their primary contests for lieutenant governor and governor, respectively, the normal large Democratic majority from the region was reduced to 20,000 votes, a factor that contributed significantly to Willis's victory. There was considerable evidence that a number of leaders in the Chandler faction—notably Hubert Meredith, who openly supported Willis—failed to support the Democratic candidate, J. Lyter Donaldson, who was strongly backed by Governor Johnson.[51] However, the defeat suffered by the Chandler faction opened the way for a new wave of anti-Chandler politicians from western Kentucky, who would become major players on the statewide political stage for decades to come.

Willis appeared to have political coattails, demonstrated by the significant cut in Democrat control in the House to 57–43, a loss of eighteen seats since 1942. Nevertheless, even with lower numbers of Democrats in the General Assembly and a Republican in the governor's mansion, Democrats retained a majority, and so organization of the legislative leadership still fell to the Democrats in each chamber. Harry Lee Waterfield, elected to the House in 1937 from Hickman County and an antiadministration member during the Chandler and Johnson administrations, traveled the state before the session with new member Adron Doran from Wingo in Graves County, seeking member support for electing him to the Speaker's position. Born in rural Calloway County and educated at Murray State, Waterfield married the daughter of the anti-Chandler agriculture secretary and local newspaper owner Garth K. Ferguson from Ballard County. Waterfield settled in Clinton, the seat of Hickman County, where he farmed and published the *Hickman County Gazette*. While Chandler and Keen Johnson opposed Waterfield, he had the backing of Donaldson, who worked behind the scenes for Waterfield, so that Waterfield eventually became the first Speaker from the First Congressional District since Henry R. Lawrence from Cadiz held that position in 1906.[52]

Equally ambitious as Waterfield, another western Kentuckian, first-term state senator Earle C. Clements from Morganfield in Union County, plotted his political rise. Like Waterfield, Clements, nearly fifteen years older than the new Speaker, was considered anti-Johnson during the session of 1942. He had considerable experience as a county officer in Union County, and his political skill had not gone unnoticed. He was Thomas Rhea's campaign manager in the pivotal 1935 gubernatorial primary against Clements' childhood friend Happy Chandler. Now he consulted with several more senior senators about the Senate leadership in the approaching session. Senator Lee Gibson, now living in Calhoun, encouraged Clements to consider running for president pro tempore, but Clements deferred to incumbent E. C. Moore, settling for the position of majority leader, with which he could control leadership decisions. His first order of business was to once more "rip" the powers of the Republican lieutenant general and Senate president, Kenneth H. Tuggle, by placing procedural matters in a committee on committees that he, Clements, would control, a move reminiscent of Governor Laffoon's hiding of Happy Chandler ten years earlier. Clements's biographer, Thomas S. Syvertsen, concludes that Democratic political leaders "were consciously hoping to cure a festering resentment among western Kentucky Democrats" left over from the elections by supporting Waterfield and Clements.[53]

The biggest issue facing Waterfield and Clements stemmed from Governor Willis's campaign pledge to eliminate the state's income tax, a proposal that gained considerable support from voters and legislators in both parties, who campaigned in its favor. However, Willis and legislative leaders paused at the repeal's $8.2 million price tag over the biennium. The reaction from western Kentucky after Willis decided against the repeal at the start of the session was mixed. On the editorial pages of the *Madisonville Messenger* and *Owensboro Inquirer,* writers commended Willis for recognizing realities and offering the promise of bipartisanship in addressing state issues, but the *Paducah Sun-Democrat* sharply criticized him for breaking a "sacred trust" given to voters and for wrongly excoriating the Johnson administration for not previously repealing the tax once the state debt was retired.[54]

Waterfield, who served as House Speaker during the entire Willis administration, and Clements, who ran successfully for a US congressional seat for the Second District later that year, helped achieve a stalemate with the administration over the income tax issue and many other financial matters. A central Democratic goal was met in the 1945 legislative races when Democrats rebounded in the House to take a 69–31 advantage. Waterfield's leadership was tested several times over the course of the 1946 session. The governor's income tax pledge was revived early in the session. After a House committee released the income tax repeal bill without any recommendation, Waterfield, with strong support from western Kentuckians John Y. Brown Sr., Rodes K. Myers, Adron Doran, and Kerby Jennings from Murray, killed the measure by a 60–36 vote.[55]

Later in the session, the Speaker also spearheaded defeat of the Moss Bill once again, with assistance from the state's public-power coalition, including the Kentucky Municipal League, the rural electric cooperatives, and the Kentucky Farm Bureau. Waterfield, aided by Senator Henry Ward's charges that private-power interests were offering lawmakers bribes to vote for the Moss Bill, held a public hearing of the entire House before the vote and joined Ward in speaking statewide on the radio against the bill. The TVA lawyer testifying against the bill told lawmakers that the Moss Bill's "practical effect" would be to bar TVA from doing business in Kentucky and to give private power "a permanent franchise" in Kentucky. During the House debate, Waterfield, whose district included the cities of Fulton and Hickman, which were actively seeking to be part of the TVA system, gave up his gavel to lead the public-power supporters, with support from A. L. "Chick" Love from Benton and J. Lee Moore from Simpson County. Rodes K. Myers, the former lieutenant governor from Bowling Green, and John Y. Brown Sr. took the lead for the private power side. After a series of amendments gutted the bill, Myers sought to pass the amended, crippled bill. When Waterfield refused to go along, Myers asked Waterfield, "Aren't you satisfied with taking the food out of the can and let us have the can?" Waterfield, taking no chances on allowing the bill to pass and giving the Senate the opportunity to put back into the bill the anti-public-power provisions contained in the original bill, succeeded in killing the bill with a commanding 60–31 vote. The public-power fight now moved from the state to the local level, where in the Jackson Purchase, for example, Paducah, the biggest prize in the war, did not vote to acquire KU until 1960, when voters rallied to support the Paducah Citizens for TVA Power, organized by the young attorney Julian Carroll, in a $7 million revenue bond purchase of KU facilities by a vote with a three-to-one margin over the very determined KU opposition.[56]

Alben Barkley held the post of US Senate majority leader just until after the elections in 1946, when Republicans took control of both houses of Congress. Against an increasingly powerful coalition of conservative, anti-Roosevelt Democrats and Republicans, Barkley supported FDR's programs during difficult votes necessary to prepare the country for the eventualities of entering World War II on the side of Great Britain against the fascist, militaristic powers of Germany, Italy, and Japan. He later characterized his relationship with the president as much like that of pitcher and catcher in baseball, with Barkley acting as catcher taking pitches from the president. He subordinated his own political ambition in 1940 to run on the Democratic national ticket for FDR's decision that serving a third term as president was essential to the nation's and the world's best interests. After distinguishing himself as keynote speaker in the Democratic National Convention in 1932 and 1936, Barkley, as permanent chairman of the convention in Chicago in 1940, played a critical role in rallying delegates made uncertain by FDR's silence regarding his intentions for a third term before they arrived at the convention. However, during a speech that reviewed FDR's many accomplished during his two terms in office, Barkley signaled to Mayor

Frank Kelly of Chicago, who caused an announcement over the loud-speaker that Illinois, New York, the United States, and the world wanted FDR, thus setting off a jubilant celebration that put in motion Roosevelt's successful nomination for a third term. The Kentucky senator, disappointed that FDR had not added him to the ticket, ignored criticism from a number of western Kentucky newspapers, including the *Earlington News,* the *Park City News* in Bowling Green, the *Fulton Daily Leader,* and the *Sturgis News,* to campaign for the national ticket and helped the president carry Kentucky by approximately 61,000 votes, 36,000 of which came from the First Congressional District. In western Kentucky, only the Republican strongholds of Butler, Ohio, and Crittenden Counties as well as Muhlenberg and Hancock Counties voted for Republican challenger Wendell Willkie.[57]

If Barkley felt any disappointment that he had been left off the national ticket, his White House ambitions—planted by his grandmother, who had grown up near Hopkinsville, where Adlai E. Stevenson Sr., one of her playmates and kinsman, was a future vice president during Grover Cleveland's administration—had not been extinguished. The Paducah senator had been mentioned as a candidate for president or vice president since former New York governor Al Smith's unsuccessful presidential campaign in 1928. And with questions arising about a fourth term for the aging, physically ailing Roosevelt and the unpopularity of Vice President Henry A. Wallace among Democratic Party regulars, opportunities could conceivably present themselves in 1944 to put the Kentuckian on the national ticket. Barkley later related that Roosevelt had encouraged the possibility of a Barkley race in 1940, but the possibility of a Roosevelt succession came to an abrupt end with the "Barkley Incident" on February 23, 1944.[58]

The president felt compelled to respond to the criticism from Wendell Willkie, his Republican opponent in 1940, that the country needed to do more to pay for the cost of the war. FDR's request for a $10.5 billion tax increase in 1944 was met with little enthusiasm from congressional Democratic leaders, who knew the difficulty that would be involved in getting the votes for such an increase from their members in an election year. When a $2.3 billion tax increase bill was sent to the president instead, Roosevelt was incensed and threatened the congressional leaders with a veto. Barkley took the lead in explaining that this was the best

Congress could do and urging the president either to sign the bill or to let it become law without his signature. Roosevelt did not budge, however, and did what he had threatened, writing one of the most scathing veto messages ever issued. The journalist Allen Drury, who covered the Senate for the United Press International at the time, wrote that the veto message had the tone of a "mad dog snarling at a postman." Rather than the normal game of pitch and catch between FDR and Barkley, the president had deliberately thrown a wild pitch by attacking lawmakers for sending him "a tax relief bill providing relief not for the needy but for the greedy," After asking for a "loaf of bread" from Congress, FDR wrote, he had received only "a small piece of crust." Barkley had made a pledge to himself in becoming majority leader that if an "irrevocable disagreement with the President ever arose, I would feel it my duty to resign [my leadership position]." FDR's veto triggered such a disagreement.[59]

The following day, as word leaked out that Barkley was prepared to give an historic speech, listeners packed the Senate gallery. Pricked by the deprecations in the president's veto message, Barkley hurled back his own by ridiculing FDR's attempt to compare his experience in the sale of Christmas trees from his Hyde Park estate with the growing of "those little pine bushes with a sturdy oak, gum, poplar, or spruce, which requires a generation of care and nurturing to produce in the forest, and from which no annual income is derived until finally it is sold[; it] is like comparing a cricket to a stallion." He defended his congressional colleagues from the president's charge that they were protecting the tax interests of the greedy before announcing his intention to resign as majority leader the following morning and calling on lawmakers to override the veto. At the conclusion, the chamber, which had been completely silent, erupted in bipartisan applause. In western Kentucky, the major newspapers generally regretted what had transpired, but they sided with Barkley. In the words of the *Owensboro Inquirer*, "Mr. Barkley has grown in stature in the eyes of the nation." In the short run, Barkley's break with the president briefly raised expectations for a Barkley presidential run.[60]

Barkley followed through on his promise to resign as majority leader, but his Democratic colleagues immediately reelected him. He was no longer viewed as "the president's man" but, as Senator Elbert Thomas of Utah proclaimed, the Kentuckian now "speaks for us to the

President." In what was one of the more unique events in congressional history, lawmakers followed through on Barkley's plea to override the veto on a tax increase by lop-sided bipartisan votes, the only time that a veto on a tax increase has ever been negated. The Barkley Incident was unforeseen by FDR, who had to scramble to conciliate the majority leader; the two exchanged appropriate apologetic notes with assurances that they could go forward as if nothing had happened, but their relationship was never the same. Barkley paid a terrible price when the president passed him over as his running mate in 1944, dismissing him as "too old" and picking Harry S. Truman instead, the much less-known Missouri senator, to replace Henry Wallace. With Roosevelt's death early in his fourth term, Barkley had missed his best opportunity to sit in the oval office.[61]

With his own reelection bid looming in 1944, Barkley campaigned for the Democratic ticket and himself, and in so doing he earned Roosevelt's gratitude when both men won fourth-term victories, and Kentucky returned to the Democratic win column. The president's victory in Kentucky was slightly higher than in 1940, with an approximate 28,000-vote bulge in the First Congressional District, where Willkie won only Crittenden County. The president's performance was not as good in the Second Congressional District, however, where the Democratic fall-off in the gubernatorial election of 1943 was to a degree reversed, but UMWA president John L. Lewis's endorsement of Willkie hurt Democrats, giving Willkie wins in the coal field counties of Muhlenberg, Butler, and Ohio as well as in Hancock County.[62]

For the third time since 1935, the 1947 Democratic primary gubernatorial campaign boiled down to a two-man race involving western Kentuckians: Harry Lee Waterfield from Hickman County in the Jackson Purchase and Earle C. Clements from Morganfield. Both men had strong ties to the Laffoon–Rhea faction, and, as the historian Thomas Syvertsen concludes, "both were leading political coalitions away from the more conservative and flamboyant politics of Chandler and his associates, and they also shared political friendships with many of the same people." They had sustained a friendship and good working relationship as legislative leaders in the 1944 session. Clements took a more circuitous route to the primary in using his remarkable political skills to outflank incumbent Second District Congressman Bev Vincent to force him to give up his own race in the 1946 primary. Before the campaign, Clements and Waterford looked for a political solution that would avoid a primary fight; Clements proposed that the younger Waterfield file for lieutenant governor with a promise that Clements would support him for governor in 1951. Waterfield, who had considerable support statewide from his House Democratic colleagues, the Kentucky Press Association, the Kentucky Farm Bureau, public-power advocates, and the school lobby, was not willing to wait his turn, though. In the end, the two promised to run constructive campaigns and to work toward party unity after the primary.[63]

Clements, less gifted as an orator than Waterfield but the consummate political organizer, focused on gaining support from county officials; from organized labor, who appreciated the congressman's vote against the antiunion US Taft-Hartley Act that year; and from tobacco growers. Waterfield won an endorsement from the *Louisville Courier-Journal,* but Clements countered by getting the backing of Jefferson County political bosses, who in return received his support of Jefferson County judge Lawrence Wetherby for lieutenant governor and influence over local patronage. Clements exploited effectively Waterfield's position on public education. Both candidates supported raises for teacher salaries, but Clements's commitment was vague. Waterfield, influenced by his close political friend Adron Doran, the former president of the Kentucky Education Association (KEA) and campaign vice chair from Graves County, endorsed the association's program, which would require an increase in state education funding from $18.4 to $34.5 million annually. This opened the door for Clements to claim that a Waterfield administration would result in higher taxes, which hurt him more than his efforts to point out Clements's questionable record on public-power matters. Despite promises to avoid mudslinging, tempers flared by the end of the campaign when the two candidates met at the annual Fancy Farm Picnic outside Mayfield. In introducing Clements, Graves County former state representative Wayne Freeman stung Waterfield for not serving during World War I (due to a chronic shoulder injury).[64]

Clements's 30,000-vote advantage in Jefferson County turned out to be his margin of victory statewide. The two men split the western

Kentucky vote, with Waterfield taking the First Congressional District and Clements the Second District by large margins. The Jackson Purchase, the heart of the Gibraltar of Kentucky Democracy, was again denied in its effort to have one of its native sons elected governor. There would be several more such disappointments in the coming years.[65]

Democratic Party unity for the November general election encountered a number of snags. Waterfield stated that he would support the party's candidate "with the same regularity and consistency with which I have always supported it," but Clements was disturbed when Waterfield arrived so late for a party unity event in Morehead in late September that he was unable to introduce Clements. Of more consequence, Waterfield missed another such event in early October at Murray, where he was once again supposed to introduce Clements, and blamed the Clements campaign for failing to invite him. Although Clements considered the snafu a "regrettable error," it took years for him to move past these snubs. Although Waterfield stayed on the sidelines during much of the fall campaign, Clements lost little time in recruiting elements of his former opponent's campaign organization, including Waterfield's close political ally Adron Doran and a number of his county chairmen from the First Congressional District. Waterfield did accompany the Alben Barkley motorcade that toured western Kentucky prior to the November election.[66]

The Republican ticket, led by gubernatorial nominee Eldon S. Dummit, was handicapped by miscues from the Willis administration, starting with the governor's backing away from the income tax repeal pledge. The historian James Klotter suggests Dummit was almost guaranteed defeat by running an anti-incumbent race against his party's incumbent governor. Dummit counted on hurting Clements for his opposition to the antilabor Taft-Hartley Act in Congress. Dummit's chances plummeted near the end of the campaign when his own campaign manager charged that the candidate's promises "are insincere and will not be fulfilled." A confident Clements accurately predicted that he would win by 100,000 votes, nearly 48,000 of them from western Kentucky, where he lost only in traditionally Republican Crittenden, Butler, and Ohio Counties. Since Ruby Laffoon, the region had its first governor who actually lived there. Democrat John A. Whitaker, the longtime Logan County attorney connected to Thomas Rhea, won the vacant Second Congressional District seat in March formerly held by Clements.[67]

Earle C. Clements was one of Kentucky's best, hardest-working governors of the twentieth century and a longtime leader of the anti-Chandler faction of the state's Democratic Party, which he took over from the recently deceased Thomas Rhea. Edward A. Farris, Clements's chief of staff, later recalled that Clements may not have been entirely scholarly in his approach to government, but he "was a very smart, uncanny-type individual in knowing the ways of men and politics and government and the direction in which public affairs ought to move." Part of his political power arose from his physicality. A former University of Kentucky football lineman, Clements was a thick-chested man of six feet. Though he had a temper, Farris said he "attempted at all times to avoid confrontation and political fights" and was at his best in moving small crowds to come around to his point of view.[68]

Clements's effort to lift the onerous $5,000 annual salary limit for state government officials from the Kentucky Constitution of 1892 illustrates the skillful exercise of his political powers. During the 1948 legislative session, the state question was placed on the ballot for November 1949, but there was considerable doubt about its passage. As early votes from rural areas trickled in on election day, it seemed very likely that the question would fail. A despondent Edwin J. Paxton, publisher of the *Paducah Sun-Democrat*, lamented, "We think the majority of us were wrong to oppose the state amendment to increase salaries." Behind the scenes, as later related by John Ed Pearce, Clements twisted arms and called in favors to cut into the rural "no" vote. One eastern Kentucky county judge who owed Clements for a personal favor Clements had done for him while in Congress stated that he could more easily "make hogs fly" than get voters in his rural county to vote for the amendment. As it turned out, pigs miraculously did fly there and in a number of other rural counties. The amendment passed in part because it fared better in western Kentucky than expected, the amendment trailing by a closer than expected 9,000 votes, made possible by wins in Trigg, Ballard, Graves, and Fulton Counties. Pearce later stated that "this single accomplishment literally saved Kentucky government."[69]

The Clements administration also played a major role in advancing the Kentucky General Assembly on the long road to legislative independence by signing legislation in 1948 to create the Legislative Research Commission, which over the years created a capacity for the legislative branch to become less dependent on governors on matters of public policy. The proposal for the commission had in the past been tied most closely with Speaker Harry Lee Waterfield during the 1944 and 1946 sessions. However, on fiscal matters, Clements was notably cautious at the start. Consistent with his message during the campaign in opposition to additional taxes, the new governor told citizens that the "the state must live within our income" and followed that pledge with a state budget that did not include any new taxes. An unimpressed editorial writer for the *Louisville Courier-Journal* termed the budget, which quickly passed both chambers without noteworthy opposition, "parsimonious." As it turned out, this was prelude. In early February, he decided to take the initiative on the issue of rural roads, which Clements and Waterfield discussed frequently during the campaign, when he asked a joint legislative session for a two-cent increase in the gasoline tax to increase spending for county and rural roads by $8 million annually and to pass the responsibility for maintaining them from county fiscal courts to the state Highway Department. Word that Clements was working on this matter became public after he called on McCracken County judge Brady M. Stewart to study it. The proposal drew enthusiastic responses from the mostly rural lawmakers and the farm community, and the bill, hurried along by what was now viewed as the "Clements steamroller," was signed into law the following week. Kerby Jennings, a Murray Democrat who was often critical of Clements, led the fight for the program on the House floor by arguing that it would get "Kentucky out of the mud" while building the economies of the state's cities by enabling farmers to get their produce to market more easily and encouraging them to spend more in nearby cities and towns. Jennings was hardly the only western Kentucky legislator to applaud the Clements initiative. The governor, who had previously entrusted the position of highway commissioner to former state senator Garrett Withers from Webster County, turned to another western Kentuckian to administer the program: Emerson "Doc" Beauchamp, a Russellville political leader who had taken over the

Logan County Democratic machine following Thomas Rhea's death. Beauchamp was well versed in the politics of county courthouse rings and road barns and understood the importance of gravel and asphalt to rural folks, a large percentage of whom lived on unimproved, dirt roads. He also understood the opportunities for additional patronage and political support to be derived from the program for the Clements faction. Clements highlighted later that the county roads program, which *Courier-Journal* writer Joe Creason, raised in Marshall County, also praised in 1950, was responsible for the improvement of 2,500 miles of rural roads by the end of his administration.[70]

Governor Clements was also a critical figure in the development of the western Kentucky tourism economy, first by acquiring properties used by TVA workers during construction of Kentucky Dam, which had been vacated following the dam's completion in 1944, and then by tapping Henry Ward as state conservation commissioner, who would oversee the development of state parks on those properties as well as other regional state parks. Local interest in the TVA properties was the focus of the Kentucky Lake Association, with Henry Ward as secretary, formed in late 1944 to promote the commercial, recreational, and sporting advantages of the lake under the management of the state parks system. Harry Lee Waterfield, spurred on by Senator Henry Ward, who was secretary-treasurer of the association at the time, had backed these aspirations in his gubernatorial campaign in 1947, but Clements was at first cautious. However, he recognized the potential that state parks on Kentucky Lake had for bolstering the development of Kentucky's tourism industry. Ward, who was also active in the Kentucky State Parks Association, encouraged candidate Clements to campaign on the matter in western Kentucky. Clements was a willing convert; he recognized that Governor Willis had blundered by not aggressively pursuing the TVA properties. With assistance from Senator Barkley, Clements persuaded TVA to hold off on selling its grounds. He called on Rumsey Taylor, the Princeton businessman closely associated with the Clements faction, to appraise the value of the grounds, and Taylor reported that they would be a steal for $250,000. After a series of very productive meetings between Clements and local officials and later between Clements and legislators from the First Congressional District, who pledged their unanimous support for the Kentucky Lake proposal, the governor negotiated the acquisition of more than 100,000 acres and buildings for $1 million that had cost TVA an estimated $2 million, and the General Assembly appropriated $70,000 for capital improvements for two state parks: Kentucky Dam State Park at Gilbertsville and Kenlake State Park, from which a parcel was later set aside for Cherokee State Park for blacks.[71]

Clements picked Henry Ward, now thirty-eight and with thirteen years of service in the legislature, to realize his hopes for the Kentucky state parks system. Dismissing Ward's support of Harry Lee Waterfield in the primary, Clements laughed that "some people might think his appointment bad politics," but Ward's long interest in parks, conservation, and development of the tourism industry as well as the leadership roles he had assumed in the free-bridge and public-power movements more than compensated. To clear concerns Ward had over giving up his position at the *Paducah Sun-Democrat*, Clements arranged a leave of absence with owner Edwin J. Paxton. As conservation commissioner, the Paducahan was also in charge of state soil and water conservation, but it was his role in establishing the state parks that marked the beginning of his legacy as one of the most outstanding Kentucky state administrators of the twentieth century. The accolades poured in from western Kentucky over the appointment. Luther Draffen, who had worked assiduously for Kentucky Dam, noted Ward's knowledge and interest in the region and predicted he would be an asset, with the combined interests of "industry, agriculture, and recreation," to making the region "one of the country's most desirable sections." Ward, who in the past had on a number of occasions criticized the Willis administration for moving too slowly on improving state parks, now felt that taking his new position "put me on something of a spot." Perhaps somewhat awed by the challenge, he surmised that "there just isn't enough state money to build and improve all the state parks that everyone wants, or to do in the existing parks everything that should be done."[72]

Ward's major task was to expand the funding for state parks. Governor Clements pitched in by directing $600,000 from his discretionary funds, nearly $280,000 of which went to Kentucky Lake state parks. By the start of the legislative session of 1950, Ward had projects under way, including new cottages at Kentucky Dam Village and Kenlake as well as additions to the lodge at Pennyrile Forest State Park; mounting of the massive Civil War anchor, museum renovations, and an expanded picnic area at Columbus-Belmont Battlefield State Park; and smaller projects at Jefferson Davis Monument and Audubon State Parks. Nevertheless, there were concerns at the time about lagging and even declining attendance figures at some of the other park sites with the large increase in visitors at Kentucky Dam State Park, by far the largest attraction in the park system. Reporting for the *Louisville Courier-Journal*, Joe Creason, a sharp observer of the Kentucky state park system, suggested that the outlook for the park system was a "gigantic question mark": "Can the State park system rightly hope to ever become a big-money maker, or is it doomed to remain, as it has so long, on the outer fringe of the folding-money class, grabbing for pennies, so to speak?" In fact, however, the energetic Ward managed to move the Kentucky state park system to a new level by securing nearly $9 million in investments for it before moving on to join Senator Clements's staff in Washington in 1955. His work helped boost attendance at the parks from less than 500,000 in 1948 to more than 3.5 million in 1954, with an accompanying 200 percent increase in tourism spending. A considerable amount of this greater attendance and expenditure took place in western Kentucky, where the state parks on Kentucky Lake (attendance ballooned at Kentucky Dam Village from approximately 34,000 in 1948 to more than 800,000 in 1949) were the most profitable in the system.[73]

The historian William Ellis has recently called Earle Clements an "education governor." His retroactive pay raise for schoolteachers in 1948 was much needed, and the state question he championed to increase the equalization assistance for the state's poorest districts, when passed, demonstrated his commitment to raising the quality of education throughout the commonwealth. In a spring 1949 special session, he risked his political future in taking on school districts, dozens of which were receiving state equalization monies but not doing enough to meet local needs for schools from property taxes. The crux of the matter was that with the amount of education funding coming from the state growing rapidly, many Kentucky counties disregarded the constitutional requirement to assess property at its full cash value; some, much to the approval of landowners, were appraising land at less than 15 percent of full value. This was an issue that Clements could have dodged at the time, and many of his political advisers were reported to have told him to do so. As the late Democratic senator J. Lee Moore from Franklin in Simpson County pointed out to his colleagues, state spending for schoolteacher salaries increased by 328 percent from 1934 to 1947, but local spending for schools increased by only 26 percent, suggesting that "there is something wrong with education in Kentucky that money isn't curing."[74]

The session got off to a rocky start when House Democrats, not eager to take up the property tax matter in an election year, bucked Clements by electing Fred Morgan from Paducah as their floor leader. Tempers flared later when Clements insisted, in a rather unusual procedure, on rolling the administration's four school bills in the House into one vote and allowing a meager thirty minutes to each side for debate. B. G. Davidson from Bowling Green and Kerby Jennings from Murray stormed from the chamber in protest. Jennings, charging that Clements's program was "socialistic" and certain to raise property taxes, was among three anti-Clements House members who resigned in the dustup (although they soon revoked their resignation). The rebellion, however, soon dissipated, and Clements's education program was passed with little incident in the Senate and approved by voters in November, but his problems over public-school spending were far from over.[75]

Adron Doran, who is remembered primarily for his twenty-three-year stint at Morehead State University, emerged during that special session as a legislative leader. Doran grew up in the little Graves County community of Boydsville on the Kentucky–Tennessee state line, which he characterized as "an isolated, unproductive, and underdeveloped section of Western Kentucky." The Dorans were strong members of the Church of Christ, and young Adron attended Freed-Hardeman College, a two-year Church of Christ college, in Henderson, Tennessee, and afterward became a minister in his faith. From Freed-Hardeman, he enrolled at Murray State, where he met Harry Lee Waterfield and future wife, Mignon McClain. She was willing to change her religious affiliation for him, but she warned Doran, whose family were Republicans, that "you'll never change me from being a Democrat," so he changed his registration. After college, Doran became a public-school educator and president of the KEA in 1946. At the time, he was principal of Wingo High School in Graves County.[76]

After being elected to the Kentucky General Assembly in 1943, Doran actively supported his friend Harry Lee Waterfield in the latter's race for Speaker and again in his unsuccessful run for governor in 1947. When Waterfield lost the primary, Doran campaigned for Clements in the general election and returned to the House in a special election after the 1948 session. Clements called upon Doran to fill in for Speaker T. Herbert Tinsley, who was unavailable for the special session and whom the governor found wanting for leadership skills that would be required in the 1949 special session. The understanding was that Doran would be the administration's candidate for the Speaker position in the 1950 session.[77]

Before the 1950 session, the KEA, disenchanted with what Clements had accomplished thus far to improve teacher salaries, attacked the governor for failing to deliver on promises allegedly made during the campaign in 1947 to endorse the goal of the KEA's program that year, to raise public-education funding to $34.5 million. Attainment of the goal would require the approval of a $13 million increase during the 1950 session. Clements avoided comment before the session, but the state press predicted an "all-out fight" would ensue after Henry Chambers, KEA president from Paducah, hinted support for a tax hike, possibly through bringing back the Ruby Laffoon sales tax. Clements refused to be cornered, but the KEA doubled down on him by producing his letter to the superintendent of Mayfield schools during the general election promising to fight for the KEA funding goal. Doran, elected House Speaker for this session, and James P. Hanratty, the new House majority leader, a thirty-one-year-old lawyer and former Federal Bureau of Investigation agent from Hopkinsville, were caught between two sides unwilling to look for a compromise. Their task was made more difficult by the return of Harry Lee Waterfield to the House, who in his district defeated the incumbent backed by the Clements administration and was now considered a leader among the antiadministration members of the House Democratic caucus.[78]

Clements broke his silence on the KEA pledge when he submitted his budget to the General Assembly early in January 1950. He said before a joint session that "at no time during that campaign, or before it, have I promised to any man, or group of men, that I would or could provide a common-school fund of $34,500,000." The statement left KEA president Henry Chambers "sick at heart" and set in motion teacher plans to protest. Harry Lee Waterfield signaled his intent to support the teachers by dismissing Clements's "theory that we can't appropriate more than anticipated revenue." An estimated 600 educators gathered in Frankfort to propose a series of tax increases on beer and whiskey, pari-mutuel wagering, and cigarettes, projected to raise an estimated $12.2 million annually. Madisonville school superintendent Harper Gatton, Governor Laffoon's former relief administrator, and Paducah Tilghman High School principal Walter C. Jetton were part of a three-member delegation deputized to present the KEA proposal to the governor, perhaps hoping that Adron Doran, their former association president, could talk to Clements in order to resolve the conflict, but Henry Chambers hinted that if no resolution could be achieved, the teachers were ready to "go fishing" until their demands were met. In fact, no compromise was reached at this stage of the conflict, and despite a series of parliamentary skirmishes between Waterfield and Doran, the House easily passed Clements's budget with only one Democratic vote against it.[79]

In western Kentucky, there were voices urging calm. The *Paducah Sun-Democrat* called on school leaders to take up House majority leader James Hanratty's invitation to develop tax-increase options and for both sides to put aside previous harsh statements in order to work together for improving the financial position of public schools. Educators meeting in Madisonville voted against a strike, and those attending a meeting in Murray indicated that they preferred to allow more time for the legislative process to work matters out. Clements, sensing division within the KEA and solid opposition from several industries over the medley of new tax sources, was not moved and told KEA leaders that they needed to raise local tax assessments to obtain the additional money desired. In some cases, as in Madisonville, where property taxes were assessed at only around 30 percent of properties' fair market value, schools took his advice, but the KEA overall was not pleased by the governor's stance.[80]

In the General Assembly, antiadministration forces attempted to bring a bill out of committee to fund the KEA request and were stopped only by a motion to adjourn. Lawmakers applauded Waterfield's statement that taking money from the state building fund controlled by the governor to use for school funding would allow Clements to participate in the tax discussions. Clements responded the following day when the House took up the previous day's motion for a vote, humbling Waterfield when the bill received only eighteen votes, five of them from the former Speaker's western Kentucky colleagues. Hanratty argued against the bill, labeling it a "blank check" that would ultimately lead to enacting a sales or coal severance tax. Speaker Doran, who did not have to vote, nevertheless voted against Waterfield to show him where he stood. Chick Love from Kuttawa, standing with Waterfield, accused many who previously stood with Waterfield and the KEA of being "yellow."[81]

After another failed attempt by antiadministration forces to discharge a bill with the KEA's tax plan from committee, the KEA leadership sent word to the state's 237 school districts to select delegates for a meeting in Frankfort to discuss next steps and to maintain contact with their legislators on the issues. Carlisle County's forty-one teachers announced days before the scheduled KEA district meetings their support for a "recess," a euphemism for strike, one of the first districts in the state to take that position. At the First District session held at Murray State, Henry Chambers angrily responded to the governor's recent comments that KEA leaders were twisting his words to local districts. Chambers, who understood Clements's pronouncement to be directed at him, offered to step down as KEA president if Clements would agree to come up with the requested revenues, but he reiterated what he had been saying for months about the governor's campaign pledge. Teachers gave Chambers and the KEA a vote of confidence, voiced their preference for a sales tax, and split over a possible "recess," with the majority wanting to see the situation develop further. The KEA then voted to maintain a "lobbying committee," with one teacher from each school district, on hand at the capitol for the remainder of the session. Teachers and parents from Madisonville, Hopkinsville, Bowling Green, and Owensboro were among the first scheduled to go to Frankfort to lobby lawmakers for the KEA program. In the end, with time in the session running short and the governor wanting to turn his attention to his expected US Senate race, he gained support for a "stopgap" two-year increase in state income taxes, expected to raise approximately $3 million annually for public schools, and promises for a comprehensive study of state taxes. As he presented his plan to a joint session of the legislature, teachers who had packed the House gallery were quiet because, after all their effort, what Clements offered fell far short of their more than $12 million increase request.[82]

Midcentury can be considered a watershed period for race relations in the commonwealth, with the Clements administration showing distinct signs of moving slowly away from Jim Crow practices on a variety of issues. Even as Kentucky imitated the segregated practices of states to the south, it had also long followed its own path on race relations by never taking away the vote from the state's blacks and allowing them to testify in court. Shortly after taking office in 1948, J. Lyter Donaldson, chair of the Kentucky Democratic State Central Committee, and Governor Clements refused to meet with southern state leaders who were revolting against President Harry Truman's Fair Deal program, with its support for black rights, and walking out of the Democratic National Convention of 1948 to form the "Dixiecrat" Party. In Frankfort, Governor Clements ended the practice of excluding Rufus Atwood, longtime president of Kentucky State College for Negroes, from presenting the college's budget along with other college presidents. The governor stood firm against the University of Kentucky Board of Trustees to prevent it from appealing a court ruling that allowed a black student, Lyman Johnson, to desegregate the college, and he nearly got into a fistfight with one of the regents to get his way. The journalist John Ed Pearce famously confirmed the governor's terrible temper after he manhandled Pearce one day in the capitol, lifting him off the floor and slamming him against the wall "in a demonstration of rhythm the artistry of which I did not fully appreciate at the moment.".[83]

Clements also supported two successful efforts in the General Assembly to water down the Day Law, under attack by court decisions, which had imposed segregation in higher education. The last bill passed at the end of the 1950 session allowed colleges to voluntarily admit black students for course studies not offered at Kentucky State College for Negroes. A number of western Kentucky lawmakers voted for it, including House majority leader James Hanratty from Hopkinsville and Adron Doran, who as House Speaker customarily did not vote on legislation. Chick Love from Kuttawa opposed it, justifying his vote by noting that "we're too far South for the two [blacks and whites] to go together." A number of private colleges, including Catholic Ursaline College (now Brescia University) in Owensboro, admitted blacks, but the public colleges for the time being continued to resist doing so. Municipally-operated Paducah Junior College, with legal backing from the NAACP, desegregated following rulings in federal courts in 1953.[84]

One significant addition to Jim Crow facilities in western Kentucky was created at this time. Cherokee State Park, 400 acres carved out of Kenlake State Park, opened in 1950 as the only state park for blacks. It had been funded by Governor Clements and, in contrast to many "separate but equal" Jim Crow accommodations, was noted at the time as "the finest 'colored' vacation site in the South," with ample picnic grounds, a bathhouse, twelve cottages, and a boathouse.[85]

Senator Alben Barkley's quest for higher office had suffered a severe setback following the "Barkley Incident," when FDR chose Harry Truman as his running mate in 1944, and he had been forced to relinquish his Senate majority leader post in 1946 when Republicans took control of Congress. Since Roosevelt's death in 1945, the vice presidency had been vacant, but the Democratic Party's sixteen-year lock on the White House was threatened in 1948. The party suffered division as conservative Dixiecrats were prepared to back the candidacy of South Carolina's Strom Thurmond and progressives were aligned with former vice president Henry Wallace. In spring 1948, President Truman's popular approval in the Gallup Poll had plummeted to 36 percent, strongly suggesting that his election chances were weak, given that the splinter candidates would undermine his chances against any one of the several potential GOP opponents. The *Paducah Sun-Democrat* explained the frustrated president's attack on the press in June as a sign that he knew "he's likely to go down in November." Indeed, the Republican National Convention that summer in Philadelphia was more of a coronation, so certain were the assembled delegates that their man would win. Clare Booth Luce, former congresswoman and wife of the owner of *Time,* electrified the GOP faithful in calling Truman "a gone goose."[86]

A downcast group of delegates arrived several weeks later for the Democratic National Convention, also held in Philadelphia; Barkley later said of the atmosphere that "you could cut the gloom with a corn knife." It fell to him to turn the mood around with his third keynote speech. Barkley, now seventy years old, demonstrated that age had not robbed him of his oratorical skills. He took aim at Republicans who had recently castigated the New Deal and at the present Congress, which had failed to address the major issues of the day. On the late President Franklin D. Roosevelt, Barkley said that he had "breathed in the nostrils of every worthy American enterprise a breath of new life, new hope, and new determination." He lashed out at the GOP candidate Thomas E. Dewey's promise to reform the federal bureaucracy and "eliminate the cobwebs" that had been allowed to accumulate during Democratic rule. According to the Paducahan, "If my memory does not betray me, when the Democratic party took over the government of the United States sixteen years ago, even the spiders were so weak from starvation they could not weave a cobweb in any department of government." To GOP attacks on the Marshall Plan and other Truman initiatives designed to prevent European countries from succumbing to the Communists, he asked, "Shall we allow humanity to sink back into a long dark night of barbarism, brutality and godless overlordship from any source in any part of the world?"[87]

Barkley was rewarded with a demonstration on the convention floor that lasted nearly thirty minutes. Truman was less than enthusiastic about what he briefly thought might be a staged effort to force the Kentuckian onto the national ticket as vice president or even as president in place of Truman. In fact, the vice presidency was very much open after Truman was unsuccessful in securing his preference, Supreme Court justice William Douglas. Truman insiders felt Barkley had little to offer the ticket due to his age and could not provide geographic balance. Barkley was aware that there was some interest in his being on the ticket, but he denied that was on his mind before the speech. The speech changed matters as Barkley and Truman now engaged in discussions that would give the Kentucky senator the chance to run on his party's national ticket, which he had dreamed about since he was a boy. However, he did not want to appear too anxious; as he told some of his supporters, he was "not interested in any biscuits that have passed around hot to other people and come cold to me." Nevertheless, Truman ultimately did offer Barkley the spot on the ticket. Wilson Wyatt, an upcoming Kentucky politician from Louisville, nominated Barkley, telling delegates that he was the "ablest man to rip the smooth but false veneer from the real record, and the real intentions of the Republican Party." Hope that the nomination would be by acclimation was thwarted by Alabama senator Lister Hill's nomination of his colleague from Georgia, Richard B. Russell. There was no contest between Russell and Barkley, however, and the Georgian quickly withdrew.[88]

Truman and Barkley came out of the convention swinging. The *Paducah Sun-Democrat,* ecstatic about its hometown politician's role in the coming election, wrote, "The Democrats will put on a fighting campaign, it is now obvious—and Alben Barkley will spark it." The story of Truman's spectacular comeback victory in 1948, initiated by a special session to challenge Republicans to enact their party platform, has often been told. The Democratic campaign kicked into high gear when Barkley's "mow 'em down" encouragement to Truman received the defiant response "I'm going to fight hard, and I'm going to give 'em hell!" as he embarked on the whistle-stop campaign across the nation, featuring his attacks on the Republican "do-nothing 80th Congress." His emphasis on the promises of his Fair Deal culminated with a victorious Truman holding high over his head the *Chicago Tribune* with the headline "DEWEY WINS."[89]

Most of the historical credit for the upset in 1948 is given to Truman, but Barkley is often not given his share of credit for his "prop stop" campaign in a DC-3, nicknamed the "Bluegrass," which took him to thirty-six states for 250 speeches and logged 150,000 miles between early September and the close of the campaign in early November with appearances in western Kentucky, as was his custom in all his elections. The Kentuckian again and again blamed the wayward agricultural policies of the GOP congressional leadership for the problems farmers and ranchers faced in the fall of 1948. In the West, he could also trumpet the benefits of the New Deal for improving the availability of electricity and water for the irrigation of crops. In closing his speeches, he would often suggest that the Democratic Party deserved the support of farmers for all that the party had done for them, not so much out of gratitude but out of "practical common sense."[90]

On that score, Barkley proved right. Though Dewey picked up Electoral College votes in the Northeast that had gone to Roosevelt in 1944, he fared poorly in the Farm Belt. Truman and Barkley picked up twenty-six more electoral votes in the Midwest than had Roosevelt in the previous election and took eight states, including the crucial states of California and Ohio, that the Dewey camp firmly believed it would pick up. The GOP candidate was aware of what happened—the farm vote switched in the days before the election. He would write after the campaign that "you can analyze figures from now to kingdom come, and all they will show is that we lost the farm vote which we had in 1944, and that lost the election." Alben W. Barkley played an important role in this loss.[91]

The upset victory gave western Kentucky and the Jackson Purchase its first and thus far only US vice president and put Barkley one step closer to realizing his presidential ambitions. Barkley carried his home First Congressional District by 35,000 and losing only Ohio and Butler Counties in the Second District. Overall, Truman–Barkley won 56 percent of the Kentucky popular vote, a higher percentage than Roosevelt received in 1944. First Congressional District voters cast a meager 1,638 votes for Strom Thurmond and the Dixiecrats; Herry Wallace polled fewer than 100.[92]

When Barkley vacated his seat on the US Senate with two years remaining in his term, Governor Clements considered taking the vacancy but instead appointed his state highway commissioner and friend Garrett Withers from Webster County. It was generally known that Withers had no intention to run in the election cycle of 1950 if Clements chose to run. Indeed, the governor did announce his own candidacy at the end of the regular session that year, sweeping aside several Democratic challengers in the primary and easily defeating, though by a somewhat smaller margin than he may have expected, his Republican opponent, Charles I. Dawson from Louisville, in the general election. The Clements campaign made certain that voters in western Kentucky would turn out for him by closing his campaign in the First Congressional District and recruiting Vice President Barkley to make a late swing through the Jackson Purchase. In a notable closing campaign speech in Mayfield, Harry Lee Waterfield, who had missed two significant opportunities to introduce Clements in the gubernatorial campaign of 1947, did so on this occasion, with Adron Doran, First District congressman Noble Gregory, and Mayfield political boss William F. Foster on hand as a show of party unity. Clements reminded the assembled crowd of his past support for popular New Deal programs and termed his opponent a "reactionary." His candidacy received endorsements from western Kentucky newspapers such as the *Paducah Sun-Democrat*, which singled out his administration's improvements of the state's park system, especially at Kentucky Dam and Kenlake State Parks. The *Owensboro Messenger* endorsed the man from Morganfield based on his record at the county, state, and federal levels, conceding his limitations as an orator but praising his ability in talking to small groups, where he "outlines his plans for building Kentucky along the lines of more fertile farms, more valuable livestock, improved homes, better roads and parks, and everything that makes life more livable to farmer and city man alike." Western Kentucky gave Clements a solid but hardly spectacular 19,000-vote win in the First Congressional District and a 15,000-vote win in his home Second District. Aside from the customary GOP wins in Crittenden, Butler, and Ohio Counties, Clements lost Caldwell County and barely eked out a win in Daviess County, where the Republicans took Owensboro for the first time since 1928.[93]

When Alben Barkley took his oath as vice president in January 1949, the World War II peace settlement was in shreds, and the possibility that the ensuing "Cold War" would become hot was very much on Americans' minds. Truman's response to the threat posed by Soviet Russia was represented by the Truman Doctrine, the Marshall Plan, and successful resistance to the Soviet blockade of Berlin. Whatever hopes may have been harbored for a peace dividend gave way to remilitarization to meet the new threat. While most eyes were focused on Europe, the Truman administration's commitment to halt the spread of communism spawned America's involvement in the Korean War in 1950, ratcheting up fears of an impending World War III. American troops were sent into combat against the Communist regime of North Korea, which had invaded South Korea in June. As the war spread to involve the Chinese Red Army, not only the necessity for Fort Campbell and Camp Breckinridge was secured, but military and civilian authorities also reconsidered the usefulness of the Kentucky Ordnance Works site near Paducah, which following the war had been reduced from 16,000 to 4,000 acres. Shortly after the Chinese army crossed the Yalu River and surprised American troops in December 1950, the announcement was made that the former KOW site would be expanded to become a massive $1 billion uranium-enrichment facility as a critical part of an accelerated program to enlarge America's atomic and nuclear bomb arsenal. The expansion of the plant was to be accompanied by the construction of additional electric power plants that would dwarf the output from the Kentucky Dam.[94]

Reasons for the Atomic Energy Commission's selection of the former KOW site was its distance from the Oak Ridge, Tennessee, the original uranium-diffusion facility; federal ownership of the KOW site; sufficient land for the facility (although rumors that the plant would need 200,000 acres were quickly erased); access to the Tennessee and Ohio Rivers and the cooperation from the TVA, KU, and other nearby power companies in Illinois and Missouri to provide the massive amounts of electricity needed for the enrichment process; and nearby coal reserves in western Kentucky and elsewhere that might be needed to generate the electricity. No contemporary accounts assign Vice President Barkley a role in the location of the plant in his home city. In later accounts, his granddaughter, Dottie Barkley, told Bobbie Ann Mason for her story on the atomic plant in the *New Yorker* magazine that "granddaddy just muscled it through," using his friendship with US House Speaker Sam Rayburn. Whether that story is accurate is difficult to gauge, but a more defendable proposition, suggested by Barkley's biographer James Libbey, who never found evidence that Barkley intervened in the selection of Paducah for the atomic plant, is that Barkley's position and connection to Paducah may have helped to tip the scales for Paducah.[95]

Construction of the plant, projected to require 10,000 workers, was soon under way. The plant would eventually have a permanent workforce of 1,600. As for the plant making the area a target for a Soviet attack, one resident sloughed it off: "Paducah is already a target, Russia would already be anxious to knock out our big railroad shops and Kentucky Dam."[96]

Family working in tobacco patch on a western Kentucky farm at the turn of the century when tobacco was the principal money crop and farmers fought the tobacco trust over reductions to prices paid for tobacco during the Black Patch War. (Courtesy of Pogue Special Collections and Archives Library, Murray State University Library)

Tobacco farmers taking their crop to market in one of many western Kentucky towns that were part of the tobacco economy. (Courtesy of Pogue Special Collections and Archives Library, Murray State University Library)

Hillman Ferry, located at Eddyville on the Cumberland River, was one of many ferries operating in western Kentucky before the rivers were bridged prior to World War II. (Courtesy of Pogue Special Collections and Archives Library, Murray State University Library)

An aerial view of the Jefferson Davis Historic Site, a memorial at the Confederate president's birthplace in Fairview, near Hopkinsville, demonstrates the strength of Confederate sentiment in western Kentucky. (Courtesy of Kentucky Department of Parks)

First Western Kentucky University president Henry H. Cherry (1906–1937), tending the campus grounds. (Courtesy of Western Kentucky University Archives)

D. H. Anderson, president of West Kentucky Industrial College in Paducah, which provided higher-education training for blacks focusing on trades open to blacks during the Jim Crow period, standing directly behind Governor A. O. Stanley as he signs the bill appropriating the first state funds establishing the college as the second public college in western Kentucky. (Courtesy of Matheson Library, West Kentucky Community and Technical College)

Rufus B. Atwood from Hickman, president of Kentucky State University in Frankfort from 1928 to 1962, left western Kentucky upon returning home from World War I. He supported Governor Chandler's decision to consolidate West Kentucky Industrial College's higher-education programs for black students at the Frankfort campus in 1936. (Courtesy of Paul G. Blazer Library, Kentucky State University)

Governor Ruby Laffoon from Madisonville (*left*) with President Franklin D. Roosevelt. Laffoon fought with New Deal authorities. (Courtesy of Hopkins County Historical Society)

Haggard outgoing governor Ruby Laffoon (*without hat*) standing beside political enemy Albert B. "Happy" Chandler (*holding hat*) at Chandler's gubernatorial inauguration in 1935. (Photograph courtesy of the University of Kentucky Special Collections)

Governor Chandler in 1959 with Robert Humphreys, former Mayfield legislator, whose long career as Chandler ally included stints as highway commissioner in both Chandler terms, numerous terms as chair of the state Democratic Party, and interim US senator after the death of Alben Barkley in 1956. (Photograph courtesy of University of Kentucky Special Collections)

Eggner's Ferry Bridge over the Tennessee River, connecting Trigg and Marshall Counties, was one of many toll bridges built in western Kentucky during the 1930s. Removal of tolls was the goal of the free-bridge movement in the region. (Courtesy of Pogue Special Collections and Archives Library, Murray State University Library)

The museum at Audubon State Park in Henderson was designed by the WPA and built by CCC workers and is one of many New Deal legacies in western Kentucky. (Courtesy of Kentucky Department of Parks)

US Supreme Court justice James C. McReynolds from Todd County being helped into his car. He was one of the "Four Horsemen," justices whose opposition to much of the New Deal resulted in FDR's unsuccessful court-packing attempt in 1937. (Courtesy of Library of Congress Prints and Photographs Division)

Senator Pat Harrison of Mississippi (*right*) shaking Senator Alben S. Barkley's hand in 1937 after Barkley won by one vote in the race for Senate majority leader, assisted by FDR's "Dear Alben" letter. (Photograph courtesy of University of Kentucky Special Collections)

The Great Ohio River Flood of 1937 inundated Morganfield and many western Kentucky river cities and propelled the construction of flood controls in the region, including a flood wall in Paducah and Kentucky Dam. (Photograph courtesy of University of Kentucky Special Collections)

The TVA's impoundment of the Tennessee River by Kentucky Dam, the largest of the TVA dams, formed Kentucky Lake and benefited western Kentucky through flood control, cheap electricity, navigational improvements, and new tourism attractions at Kentucky Dam Village, Kenlake State Resort Parks, and Cherokee State Park, the only state park created for blacks during the segregation era. (Courtesy of Kentucky Department of Parks)

Governor Earle C. Clements (*center*) from Morganfield, one of Kentucky's most powerful political figures of the twentieth century, with new conservation commissioner Henry Ward (*right*) from Paducah, who would make great contributions to western Kentucky parks and roads over a long career as a state administrator. (Photograph courtesy of University of Kentucky Special Collections)

Three western Kentucky political leaders: Adron Doran (*on left*), House Speaker during portions of the Clements and Wetherby administrations and Morehead State University president (1954–1977); Harry Lee Waterfield (*background*) from Clinton, House Speaker (1943–1947) and lieutenant governor (1955–1959, 1963–1967); and two-term governor Happy Chandler (*front center*) (1935–1939, 1955–1959). (Courtesy of Pogue Special Collections and Archives Library, Murray State University Library)

US Senate majority leader Lyndon B. Johnson (*end of table*) meeting with the Democratic Policy Team. Assistant Majority Leader Earle C. Clements is at LBJ's far left and former vice president Alben Barkley from Paducah is seated to LBJ's right. Barkley's defeat of Senator John Sherman Cooper helped give Democrats control of the US Senate in 1955. (Photograph courtesy of University of Kentucky Special Collections)

Future governor Wendell Ford (*left*) from Owensboro with Governor Chandler holding fake paper announcing his nomination as a Democratic presidential candidate in 1956. (Photograph courtesy of University of Kentucky Special Collections)

Emerson "Doc" Beauchamp (*right*), Logan County political boss in the Clements faction of the Democratic Party, held many state offices, including lieutenant governor during the Wetherby administration. Here, as agriculture commissioner during the Combs administration, Beauchamp is seen inspecting tobacco. (Photograph courtesy of the Kentucky Department for Libraries and Archives)

Governor Bert Combs (*left*) and Henry Ward, highway commissioner from Paducah, before the Western Kentucky Turnpike groundbreaking at Leitchfield in October 1961. (Courtesy of Pogue Special Collections and Archives Library, Murray State University Library)

Lieutenant Governor Harry Lee Waterfield poses with (*left to right*) civil rights leaders Jackie Robinson, *Louisville Defender* publisher Frank Stanley Jr., and Martin Luther King at a march for a state civil rights law in Frankfort in 1964. The bill failed that year, but Governor Ned Breathitt from Hopkinsville passed the South's first public-accommodations civil rights law in 1966. (Courtesy of Pogue Special Collections and Archives Library, Murray State University Library)

A massive shovel used for strip mining crosses Western Kentucky Parkway. Damage to land in eastern and western Kentucky coal fields led Governor Breathitt to successfully push legislation requiring mine operators to undertake land reclamation in 1966. (Courtesy of Muhlenberg County Library)

Bumper sticker for Governor Breathitt's preferred Democratic slate for 1967, but former Governor Bert Combs backed out, paving the way for the unsuccessful gubernatorial campaign of Henry Ward, highway commissioner from Paducah during the Combs and Breathitt administrations. (SCL photographs, courtesy of Special Collections Library, Western Kentucky University)

Katherine Peden from Hopkinsville was economic-development recruiter in Governor Breathitt's administration, here photographed with legendary Western Kentucky University basketball coach Ed Diddle (*seated center*) and Governor Breathitt (*seated next to Diddle*) at a Bowling Green economic-development announcement. Peden cracked the glass ceiling by winning the nomination in 1968 as Kentucky's Democratic candidate for the US Senate. (SCL photographs, courtesy of Special Collections Library, Western Kentucky University)

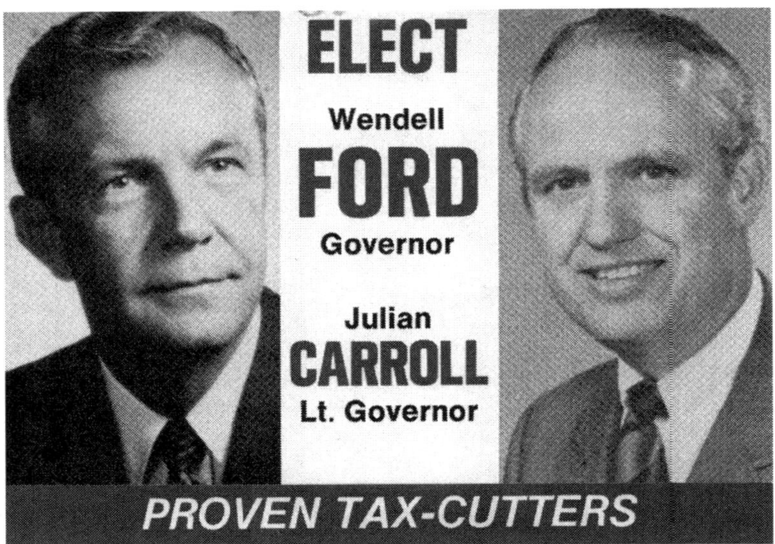

Western Kentuckians Wendell Ford and Julian Carroll used their unsuccessful opposition to "Nunn's nickel" in their successful general election campaign for governor and lieutenant governor in 1971. (SCL photographs, courtesy of Special Collections Library, Western Kentucky University)

Governor Wendell Ford working from his capitol office after tornadoes hit Kentucky in April 1974. (Photograph courtesy of the Kentucky Department for Libraries and Archives)

Governor Julian Carroll, the only governor from the Jackson Purchase, celebrates the twenty-fifth anniversary of the Bookmobile Program at the Kentucky State Fair. (Photograph courtesy of the Kentucky Department for Libraries and Archives)

Republican Lawrence "Larry" Forgy from Logan County, campaigning for governor in 1992, a close race that he lost to Paul Patton. (SCL photographs, courtesy of Special Collections Library, Western Kentucky University)

Happy Days and the Last Hurrah of State Democratic Party Factionalism

Kentucky at midcentury had reason to take a hard look at itself in comparison with other states. A number of public and volunteer studies were under way before the end of World War II to gather measures to determine the direction it was going. Perhaps the most outstanding of these studies was done by the Committee for Kentucky, established by Governor Simeon Willis, which issued its final report, *Program of Action for Kentucky*, in January 1950. The committee had a considerable western Kentucky influence, with Lone Oak's Maurice Bement, who had worked for the federal National Youth Administration, serving as executive director and former Henderson newspaper man James W. Armstrong in charge of community services programs. Before its work ended, the committee had a number of successes in state legislation and at the local level, as in Henderson, which improved its summer programs for young people, addressed juvenile-delinquency issues, initiated a local development program, and implemented a civil service. However, the committee bluntly concluded that the commonwealth by the early 1940s "had come upon sorry days." Nevertheless, the western Kentucky press praised the committee's efforts, which had awakened an interest in improving public education, conserving the state's natural resources, and improving the transportation infrastructure.[1]

Though there had been considerable progress achieved in western Kentucky during recent decades, it was not reflected in the census of 1950. The region's population continued to be stagnant, with only Calloway, Christian, Daviess, Graves, Henderson, Hopkins, Logan, McCracken, Simpson, and Warren Counties reporting gains since 1940. In contrast, Ballard, Butler, Carlisle, Hickman, Livingston, Lyon, Muhlenberg, Ohio, Trigg, Union, and Webster Counties had been staggered with population declines greater than 10 percent. Only Calloway and McCracken in the Jackson Purchase showed gains. The years had been perhaps hardest on rural areas, from which most black farmers had moved on between 1925 and 1954, as had many tenant farmers and sharecroppers, other than from the cotton farms located in Fulton County. Progress in addressing the sense of isolation in the region had been real but still lingered. This was illustrated by the movement in the early 1950s to improve rural telephone service by replacing antiquated equipment dependent on local switchboard operators with more modern rotary dial phones. Repeating the model of creating rural electric cooperatives to offset failures of private utilities to deliver services to isolated farmhouses, federal and state legislation authorized rural telephone cooperatives (RTCs), which could apply for low-cost federal loans. Locals quickly established the Ballard County RTC; the Hickman, Fulton, Clinton RTC; West Kentucky Rural Telephone Co-Op to serve five Jackson Purchase counties; and the Logan County Rural Telephone Company, with subscribers in Butler, Muhlenberg, Logan, Simpson and Todd Counties.[2]

After World War II, there were large job losses in several factories that had been engaged in munition manufacturing, and several legacy businesses closed, such as the Owensboro Wagon Company, which had tried to hold on following automobiles' replacement of the horse and buggy by producing coolie carts for lend-lease to Chiang Kai-Shek's nationalist China, and the Mengel Box factory in Hickman, which had a workforce of 600 producing airplane parts at the start of the war before a fire in 1942 closed it. A listing of Kentucky businesses in mid-1950 reveals a significant industrial base in western Kentucky, with thirty-eight plants employing more than 100 workers. The largest among them were the General Electric Tube Plant (formerly Ken-Rad) in Owensboro, which at the end of the war employed more than 3,800 as a major producer of vacuum tubes; Green River Steel, also in Owensboro, with more than 500 workers; Bowling Green Manufacturing, employing 800; the Illinois Central Railroad Shop, employing more than 1,500; and, most recently, the uranium-enrichment plant in Paducah, employing as many as 22,000 workers during the construction period. The region was sprinkled with a number of cut-and-sew factories employing women in largely low-wage jobs, the biggest of which were Merit Clothing with a workforce of nearly 2,000 and Curlee Clothing with more than 500 workers, both located in Mayfield; Union Underwear in Bowling Green with more than 1,000 workers; Enro Shirt in Madisonville with nearly 250 employees; and Henry I. Siegel with more than 400 workers in Fulton.[3]

Postwar western Kentucky's political and business leaders looked to complete long-term projects interrupted by the struggle against the fascist powers. One such project, started in the early 1930s with the creation of the Tri-State Short Route Association, boosted a federal highway between Vincennes, Indiana, and Nashville and passing through Owensboro, Livermore, Central City, and Russellville that would cut out more than fifty miles from the US 41 route running in Kentucky from Henderson to Hopkinsville. The association, with E. G. Lindeman, a chair factory owner from Livermore, as its leader, had made significant progress before the war with the bridging of the Ohio River at Owensboro and of the Green and Rough Rivers at Livermore and with the laying of a good macadam road from Central City in Muhlenberg County to Nashville, but federal designation eluded supporters until the 1950s. Until then, the road, then designated Kentucky State Highway 75, was in relatively rough shape between Livermore and Central City. This did not deter those citizens now organized as the Highway 75 Association, with new leadership from Island state representative Archie Moore and Owen Coin, retired National Guard colonel, from Livermore, from lobbying state and federal highway leaders to end the tolls on the Glover Cary Bridge over the Ohio River at Owensboro and to add Highway 75 to the federal highway system. At a meeting in Russellville in October 1952 attended by more than 700 people, Coin wryly commented that the campaign for a federally designated road had gone on so long that it might be "considered a religion and not a road project." However, the Kentucky Highway Department provided more than $450,000 for road widening and grading improvement for the Livermore to Central City stretch, and federal designation was achieved in July 1953, a few months before Coin's death in a traffic accident on what became US Highway 431. The Highway 75 Association, now under the leadership of former Central City mayor Albert Harding, changed its name to the US Highway 431 Association and set out to convince vacationers and commercial travelers going south from Chicago to Florida to take this new route.[4]

In contrast to the long gestation of the US 431 project, economic prospects in the Jackson Purchase appeared to perk up almost overnight when in the midst of the Korean War the Atomic Energy Commission announced in December 1950 it would be locating a new uranium-enrichment plant just west of Paducah on the previous site of the Kentucky Ordnance Works. Efforts were made to downplay the enormity of the project and the disruptions it would cause to local communities. The reality was that every component of Paducah and McCracken County's public services—housing, school, transportation, public safety, and public utilities—was stressed to accommodate the 23,000 initially temporary construction workers and the approximately 1,600 operational workers hired by Union Carbide for the plant. The projected 2,000 megawatts per hour that the new uranium-enrichment plant required made it the world's largest single-user facility at the time, using as much as 4 percent of the nation's electricity capacity. Additional thousands of construction workers were engaged in building the new TVA Shawnee Steam Plant in nearby Grahamville and the Joppa Steam Plant a few miles down the Ohio River in Illinois.[5]

In response to the additional demands placed on Paducah and the communities within a sixty-mile radius of the plant, Western Baptist Hospital and Heath High School were constructed in Paducah, and schools elsewhere were expanded. Bond issues added much needed capacity to water and wastewater-treatment systems. The retail sector doubled in McCracken County after plant construction, providing profits to merchants and higher wages to employees. However, the plant's impact soon gave Paducah a negative public image as labor unrest resulted in more than 150 strikes during the construction of the plant and associated power plants—all brought to the nation's attention by *Colliers* magazine in 1953, which termed what was taking place a "national disgrace," attributable to the Atomic Energy Commission's failure to foresee and plan against the clashes between outside veteran construction workers from previous large-scale government projects and the locals they considered "country bumpkins." Local leaders tried to shoulder some of the blame for failing to stay ahead of public-service needs associated with the influx of such a large number of outside workers and their families.[6]

Repercussions from the establishment of the uranium-enrichment plant were also felt in the Western Kentucky Coal Field, which was called upon to supply the coal needed to provide heat necessary to convert water to the steam that turned the electrical turbines. In fact, the 1950s began a period of rapid development in the coal field in terms of total coal output and worker productivity. From 1960 to 1970, coal extraction nearly doubled from 65 to 125 million tons per year. UMWA involvement had remained roughly the same as it was before the war, when operators in the mostly western counties fought successfully the union's efforts to organize there, but it achieved a dramatic breakthrough when West Kentucky Coal Company, among America's largest coal producers and determined to prevent UMWA organization of its mines, abruptly decided in late 1953 to recognize the union. The Cleveland industrialist Cyrus Eaton, using money funneled to him from UMWA president John L. Lewis, who wanted to unionize West Kentucky Coal, had acquired a major financial interest in the company and persuaded the board of directors to reverse its policy on collective bargaining. This development, which had a major impact in Hopkins and Webster Counties, was not well received in some quarters. The editorialist for the *Madisonville Messenger*, for example, blasted the move but drew a small measure of satisfaction that local union leader Ed J. Morgan "and his assorted punks, bruisers and highway wobblers here have no cause to strut with importance of this victory" and called for the remaining nonunion mines in the region to resist pressure to unionize. The UMWA–Eaton relationship became a major story in the early 1960s, when several small coal operators successfully sued Lewis and those to whom he had loaned union funds in order to give the union a stronger hand in the mines. A federal court in Nashville dismissed monopoly charges against Eaton and West Kentucky Coal but found Lewis and the UMWA guilty of conspiracy.[7]

Of even greater significance were improvements on the Green River during the 1950s. Since 1900, navigation on the river, which flows 370 miles in Kentucky from its source in the Appalachians downriver to the Ohio River near Henderson, passing through the heart of the Western Kentucky Coal Field, had suffered due to neglect. The historian Eileen Hagerman does an excellent job in presenting how local forces helped restore navigation on the river, which played a significant part in expanding coal production from the Western Kentucky Coal Field. The central figure in this turnaround was Carl Reis, operator at the Green River Coal Company near Mogg, a few miles north of Central City, who would come to be known as "Mr. Green River." He had been a leading local voice in landing KU's $10 million Green River coal-fired plant near Mogg. In September 1951, he joined James R. Hines from Bowling Green, owner of a towing service on the Green and Ohio Rivers, to form the Green River Valley Citizens League (GRVCL). At the organizational meeting held in Central City, Reis and Hines brought together coal and other interests from Henderson to Bowling Green to support river improvements, with the goals of increasing coal production, abating chronic flooding in the lowlands of McLean and Daviess Counties, and spurring industrial recruitment. Although Hines was elected president of the GRVCL, much of the leadership fell to Reis, who assumed the modest title "president emeritus." The GRVCL looked to the federal government to rebuild the locks and dams on the lower Green River at Spottsville and Calhoun-Rumsey so that they could accommodate modern coal barges as well as to provide a nine-foot-deep channel upriver at least to the Rochester Dam on the border of Muhlenberg and Butler Counties. Initial resistance by farmers in McLean and Daviess Counties, who formed the Green River Agricultural and Drainage Association, was diminished by assurances that their concerns would be addressed.[8]

The initial cost of the river improvements was estimated to be $6 million, but it soared with the inclusion of conservation costs at a congressional hearing held in Central City. Reis was undaunted, however, offering that the improvements would reduce transport costs on coal destined for the Paducah uranium-enrichment plant enough to justify the expenditure. The Army Corps of Engineers prepared a $16.4 million plan in February 1953 for dredging and for the Spottsville and Calhoun-Rumsey dam and lock improvements. Congress appropriated those monies in the next two sessions, but floods in the Green River Valley in 1955 raised local and congressional interest in dam projects on the Barren and Rough Rivers and Nolin and Pond Creeks, all tributaries of the Green River, that were projected to cost $35 million. The final appropriation provided money for Green River improvements below the Rochester Dam and money for repairs at the Rough River Dam, all of which left farmers, conservationists, and GRVCL supporters from Bowling Green and the Barren River area disappointed that their interests, as Hagerman suggests, had been sacrificed for those of the coal operators.[9]

Nevertheless, several thousand local citizens were on hand at the Calhoun–Rumsey locks and dam for the celebration of the Green River improvements on July 14, 1956. A reporter present projected a "new era" for the Green River Valley. Certainly, the GRVCL could claim that its goal to increase commerce on the river was met as the barge traffic, which was only 350,000 tons in 1946, grew to more than 9 million tons in 1959. The expanded use of giant shovels in the Western Kentucky Coal Field, such as "Big Hog"—the world's largest shovel, tall as a twenty-story building and capable of removing 100,000 cubic feet of earth to yield 14,000 tons of coal daily—gashed the earth at the Peabody Coal Company's mines near Paradise in Muhlenberg County. Strip or surface mining in the western field nearly doubled in the 1960s from 18.5 million tons to more than 33 million tons annually. All of these developments led TVA to announce in 1959 plans to build its largest coal-fired plant, the $100 million Paradise Fossil Fuel Plant, not in the Tennessee Valley but in the Green River Valley, to take advantage of the river for shipping coal to the plant. To secure the plant's needed coal and to manage its energy cost, TVA reached a $195 million agreement with Peabody Coal whereby Peabody would supply the plant 4 million tons of coal annually below market rates over the following seventeen years.[10]

In 1952, Vice President Alben Barkley had one last opportunity to fulfill his ambition to win the White House. It came after President Truman's popular approval plummeted following his controversial dismissal of General Douglas A. MacArthur and the nation had experienced the ups and downs of the Korean War, both of which led to Truman's unexpected announcement at a national Jefferson-Jackson Day dinner in late March that he did not intend to run for reelection. Barkley's name, based on his strong popularity among voters, immediately was placed among the most likely Democratic potential candidates, despite his advanced age at seventy-four. The "Veep," a nickname originally given to Barkley by a grandson, was viewed affectionately during his very public courtship of and marriage to his second wife, Jane Hadley. However, Truman was determined to play a major role in the selection of his party's nominee, and he conducted a series of discussions with a number of politicians, including US Supreme Court justice Fred Vinson from Kentucky and Governor Adlai E. Stevenson II of Illinois, both of whom, however, refused to accept the president's support. In the meantime, Barkley announced that he would be "willing-to-run if drafted" after Kentucky Democrats in mid-May pledged the state's twenty-six votes for its "favorite son" at the Democratic National Convention. His prospects excited enthusiasm in western Kentucky, especially in the Jackson Purchase. In a *Paducah Sun-Democrat* editorial before the Republican National Convention in late July, the writer boasted that Barkley, despite his age, measured up well against the top GOP presidential candidates, General Dwight D. Eisenhower and Senator Robert Taft of Ohio, and would, based on his political track record, help unify the ideological and sectional rifts in the Democratic Party.[11]

Truman and Barkley had avoided discussing Barkley's candidacy until days before the delegates were scheduled to arrive for the Chicago Democratic National Convention in July. Clearly, Truman was concerned by Barkley's age, but he was also alarmed by health issues that could take a heavy toll on Barkley if he were elected. In a memorandum reviewing the credentials of several candidates days before their meeting to discuss Barkley's presidential chances, Truman noted that the Kentuckian "wants to be President more than anything else in the world" but that his eyesight was so poor it could take him five minutes to sign his name. "My good friend Alben would be dead in three months if he should inherit my job!," he wrote. Nevertheless, after Truman's search for another candidate that he could endorse failed, he gave Barkley his support. Truman preferred not to make his choice known publicly, but he and Barkley felt confident that Barkley could count on the backing of the Kentucky, Illinois, and Missouri delegations on the first ballot, after which Barkley's popularity with the delegates and Truman's influence would secure the nomination for the Kentuckian by the third round.[12]

Before the meeting adjourned, Truman advised Barkley that in order to prevent his age from becoming a disqualifying issue, especially with labor leaders, he should meet with them individually. The Veep arrived in Chicago, and in a show of vitality he walked briskly from the train station to his hotel in the July heat. Before arriving, he had talked to several leading figures in organized labor, which he had strongly supported his entire political career. Some encouraged his candidacy, but in a rather confused sequence several others, most notably United Auto Workers president Walter Reuther, released a statement shortly after the VEEP's arrival at the convention that labor would not back Barkley due to his age. Barkley learned of this rejection only after he invited a group of the labor leaders to a morning breakfast. He was convinced that the real reasons for the statement were that they felt he was too close to Dixiecrats and conservative politicians and that other candidates had convinced labor they would be more amenable to labor's interests. The announcement was quickly repudiated by labor friends of Barkley, including UMWA president John L. Lewis, who urged Barkley to continue his fight for the nomination. Nevertheless, Barkley sensed that labor's statement was the "kiss of death" for his candidacy, and so he announced his decision to withdraw from the race. Barkley reminded Democrats that "they should serve the best interests of all segments of our life. . . . [H]owever, I have learned that certain self-anointed political labor leaders have taken it upon themselves to announce their opposition to me." He planned to leave the convention immediately to return to Paducah, but Truman insisted Barkley be added to the convention agenda. In his final speech at a Democratic National Convention, Barkley, who was given an exuberant, twenty-four-minute parade, told the assembled delegates that he was proud to have been "a humble mechanic" in both the New Deal and the Fair Deal. Ironically, Governor Stevenson II, Barkley's distant kinsman whose father, Adlai E. Stevenson Sr., was vice president from 1893 to 1897, who had initially refused Truman when asked to become a candidate, ultimately won the nomination, confirming the Veep's belief that Stevenson had never ruled out the nomination. Stevenson gave brief consideration to Barkley as his running mate, but another vice presidential term held little attraction, so Barkley was not unhappy when that offer did not develop, and the issue became moot when Dwight D. Eisenhower won the general election.[13]

Barkley's retirement from public office was brief. Kentucky Democratic leaders coaxed him into challenging incumbent GOP senator John Sherman Cooper in 1954. Despite his age, Barkley conducted a vigorous campaign. Speaking to large Jackson Purchase crowds near the end of the campaign, he blamed the GOP for World War II by failing to join the League of Nations and attacked the Eisenhower administration for its trickle-down economics and its "throw away, give away, steal away" program. Voters in western Kentucky turned out for its longtime champion, with the First Congressional District providing half of his winning 70,000 votes. This Democratic pickup had national implications as it, along with Oregon independent Wayne Morse's decision to support the Democratic caucus, gave Lyndon B. Johnson of Texas the majority leader position in the US Senate. Johnson's party whip, Senator Earle C. Clements of Kentucky, also advanced to majority whip.[14]

Barkley's long political career ended on April 30, 1956, when he collapsed during a speech at Washington and Lee University. His final words in addressing his recent years as a back bencher in the Senate were: "I had rather be a servant in the House of the Lord than to sit in the seat of the Mighty." Barkley's death was a national event. A special funeral train carried his body back to Paducah. At the funeral were former president Harry Truman, Adlai E. Stevenson II, twenty-four US senators, including Majority Leader Lyndon Johnson, and Kentucky's political elite, including the Veep's one-time political adversary Governor Happy Chandler. The *Paducah Sun-Democrat* declared that with Barkley's death the end of a political era was taking place, a sentiment also voiced by the *St. Louis Post-Dispatch*'s eulogy, repeated in the *Paducah Sun-Democrat*, that "with his passing goes the last of an indestructible party fealty, lively Fourth-of-July forensics, hard hitting eloquence which was never mean but never asking or giving quarter."[15]

The intense factionalism that characterized Kentucky Democratic politics during the 1930s had abated during Happy Chandler's tenure as baseball commissioner, starting in 1945 and coming to an end in the summer of 1951. Chandler considered throwing his hat in the ring for that year's Democratic gubernatorial race against incumbent Lawrence

Wetherby, who had the full backing of the Clements faction. Chandler's political friends persuaded him that the timing was not right and that the governor's race in 1955 would give him time to rebuild his political support. In the meantime, he expressed an interest in the vacancy created by the unexpected death of US senator Virgil Chapman in March 1951, which Governor Wetherby now needed to fill. A return to the Senate would advance Chandler's prospects for a spot on the Democratic national ticket in 1956, but the governor chose instead Congressman Thomas R. Underwood from Lexington, a former managing editor of the *Lexington Herald* and a Hopkinsville native whose father had edited the local newspaper. Whether with this decision Wetherby missed a chance to avoid a return to the factional infighting of the past is difficult to judge given the large egos of Chandler and Clements and their political lieutenants.[16]

The Clements faction retained a strong hold on commonwealth politics during the Wetherby administration, and western Kentucky political leaders were a very visible part of it. In addition to former governor and current US senator Earle Clements from Morganfield and Russellville's Emerson "Doc" Beauchamp, rural road administrator in the Clements administration, who was elected lieutenant governor on Wetherby's statewide slate, the Clements faction included Paducahan Henry Ward, who carried over as conservation commissioner. In the General Assembly, Adron Doran, the House Speaker from Graves County, and his majority leader, James Hanratty from Hopkinsville, retained their posts under Wetherby for the 1951 special session and the 1952 regular session. Doran joined the governor to give commonwealth teachers $9 million in pay hikes in the special session, which enabled the two to mend fences with the Kentucky Education Association but put Earle Clements in a bad light given his fight with the KEA over teachers during the 1950 regular session. Doran, who had finished his doctorate in education at the University of Kentucky, decided not to run for reelection to the House in 1953. To fill Doran's shoes, House Democrats picked Charles Burnley, a railroad fireman from Paducah, as Speaker for the 1952 and 1954 sessions. Burnley joined Harry Lee Waterfield and Doran as Speakers from the Jackson Purchase since 1944.[17] Wetherby supported Doran's appointment as president of Morehead State in 1954.

Wetherby's impact on western Kentucky politics was marked first by his refusal near the end of his term to join other southern governors in fighting implementation of the controversial *Brown v. Board of Education* (347 US 483) Supreme Court ruling striking down Jim Crow segregated public schools, thereby blunting, at least temporarily, much of the initial bluster against desegregation that took place in many southern states. Second, he tackled congressional redistricting in the 1952 session after the 1950 census cost the commonwealth one of its nine congressional districts. The First Congressional District remained safe for Democrats, even though it now included the Republican strongholds Butler and Ohio Counties as well as Muhlenberg County, where the GOP was competitive. The redistricting plan also sustained for the time being the stalwart Democratic western Kentucky political leadership in the Second Congressional District from Congressman William Natcher of Bowling Green, who would hold that seat until his death in 1994, as well as from Senator Earle Clements, Doc Beauchamp, former US senator Garrett Withers from Webster County, and Clarence W. Maloney from Madisonville.[18]

With the Democratic gubernatorial primary approaching in 1955, Kentuckians braced for an intense campaign on a scale that would rival the Chandler–Barkley US Senate primary in 1938. Chandler, the Henderson County native and former governor and US senator currently living in Versailles, was prepared to launch his political comeback as the standard bearer for his faction. He had been a frequent, if not always accurate, critic of Governor Wetherby's spending on office furnishings and Senator Clements's efforts to control state decision making from Washington. Chandler lashed Clements for supporting Senate majority leader Lyndon Johnson's efforts to redirect tax revenues from offshore oil drilling to coastal states rather than placing those monies in federal coffers that would benefit Kentuckians. The Clements faction's delay in picking an opponent to run in the primary against Chandler was of little concern to Chandler because his strategy was to run against Wetherby and Clements, referring to them derisively as "Wetherbine" and "Clementine."[19]

There was initial strong support for Clements himself to run, but he took himself out of contention early. Doc Beauchamp, the Russell-

Kentucky. Political columnist John Ed Pearce does explore the governor's accomplishments at the time in more detail, but he also concludes that they did not measure up to those from the first term. In fact, this second term was beset by numerous political conflicts, many of which were self-inflicted.[25]

As Bert Combs predicted, the most pressing issue the new governor faced was a shortage of revenue with which to meet his campaign commitments, in particular the schools' minimum-foundation program, which he had said could be funded without a tax increase. To accomplish his legislative agenda in the 1956 session, Chandler surrounded himself with western Kentucky political leaders, including Lieutenant Governor Waterfield, now presiding over the Senate and the Legislative Research Commission, which he had championed as House Speaker a decade earlier; Senate majority floor leader William Sullivan from Henderson; Senate president pro tempore E. W. Richmond from Owensboro; and House majority floor leader Fred Morgan from Paducah. Charles Burnley, House Speaker from Paducah in the 1954 session, was also on hand to assist after making the conversion from Combs supporter to Chandler advocate. In the key post of state highway commissioner, a source of political patronage and road contracts used to bargain for legislative support, Robert Humphreys from Graves County returned for a second hitch after holding that post during Chandler's first administration.

Chandler went back to his first-term strategy of delaying fiscal matters until after the 1956 regular session. Both Democratic gubernatorial candidates had pledged during the primary in 1955 to fund the minimum-foundation program established in 1954 to assist the poorest school districts in the commonwealth, but Chandler vehemently insisted that he could not do so without raising taxes. Despite his procrastination on fiscal matters, it soon became abundantly clear that program cuts of $19 million ($181 million in 2020) had to be made and additional taxes levied to balance the budget. This news provided oxygen to the anti-Chandler forces in western Kentucky. A *Paducah Sun-Democrat* article warned the governor that the explanation for his election was unrelated to his political background, his experience as baseball commissioner, and "his winning smile" but rather to "a promise to the people which he knew was impossible to carry out." The budget that Chandler rammed through the legislature called for spending $52 million that the state did not have. Emboldened anti-Chandler rebels made a strong effort to halt the Chandler steamroller but lost a motion by House member Edward T. "Ned" Breathitt from Hopkinsville to postpone action on the budget so that legislators would have time to consider the taxes that would be required to balance it. Fred Morgan, the majority leader from Paducah, termed the motion "a vote against schools." Breathitt was one of the leaders pushing to pass a sales tax in the subsequent special session, but Morgan once again led the administration forces to defeat the proposal on a 37–50 vote. The governor's plan had significant increases in the income tax instead, and it passed in the House. It faced rough sliding in the Senate, though, where after four hours of debate it passed by a narrow 21–15 vote (one more than the twenty votes required for emergency bills). Western Kentucky senators generally supported Chandler, with Senate majority leader William Sullivan leading the Chandler forces, but Clarence W. Maloney from Madisonville, a leader in the opposition, hammered the governor for breaking his no new taxes campaign promise.[26]

After Chandler vowed during the contentious primary to "retire" Senator Clements and Lieutenant Governor Doc Beauchamp back to their western Kentucky farms, Democratic Party unity gave way to perhaps the most vicious factional warfare seen in Kentucky since the Laffoon administration in the 1930s. Chandler waded into the US Senate primary of 1956 by supporting Clements's opponent and steamrolling legislation that moved the primary from August to May, making it more difficult for Clements to campaign while the Senate was in session. Matters only grew worse with Senator Barkley's death in April, ironically too late for the May primary because of the new election calendar. To fill Barkley's seat for the time being, Chandler picked longtime political supporter and current state highway commissioner Robert Humphreys from Graves County, but it fell to Kentucky's Democratic Central Committee, still controlled by the Clements faction, to make the final decision on the party's general election nominee, and the committee instead picked by a 35–0 vote former governor Lawrence Wetherby. That snub of Chandler effectively, in the words of one observer, "tossed harmony talk into a cocked hat." With tempers high on both sides, the factions clashed during the June party reorganization, which was replete with threats from Chandler supporters in western Kentucky that state employees would be fired if they did not recruit others to precinct conventions. Ruthlessly, Chandler wrenched control of the Democratic Party organization from the Clements faction.[27]

Smarting from his recent defeat at the hands of the Democratic Central Committee, Chandler took the fight to local and state Democratic conventions in late June, with control at stake over the Kentucky delegation that would go to the 1956 Democratic National Convention and with hopes that he, as the Bluegrass State's "favorite son," might emerge as part of the national ticket. Trailing as he did the front-runners Adlai Stevenson, Governor Averill Harriman of New York, and Senator Estes Kefaufer of Tennessee, his chances rested on the slim possibility that he would emerge as the compromise candidate to break a convention deadlocked after four rounds of balloting. One of the most conservative candidates, he hinted to the Alabama delegation that his administration would be friendlier to southern states opposed to additional pressure coming from Washington to integrate public schools. Chandler's strategy completely failed: Adlai E. Stevenson was renominated on the first ballot, and Chandler received a humbling 36½ of the needed 686½ votes. Robert Humphreys, perhaps trying to put a good face on the matter, commented after the vote that Chandler "got 6½ votes more than I thought he would get." The drubbing pleased the leaders of the anti-Chandler forces, Earle Clements, Doc Beauchamp, and Lawrence Wetherby, who refused to participate in the demonstration in support of Chandler that took place after his name was put into nomination on the convention floor, preferring to be engaged in a political discussion with former president Harry Truman, who had brushed Chandler aside at least twice when Chandler sought the former president's support in recent weeks. This proved to be Chandler's last chance for a spot on the Democratic national ticket. All that remained for the fulfillment of his national political aspirations was a late scratch as George Wallace's vice presidential running mate for the law-and-order and states' rights (with respect to segregation policy) American Party in 1968.[28]

Despite his assurances that summer that he would support "every 'durn'" Democrat on the ballot, the governor stayed on the sidelines during the general election and did nothing to rally state workers for the Democratic presidential ticket or for Clements and Wetherby's US senate races. In western Kentucky, Lieutenant Governor Harry Lee Waterfield and lame-duck Senator Robert Humphreys stumped for the Democratic candidates and the Chandler administration's $100 million road bond issue (which paid off as the First Congressional District provided nearly 26,000 of the 32,000 votes by which the measure passed). Chandler could also draw some satisfaction from the Republican sweep in the statewide races. Eisenhower easily won Kentucky, losing only the First Congressional District, which also produced majorities for Clements and Wetherby. Wetherby had the difficult task of defeating popular John Sherman Cooper. Many thought Clements would survive his contest against the relatively unknown Thruston B. Morton, but he instead lost by a mere 7,000 votes despite a large margin in the Democratic bastion First Congressional District and a relatively slim lead in his home Second District, where Daviess County and Owensboro disappointedly gave Morton a 2,078-vote majority.[29]

Much has been said about the Clements defeat. Most notably, Robert Caro, acclaimed biographer of President Lyndon B. Johnson, uses Clements's loss to prove LBJ's ruthlessness. According to Caro, as Senate majority leader at the time Johnson applied undue pressure to force Clements, Senate majority whip, to vote for a bill in 1956 that lowered the age for persons with disabilities to qualify for Social Security benefits, part of the Senate Democratic caucus's legislative program designed to promote Johnson's quest for a presidential bid that year or in 1960. The measure was strongly opposed by the American Medical Association, and Clements's reelection chances, as LBJ was well aware, would be jeopardized if he voted for it. Caro follows Bobby Baker, Johnson's trusted aide, and national columnists Rowland Evans and Robert Novak as the sources for pinning Clements's defeat on LBJ's pressure on the Kentucky senator to vote for the disability bill. Baker said of this vote: "Of all the votes that I've ever seen that was mean and cruel and defeated a man," this was the meanest and cruelest and caused Clements to lose his race that year." However, the criticism of Johnson in this case goes too far. During an interview for the LBJ Presidential Library in 1977, Clements conceded that the vote was "important" but not *the* decisive factor in the election outcome. In fact, Chandler's support of

Democratic candidates during the general election would most likely have allowed Clements to be reelected.[30]

Governor Chandler was a central figure in the events that unfolded at the start of the school year in 1956, when several school districts in the western coal fields became embroiled after black students sought to attend white schools. This was two years after the landmark US Supreme Court decision in *Brown v. Board of Education* called for an end to segregated schools, but there had been little change in western Kentucky schools, as a survey by the *Paducah Sun-Democrat* revealed: of the nineteen school districts in its readership area, only five—Marion, Murray, Calloway, Mayfield, and Paducah schools—reported "token enrollment" of blacks in previous "white schools." The survey noted no racial tensions at those schools, in contrast to what was taking place in the school districts in Henderson County, Sturgis in Union County, Clay in Webster County, and Madisonville in Hopkins County. In the case of Madisonville, where the local chapter of the National Association for the Advancement of Colored Persons (NAACP) filed a federal lawsuit in July 1956 on behalf of twenty-one black students, matters never took a violent turn. The *Madisonville Messenger* on July 14, 1956, however, lashed out against the suit by listing each black student's name and home address to intimidate the students' families. After Virginia's governor pledged "unyielding resistance" to pressures to desegregate his state's public schools, the paper, to show support for whites' defiance in Clay and Sturgis, wrote that Kentuckians should "regret the day when we severed our state from the Old Dominion."[31]

Developments in Clay and Sturgis quickly threatened to erupt in violence, spurred on by the White Citizens Council, an organization established to block school integration. Governor Chandler was raised in the area and knew personally the mayor of Clay, who told him that regardless of any federal law on desegregation, "ain't no n—— going to school down here." Chandler was hardly progressive on race, but he was not cowed by the racist views of the Clay mayor and believed blacks deserved greater opportunities given the sacrifices they had made during World War II and the Korean War. He had demonstrated his position by standing up as baseball commissioner against baseball owners in the controversy over the Brooklyn Dodgers' signing of Jackie Robinson.

In the case of Sturgis and Clay, he refused to back down to local white leadership and sent the Kentucky National Guard and state police to quell potential violence that threatened the black students. In his autobiography, he explained that, in contrast to the later actions of Governor Orville Faubus in Little Rock, Arkansas, who in following the southern "massive resistance" strategy used the National Guard to prevent black students from desegregating Little Rock schools, "my instructions were that the troops were not to put anybody in school, but they were not to let anybody stop anybody who wanted to go to school." James Howard, one of the Sturgis black students, later defended Chandler's decision to intervene, suggesting that without it "there is little question in my mind that more would have happened other than having rocks or eggs or tomatoes thrown at us."[32]

Local white citizens, feeling that matters would have been better handled if the governor had not intervened, were critical of him. An editorial in the *Sturgis News* stated that "our only comment is that we regret that he is to be at the helm of our state government for several years yet, because he had demonstrated that we cannot expect from him the sound, sensible government of his two predecessors [Clements and Wetherby] whom he so loudly condemns." Passions ultimately cooled, and the justification that local school authorities needed to return the black students to their segregated schools came when Kentucky's attorney general Jo M. Ferguson issued an opinion holding that integration of local schools needed to be in accordance with local school board plans. Because the districts in question did not have plans, the transfers of the black students were denied. Ferguson, who considered himself a southerner and a "gradualist" on civil rights, sought to give as much discretion to the local districts as possible regarding desegregation in the absence of clear timetables from the federal courts. White boycotters at the Sturgis school were exhilarated when, after nearly a month of turbulence, word of what was taking place came down from the Union County School Board and shouted, "Let's don't ever try it again."[33]

Ferguson understood at the time that his opinion might not comply with US Supreme Court rulings that school districts must not delay in implementing the *Brown* decision. He was correct, and federal district court judge Henry Brooks in Owensboro ruled in favor of an NAACP suit representing clients from Hopkins, Webster, and Union Counties that school districts there were to begin desegregation at the start of the 1957–1958 school year. Even with this ruling, new plans adopted by those county school boards delayed integration by permitting the continued operation of schools for blacks into the mid-1960s. Union County, for example, operated Dunbar High School for blacks through the 1964–1965 school year, when the new Union County High School opened. But Paducah, Owensboro, Marion, Dawson Springs, and Russellville schools were integrated by 1956. A number of school districts allowed black students to transfer to "white schools." Providence Rosenwald in Webster County, Owensboro Western, Princeton Dodson in Caldwell County, Murray Douglass, J. W. Million in Earlington, Drakesboro Community in Muhlenberg, Paducah Lincoln, Mayfield Dunbar, Henderson Douglas, Franklin Lincoln in Simpson County, Bowling Green High Street, Madisonville Rosenwald, and Hickman Riverview in Fulton County were segregated black high schools that remained open until, under threat from the Kennedy and Johnson administrations in the 1960s to cut federal funding for noncompliance with the *Brown* ruling, school districts closed them.[34]

School desegregation struck a crippling blow to Jim Crow in western Kentucky. The *Brown* ruling erased the barrier at Western Kentucky and Murray State Colleges, which had chosen to remain segregated despite recent legislative changes in the Day Act that would have permitted black students to enroll. Mary Ford Holland, a forty-eight-year-old teacher in Lyon County, quietly enrolled at Murray State in the summer of 1955 as the college's first black student. Desegregation was approved in a unanimous vote of the Council on Public Higher Education in 1956, but by 1963 Western Kentucky College had only ninety-six black students. When Western beat the University of Kentucky in basketball in 1971 with a starting line-up featuring star black players en route to a birth in the NCAA Final Four, the presence of black students on campus was more accepted. However, there were discordant notes in the black community that suggest that for affected blacks the closing of black schools left a bittersweet memory. The feminist writer belle hooks, for example, says that when she and other students at Crispus Attucks High School in Hopkinsville were forced to attend the integrated school, "we prepare[d] ourselves to go willingly to what [would] be kind of a slaughter, for parts of ourselves [had to] be severed to make this integration of schools work." More bluntly, Vivian Caldwell, a teacher at the all-black Hickman High in Fulton County, called desegregation a "big mistake" because it removed an important community focus for blacks. For future black students, too many western Kentucky school districts' failure to emphasize the importance of racial diversity in school faculty and administration deprived them of essential role models.[35]

Twentieth-century advances wrought by electrification, widespread usage of motorized vehicles to travel improved roads, and the introduction of radio and television into farm homes made rural living in western Kentucky less isolating. Nevertheless, the town and country divide remained. Such was the conclusion of Bobbie Ann Mason, one of Kentucky's premier writers, who grew up outside of Mayfield at midcentury and identified with country folk. She describes herself in her autobiography as a young person "acutely conscious of being country," feeling "inferior to people in town because we grew our food and made our clothes while they bought whatever they needed," and living in a "state of psychological poverty."[36]

A number of rural institutions were eroding. Country stores, considered essential communications centers of rural society, were under great stress due to competition from chain stores and later from "box stores" and shopping malls in nearby towns, which could be easily reached by travel over western Kentucky's greatly improved highway system. As one writer suggested, country stores—which had dotted the countryside for more than a century, providing rural families with their essential needs, offering a "sledge hammer and a Moon Pie under the same roof," and acting as banks and post offices—were rapidly disappearing by midcentury. Others such as Wyatt's Grocery in Roaring Springs and Linton's Groeninger's, both located in Trigg County, as well as Fruit Hill Grocery and Honey Grove's Shanklin's Grocery in Christian County and Barnes Store in Caldwell County kept their doors open well past 1950, but as one writer lamented in a story about Kentucky country stores in 1986, "the days when country stores dotted every crossroad in rural America are gone."[37]

Like country stores, community schools in western Kentucky were rapidly dwindling in number after 1950 under pressure from education reformers, who believed school consolidation was good education policy. William Ellis, the historian of Kentucky education, reminds readers that school consolidation was a consequence of the Country Life Movement in the early twentieth century, which replaced hundreds of one- and two-room schoolhouses with larger school buildings located in small communities throughout the region. Crittenden County, with a school-age population of approximately 2,000, had forty-six schools, including rural high schools at Tolu, Marion, Francis, Shady Grove, and Mattoon, plus Marion High School operated by the Marion Independent School District. All of these high schools were consolidated into Crittenden County High School in 1957. By midcentury, the school-consolidation policy, with the backing of the State Board of Education, pressured many counties both to reduce the number of school boards and to eliminate those high schools that fell below enrollment thresholds to be fully accredited in favor of larger schools that offered an expanded curriculum. The local pushback was strong because residents looked to its schools as social centers and argued that existing smaller schools offered greater extracurricular opportunities than consolidated schools.[38]

There were a variety of circumstances behind county consolidations in western Kentucky. In Trigg County, school revenues became tight as land was taken off the tax rolls with the development of Kentucky Lake and Camp Campbell, forcing the school board to close 16 one-room school houses; Trigg County High School was one of the earliest high school consolidations, taking place in 1937. Ballard Memorial High School in LaCenter, at urging from Frankfort, took the place of five much smaller schools in Barlow, Bandana, Blandville, Wickliffe, and LaCenter's old Ballard High School. Fulgham and Columbus schools in Hickman County consolidated in 1978 due to serious fire and safety concerns. A long battle between Frankfort and consolidation opponents in Logan County ensued over consolidation of the county's five high schools (Lewisburg, Adairville, Auburn, Olmstead, and Chandler Chapel) all of which were operating with provisional or emergency authorization that lasted nearly fifteen years, until the schools were consolidated to form Logan County High School in 1982. Tempers rose to the point that consolidation opponent Rev. Bob Brown, a former chair of the State Board of Education, suffered a deadly heart attack in 1980 while speaking to the Kentucky School Administrators Association. Warren County consolidation in the mid-1960s involved threats to remove accreditation for all county schools, freeze construction money, and suspend several local school board members. In cash-strapped Graves County, voters several times refused to approve funding to consolidate the five high schools at Symsonia, Farmington, Sedalia, Wingo, and Lowes (Cuba High School, winner of the boys Sweet 16 basketball tournament in 1952, closed in 1977) into Graves County High School, but consolidation moved forward in the early 1980s.[39]

School consolidation was a protracted matter in Hopkins and Muhlenberg Counties in the heart of the Western Kentucky Coal Field and would not be completed until the turn of the twenty-first century. The large number of Hopkins high schools was reduced in the early 1960s with the consolidation of Dalton, Charleston, and Nebo High Schools into West Hopkins High School. Lagging attendance at Earlington High School, the victor of the state basketball championship in 1967, forced its closure in 1975, when the town's independent school board merged with Hopkins County School Board and students enrolled at Hopkins South and Hopkins West High Schools. Overcrowding at Madisonville High School was resolved with the opening of Madisonville North Hopkins High School in 1968. Finally, the number of high schools in Hopkins County was cut to three in 1996, including Dawson Springs High School, operated by an independent school district, and Hopkins Central High School (consolidating Hopkins South and Hopkins West) near Mortons Gap in the south part of the county. Muhlenberg County schools, buoyed by payments from the TVA for the Paradise Steam Plant located near Drakesboro, delayed consolidation for even longer than neighboring Hopkins County. With Greenville, Central City, Drakesboro, Graham, Muhlenberg Central, Hughes-Kirk (Beechmont), and Bremen High Schools, Muhlenberg County was home to seven high schools when two new schools, Muhlenberg North and Muhlenberg South High Schools, opened in 1990. The consolidation was made easier by the district's decision to retain grades one through eight at the former high schools. However, local anger was rekindled in the new century when the county school board shuttered in 2005 the Drakesboro, Hughes-Kirk, Graham, and Lake Malone schools, leaving a large void in those rural communities, and later when the two high schools were consolidated into one high school operating on two campuses.[40]

For the local communities, there was a tremendous sense of loss associated with consolidation. Schools were an important part of the local economies and a gathering place for social functions. For many, there was a strong attachment to the local teams. A writer on the sports beat for the *Paducah Sun-Democrat* in 1973 recalled the many schools that had fallen victim to consolidation in western Kentucky: Bandana, Wickliffe, Clinton, Harden, Sharpe, Calvert City, New Concord, Almo, Fulgham, Bardwell, and Cayce. Sports certainly fueled the anticonsolidation forces in Hopkins and Muhlenberg Counties, where the trade-off between expanded curricula and fewer opportunities to compete in extracurricular activities was hotly debated. There was a proud sports tradition at the seven Muhlenberg high schools, perhaps most keen at Central City High School, which had the winningest boys basketball program in the commonwealth at the time it closed.[41]

Political controversy continued to dominate Governor Chandler's second term; this certainly was the case when in January 1957 the death of the clerk of the Kentucky Court of Appeals, at that time the highest court in the commonwealth, led to the court's appointment of western Kentuckian Doris Owens to the vacant office. Chandler saw this appointment as an encroachment on his authority to fill vacant elected constitutional offices, so he ordered the state treasurer to stop payment of Owens, a native of Wickliffe whom one reporter described as a "modest, retiring, a gentlewoman" with twenty-three years of experience in the courts. When the issue came before the Court of Appeals, the court ruled against Chandler. Chandler would not let go of what he considered to have been an affront, however, so he backed his own candidate when Owens ran that May in a primary to keep her office. She routed her opponent, and the *Louisville Courier-Journal*, which by this point was decidedly hostile to the governor, called Owens's victory the governor's worst political defeat. One political observer concluded that many voters who might not have been enthusiastic to vote for a woman could not overlook the governor's egregious treatment of her, as when he boasted, "We'll beat the old maid without end!" The conflict also caught up Treasurer Henry Carter, who disobeyed the governor on the pay issue, and Attorney General Jo M. Ferguson, who refused to side with Chandler's efforts to suspend Carter.[42]

The Kentucky General Assembly races in 1957 provided an opportunity for the Clements faction to gain momentum in the lead-up to the gubernatorial primary in 1959. The Chandler forces were routed in the First Congressional District, where antiadministration candidates lost only two legislative races. The *Paducah Sun-Democrat* stoked anti-Chandler sentiment with a scathing editorial at the end of the 1957 session that took Chandler to task for breaking his campaign pledge on taxes and charged Paducah solons Senator Joe Grace and Representatives Fred Morgan and Charles Burnley with being "Happy's Charlie McCarthys" for allowing the governor to pull their strings. When Joe Grace decided against running, anti-Chandler candidate Strother Martin, a former senator, defeated Tom Garrett for the open Senate seat. Morgan and Burnley also lost their primary bids, replaced by anti-Chandler candidates R. C. McGuire and Charles A. Williams. Other antiadministration victories went to incumbent Shelby McCallum from Benton, Lon Carter Barton of Mayfield, George Lovelace of Barlow, Joe E. Nunn of Cadiz, and Everett Cook, representing Livingston and Crittenden Counties. Farther east, Chandler could take some satisfaction with the reelection of Senate president pro tempore E. W. Richmond from Owensboro and election of freshman senator Frank Bassett from Hopkinsville, son of the former mayor and a popular physician, who replaced antiadministration senator Clarence Maloney under a rotational agreement between Hopkins and Christian Counties. Otherwise, the Clements faction fared well in the Western Kentucky Coal Field. Perhaps the biggest defeat was that of Senate majority leader William Sullivan of Henderson by anti-Chandler candidate J. Murray Blue from Providence. Happy was disappointed when Casper "Cap" Gardner, mayor of Owensboro, lost to incumbent state representative Pat Tanner, one of Chandler's harshest critics. In Bowling Green, Rodes K. Myers, lieutenant governor during the Keen Johnson administration but now considered a Chandler candidate, lost to Paul Huddleston, who would have one of the most anti-Chandler voting records among Democrats in the 1958 legislative session. Another Chandler opponent winning a first term in the state house was Edgar Arnold, managing editor of the *Madisonville Messenger*.[43]

Nevertheless, Governor Chandler, with strong Democratic majorities in both chambers after the general election, boasted that his legislative program for the upcoming session was vouchsafed by his supporters, especially in the Senate Democratic caucus. But according to one count, support for him was very evenly divided after his effort to discipline Mayfield senator Wayne Freeman backfired and his failure to support Owensboro senator E. W. Richmond in the race to retain the president pro tempore post drove Richmond into the opposition camp. Richmond retaliated by preventing Robert Humphreys, chair of the Kentucky Democratic Central Committee, from presiding over the caucus's organizational meeting and by successfully calling for the election of Senate offices to be conducted by secret ballot. Richmond's strategy culminated in the defeat of the governor's candidate for Richmond's former position.[44]

In the House, an anti-Chandler insurgency referring to themselves as "the rebels"—including western Kentuckians Paul Huddleston from Bowling Green, Lon Carter Barton from Mayfield, R. Douglas Ford and Pat Tanner from Owensboro, Tom Wathen from Morganfield, and McCracken County's two new representatives, R. C. McGuire Jr. and Charles A. Williams—was prepared to challenge Chandler in the 1958 session. With strong backing from the Jefferson County legislative delegation, which was on the outs with the governor, "the rebels" successfully amended his budget in the House by taking $1.5 million linked to the controversial removal of the State Health Department from Louisville and using it instead for purposes popular with rural western Kentucky voters, such as mosquito control and efforts to limit the spread of brucellosis in the state's dairy industry. In a well-coordinated legislative strategy, Paul Young from Logan County at the last moment switched his vote on a procedural motion that opened up the budget for a series of amendments.[45]

The task of putting together a budget that would pass in the General Assembly fell to Lieutenant Governor Harry Lee Waterfield, the Hickman County Democrat and presumptive gubernatorial candidate of the Chandler faction for 1959, in his position as Senate president. He cobbled together what the *Paducah Sun-Democrat* suggested looked like a return to the bipartisan combine of the 1920s, comprising fifteen Democrats, including E. W. Richmond and George Overbey, who found their way back into the governor's good graces, and eight Republicans. With that "combine," funding for the Health Department move was restored, but Chandler conceded to a series of amendments and promises to Republicans for road contracts, patronage, and help on legislation. The amended bill passed by a 24–5 vote, splitting the western Kentucky vote, with Strother Melton, Wayne Freeman, J. Murray Blue, and John Willis from Muhlenberg County in the opposition.[46]

With the 1958 session completed and one year before the primary election for governor, politicians in Kentucky began to focus on the Democratic gubernatorial candidates. However, the congressional primaries that year also provided an opportunity for the two Democratic factions once more to test their relative strength and add to Kentucky's political lore. Governor Chandler had perhaps unwittingly helped set the stage for this melodrama when during the 1956 session he had initiated the drawing of a new congressional map that moved Logan County into the First Congressional District in hopes that splitting Doc Beauchamp and Earle Clements into different districts would weaken the anti-Chandler forces in the Second Congressional District. It was certainly reasonable to expect that Beauchamp would pose a minimal threat to Congressman Noble Gregory, who had held the First District seat for twenty years. To oppose Gregory, the Clements faction backed Frank Stubblefield from Murray, who had some political experience as a railroad commissioner. Stubblefield did well, winning Calloway in a landslide, beating his opponent in Lyon and Marshall Counties, and running competitively elsewhere. Nevertheless, it appeared at first that Gregory was the victor. Al Smith, news editor of a Russellville newspaper and longtime host of Kentucky Educational Television's program *Comment on Kentucky*, later recalled receiving a call from the *Paducah Sun-Democrat* asking for the Logan County returns in order to call the election for Gregory. Smith knew that those results were in the hands of Beauchamp, a master of the hard-knuckle campaign politics of the day who controlled the Logan County election board. Beauchamp held back reporting the Logan returns, however, until after learning results from other counties, and then he manipulated the Logan County results sufficiently, including a 127–1 drubbing of Gregory in Beauchamp's home Schocoh precinct, to achieve a one-sided 2,274–443 Stubblefield win in Logan County, which gave him the Democratic nomination by 432 votes. Chandler announced that "everybody in Kentucky knows they have been stealing Logan County for years" and called for state and FBI criminal investigations and voter recounts in several counties to overturn the election results. In the end, though, Stubblefield held onto his new seat, and Harry Lee Waterfield lost a valuable political asset in western Kentucky for the approaching gubernatorial race.[47]

In March 1958, Edward J. Paxton, publisher of the *Paducah Sun-Democrat*, surveyed the field for his "winter book" of potential Democratic gubernatorial candidates for next year's primary. Among those listed were three western Kentuckians: Harry Lee Waterfield, the favorite and standard bearer of the Chandler faction seeking to become the first governor from the Jackson Purchase in his second try, and two anti-Chandler aspirants in Cadiz agricultural businessman Smith Broadbent and Rumsey Taylor of Princeton, who had been campaign chair of Bert Combs's unsuccessful gubernatorial race in 1955. Not on Paxton's list was Earle Clements, the former governor and US senator from Morganfield, who could claim the top spot in his faction. Clements took himself out of the race quickly, but there was a clear suggestion that he would exercise a strong voice in who would ultimately run against the favorite Waterfield. By summer, the field had been winnowed to Wilson Wyatt, the former Louisville mayor, and Bert Combs, strongly backed by Clements. Squeezed out of the race, Rumsey Taylor, in what some viewed as a slap at Combs, threw his support to Wyatt. The delay in deciding which of the two anti-Chandler candidates would run bolstered Waterfield's chances. Finally, Clements, with convincing polling data to that point, brokered a mid-January compromise in which Combs took the top spot on the ticket and Wyatt the second spot as lieutenant governor. Waterfield, campaigning in Madisonville when he learned the news, expressed little apprehension about the united ticket, soon to be dubbed "The Team You Can Trust," and quipped, "The owl and the pussy cat laid down together eight months too late . . . eight months too late." To encourage western Kentucky Clements faction voters to show up for the May primary, Doc Beauchamp filed for agriculture commissioner.[48]

The Democratic gubernatorial primary of 1959 featured two seasoned candidates, both of whom were careful to avoid discussions about additional tax revenues because they had lost their previous gubernatorial bids in large part on the perception that if elected they would raise taxes. Waterfield had the advantages of campaign funds and support from the state workforce that came with being the administration's candidate, but he also had to run on Chandler's spotty record for the past four years and the intense built-up enmity against the governor. Based on that, Combs and Wyatt, with Clements at the campaign's headquarters, decided to focus their campaign against Chandler. John Ed Pearce later said that "it was not the most intellectual campaign ever waged." Combs used a publicized incident in which game wardens at a wildlife refuge in Ballard County near the Mississippi River caught the governor illegally shooting geese. Combs's supporters repeatedly disrupted Waterfield campaign events with duck and geese calls, often entertaining those in attendance by prodding caged geese with hot sticks and shouting, "Happy killed my pappy!" Waterfield pleaded with Chandler to pay the fine and put the matter to rest, but he would not do it. The "crippled goose" caper, Waterfield later said, "hurt me as much as any one thing in the campaign." Chandler's efforts to belittle Combs and Wyatt by calling them "the little judge" and "ankle blankets" (Wyatt wore spats) paled by comparison.[49]

In the end, Combs won by more than 33,000 votes, largely due to the strong anti-Chandler vote in Jefferson County, where the governor had been engaged in a war with local political leaders and the *Louisville Courier-Journal*. Waterfield had counted on a 25,000-vote majority in the First Congressional District, his home base, to offset his losses in Louisville, but he had to settle for only a modest victory there and lost in the Second District. Waterfield rolled up a 10,000-vote margin in the Jackson Purchase by losing McCracken County only by a small margin. Combs took the urban areas of McCracken, Warren, Christian, and Daviess Counties as well as Hancock, Hopkins, Livingston, Logan Lyon, Muhlenberg, Trigg, Union, and Webster Counties. The Jackson Purchase thus failed once again to see a major Democratic candidate from there move on to the general election. Waterfield was gracious in defeat, but not Chandler, even though he could take some measure of bitter satisfaction in the primary defeats of western Kentucky rebels Paul Huddleston from Warren County, Edgar Arnold from Madisonville, and Charles Williams and R. C. McGuire from McCracken County. Upon learning the election outcome, Happy weakly vowed to work for the Democratic ticket in the general election but generally held back use of state resources under his control and warned that he might return to "clean 'em out" in 1963. He loudly complained when campaign organizers failed to invite him to an appearance by former president Harry S. Truman in Paducah in late October to support the Combs ticket and suggested less than two weeks before the general election that the "salvation of this state" lay in Combs losing. Chandler's bolt had little impact, though, as Bert Combs smashed Republican candidate John Robsion by a record 180,000 votes.[50]

When Bert Combs was inaugurated in December 1959, western Kentucky was for the first time since 1931 shut out of the two top elected offices in the executive branch, with the exception of Republican Simeon Willis's term of office. However, the region was well represented among the down-ballot statewide posts, with Doc Beauchamp returning to Frankfort as agriculture commissioner after a four-year absence and Doris Owens winning a full term as Court of Appeals clerk. In addition, a number of key administrative positions went to western Kentuckians, including Carlos Oakley from Morganfield as commissioner of welfare, despite losing his primary race for state superintendent of education; former attorney general Jo M. Ferguson from Muhlenberg County as commissioner of economic security; Edward T. "Ned" Breathitt, former Hopkinsville state representative, as personnel director; and Owensboro native Wendell Ford, son of former state senator E. M. Ford and political protégé of J. R. Miller, as assistant executive secretary in the governor's office. Combs's most controversial appointment was Earle Clements, former governor and US senator from Morganfield, as state highway commissioner. The appointment was certainly deserved, given the former US senator's crucial backing of the new governor in his two races, and it was well received in western Kentucky, but it also raised questions, especially at the *Louisville Courier-Journal*, about which man would be in charge of the new administration.[51]

The 1960 session of the General Assembly proved to be an historic one. The new governor had long been convinced that essential state services, especially public schools, were underfunded. The remedy would require a substantial tax increase, which unwitting voters assisted him when they approved in November a veterans' bonus. Ironically, the constitutional amendment for the bonus, passed with Governor Chandler's support on the final day of the 1958 legislative session, was to be funded with an unspecified general sales tax. Chandler had built his political career on his opposition to Governor Ruby Laffoon's sales tax, but now Governor Combs, who knew that the bonus provision could be funded by a sales tax of less than a penny, plunged forward, after the Kentucky Court of Appeals ruled favorably on the wider use of the sales tax, to propose to lawmakers a three-cent sales tax.[52]

Combs showed considerable legislative skills by supporting a series of politically advantageous exemptions to the tax, including coal sold to produce electricity and a number of agricultural items, and nearly $21 million in income tax cuts. In contrast to the struggles Governor Ruby Laffoon faced in passing a sales tax in the early 1930s, the expanding public sector developed since the New Deal weighed in favor of Combs, but the new antiadministration forces had strong leadership from former Chandler majority leaders Senator Frank Bassett from Hopkinsville and Representative Fred Morgan from Paducah, back in the House after avenging his defeat in 1957. Nevertheless, the governor pushed aside Bassett and Morgan's delaying tactics to win approval for his $80–120 million tax increase in early February with a bipartisan 84–9 vote in the House and a 28–8 vote in the Senate. Morgan claimed himself to be a "voice in the wilderness" during the floor debate. Western Kentucky was split as House Democrats Tom Wathen from Morganfield and Henry C. Neel representing Henderson as well as Senators J. Murray Blue from Webster County and E. W. Richmond from Owensboro—all representing districts bordering Indiana, which lacked the sales tax—joined Bassett and Morgan in voting against the tax.[53]

The legislature soon enacted the state's first $1 billion budget, which the governor proclaimed would lift the commonwealth from "her old depressing place at the bottom of the ladder." Western State College and Murray State College received new classroom buildings and dormitories to cope with the rapidly rising student enrollments, and Combs promised to provide for the construction of a superhighway in western Kentucky stretching from Elizabethtown to the tourist areas around Kentucky Lake to balance his prior commitment to a similar highway in eastern Kentucky. In contrast to the sales tax bill, the budget sailed through the General Assembly on unanimous votes. Fred Morgan, whose only objection to it was the money allocated to support the Louisville Symphony

Orchestra, called it the "best state budget I've ever seen." State roads and parks were also winners in the session with the passage of a $100 million bond proposal for voters to consider. Among the other accomplishments during this session was passage of a merit-system law that greatly reduced the state's reliance on patronage employment and ended the onerous assessments of state employees' paychecks for political party purposes, authored by Owensboro's Pat Tanner, who said during his House debate that state workers would "no longer be a tool and victim of each political campaign."[54]

Governor Combs proudly summarized the results of his first session: "Now we have a program which Kentucky has needed for years to help us achieve the progress our people deserve in the fields of education, health, welfare, industrial development, and agriculture progress." But the mood soured when the *Louisville Courier-Journal* broke the news of a political scandal that shook the ruling Democratic faction and dogged Combs for the remainder of his term. The scandal's source was a $346,000 lease-purchase arrangement at the Kentucky Highway Department, which Earle Clements directed, for thirty-four large, used dump trucks of little use to the agency from a Louisville auto dealer who had been the finance head of the Combs campaign. The political fallout caused a rift between Combs and his political mentor that ultimately led to Clements's resignation in order to work for the Kennedy–Johnson presidential campaign later that summer. Clements's anger soared when the governor preempted any possibility of his returning to the Highway Department when he announced plans to appoint a permanent replacement. Before leaving his post, Clements did concur with the governor's choice of Henry Ward, the Paducah native who had developed a very close relationship with Clements as his conservation commissioner. Ward's value to the Combs administration included his ability to sell voters on the highways and state park bond issue in the upcoming election in November.[55]

The rift between the governor and Clements had a significant impact on the leadership of the Clements faction when the former governor soon transferred his political allegiance to Happy Chandler, a longtime political opponent dating back to the gubernatorial primary in 1935, when Clements had chaired Thomas Rhea's unsuccessful campaign against Chandler. J. R. Miller, the Owensboro "kingmaker," met with Clements to proffer Combs's desire to bury the hatchet, which earned Miller "the cussing of his life" for colluding with Combs, whom Clements considered a "dirty lying S.O.B." Harry Lee Waterfield helped mediate a reconciliation between Chandler and Clements in September 1960, driven by mutual hostility for Governor Combs. One prominent former Clements supporter pronounced him "politically dead" in state politics. In the meantime, anti-Combs legislators, in particular Senators Rex Logan from Smiths Grove in Warren County, George Overbey from Murray, and newly elected "Cap" Gardner from Owensboro, exploited the truck scandal to limit Combs's accomplishments in the 1962 session. With less than stellar support in the region for the governor, western Kentucky was shut out of the Democratic leadership during his term. The only western Kentuckian in a legislative leadership position during the Combs administration in the 1962 regular session was House minority leader Wayland Render from dependably Republican Ohio County.[56]

Combs's strong record and Earle Clements's efforts on behalf of his close friend Lyndon B. Johnson were not sufficient to put the commonwealth in the win column for Democratic candidate John F. Kennedy in 1960. The state party called upon Smith Broadbent, the Cadiz farmer/businessman to coordinate all its campaign efforts and chose former governor Keen Johnson, originally from Lyon County, as its nominee to run against incumbent GOP US senator John Sherman Cooper. Kennedy's hopes to carry Kentucky against Republican vice president Richard Nixon depended heavily on Democratic votes from western Kentucky, the state's Gibraltar of Kentucky Democracy. To that end, in early October Kennedy made campaign speeches to enthusiastic crowds in Paducah and Bowling Green, with Governor Combs and many Democratic leaders across Kentucky there to support the Massachusetts senator. Kennedy did carry western Kentucky, but his 16,000-vote majority was the lowest in a presidential election since Al Smith's disastrous defeat in 1928. Richard Nixon won not only traditionally Republican Crittenden, Ohio, and Butler Counties but also Daviess, Warren, McLean, Hancock, Muhlenberg, Caldwell, and Livingston Counties. Despite a narrow margin in the First Congressional District for former governor Keen Johnson, John Sherman Cooper retained his US senate seat with a landslide win statewide. Combs could find some solace that voters passed his $100 million road/state parks bond issue in the November election, which carried easily in western Kentucky. Voters once more rejected a constitutional convention, despite a healthy 16,000-vote majority from the First District.[57]

By this point, the 1963 campaign was already shaping up to be a reprise of Chandler's 1935 election to his first term as governor, propelled by his promise to repeal the state's recently enacted sales tax. He gave every indication, when he entered into the 1961 Democratic primaries that he intended to run against Lieutenant Governor Wilson Wyatt, the presumptive candidate of the Combs faction. After Combs predicted that his legislative candidates looked strong before the primary, the former governor quipped, "When the governor gets all the noses counted, he may find out he's like Little Bo Peep—he lost his sheep." In fact, the results were mixed. Combs fared well in western Kentucky state House races when John Dixon beat Frank Bassett, who had been forced to give up his Senate seat to Fred Nichols, a Combs supporter from Madisonville, under a rotational agreement between Christian and Hopkins Counties. Tom Wathen from Morganfield and Henry Neel from Henderson, both of whom voted against the sales tax, also were defeated by Combs's candidates. In addition, the Combs forces gained two new faces of great interest in the House in Paducah attorney Julian Carroll, who leveraged his successful work on a campaign to permit the city to acquire KU's facilities in order to start a long political career, and Louise Kirtley, the former Owensboro city attorney and first woman in Daviess County to file for state office.[58]

Critical to Combs's legacy and the future of the sales tax was the selection of a candidate capable of winning the gubernatorial primary in 1963. It had been widely assumed in 1959 that Wilson Wyatt, who had given up his quest for the governor's mansion under the arrangement brokered by Earle Clements, was owed that opportunity, but he chose instead to challenge first-term GOP incumbent US senator Thruston Morton in 1962. Without question, Combs hurt Wyatt's campaign by failing to wait until after the November general election before choosing who was to run opposite Chandler, but he felt that protection of his programs dictated his course of action. Combs seemed especially interested in a number of potential candidates from the other side of the state. Young congressman William Natcher from Bowling Green drew consideration, as did current highway commissioner Henry Ward from Paducah. The choice ultimately came down to Court of Appeals judge John Palmore from Henderson and Edward T. "Ned" Breathitt from Hopkinsville, the former state representative who had served in the Combs administration as director of personnel. Palmore's candidacy would be hampered by several rulings he had made that many considered antibusiness, and his mentor, Earle Clements, discouraged him from running as Combs's man. Ned Breathitt threw his hat in the ring in May 1962, thereby giving him ample time to build his campaign. He came from a distinguished Kentucky political family dating back to Governor John Breathitt (1832–1834) and more recently James T. Breathitt, elected lieutenant governor in 1927. Ned Breathitt had strong anti-Chandler credentials as a leader among House "rebels" in 1956, and he provided a youthful, clean image that gave him an advantage over his much older opponent in the new age of politics when television played an ever-bigger role.[59]

The Democratic campaign for 1963 shaped up by late 1962 as a contest centered on men from western Kentucky. In addition to Chandler and Breathitt, Princeton's Rumsey Taylor, Combs's campaign chairman in 1955 who had switched his allegiance to Wilson Wyatt in the race in 1959, also announced his candidacy, but he soon withdrew and, with great surprise to some political observers, gave his support to Chandler. Considerable interest was focused on the lieutenant governor race. Henry Ward gave strong consideration to running with Breathitt but due to health reasons decided in December against it, so Breathitt ran in the primary without a running mate. This would have its political advantages in western Kentucky if Breathitt won the primary; Breathitt's wife was related to Robert Humphreys, who could aid Breathitt so long as he did not attack Harry Lee Waterfield. In the Chandler faction, strong consideration was given to running Paducahan Fred Morgan, the former Chandler House majority leader, but several of the former governor's closest political advisers convinced him that putting Waterfield in the lieutenant governor slot would be a greater asset for the campaign. To bolster Breathitt's chances in western Kentucky, Doc Beauchamp filed for state treasurer, and Henry Ward, Smith Broadbent, and J. R. Miller, all of whom had been longtime leaders in the Clements faction, were enlisted to support Breathitt. He added political newcomer Katherine Peden, his high school classmate from Hopkinsville, local radio executive, and former chair of the National Professional and Business Women's Clubs, as a campaign cochair. They, along with Governor Combs, would fill the void left by Earle Clements, who now sided with his former adversary Happy Chandler.[60]

Ned Breathitt proved to be a savvier candidate than Combs had been in 1955. He studiously avoided going on the record or hinting that he would favor a tax increase, and he was quick to adapt to the joke telling and back slapping that Kentucky voters liked from their candidates. In a campaign visit to Paducah in mid-April, Breathitt pledged to retain the sales tax and offered a strong western Kentucky program centered on completing the Western Kentucky Turnpike started by Governor Combs and developing tourism opportunities associated with Kentucky Lake, Barkley Lake from the soon-to-be-impounded Cumberland River, and the Between the Rivers region. As Combs did in 1959, Breathitt kept Chandler on the defensive. The campaign made effective use of the charge that a Chandler relative was raising money for his campaign with promises of future rewards under a third Chandler administration. "Fill your sack for Billy Jack!" theatrics disrupted Chandler campaign events. However, it was the younger man's edge on television that was decisive. Certainly, the contrast between the youthful-looking Breathitt and the elderly former governor worked to the former's benefit. However, Breathitt's campaign resorted to "dirty tricks" near the end of the primary campaign by producing and purchasing television air time through a "Citizens for Better Government" organization to broadcast a thirty-minute program entitled *The Chandler Years in Review—The True Story of What A. B Chandler Has Done to Kentuckians.* The negative content of this program incensed Chandler, who filed a complaint with the Federal Communications Commission. The commission later fined WHAS-TV in Louisville for an "extremely serious violation" of commission rules in failing to fully identify for viewers the program's origins, but the damage was done.[61]

In the weeks preceding the primary election, most political observers predicted a close outcome; few would have predicted Breathitt's smashing 62,000-vote win in a record primary turnout. Western Kentucky contributed 22,000 of those votes, as Chandler carried only Harry Lee Waterfield's home Hickman County, Ballard County, and Carlisle

County in the Jackson Purchase; the Republican-leaning Crittenden, Butler, and Ohio Counties; his home county of Henderson; and McLean County. The magnitude of Breathitt's victory led the *Louisville Courier-Journal* political columnist John Ed Pearce to write an epitaph for Chandler and Clements, who, he stated, now "join the ranks of the sometimes remembered old governors of the state . . . all part of the color and the lore, but no longer useful instruments of political force in Kentucky." Although Chandler tried to shrug off the loss as somewhat of a personal "relief," there was no question that voters had rejected him. Chandler contributed to that sentiment when he recited from Rudyard Kipling's poem "Recessional" that "the shooting and the tumult dies, and the captains and kings depart" during an election-eve telecast.[62]

The Chandler faction did have one significant victory as Harry Lee Waterfield topped Breathitt's vote total in the lieutenant governor primary, giving western Kentuckians the top two spots on the Democratic ticket for the third time since 1931. Breathitt and Waterfield wasted little time before meeting at Waterfield's farm outside Clinton to map out their general campaign strategy and reaching agreements that would give Waterfield a meaningful role in a Breathitt administration. Unity was critical; they recognized that they faced a tough opponent in Louie B. Nunn, the former Barren County judge, who with his brother Lee, a Richard Nixon strategist, had engineered GOP wins in both US Senate races in 1956. The two Democrats built a solid campaign organization in western Kentucky around Breathitt supporters Katherine Peden, J. R. Miller, Public Services Commission chair David Francis from Bowling Green, former Murray State president Rainey T. Wells's grandson Wells Lovett from Owensboro, Smith Broadbent, and Doc Beauchamp, who were joined now by Waterfield organizers William F. Foster and Robert Humphreys.[63]

Perhaps the biggest campaign issue in the general election was Governor Combs's executive order prohibiting racial discrimination in services provided by or regulated by state agencies, which he issued shortly after the primary. Reactions to the order were mixed in western Kentucky, largely supportive in Paducah, according to published reports, but the *Madisonville Messenger* issued a front-page editorial staunchly criticizing the governor for subverting property owners' constitutional rights and exercising powers that he did not have. Nunn capitalized on the emotions that the order stirred up among white voters, particularly in western Kentucky, using it as a wedge issue that could propel him to victory. He appeared on television statewide in mid-July surrounded by American and Kentucky flags, state statute books, and a very large Bible to denounce Combs's use of an executive order rather than taking the issue before the Kentucky General Assembly. He told listeners, "This is a very dark day," and "we have an example of dictatorship by the governor of the Commonwealth of Kentucky." The executive order was discussed widely in western Kentucky during the campaign, but the press discounted its impact at the polls. One veteran *Paducah Sun-Democrat* columnist probed a local Democrat who was voting for the Republican candidate Nunn, finding his reasons for doing so confused, but conceded that there were in fact "Nunn Democrats" who were "scattered and frail but devilishly loud." Newspaper editors surveyed shortly before the election were in consensus that Breathitt would win easily, despite Chandler's bolt in support of the Republican ticket. The editor of the *Mayfield Messenger* projected that Breathitt would win by between 75,000 and 100,000 votes, and the *Paducah Sun-Democrat* editor expected him to carry the First Congressional District by up to 40,000 votes.[64]

Breathitt did appear to have the election in hand, as early returns indicated. Several news organizations were about to call the election for him, but some observers thought it best to wait. Allen Trout, the *Courier-Journal* reporter, told Harry Lee Waterfield's son that it would be best to wait, advice that was passed to Hickman County native Don Mills, Breathitt's campaign spokesman. Trout was right as Breathitt's lead indeed started to falter. During the anxious wait, his anxiety level was raised by the possibility of a Waterfield double-cross after he found Waterfield huddled with Earle Clements (who had not joined Chandler in his bolt from the party). In the end, that suspicion proved false, but it was a harbinger of future distrust between Breathitt and Waterfield that would play a major role in the new administration. In fact, the Gibraltar of Kentucky Democracy's 27,000-vote win was crucial for Breathitt, who avoided an upset by edging Nunn by 15,000 votes. In western Kentucky, Nunn won only Crittenden, Muhlenberg, Butler, and Ohio Counties, but Breathitt escaped with the smallest wins in Carlisle, Fulton, Livingston, McLean, and Simpson Counties of any Democratic nominee in forty years. Breathitt credited Waterfield's backing as a major factor in his victory.[65]

Large federal public-works projects, such as those creating Kentucky Dam and Kentucky Lake as well as the massive uranium-enrichment plant near Paducah, continued to play a large role in the development of western Kentucky in the 1950s and 1960s. Indeed, with the completion of Kentucky Dam, leaders in Kentucky and Tennessee moved on to fight for improvements on the Cumberland River, which entered Kentucky from Nashville before emptying into the Ohio River at Smithland, a short distance from the mouth of the Tennessee River. To that end, the Cumberland Valley Association and the Lower Cumberland Valley Association (LCVA) were formed in the early 1950s for the purpose of taming the Cumberland River in order to prevent periodic flooding and associated soil erosion along the river. Their aim was to convince federal authorities to build a multipurpose dam in the lower Cumberland Valley for electricity generation, navigation, flood abatement, and recreation, with a price tag of $130 million. The LCVA, with strong support from the Paducah Association of Commerce, lobbied the US Army of Corps of Engineers and the Kentucky and Tennessee congressional delegations for what at that time were called Cumberland Dam and Lake Cumberland. Although an initial appropriation for planning improvements on the Cumberland River was included in President Truman's final budget, further progress was slowed during the Eisenhower appropriation as he was generally reluctant to support massive public power initiatives. TVA and the Army Corps of Engineers reached consensus that a high dam in the lower valley rather than a series of low dams was needed. Supporters claimed some measure of success in the 1956 congressional session with a $200,000 appropriation for the planning of a high dam near Grand Rivers in Livingston County. Senator Earle Clements, with tardy but eventual support from Congressman Noble Gregory, took the lead in gaining bipartisan support to give the recently deceased Alben W. Barkley's name to the dam project and resulting lake and to appropriate the $1.3 million to finish the planning and begin construction.[66]

Barkley Dam, dedicated by Vice President Hubert Humphrey in August 1966, is located approximately 30 miles upriver from the mouth of the Cumberland River and was built at a final cost of $142 million. In addition to the dam's navigational and flood-control benefits, it generates up to 130,000 kilowatts per hour. Lake Barkley, which dislocated numerous farmers and resulted in the relocation of parts of Kuttawa and Eddyville, is more than 130 miles long, stretching into Tennessee as far as the Cheatham Dam, thirty miles north of Nashville. With Kentucky and Barkley Lakes running parallel in western Kentucky for nearly 50 miles, they created one of the commonwealth's preeminent recreational areas. Lake Barkley soon became home to Lake Barkley State Resort Park, funded by a bond issue developed by Governor Breathitt in 1964 and costing an estimated $8 million.[67]

Transportation to those attractions, however, was slowed by a lack of limited-access superhighways like those being built nationwide as part of an interstate highway system. In western Kentucky before 1960, there were no such roads. Governor Wetherby had made a modest start with the construction of the Kentucky Turnpike, a toll road from Louisville to Elizabethtown that would be incorporated into I-65. Happy Chandler was distinctly cold to such projects, but Governor Combs was a proponent of the superhighways and their role in expanding tourism in the commonwealth. Most of the proposed federal interstates were designed for north–south traffic, ignoring the need to facilitate east–west travel in a state that measures more than 400 miles from Hickman on the Mississippi River to Ashland at the West Virginia border. During the Combs administration, the state, with Henry Ward (ironically a leader in the free-bridge movement of the 1930s and 1940s) taking the lead as state highway commissioner, became heavily engaged in construction of interstate highways, heavily subsidized by the federal government, *and* turnpikes, toll roads paid for by bonds, starting with the Mountain Parkway, which Combs pushed through quickly after taking office. By 1970, the state boasted more than 1,000 miles of modern, limited-access superhighways, a considerable portion of which were located in western Kentucky. I-65, running from Louisville through Bowling Green to the Simpson County town of Franklin on the Tennessee state line, was completed in 1969. The highway had a very significant impact on Bowling Green by strengthening its ties to both Louisville and Nashville, propelling it past Owensboro in the future as the largest city in western Kentucky and as the third largest in the state, behind only Louisville and Lexington, in the twenty-first century.[68]

Of greater importance to tourism in western Kentucky and residents of the region was the completion of the Western Kentucky Turnpike. Two alternative routes were originally discussed: a northern route, following US 60 along the Ohio River from Louisville through Owensboro to Paducah, and a southern route, following US 62 from an I-65 interchange at Elizabethtown to Princeton. The southern route, despite sharp opposition from the Northwest Kentucky Highway Improvement Association, which supported a compromise route connecting Elizabethtown and Princeton but running through Fordsville in Ohio County and Providence in Webster County, was selected because it served an area without an already planned interstate. Governor Combs attempted to smooth ruffled feathers among leaders in Owensboro and Henderson by calling for a more southerly route for I-64 in Indiana, which would be more convenient to those cities, and announced plans for construction of the 127-mile toll road, the Western Kentucky Turnpike, which was completed in October 1963 at a cost of $118 million in bonds.[69]

A much more complicated matter, one that would engage Henry Ward during most of his tenure at the Highway Department, involved coming to agreement on I-24—which would connect western Kentucky to St. Louis and Chicago in the north and to Nashville and Chattanooga in the south—between the governors of Kentucky, Tennessee, Illinois, Indiana, and Missouri and the federal Bureau of Public Roads. Ward announced at a meeting in Paducah in March 1961 that Governor Combs supported a straight-line route from Hopkinsville to join the Western Kentucky Parkway near Princeton, which would provide a free road through the lakes area before bending to the west below Paducah and then crossing the Ohio River between Barlow and Wickliffe. When the federal Bureau of Public Roads established Nashville and Cairo, Illinois, as "control points" for the Kentucky portion of the interstate, it was nearly certain that I-24 would be built through the Jackson Purchase. However, a competing, older plan that would connect Paducah, Murray, and Mayfield was backed by the I-K-T Committee. Local support for Ward's plan came from the Western Kentucky Superhighway Association. The I-24 issue ultimately was resolved by the governors who hammered out a compromise that followed for the most part Ward's I-24 plan but also included construction of an interstate highway from Caruthersville, Missouri, across the Mississippi River to Dyersburg, Tennessee, the only river bridge between Memphis and Cairo, Illinois. The new plan modified Ward's original route by crossing the Ohio River over a new bridge connecting Paducah and Metropolis, Illinois, as an alternative to the aging Irving S. Cobb Bridge. Further delays and agreements, including one between the governors of Kentucky and Tennessee to improve US 51 between Memphis and Fulton, Kentucky, held up approval for planning on I-24 until August 1964. Groundbreaking ceremonies for I-24 took place in 1967, but it was not completed until May 1980, twenty-two years from when it was announced, at a cost of more than $242 million for the Kentucky portion.[70]

No additional interstates would be built in western Kentucky in the twentieth century, but additional toll roads were. The decision on the I-24 route left a significant section of the Jackson Purchase dissatisfied. Gubernatorial candidate Ned Breathitt attempted to mollify the bruised feelings left from the routing decisions over I-24 by announcing during a speech in Mayfield early in his campaign that during his term in office he would build a toll road from I-24 near Eddyville to Fulton on the Tennessee state line. When built, this fifty-two-mile road served Marshall, Graves, Calloway, Hickman, and Fulton Counties and to one columnist at the *Paducah Sun-Democrat* was one of the final links to those who dreamed of superhighways connecting the far reaches of the commonwealth. In the summer of 1964, Breathitt announced plans for the Pennyrile Parkway, which would provide a four-lane superhighway from Henderson to the Tennessee state line south of Hopkinsville by adding toll sections to both ends of the US 41/Madisonville Bypass.[71]

The new administration that took office after the elections in 1963 had a very pronounced western Kentucky influence, starting with Governor Breathitt and Lieutenant Governor Waterfield, and included two other statewide-elected officers from the region in state treasurer Doc Beauchamp and Murray's Harry Sparks, whose candidacy was supported by Breathitt and Chandler, as state school superintendent. Henry Ward retained his powerful position as highway commissioner, and Katherine Peden was brought in from the Breathitt campaign to serve as commerce secretary. The state's two top legislative posts also went to western Kentuckians: Shelby McCallum from Benton, the governor's longtime business associate and friend, was tapped as House Speaker, and former Owensboro mayor and Chandler supporter Casper "Cap" Gardner, with the backing of Harry Lee Waterfield, was chosen as Senate majority leader. Gardner's selection was a controversial one, with some Breathitt supporters at the presession conference in December at Kentucky Dam State Park feeling that the governor should have picked someone more aligned with him. The choice as it turned out would be one of several sources of friction that developed between Breathitt and Waterfield that led to a split in the coming months.[72]

Underlying the partnership achieved at the start of the general-election campaign was that Waterfield, in return for a meaningful role in the Breathitt administration, pledged support for Breathitt's budget and for legislation important to the governor. Breathitt agreed to share with Waterfield the appointment of county contacts, give him a lead role in industrial recruitment, and allow him, as the presiding officer in the Senate, considerable latitude in the legislative arena. However, from the outset, when Breathitt misinterpreted Waterfield's huddling with Earle Clements while waiting on election returns as a conspiracy aimed at sidelining him for a power-sharing arrangement in a Nunn administration, the trust level between Breathitt and Waterfield was less than complete. Hugh Morris, a columnist for the *Louisville Courier-Journal*, rightly warned before the start of the session that Breathitt's control of the legislature was too dependent on the "mutual trust and affection" between him and Waterfield to block formation of antiadministration coalitions of Democrats and Republicans that could prove obstructionist.[73]

The session started off slowly. A tight fiscal situation and a campaign pledge not to raise taxes caused Breathitt to delay filing the biannual budget plan until early February, and when it was filed, it became a test of his legislative strength. In the House, Fred Morgan, the former Chandler majority floor from Paducah, prevailed easily on his motion to hold up consideration of the budget, wryly reminding his colleagues that Breathitt had been involved in stalling consideration of the Chandler budget in 1956. In fact, the budget bill took several weeks to pass, by which time the first public signs of a rift between Breathitt and Waterfield were registered.[74]

The conflict arose over a budget-oversight bill that Waterfield backed, consistent with his interest in legislative oversight dating back to his days as House Speaker in the mid-1940s. After passing the Senate, the bill came up for a House vote, at which time Breathitt, who now accused the lieutenant governor of pushing through a "ripper" bill, successfully gathered the votes for its defeat. Waterfield refused to back down and accused the governor of reneging on his support of the measure. Although Waterford attempted to downplay the significance of the dispute by suggesting that it would not cause a political break with Breathitt, he did add that "it is not proper for me to ignore or change the facts leading up to the dispute to resolve the matter nor is it proper for the Governor to make such charges." He further courted Breathitt's displeasure when, in denying that he would withhold his assistance in passing Breathitt's legislative program, he noted, "Lord knows, he needs it."[75]

As it turned out, the 1964 session was, as the historian Kenneth Harrell describes it, "clearly a disappointment." The General Assembly passed only a watered-down measure to regulate strip mines, and on civil rights, perhaps the centerpiece of Breathitt's legislative program, it utterly failed. He had vowed to pass a civil rights act dealing with the elimination of Jim Crow segregation related to public accommodations, addressed in Bert Combs's executive order, but was delayed to give Congress time to pass its legislation on the matter, which would pave the way for a Kentucky act. However, Breathitt committed himself to forcing the issue at the end of legislative session if the federal legislation stalled.[76]

There were certainly trepidations about the civil rights issues in western Kentucky at the time. The oral historians Catherine Fosl and Tracy E. K'Meyer recount in *Freedom on the Border: An Oral History of the Civil Rights Movement in Kentucky* how young blacks used sit-in tactics to break down barriers preventing business establishments from serving blacks in a number of western Kentucky communities such as Bowling Green, Hopkinsville, Owensboro, and Franklin in Simpson County. Hecht Lackey, founder of WHOP radio in Hopkinsville and recent mayor of Henderson, pointed out the progress he had observed in Paducah on public accommodations for blacks during a forum organized by the Kentucky Human Rights Commission in 1964. Nevertheless, Senator Tom Garrett of Paducah in mid-January termed the civil rights issue "one of the most touchy problems that the governor will have." After Carl Perkins, congressman from eastern Kentucky, was the only vote for civil rights in the state's congressional delegation, and it appeared certain there would be a protracted filibuster in the US Senate, the *Paducah Sun-Democrat* counseled Breathitt that the Kentucky delegation's vote should signal that the commonwealth was not ready to pass his civil rights legislation. It was better to defer to the judgment of barbers, beauticians, and other businesspeople who "are already highly selective in accepting customers, regardless of their race and color."[77]

Kentucky civil rights advocates, aroused by Governor Combs executive order and efforts to pass federal legislation on public accommodations, demanded a state law and were determined to press the issue. Legislation was drafted, and plans went forward for a march on Frankfort to register support for reform, scheduled to match the governor's timetable for taking up his legislation near the end of the session. The march, sponsored by the Congress of Racial Equality and a newly established Allied Organization for Civil Rights in Kentucky, was expected to draw 50,000, led by Martin Luther King Jr. and Jackie Robinson, who broke the color barrier in major league baseball. In western Kentucky, plans for attending the march quickly developed in urban centers, with leadership coming from black preachers. In Owensboro, the Allied Organization—with O. B. Smith from Zion Baptist Church, W. R. Brown from Fourth Street Baptist Church, and J. Van Alfred Winsett from Center Street Baptist Church—organized approximately 100 locals planning to attend the event. The Non-partisan League of Paducah, with W. G. Harvey as president, made arrangements there. A delegation of approximately 150 from Hopkinsville, joined in the march by Governor Breathitt's fifteen-year-old daughter, traveled to Frankfort.[78]

Despite freezing temperatures and a blustery wind for the walk on March 5, an estimated 10,000 persons participated in a peaceful demonstration. King and Robinson, along with Frank Stanley Jr., publisher of the *Kentucky Defender*, met briefly with Governor Breathitt to discuss the public-accommodations legislation's prospects. However, the march's real audience—the members of the Kentucky General Assembly—was for the most part unmoved. This was certainly true of the western Kentucky delegation, which failed to provide any semblance of progressive leadership toward passage of the legislation in the remaining two weeks of the session. Several General Assembly voices from the region refrained from criticizing the marchers, such as Lieutenant Governor and Senate president Harry Lee Waterfield and Senator Owen Billington from Murray, who judged, "I don't think it will have any ill effect." However, Senator Thomas Brizendine from Simpson County declared, "It's not right to put pressure on the Legislature this way"; similarly, House Speaker McCallum felt that "the Legislature should not act under duress." Future governor Julian Carroll, then a second-term state representative from McCracken County, suggested that "the better strategy would have been for marchers to focus their effort on lobbying their legislators." Richard Frymire, state representative from Madisonville, joined Carroll in criticizing civil rights advocates for failing to work with legislators to develop a compromise bill that might pass the legislature. Senate majority leader "Cap" Gardner dismissed the march as a "very poor idea," suggesting that a march ten times as large would not make any difference to him and that civil rights legislation would be considered in the Kentucky Senate only if the House passed it first.[79]

All efforts by the governor and civil rights advocates failed in the last days of the session as the Rules Committees in the two chambers took control and blocked passage of the public-accommodations bill. A hunger strike staged in the House gallery failed to move lawmakers. Former House minority leader Wayland Render from Ohio County dismissed the strike in the strongest terms and said civil rights legislation could pass only "if all outside interests would keep hands off and allow us to proceed in a serene manner." Breathitt made an impassioned plea before the House Rules Committee but could not muster a majority of votes to move the bill. Efforts on the floor to discharge the civil rights legislation in both chambers did not come close to gaining enough votes to force a floor vote. It was apparent that without a federal law the Kentucky General Assembly was unwilling to pass one of its own. Ultimately, in order to end the hunger strike, Breathitt promised that after the federal Civil Rights Act was enacted, he would consult with lawmakers to gauge whether he should call a special session to consider a Kentucky law. The *Courier-Journal* savaged Breathitt's performance on this issue, for which he "came too late with too little" and ended up "capitulating to the obstructionists."[80]

Breathitt kept his special-session promise after Congress finally enacted the Civil Rights Act of 1964 in early July. In mid-May, he met with mayors from more than forty cities and towns, including Bowling Green, Central City, Franklin, Henderson, Mayfield, and Murray, who gave him unanimous support for a Kentucky public-accommodations law. This support had little impact on state legislators, however, when the governor invited them to a meeting in late July to discuss the chances of the civil rights bill in a special session. He pleaded that their votes for the civil rights bill "would be notice to all our citizens and to all the world that we believe in the principles of justice and fair play and that we are ready, willing and able to promote those ideals without outside help." Disappointed, Breathitt secured only twenty-three pledges from state representatives and twelve from state senators to support the legislation. The *Paducah Sun-Democrat* editorial writer, although crediting Breathitt for acting in "good faith" and conceding that the commonwealth would benefit from its own civil rights bill, pragmatically concluded that voters were opposed to it.[81]

By this time, it was abundantly clear that Breathitt had to make fundamental changes in his administration or run the risk of his term in office being judged a complete flop. Failure, in his opinion, could be reversed only by taking steps necessary for him to secure control of the General Assembly, including the neutralization of Waterfield and Gardner's influence in the Senate. The issue that finally caused Breathitt and Waterfield to split involved grievances arising from Waterfield's promised leadership role on economic-development matters. Commerce Secretary Katherine Peden, the governor's Hopkinsville high school classmate and campaign cochair, found herself at the center of the conflict, which ultimately forced Breathitt to choose between her and Waterfield or find himself isolated within his own administration. The governor supported Peden, on whom he counted heavily to fulfill his campaign pledge to add new jobs in the commonwealth. In early May, the matter became public after Peden objected to Waterfield using his position as chair of the Kentucky Economic Development Commission to advance his prospects in the gubernatorial campaign of 1967 by hiring Carlos Oakley, a former Morganfield school superintendent and welfare director in the Combs administration, and a photographer. The more senior lieutenant governor called her criticisms "a lot of foolishness" and demanded the governor resolve the conflict. Ultimately, Breathitt "fired" the lieutenant governor by removing him from the Economic Development Commission with a public rebuke in a letter to Waterfield: "I do not see how it will be possible to work together in this particular and vital area when you have publicly attacked me and my closest personal and political friends." Reaction in western Kentucky, at least in the local media, seemed understanding. In a *Paducah Sun-Democrat* editorial, the writer said differences between Breathitt and Waterfield had been there since January. Waterfield's political ambitions were known, but he was aware that the likelihood of getting Breathitt's support for a gubernatorial race was nearly nonexistent. On his part, the governor felt he had "leaned over backward" to avoid the break.[82]

Once the pretense of factional unity had been set aside, Breathitt and Waterfield understood that their political fortunes would turn largely on who would emerge victorious from the Democratic primaries of 1965. Western Kentucky was perhaps the most important battleground. In a Senate-seat race, Senator Cap Gardner from Owensboro, Waterfield's handpicked majority leader for the 1964 session, faced Wendell H. Ford, the former administrative assistant to Governor Combs, who was recruited by Breathitt. Both Gardner and Ford were viewed as politicians who aspired to higher office. Some felt that Gardner, as majority leader and a former resident of Hancock County, had an edge, but Ford had the backing of influential utility executive J. R. Miller. Ford scored political points by criticizing his opponent for failing to improve highway access to Owensboro, and in the end he won in a 305-vote upset. Breathitt choices also won two other key western Kentucky senate races. In the Henderson area, William Sullivan, the Senate majority leader under Chandler in 1956, running now as a Breathitt supporter, avenged his loss in 1957 by beating incumbent Senator J. Murray Blue from Clay. Breathitt candidate Floyd Hayes Ellis from Bowling Green won a contest over a Waterfield man from Leitchfield for a Senate seat formerly held by Rex Logan, leader of the anti-Combs forces who was driven from office in 1963 by Combs's redistricting bill that merged part of Warren County with Breckinridge, Edmonson, Grayson, and Ohio Counties. However, Waterfield could claim a win in the Hopkins, McLean, Caldwell, and Lyons Counties district by his candidate Richard Frymire against the Breathitt-backed candidate. Frymire, a young former military pilot and attorney from Madisonville, had gained recognition from the press for his outstanding work as a state representative and, according to an Associated Press writer, "now becomes the most politically attractive candidate of the antiadministration faction." He had refused Breathitt's backing when Breathitt demanded support for his legislative program. Nevertheless, Governor Breathitt was the clear victor statewide by winning seven of the ten key Democratic primary races and knocking off Cap Gardner.[83]

Before the showdown in the new legislature, Breathitt was forced to call a special session in August 1965 over property taxes, which would increase sharply due to a Kentucky Court of Appeals ruling in June requiring property to be assessed at its full value. The ruling, if allowed to go into effect, threatened to set off a tax revolt by tripling property taxes (a result welcomed by the educational interests that had initiated the suit) and jeopardized both the anticipated Democratic majorities in the legislature and Breathitt's road bond program on the November ballot. Waterfield and Breathitt presented competing plans before the special session convened, which was complicated by the ongoing feud between them. Breathitt was ultimately forced to cobble together a bipartisan majority of twenty-one senators in a very disputatious session in both chambers. An effort to reconcile the two men failed, and Waterfield uttered that if Breathitt "would attend to his executive offices and leave the legislature alone, we'd get along better." In the waning days of the session, with the governor in control of the General Assembly, an enraged Waterfield undertook a series of actions to block Breathitt's legislation, starting with a motion to adjourn the Senate before action on the bill could be taken, but the Breathitt forces were in control and ignored Waterfield's tactics. The bill passed, but in sending it to the governor for signing, Waterfield included with his own signature a note stating that "it is the judgement and the discretion of the lieutenant governor and the senate president that HB 1 has not been validly enacted." It had not been a smooth session by any stretch of the imagination, but Breathitt took from it newfound respect for him in Frankfort that would carry forward into the 1966 session.[84]

Waterfield continued his opposition to Breathitt in the coming months by spearheading whatever opposition there was to the governor's $176 million road bond issue. The administration had a strong hand as it argued that the bond issue would be matched by $700 million in federal spending, but Waterfield warned against the growing state debt. His efforts fell far short; in western Kentucky, the only county in the First Congressional District to vote against the measure was Waterfield's home Hickman County. One Paducah columnist considered his defeat on the bond issue, combined with those during the special session, as Waterfield's "third strike," signaling that he "is through in Kentucky—at least as far as active vote getting is concerned."[85]

Waterfield, however, continued his fight at the start of the 1966 regular session, but Breathitt crushed him by excluding him from the Senate Democratic caucus as it chose legislative leaders loyal to the governor and then by "ripping" his powers, much as Governor Laffoon had done to Happy Chandler and Earle Clements to Kenneth Tuggle when they were lieutenant governors, by creating a "committee on committees" to guide Senate activities. However, Waterfield had supporters in the Democratic caucus, led by Richard Frymire, who staged a walkout during the caucus. Joining Frymire were Thomas Brizendine from Simpson County and Owen Billington from Murray. Waterfield's hopes rested on the slim possibility of forging a bipartisan Senate coalition; but the 22–10 Senate vote on the amended rules was unequivocal. A clearly frustrated Waterfield reacted to his defeat by reminding senators of the partnership that he had entered into with Breathitt to win the election: "I don't take credit for electing him . . . , but I could say I could have beaten him."[86]

Despite the ripping of Waterfield's powers as Senate president and the electoral defeat of former Senate majority leader Cap Gardner, western Kentucky continued to have a strong voice in the 1966 session, starting with Hopkinsville native Governor Breathitt. His Benton friend and business associate Shelby McCallum returned for a second term as House Speaker, and former House Speaker during the Laffoon administration and Union County native John Y. Brown Sr. (currently representing Fayette County) returned as House majority floor leader. Breathitt built up momentum by presenting his budget at the opening of the session and passed it with little difficulty. Back on his legislative program were enactment of a Kentucky civil rights bill and strip-mining legislation. Prior to the session, legislators understood that their cooperation on the governor's legislative program was expected if they wanted his help on patronage and other matters vital to them. Breathitt's chances of passing a civil rights bill benefited from a general belief that a state law that would give Kentucky enforcement powers over the federal act would be preferable to federal intrusion.[87]

With Brown managing the administration's civil rights bill in the House, the measure moved quickly through the General Assembly, but not without a number of amendments to satisfy concerns that western Kentucky lawmakers had with it. Passions were high when the bill made it to the House floor; Brown termed it the "most important piece of social legislation that the legislature of Kentucky has ever had before it," and R. E. Hale from Owensboro said, "I have been ready to vote for such a bill for 60 years, since I was a boy." In contrast to the outcome in 1964, a majority of western Kentucky legislators, with a few exceptions, such as Lloyd Clapp from Wingo and William H. Maddox of Hickman, were part of the majority in a 76–12 vote in favor of the civil rights bill. In the Senate, there was little doubt about the bill passing, but Harry Lee Waterfield unleashed a series of critical remarks, attempting to call into question Breathitt's commitment to civil rights. He related that when the topic had come up in their unity meeting after the primary of 1963, Breathitt had commented that his administration would "go easy on it," and that it was only later, said Waterfield, that Breathitt "got mildly for it." In the final vote, George Brand from Mayfield was the lone vote against the bill. In the public signing near the Lincoln statue in the capitol rotunda, Breathitt announced that he hoped that the Kentucky Civil Rights Act of 1966, the first passed by a southern state, would spur other southern states to enact similar laws. Kentucky and Governor Breathitt were hailed for their efforts: in an editorial in the *Paducah Sun-Democrat,* which two years earlier had defended lawmakers for refusing to pass civil rights legislation because of voter opposition to it, now congratulated the governor and those who voted in favor this time and noted that "it should be a matter of quiet pride to Kentuckians that their state is the first below the Mason-Dixon line to adopt civil rights legislation." Outside the state's borders, Martin Luther King Jr. called the bill a "milestone for a Southern state," and Ralph McGill, the progressive editor of the *Atlanta Constitution,* lauded the bill for "making 'states rights' acceptable."[88]

Breathitt did not relax after the legislature passed a weak mine-reclamation bill in 1964. As chair of the natural-resources committee of the National Governors Association, he studied effective reform efforts in Pennsylvania and sought, albeit unsuccessfully, to secure an interstate mining compact with hopes that a solution could be achieved to answer Kentucky coal operators' objection that a tough mining law would put them at a competitive disadvantage. He made no secret in the months leading up to the 1966 session of his intention to seek legislation similar to that in Pennsylvania. The industry's public image had suffered in recent years, starting with the *Louisville Courier-Journal's* Pulitzer Prize–winning exposé "Kentucky's Ravaged Land," published on January 5, 1964. Unlike much of the coverage of the coal industry's negative effects that depicted landslides and flooding in Appalachia, the *Courier-Journal* exposé provided balanced coverage of the two Kentucky coal fields that demonstrated in vivid imagery the need for strong regulation of strip mining. In the western field, the relatively flat topography had made the use of large shovels more prevalent and profitable there. While extracting the coal near the surface, though, strip mining created large spoil banks composed of dirt, shale, slate, rocks, and other wastes. The resulting runoffs choked streams and polluted water supplies, such as in the Clear Creek watershed between Madisonville and Providence. Local residents were initially hesitant to criticize the mining industry because it was the "goose that laid the golden egg," but one Hopkins County farmer with a 500-acre spread who was the president of the local branch of the Kentucky Farm Bureau conceded that "there are a lot of farmers like me who are hard against what the mines are doing." A store operator in the Hopkins–Caldwell County border community of Charleston complained of the mosquitoes, so plentiful that Hopkins County initiated a $10,000 fund drive to purchase an airplane for their control in 1966 and attributed them in large part to the failure to reclaim mined land: "These dudes bite just like wasps." Reporters concluded that "West Kentucky remains a paradox of rolling, successful farms lying cheek to jowl with a wasteland of stripped earth." Reformers greatly benefited from the public outrage against coal operators in the November 1965 incident involving Ollie Combs, a frail, elderly widow arrested for attempting to block strip mining on her property in Knott County by physically standing in the way of a bulldozer. She helped rally the public to the need for laws to rein in the coal interests in the commonwealth.[89]

In his opening speech for the 1966 legislative session, Breathitt told lawmakers that the strip-mining law of 1964 had proved "not adequate to protect the people or their land and to deal fairly with the coal industry." To acquaint them with the seriousness of the problems in the coal fields, the Breathitt administration arranged for them to tour strip-mined areas of the state. Sixteen legislators were flown to Muhlenberg County in the Western Kentucky Coal Field for visits to mining areas there and in nearby Ohio and Hopkins Counties. The majority, including freshman senator Wendell Ford of Owensboro, came away in favor of stronger reclamation requirements, but another new senator, Richard Frymire of Madisonville, where coal mining was a major part of the local economy, announced his opposition to any measure that "impairs the ability of our coal area to compete with other states." His position was backed by statements from Peabody Coal officials that new requirements to restore stripped lands to their original contour would increase costs by more than $1,000 per ton for each acre, thereby putting Kentucky coal operators at a definite disadvantage.[90]

Mining interests in western Kentucky complained loudly of the governor's tactics. The legislators' visit, they complained, was to recently mined areas in the Western Kentucky Coal Field, not to older mines where reclamation efforts had already been undertaken. The vice president of Badgett Mine Stripping Company in Madisonville stated that Breathitt's program "hit us right smack in the face" and simply aimed at satisfying the position held by the *Louisville Courier-Journal*. A *Madisonville Messenger* editorial lashed out at coverage of the mining issue in the *Courier-Journal,* accusing that paper of displaying hypocrisy for taking a decidedly "more charitable attitude toward the distilling industry than it has toward coal mining" and for failing to take into account reported industry estimates that the reclamation costs of the new bill would put Kentucky coal at a competitive disadvantage with coal from other states.[91]

The legislative tour was followed by three days of joint public hearings to give all sides an opportunity to speak on the mining legislation. A spokesperson from the Kentucky Natural Resources Cabinet stated that it had more than 6,000 letters for stronger reclamation requirements compared to 148 against them. The powerful Kentucky Farm Bureau, whose members opposed the damage that strip mining did to the land, supported the bill, as did conservation districts statewide. Several speakers testified that pollution in the Tradewater River watershed in the Western Kentucky Coal Field was so great that the watershed could not sustain local wildlife and that the town of Sturgis in Union County had been forced to stop using water from that river. The tourism industry, which claimed to bring more money to the economy of Kentucky than did the coal industry, joined with environmentalists in backing tougher curbs on strip mining. Harry Caudill, a close college friend of the governor and author of *Midnight Comes to the Cumberland* (1963), a classic environmentalist perspective of the harmful impacts of coal mining at that time, and the Widow Combs called for a complete ban on strip mining on the final day of the public hearings. Breathitt told lawmakers that the legislation would not damage the economic viability of Kentucky's coal operators. He presented a stark choice between the preservation of the natural resources "with which a good God has endowed this beautiful Commonwealth" and their exploitation "by a comparatively small number of powerful corporations, many of them absentee-owned, who would claim the privilege of exhausting our children's inheritance to produce cheap fuel."[92]

Although coal operators felt they were not given the time to fully present their position to lawmakers, Breathitt pressed the General Assembly to pass his legislation. After a motion offered by Fred Morgan of Paducah to delay consideration on the bill was defeated, Breathitt forces cut off any amendments to it. To the critics of "the Breathitt steamroller," House majority floor leader John Y. Brown Sr., drawing from his many years in state and federal politics, answered that when confronted with a governor's steamroller, they should simply "lie sideways and you get your pants pressed at the same time." The House passed the bill 83–10, but its toughest test came in the Senate. Richard Frymire, the Hopkins County senator and Waterfield supporter, attempted to water down the measure with a series of amendments in favor of the coal industry. In a tense vote, Breathitt's forces consistently held their ground in a series of 20–17 votes. Only seven Democrats, including antiadministration western Kentucky senators Thomas Brizendine from Simpson County and Owen Billington from Murray, voted with Frymire. In the end, however, Frymire, who said he favored reclamation, was part of the 36–2 majority that passed the bill.[93]

Measuring the impact of the new legislation on the coal industry in Kentucky is difficult. One historian's examination of the administrative enforcement efforts suggests that after Breathitt left office, future administrations were lax in punishing violators. An industry timeline for Kentucky coal overlooks the legislation, suggesting that the teeth in reclamation began with the federal Surface Mine and Reclamation Act of 1977. Western Kentucky, coal production did not slow down. Although mining employment in the Western Kentucky Coal Field was halved before the turn of the twenty-first century, it is more likely that the causes for that reduction were the area's high-sulfur coal, competition from less-expensive natural gas, and improvements in production.[94]

Passage of the strip-mining bill in late January completed consideration of the "Big 3" measures in Breathitt's legislative program (his budget bill was the third). An additional thorny issue, congressional redistricting, of great interest to western Kentucky, came up late in the session after Breathitt was warned that unless the legislature acted, the federal courts would redraw the districts. The continued population drain in western Kentucky over the past few decades now forced lawmakers to make substantial changes to the area's two districts. The plan, which easily passed in both chambers, diluted the influence of western Kentucky in the state's congressional delegation by expanding the First Congressional District eastward to pick up Union, Webster, Henderson, Hopkins, and McLean Counties from the Second District; Simpson County was added to the Second District. The fifteen counties now outside the Jackson Purchase represented more than 60 percent of the First District's total population. The Second District also expanded eastward to pick up Hardin, Bullitt, Nelson, Spencer, LaRue, Washington, and Marion Counties, but both districts were still considered safely Democratic. All of western Kentucky except Hancock, Daviess, Ohio, Warren, and Simpson Counties lay in the First District.[95]

On balance, the Breathitt turnaround, not seen since Governor Laffoon's administration, had been remarkable. Although he counted as disappointments the failures to pass a ban on capital punishment and to abolish broad-form deeds used in eastern Kentucky to allow coal operators entry onto private property, as in the case of Widow Combs, the media praised the governor's performance. The *Paducah Sun-Democrat* called his record "one of the best in Kentucky's modern history," made even more remarkable by the fact that it had come in his second legislative session, "at which past governors have generally sought to avoid controversy and stuck to routine housekeeping bills." The *Owensboro Messenger-Inquirer* was slightly less effusive in its praise due to questions about the impact of the strip-mining bill on the coal industry and about providing money for teacher salary increases outside the budget, but it concluded that "his programs for improving and updating Kentucky political institutions, for social progress, for conservation of natural resources are the best this state has seen in many an administration."[96]

Among the Breathitt institutional reforms in 1966 were the strengthening of the coordinating body for the state's higher-education institutions, renamed the Council on Higher Education and governed by lay members, and the upgrading of the regional colleges to university status to enable them to expand their graduate programs, especially in the liberal arts. The post–World War II period was marked by the expansion of public services in western Kentucky. Opportunities to attend state-funded higher-education institutions there expanded in the second half of the twentieth century. GI Bill benefits created for World War II veterans enabled thousands to afford the cost of a higher education. Murray State University and Western Kentucky University, two of the state's regional universities (elevated to university status during the 1966 session), with an open-enrollment policy and comparatively low tuition, opened their doors to these students and expanded classroom and housing facilities to accommodate them. Murray's Ralph H. Woods and Western's Kelly Thompson joined Adron Doran, the former Kentucky House Speaker from Graves County, at Morehead and Robert Martin at Eastern to provide strong presidential leadership for the regional colleges. According to Lowell Harrison's history of Western Kentucky University, $21 million ($185 million in 2020) was spent on its construction from 1955 to 1965 to keep pace with the college's exploding student population. By 1969, Western Kentucky University enrolled nearly 11,000 students; Murray State, which had kept pace with enrollment at Western for decades, now began to experience more gradual growth, reaching approximately 9,100 by 2000.[97]

The existing system of Kentucky public four-year colleges proved inadequate to meet the postwar demands for state residents interested in college educations in terms of available space and accessibility. A system of community colleges slowly developed that achieved official recognition in 1962 when the General Assembly passed legislation creating the community college system under the control, strongly opposed by the four regional colleges, of the University of Kentucky. Two-year institutions had existed in western Kentucky in a number of communities in the past. Governor Chandler had closed the black two-year college in Paducah, West Kentucky Industrial College, in 1938 when its educational mission was merged with Kentucky State College in Frankfort and the Paducah campus became home to West Kentucky Vocational School, a residential vocational school for blacks with a high school curriculum. Paducah Junior College, now under the control of the city, arose in its place to educate local white students. Henderson Community College, originally called the University of Kentucky Northwest Center, was created during Happy Chandler's second term near his home town of Corydon under the control of the University of Kentucky. Hopkinsville Community College, authorized in 1962 as part of the University of Kentucky's community college system, started offering classes in September 1965. Paducah Junior College, which opened its doors in 1932 as a private institution before coming under municipal control in 1962, had moved its campus in 1964. However, it was underfunded in comparison with the state-operated community colleges, which led to negotiations with the University of Kentucky so that it could be added to the university's community college system in 1968. Bowling Green Community College, operated by Western Kentucky University, functioned independently of the University of Kentucky system.[98]

Other western Kentucky cities also sought to boost economic-development prospects programs by establishing a public higher-education presence to train the local workforce. This was the case with Madisonville, located midway between Henderson and Hopkinsville, which had lost out to Cookeville, Tennessee, for a new plant in large part because Cookeville had a four-year college. Madisonville business and civic leaders sought to remedy that deficiency when a consortium was established by Murray State, Western Kentucky, and the University of Kentucky in 1961 that later evolved into Madisonville Community College in 1968. The cooperation that prevailed among the partners in Madisonville was lacking in Owensboro, the largest city in the commonwealth without a public college, until a Graduate Extension Consortium was created in 1969 involving the two Owensboro private colleges, Brescia and Kentucky Wesleyan, and Western Kentucky University. This arrangement worked well and soon had more than 1,000 students enrolled, but friction ensued when Murray State University became involved. Western Kentucky ultimately supplanted Murray State with the promise of a future regional campus, but physical realization of a regional Western Kentucky University campus was achieved in 2009.[99]

The changes taking place in the region's higher-education institutions generally weakened the role for private colleges. For example, Bethel College in Hopkinsville, a Southern Baptist school, closed its doors after more than a century when Hopkinsville Community College arrived on the scene. Where no state-supported colleges exist, such as Owensboro, private institutions such as Brescia University, a Catholic institution that had evolved from Mt. St. Joseph College and had received accreditation as a four-year college in 1957 and upgraded to university status in 1998, and Kentucky Wesleyan College, a Methodist-affiliated school that relocated from Winchester in 1951, are well established into the twenty-first century. Mid-Continent University, which began in 1949 as a two-year college in Clinton before moving to Mayfield as Bible Baptist College of Mayfield and changed its name to Mid-Continent College in 1993, was the self-styled "best-kept secret" in the Jackson Purchase. Its enrollment grew significantly after establishing an accelerated bachelor-degree program offered at a number of sites before closing, with a student enrollment of approximately 2,000, in 2014 due to financial difficulties.[100]

For the estimated 2,500 to 5,000 residents living in the Between the Rivers or Land between the Lakes (LBL) area, President Kennedy's announcement in 1963 that a federal recreational area would be established on LBL was exciting news. Most residents first assumed that the plans would involve the 65,000 acres of the Kentucky Woodlands Natural Wildlife Refuge and that there would be additional tourism dollars and jobs added to the local economy. They were disappointed and angered by the announcement from the TVA that it intended to take control of the entire area, with plans to remove all businesses and homes.

The towns of Golden Pond and Twin Lakes on the Kentucky side and the Tennessee community of Model would be leveled.[101]

The local historian Betty Jo Wallace's book *Between the Rivers: History of the Land between the Lakes* (1992) tells the story of the one-sided struggle that ensued over the next decade as local residents unsuccessfully attempted to defend their lifestyle by organizing into the Tri-County Organization for Constitutional Rights, led by county officers in Trigg and Lyon Counties against a federal bureaucracy that was determined to have its way. On the other side, the Between the Lakes Development Association, which represented tourism interests outside the Between the Rivers area, chaired by Smith Broadbent counted on benefiting from projected retail sales from LBL visitors' spending, which was projected to increase from $660,000 to more than $10 million annually. Many Between the Rivers landowners settled for the price that the TVA offered for their land. Holdouts lost their last hope when a federal judge approved the TVA's authority to acquire resisters' land by condemnation procedures under its authorizing legislation in late 1967.[102]

The LBL recreational area has been a source of great controversy over the years. Cadiz-born author John Egerton strongly condemned the development plans for the LBL—in a tone reminiscent of the Southern Agrarians of the Great Depression in *I'll Take My Stand* (1930) — in *The Americanization of Dixie* (1974). To Egerton, the LBL project was one of the clearest examples of the federal government treating southern history and people as "a thing to be bought or sold or stolen." Displaced Between the Rivers residents and their descendants continue to fight for a voice in what was done with their former home lands. The controversy has been exacerbated by the project's failure to meet its planners' expectations. Locals from the start were puzzled over why large numbers of visitors would choose to travel long distances for recreational purposes to a land populated by large numbers of snakes, ticks, and mosquitoes and with few spectacular natural vistas. Indeed, the number of visitors plateaued at around 2 million annually by the early 1970s, but as high energy prices and unrealized increased leisure time affected travel patterns, LBL visitors from long distances proved much fewer than projected. In the view of the University of Tennessee geographer Ronald A. Foresta, LBL began as "the most important and exciting recreational idea" of the 1960s but fell considerably short of its original vision in the decades to come.[103]

Western Kentucky was in a position to expand its economy during the third quarter of the twentieth century by creating new jobs and encouraging industrial investment in the area. The large General Electric plant in Owensboro, formerly known as Ken-Rad, employed as many as 6,600 workers producing vacuum tubes in the mid-1960s; the completion of the gaseous-diffusion plant added more than 2,000 jobs in the Paducah labor market to produce weapons-grade uranium for the Cold War; and the large clothing factories in Mayfield, most notably Merit Clothing managed by Democratic boss William F. Foster, employed more than 2,000 in the 1950s. The expanding economy took advantage of an ample labor force, improved transportation, and the low-cost, abundant electricity that provided air-conditioning in area homes and workplaces to make the stifling heat of western Kentucky summers bearable. Ned Breathitt kept his campaign pledge of 1963 to expand the commonwealth's economy. Commerce secretary and Hopkinsville native Katherine Peden made her reputation as an industrial recruiter for Kentucky through her "Come to Kentucky—It's a Profitable Move" campaign, which led to 749 industrial investments by new or existing industries that pumped more than $1.2 billion into the manufacturing sector and created a 23 percent increase in factory jobs.[104]

Western Kentucky was a beneficiary of this development. General Tire started production at its Mayfield plant in 1960 and ramped up to more than 2,000 factory jobs. Kentucky Dam became an incubator for the development of a significant number of chemical plants in Calvert City, so that 26 percent of the Marshall County labor force was involved in manufacturing by 1988, and per capita income soared. Madisonville, in the heart of the Western Kentucky Coal Field, was a major benefactor of this burst of new industry by landing Goodyear, General Electric, National Can, and Mid-American Canning plants, which added more than 1,000 factory jobs, and the construction of a York air-conditioning plant expected to add 700 jobs gained the town recognition in 1971 as one of thirteen All-Kentucky Cities. Russellville, through cooperation of local government and business leaders that upgraded public utilities and sold industrial revenue bonds, recruited the Rockwell and Emerson

Electric plants, which anchored an industrial workforce in Logan County greater than 2,000. Throughout the region, small cut-and-sew factory operations provided jobs for a largely female workforce. Factory jobs were also added in smaller communities, such as the nearby Todd County town of Elkton, where more than 100 new manufacturing jobs were created as Aluminum Refrigerator Doors of Chicago expanded there in 1965.[105]

New industry created opportunities for a new generation of leaders in western Kentucky, such as Owensboro's J. R. Miller, a Mississippi native, who parlayed a career in rural electrification at the Green River Rural Electric Cooperative to become a Democratic kingmaker and a principal backer of Wendell Ford in his rise from the state Senate to the governor's mansion and then the US Senate. Miller, who nursed his own political ambitions as chair of the Kentucky Democratic Party in the early years of the Ford administration and later as mayor of Owensboro, had a large vision for what inexpensive electricity could do in the development of western Kentucky, which led to the creation of Big Rivers Electric Corporation in 1961 as the controversial wholesale distributer of electricity to thirteen western Kentucky counties by the mid-1970s and of the Green River, Henderson-Union, and Meade County rural electric cooperatives. By the mid-1960s, Big Rivers provided electricity from its initial 65,000-kilowatt plant (expanded to nearly 2 million kilowatts from four power plants in the region after 2000) to the new aluminum-smelting plants located near Hawesville and Lewisport on the Ohio River in Hancock County and at Sebree on the Green River in Webster County, which provided 1,700 industrial jobs in thirteen western Kentucky counties.[106]

Governor Breathitt's last hurdle in establishing himself as one of the commonwealth's strongest twentieth-century governors was to prevail in picking his successor. Breathitt's first choice was former governor Bert Combs, whose statewide recognition and popularity would have made him the favorite. Breathitt courted his political mentor, who at one point accepted Breathitt's offer, with Henry Ward as his lieutenant governor to provide the geographical balance from western Kentucky that would be valuable in the Democratic primary against expected rival campaigns headed by either Happy Chandler or Harry Lee Waterfield. However, Combs quickly decided against running due to family considerations. Breathitt then in mid-November 1966 tapped Henry Ward, the native Jackson Purchase journalist and politician with an outstanding administrative record for building the commonwealth's state parks and highway systems under four governors. Ward was viewed as a scrupulously honest public figure, who in announcing his candidacy recalled his political independence from governors dating back to 1933, when he first was elected to the General Assembly: "I have supported them when I thought they were right and opposed them—sometimes right vigorously—when I thought they were wrong." Ward, who had spent many years as a journalist at the *Paducah-Sun-Democrat*, could expect strong backing from most of the state's most powerful news outlets, especially the *Louisville Courier-Journal*. To ensure his credibility with Democratic leaders across the commonwealth, Ward secured Combs's commitment to manage the campaign; however, Combs soon had to step aside after President Johnson appointed him to a federal judgeship. Ward built a strong organization in western Kentucky with backing from former Chandler/Waterfield supporters Rumsey Taylor in Caldwell County; Fred Morgan, the Paducah state representative and former Chandler majority leader; William F. Foster, the Mayfield political boss who had caused such a stir by changing horses in 1955 to support Chandler (although Foster died before the May primary); and Smith Broadbent, the political boss from Cadiz. The Jackson Purchase hoped that Ward would break through to become the area's first governor.[107]

The Democratic primary in May 1967, a somewhat crowded field, featured, in addition to Ward, two other western Kentucky veteran politicians: Happy Chandler, who arose from the premature grave that political pundits had assigned him to following his decisive defeat in 1963, and current lieutenant governor Harry Lee Waterfield, back for a third try at the top rung of the state's political ladder. Chandler campaigned vigorously by blasting the past two gubernatorial administrations with which Ward had been closely associated for their big-spending and high-taxing records. In Owensboro, Chandler hoped to encourage anti-Ward sentiment by reminding locals that Ward had done nothing in nearly eight years as highway commissioner to address the city's cry for access to superhighways, and in Ward's hometown of Paducah Chandler promised a public four-year state college if elected. Chandler repeated often, "You don't have to know Henry Ward to dislike him, but it helps." Ward refrained from slinging back the mud slung at him. In a final swing through the Jackson Purchase, however, at the end of the campaign, Ward launched out against "phony candidates, phony issues and phony promises." He effectively turned aside accusations that he had "deserted" the Jackson Purchase after joining the Clements administration in 1948 by reminding voters of the many state parks and highways that he had played a hand in shaping while in Frankfort. He castigated former governor Happy Chandler for being against state parks and superhighways: "A park system under him would be the deteriorating, wasp-infested place that Kentucky Dam Village became during his last administration." In endorsing Ward, the *Paducah Sun-Democrat* charged that Chandler had demonstrated over the course of his political career that he was not a Democrat, but a "Chandlerite."[108]

Predictions of a close race erred as the crowded field split the anti-administration votes, giving Ward a nearly two-to-one margin statewide over runner-up Chandler. In western Kentucky, Ward dominated by receiving more votes than Chandler and Waterfield combined, with the latter carrying only his home Hickman County. Chandler fared slightly better in winning his home Henderson County as well as Union and Carlisle Counties. Ward's 95,000-vote landslide once again suggested Chandler had lost his magic among Kentucky Democrats and that the Chandler faction was in a precipitate decline. Bill Powell at the *Paducah Sun-Democrat* concluded: "At the age of 68, almost 69, the old warrior has fought his last political battle. He should have done thus in 1963."[109]

Ward now faced Louie B. Nunn, the narrow loser in the gubernatorial general election in 1963 who now narrowly won his Republican primary. The size of Ward's primary victory gave many Democrats confidence that victory in November was a certainty. However, the campaign had its share of problems that concerned the candidate. First, the loss of Bert Combs as campaign manager and senior statesman had created a leadership vacuum in the campaign that was never filled. One columnist indicated after the election that Governor Breathitt's campaign influence was very small, even in western Kentucky. Further, Ward was frustrated that the months between the primary and the fall general election sapped his organization of needed momentum. In addition, the political winds in the nation seemed to be shifting, particularly in the South, where "backlash" from many voters unhappy over the antipoverty campaign, the Vietnam War, and perceived liberal national policies regarding civil rights offered opportunities for Republicans to pick up votes in areas, such as western Kentucky, where Democrats had been dominant. Ward responded that those matters were "next year's business." He also worried that a lower-than-expected Democratic turnout for the primary election might indicate many voters intended to vote for the GOP in November. In addition, the much more senior Ward, now fifty-eight years old, was disadvantaged by the more youthful, telegenic Nunn, a repeat of the Democratic primaries in 1959 and 1963, when younger candidates held the upper hand as television assumed an increasing importance in election outcomes. Finally, Chandler bolted once again to support Louie Nunn against what he called the "bankrupt" policies of Combs, Breathitt, and President Johnson. For his part, Nunn departed from his previous campaigns by being less negative and aggressive.[110]

Though both candidates pledged not to raise taxes, Nunn rallied his crowds by calling Ward the "tax man" and reminding listeners that Ward had been part of the Combs administration, which had put through the sales tax. For his own part, Ward touted his long experience in state government. His campaign slogans were "Henry Ward—Sound Builder for Kentucky" and "Henry Ward—Tell It the Way It Is." Allan Trout, the veteran *Courier-Journal* political columnist, surmised that political factions in the commonwealth were destined to falter after two administrations because governors have to disappoint constituents' requests so often that "attrition of time beats the party." Another writer at the paper suggested that Nunn was simply more "salable" to the voters than Ward, who came across as "a gruff, assured man who, after 13 years as a key administrator under four Democratic governors, was in the habit of giving orders and commanding obedience" and who "half believed handshaking cost him votes." One Ward supporter later concluded that he would have been a great governor if he only could have been appointed to the office.[111]

Election results were disappointing to Ward supporters in western Kentucky as Nunn won with a comfortable 21,000-vote margin statewide. Ward joined Jackson Purchase natives Alben Barkley in 1923 and Harry Lee Waterfield in 1947, 1959, and, for the third and last time, 1967 in failing to win after waging strong gubernatorial campaign bids.

Ward needed at least a 30,000-vote win in western Kentucky, considered a critical battleground area, but Nunn, who had angered organizers at the Fancy Farm Picnic when he was a no-show, said weeks before the election that Chandler Democrats were working at the precinct level to elect him so that if he failed to win the First District, he certainly would come much closer than he had against Breathitt. Although Nunn lost in the First District, Ward's majority there was a disappointing 15,457 votes. In western Kentucky, Nunn won only in Crittenden, Caldwell, McLean, Ohio, and Butler Counties, but he polled competitively throughout the Jackson Purchase, other than Ward's home McCracken County, and held the Democrat to a disappointing 17,000-vote edge.[112]

For the first time since 1947, a Republican would reside in the governor's mansion. Downcast Democrats could, however, find some solace in relative political newcomer Wendell Ford's 16,000-vote victory in the lieutenant governor's race. The Owensboro state senator, a protégé of utility magnate J. R. Miller, with his statewide network in the public-power advocates, had won a very close primary contest. His victory not only put him in the position, as the highest-ranking Kentucky Democrat, to control his party's organization but also raised expectations that he would be the Democratic frontrunner in the gubernatorial race in 1971.[113]

Election results from the 1963 and 1967 gubernatorial elections gave rise to concern that the Democrats in Kentucky were losing control in both Frankfort and Washington, where Kentucky was represented by two Republican senators. Some suggested that civil rights reforms were the cause. Ned Breathitt survived the stiff challenge from Republican Louie Nunn, who effectively exploited Governor Combs's civil rights executive order in 1963. Passage of legislation in Washington in 1964 that struck down much of the South's Jim Crow segregationist public-accommodation provisions, followed in 1966 by a companion law in Kentucky strongly supported by Breathitt, certainly played a role in Nunn's narrow defeat of Henry Ward in 1967. Western Kentucky seemed to prove this point as the Gibraltar of Kentucky Democracy: generally considered the most conservative region in the commonwealth on racial issues, failed to deliver its normally solid Democratic majorities. Nevertheless, Democrats could take future hope in the down-ballot races that year, including the one for lieutenant governor with the election of Owensboro's Wendell Ford.

5

From Democratic Resurgence to the Collapse of the Gibraltar of Kentucky Democracy

The political fortunes of the Kentucky Democratic Party in the late 1960s were at low ebb. The GOP had held both US Senate seats since 1956 and captured the governor's mansion in 1967, ending twenty years of Democratic rule. Although the factional division among Democrats was clearly weakening, it played a key role in the defeat of Henry Ward from Paducah in the governor's race when Happy Chandler campaigned reportedly in up to sixty counties for Republican Louie Nunn. Nunn's win also reduced the Democrat's majority in the General Assembly, giving hope that the Republican surge could in the near future sweep them into power in one or both chambers. Western Kentucky's state House delegation included Republicans George Greer from Owensboro (who beat Louise Kirtley, seeking a third term); Lindell Richey of Muhlenberg County; T. C. Simmons from Allen County, whose district included Simpson County; Theron Kessinger from Beaver Dam; and Quentin Wesley from Sturgis. The unusually large number of Republicans from the region contributed to a narrow 56–44 Democratic majority in the 1968 session. If there was a bright spot for Democrats to be found in the 1967 elections, it was the election of Owensboro state senator Wendell

Ford as lieutenant governor. He dealt Governor Nunn an early defeat by helping elect newcomer Delbert Murphy to fill Ford's Senate seat in a close special-election race against now independent former senator Cap Gardner and the governor's choice, Republican William J. Richard, who had lost his race for state representative to Don Blandford.[1]

For the first time since 1946, legislative Democrats organized themselves without interference from the governor at what was now the traditional presession conference held at Kentucky Dam Village State Park. New lieutenant governor Wendell Ford from Owensboro filled the vacuum by cobbling together a leadership team that united the two competing Democratic factions in the Senate, for which Democrats chose former Chandler majority leader William Sullivan from Henderson as president pro tempore and Madisonville's Richard Frymire, who had been aligned with Waterfield in the 1966 session, as majority leader. In the House, Paducah's Julian Carroll, now in his third term, actively campaigned for the Speaker position, nudging aside fellow Paducahan Fred Morgan. Once Morgan acceded to Carroll's locking down the top spot, Carroll threw his support to Morgan for majority leader, giving Paducah a previously unheard-of hold on the two most powerful posts in the Kentucky House of Representatives.[2]

When Nunn took office, he was faced with a serious budget crisis that had forced Governor Breathitt to cut spending by $24 million before he left office. After campaigning on a "no new tax" pledge, Nunn now faced the rather daunting choice between severe budget cuts or a significant tax increase. Democratic leaders prior to the session had rejected obstructionist tactics; Senator Frymire told a Hopkins County Kiwanis group that "the attitude of the Democrats going to Frankfort next month will not be to obstruct the governor's program or to rip him of power." That cooperative spirit was short-lived, however, as Nunn delayed introduction of his fiscal program until late February. Efforts to put Democrats on the spot by combining the budget and tax hike into a single bill was turned aside when Speaker Julian Carroll declared that the combination violated constitutional provisions limiting legislation to one subject. When the tax bill, containing a two-cent sales tax hike (soon known as "Nunn's nickel") was filed, promises of Democratic cooperation with the governor were forgotten. Carroll suggested that the state should live on its existing tax sources; Fred Morgan filed a Democratic plan combining a much smaller sales tax increase with numerous exemptions and a host of other tax hikes; Wendell Ford staked out his position, terming Nunn's nickel a "rough bite on the people," and called for a plan that would lessen the impact on "widows, widowers, old age pensioners, those on Social Security, and those in low-income brackets" by exempting food and other necessities from the sales tax; and William Sullivan was dismayed that Nunn's plan would raise the sales tax and concluded that the General Assembly would not support it. Other western Kentucky lawmakers not part of the leadership also voiced opposition, such as Wingo representative Lloyd Clapp, who reminded the governor of his no-tax campaign pledge but indicated he might support a penny hike on nonessential items such as liquor. Nunn clearly could not count on Democratic leaders to help pass his tax bill.[3]

Governor Nunn held a strong hand in his fight with Democratic legislators given the power to grant local favors and the hundreds of millions of dollars that the new taxes would add to the state coffers. The slim majority Democrats held in the House made Nunn's job easier if he could hold the Republican minority together. The opposition experienced a brief victory when it exempted groceries from the sales tax by a 48–47 vote in the House. However, the governor managed the following day to remove the exemption by twisting the arms of the few Republicans and sufficient Democrats who had voted for the amendment and passed his tax plan with a comfortable 59–34 majority. Among the Democrats who switched their votes were western Kentuckians Lloyd Clapp and Bill Cox from Madisonville; Majority Floor Leader Fred Morgan, who had publicly stumped for his own lower-tax plan, now reluctantly voted with Nunn, citing as his reason his campaign pledge to teachers in his district. However, it is the Bill Cox story that is most remembered after he explained to House members that Nunn had twisted his arm by threatening to veto a bill to create Madisonville Community College and withhold $1 million in projects for Hopkins County. Cox, a first-term lawmaker, realized that by changing his vote he could not be reelected, but he believed the community college and local projects were worth the sacrifice. Richard Frymire, also from Madisonville and Senate author of the college bill, felt Nunn had bluffed Cox.[4]

Lieutenant Governor Ford and Senate Democratic leaders hoped to stop Nunn's nickel by focusing on the regressive impact of the sales tax on Kentucky's workers and its adverse impact on border merchants, who would be handicapped against competitors in other states with lower sales taxes. The Henderson and Owensboro Chambers of Commerce protested the sales tax for that reason, and Henderson merchants sent a delegation to lobby against the plan in the Senate. The end result was similar to that in the House as Nunn secured in the last week of the session sufficient Democratic votes in the Senate to defeat Ford's efforts to hold the increase to a penny and exempt food. However, the leadership was successful in preventing the western Kentucky delegation, with the exception of Carl Hadden from Elkton, in joining the Nunn camp. Eight Democrats—notably former governor Lawrence Wetherby, whom Frymire alleged to have been protecting the interests of Brighton Engineering, a major road builder where he held a prominent position—bolted their Democratic colleagues to vote for Nunn's nickel.[5]

In the end, the 1968 session was a notable experiment in divided government that reflected well on both the governor and the General Assembly. The legislature succeeded in building on the civil rights momentum from the 1966 session by making Kentucky the first southern state to pass open-housing legislation. Concerns that a "white backlash" would punish lawmakers for voting in favor of civil rights legislation after the fallout from Governor Combs's executive order nearly cost Ned Breathitt his election in 1963 were missing in 1968. Western Kentucky legislators played significant roles, especially Paducah senator Tom Garrett, who helped secure votes for the bill in exchange for Senator Georgia Davis Powers's help on a daylight-savings-time bill, and Hopkinsville representative John Hardin, who gave an impassioned floor speech for the bill, which was passed the last day of the session. Hardin urged representatives to cast their votes in favor of the bill, calling it "a fine step toward the cure of this sickness called discrimination." No western Kentuckians senators voted against the bill (Mayfield senator Carroll Hubbard and Christian County senator Pat McCuiston failed to vote even though they were present). Jim Bruce from Christian County, Lloyd Clapp, and Charles Lassiter from Murray voted against the bill in the House.[6]

Interstate and parkway construction plans to this point bypassed Owensboro, much to its displeasure, which had long believed that the state paid insufficient attention to its transportation needs. In a pithy editorial in the *Owensboro Messenger-Inquirer,* the writer objected to plans for the Jackson Purchase Parkway, which, he stated, would serve "only cities and towns of relatively low population," leaving "the Owensboro area about the only major part of Kentucky for which modern highway plans have not been made or announced." In a message directed at the state's Democratic leadership, the editorialist wrote that neglect of the city's highway needs not only put it at a disadvantage economically but also weakened its support for the Democratic Party at the polls. The complaints did not fall on deaf ears in Frankfort. In 1965, Henry Ward pledged to a visiting Owensboro delegation, led by Mayor Dugan Best, his support for a potential interstate through Owensboro that would connect Lafayette, Indiana, and Hopkinsville, but then he damped down enthusiasm by adding that approval for the road could not come earlier than 1970. Emotions spiked a short time later when state highway maps depicting completed and planned superhighways in the commonwealth again left out Owensboro. Remembering that initial exit signage on the Western Kentucky Parkway failed to direct motorists to Owensboro, the *Messenger-Inquirer* complained that "Kentucky's fourth largest city was completely bypassed." Another editorial lamented that "every day it is becoming more and more apparent that the opportunity for highway equality in our area is diminishing rather than decreasing."[7]

The pessimism was perhaps exaggerated. Pressure soon built around parkway plans to link Owensboro to the planned Pennyrile Parkway, which connected Henderson and Hopkinsville. In addition, by the fall of 1966 planning for the Green River Parkway connecting the city with Bowling Green, with important interchanges with I-65 and the Western Kentucky Parkway, was also well under way. The planned new parkway was a central issue in the gubernatorial general election in 1967 pitting the former highway commissioner Henry Ward against Louie Nunn, the unsuccessful GOP candidate in 1963. Ward, hoping to secure western Kentucky in what was anticipated to be a close contest and with Owensboro's Wendell Ford as candidate for lieutenant governor at his side, pledged support for the four-lane highway as a free road, if possible, or a toll road that would cut the distance to Bowling Green by fifteen miles and would include an extension to a new Ohio River bridge with Indiana's construction of an additional modern highway to I-64. The Democrats' road pledges were rewarded with the *Owensboro*

Messenger-Inquirer's endorsement after Nunn ruled out the possibility of a new parkway linking the two western Kentucky cities.[8]

Thus, Louie Nunn's election in 1967 raised concerns that plans for a road from Owensboro to Bowling Green would be shelved, but the new administration, which had campaigned hard in the Second Congressional District for new roads, quickly announced plans to build four-lane US 231 to the Western Kentucky Parkway. By summer, it was apparent to the new administration that to honor candidate Nunn's road pledges, Governor Nunn would need to consider additional state parkways. Bundled together into a $374 million package for consideration by the Kentucky Turnpike Authority, Owensboro, with WOMI radio general manager Hugh Potter and Daviess County judge Pat Tanner leading the way, encouraged the five-member authority, one of whom was Lieutenant Governor Wendell Ford, with two parkways benefiting his hometown, to approve the package. The vote was 4–0 (Democratic attorney general John Breckinridge abstained due to concerns that the additional state debt involved was "reckless"). The Ohio River bridge would be long in coming, but the Audubon Parkway opened in 1970, and the Green River Parkway (later the Natcher Parkway) opened in 1972. Now governor, Wendell Ford predicted at the dedication of the Green River Parkway that more than 2.1 million vehicles would use the road in its first year and would open up potential economic growth in Owensboro similar to that experienced by Elizabethtown at the intersection of the Western Kentucky Parkway and I-65. Road users continued to pay tolls on these two roads into the twenty-first century, but tolls on the Western Kentucky Parkway were removed in 1987, and tolls on the Pennyrile and Purchase Parkways were terminated in 1992.[9]

Although women in the commonwealth had been able to vote since 1920, they had not for the most part assumed a significant role in elected state political offices, especially in western Kentucky. The exception was Doris Owens, the Wickliffe clerk of the Kentucky Court of Appeals who had been caught up in a fight between Governor Chandler and the court over her appointment in 1957 and had gone on to win statewide election to the position twice. This situation slowly changed in the latter half of the twentieth century as several women were elected to the General Assembly. Most commonly, they were widows elected to serve in the place of their deceased husbands, as in the cases of Carolyn Moore from Simpson County, widow of Senator J. Lee Moore and the first woman senator in Kentucky in 1949, and Minnie Poindexter Webb, the widow of Senator Henry E. Webb Jr. from Todd County in 1954. Allie Mae Linton from Russellville, sister of powerful Democratic kingmaker Emerson "Doc" Beauchamp and widow of a former state representative, was elected to the House from Logan County in 1948 following the resignation of Thomas A. Noe to become Russellville city attorney. She represented her district through the partial term and in a full term to 1952. Louise Kirtley, elected to the House from Owensboro in 1961, was different from her predecessors in that the former city attorney and first lawyer of her gender elected to the General Assembly ran on her own record and served two terms before losing in a reelection bid for a third term in 1965 and again in 1967.[10]

In this context, Katherine Peden's US Senate campaign in 1968 blazed a new trail for western Kentucky women. She had already made a significant national record in the private sector as an executive at WHOP radio in Hopkinsville president of the National Federation of Business and Professional Women's Club, and as an effective industrial recruiter while serving as commerce secretary during the Breathitt administration and had doubled his campaign pledge to add 75,000 nonagriculture jobs to the state. Among her successes included the announcements of several new plants in western Kentucky: Southwire, an aluminum-processing plant in Hawesville projected to employ 900; West Virginia Pulp and Paper in Wickliffe with 300 workers; Firestone Tire in Bowling Green with an expected 400 workforce; Eli Lilly and General Graphite in Murray with more than 400 employees; Harvey Aluminum in Lewisport; and B. F. Goodrich in Calvert City. Before leaving office as commerce secretary, Peden facilitated a national firm involved in business relocations to update its outlook for the Jackson Purchase and the Daviess and Hancock Counties areas. For her successes, President Johnson appointed her to the Kerner Commission, which was charged with investigating the causes of urban riots in the mid-1960s.[11]

Peden had briefly considered running against US representative Frank Stubblefield for the First Congressional District, but she was the first Democrat to throw her hat in the ring to challenge two-term GOP incumbent US senator Thruston B. Morton once Breathitt decided against entering the race. She explained that Kentuckians would elect her because they "want a senator who will do more for Kentucky." Even though her right-of-center political philosophy fit well with Kentucky voters, she was considered an underdog against Morton, but after he announced in February 1968 his decision not to seek reelection, interest in the race picked up. From Washington, President Johnson, who was still planning his own reelection campaign, sent word to Kentucky Democrats that Morton's seat was winnable and urged them to back the most viable candidate possible. That description best fit Breathitt, but he kept his promise to back Peden. This did not deter others from filing, urged on by the belief in many circles that Peden would be unsuccessful against a strong GOP candidate, a notion that she attributed to her gender. But she asserted that she was a "woman of courage" who wanted to "serve Kentucky in the U. S. Senate." A host of contenders soon came forward. Among them were west Kentuckians Julian Carroll, who announced following the legislative session but left the race in early April, and the old warhorse John Y. Brown Sr. from Sturgis, who, when the press discounted his chances after six consecutive statewide campaign defeats, humorlessly quipped that "Joshua marched around Jericho six times and the wall stood, but the walls tumbled down on the seventh." Henry Ward, now back at the *Paducah Sun-Democrat,* predicted before election day that the favorites were Peden, Brown, and Foster Ockerman, a powerful figure in Kentucky Democratic politics who had been one of Ned Breathitt's campaign chairs in 1963. Thelma Stovall, who had held statewide offices since 1955, stumped for Peden. At one rally in Gilbertsville, she warned approximately 300 women from the First Congressional District to be on guard against those who would make them believe women could not win high office. In a crowded field of twelve, voters picked Peden over Brown in a light turnout by more than 30,000 votes. She swept western Kentucky with the exception of Union County, Brown's home county. Her Republican opponent was Marlow Cook, a county judge from Louisville. In a slap at the unpopular Governor Nunn, Peden suggested Republicans may have been wiser had they "not picked another county judge," but the *Paducah Sun-Democrat* predicted that the two attractive candidates promised to give voters a "fascinating race."[12]

In fact, the two waged a heated battle, starting with the Fancy Farm Picnic, which featured considerable barbs from the candidates, especially over Nunn's nickel. Although Nunn was a no-show once again, Peden attacked Cook's failure as a Jefferson County judge to rally Louisville area Republican legislators against Nunn's nickel. However, the race turned on national issues as images of Vietnam War protests and urban race riots following Martin Luther King Jr.'s assassination were constant fare on television news. Peden took advantage of her experience on the Kerner Commission to tell the Fancy Farm crowd that "the domestic crisis faced by the nation today can be solved only by respect for law and order and recognition of social justice for all our people," but she was more restrained on Vietnam in expressing her hope that the Paris peace talks might bring the war to an end before she took office in January. She scored additional points against Cook that fall in her response to the civil disturbances that erupted in Louisville.[13]

But 1968 was not a good time for a Democrat to run statewide in Kentucky, with the national party in shambles and its candidate, Vice President Hubert Humphrey, seemingly tethered to an unpopular president and running against a strong law-and-order candidate in former GOP vice president Richard Nixon and in western Kentucky against a third-party candidate, segregationist George Wallace. Humphrey found sufficient momentum in the last month of the campaign to hold off in Kentucky what some felt could have been a Wallace majority in the First Congressional District and achieved a solid, although not spectacular, showing. Nixon and Wallace combined (Wallace won in Christian, Logan, Muhlenberg, Caldwell, and Butler Counties) had considerably more votes than did Humphrey. Nixon won the traditionally Republican Butler, Crittenden, and Ohio Counties, but he surprised the pundits by winning Logan, Caldwell, and Muhlenberg Counties. Peden outperformed the national party, however, carrying western Kentucky by nearly 30,000 votes and winning approximately two-thirds of the state's counties. Cook's only victories in western Kentucky were in Butler, Caldwell, Crittenden, Hancock, and Ohio Counties. Peden, however, was disadvantaged by refusing to accept large contributions from wealthy contributors who might expect favors in return and by being unable to compensate with sufficient backing from party sources. In the days after the election, she criticized the Kentucky Democratic Party, controlled by Wendell Ford and J. R. Miller, saying that "for the first time in 20 years, there was no Democratic state organization to help me." Although her prospects for a future political race seemed viable, she left politics to return to the private sector, and no other western Kentucky women have followed her path by waging a credible campaign for a major statewide or national office.[14]

Democrats quickly rebounded from their defeats in the November election. A few days after the election, party leaders met in Louisville, and as they looked ahead to future state legislative contests and the gubernatorial race in 1971, they were in fact buoyed by Peden's stronger-than-projected performance and the stronger-than-expected Democratic vote in Jefferson County, which J. R. Miller termed the "miracle of the campaign." Still, few could have forecast in that moment that Democrats would soon embark on a resurgence keyed by taking back the governor's mansion in 1971 and achieving a lock on statewide elected offices, with the notable exception of the US Senate, through 2004. The Democratic resurgence began with the close partnership between Lieutenant Governor Wendell Ford, the highest-ranking Democratic elected official in 1967, and his closest political ally, J. R. Miller, the state party chair—both from Owensboro. Since arriving in Kentucky from Mississippi as a young man, Miller had built a powerful career in the public-power sector as head of the Green River Rural Electric Cooperative and had become a leader in the state's public-power network, which had enabled him to gain recognition as one of the "kingmakers" in the Clements/Combs faction. As the factions faded, Miller's political influence did not. Both Ford and Speaker Julian Carroll, who provided legal services for Miller's power operations, were associated with him. One *Louisville Courier-Journal* reporter described Miller as "a man of driving, relentless energy, a man who understood and sought power." In June 1968, Miller took over as Democratic Party chair after Lawrence Wetherby's party position became untenable when he voted for Nunn's nickel. Contemporaries considered Miller's political skills the best since Earle Clements. He and Wendell Ford shared the same goal of opening up the Democratic Party to new blood by encouraging Democratic youth organizations, headed up by Hickman County native Don Mills, Governor Breathitt's press secretary and now editor of the *Lexington Herald*, and by giving younger Democrats leadership roles. This tactic was demonstrated in the selection of younger delegates to the 1968 Democratic

National Convention in Chicago (Happy Chandler was pointedly left out due to his failure to support Democratic candidates in the general election of 1967).[15]

In 1969, the state legislative races provided an opportunity for the new Democratic leadership to make significant gains that would prove important in the 1971 gubernatorial race. First, Democrats took control by upsetting the GOP in Jefferson County in the Louisville mayor and county judge races and by defeating two incumbent GOP state senators, with Mills crediting young people for playing a "key role" in these wins. Democrats stormed back in the House, taking advantage of voter anger over Nunn's nickel to extend their majority to 72–38. Because of his vote for Nunn's sales tax increase, Fred Morgan, the veteran former House majority leader from Paducah, was upended by Austin Wenz in the Democratic primary. Miller and Ford found great satisfaction in the results of the general election, after which Miller told listeners that he "was delighted that the people of Kentucky have decided that their best interest resides with the Democratic party." In western Kentucky, Democrats—with the exception of Theron Kessenger in his reelection to the safe House seat formed that included strongly GOP Ohio and Butler Counties—defeated Republicans George Greer in Daviess County, Lindell Richie in Muhlenberg County, and Quentin Wesley in Union County. Nunn had ceded Democratic gains in the House, but he had high hopes in the Senate, where he had found sufficient Democrats willing to vote with him in 1968 and hoped to improve his position in 1970. The results for the Senate were mixed, however, as Democrats lost one seat, but Ford was pleased that incumbent Owensboro senator Delbert Murphy turned aside Cap Gardner, the former Democratic Senate majority leader running as a Republican with strong backing from Nunn.[16]

Although western Kentucky lost its two majority leaders from the 1970 session (Senator Richard Frymire was called to military service), the region remained strong in the legislative leadership. In addition to Lieutenant Governor Ford, who was also president of the Senate, House Speaker Julian Carroll and Senate president pro tempore William Sullivan from Henderson returned. They were now joined by Paducah's Tom Garrett as Senate Democratic caucus chair. Money dominated the session because the previous session's tax increase had provided ample money for funding state obligations, and Governor Nunn sought to repair his party's image by calling for the elimination of the sales tax on prescription drugs and several other items. However, his budget failed to address teacher pay hikes, to the dismay of the Kentucky Education Association, which sought a $1,000 per year pay hike that teachers felt they were due for supporting Nunn in the sales tax effort in 1968. Instead, Nunn put legislative Democrats on the defensive by leaving an undesignated $18 million, far short of the amount needed to satisfy teacher demands, for legislators to use for either teacher salaries or tax cuts. Talk of "strike" surfaced quickly, but the *Paducah Sun-Democrat* cautioned that "a public subsisting on a 50th per capita income is not going to tax itself to provide its school teachers with salary levels of the 35th or better rank, whether or not they go on strike."Teachers were not easily deterred by such warnings. When the KEA gathered in Frankfort in late January, teachers from western Kentucky were among those who appeared willing to strike if necessary. Martha Dell Sanders, a former Kentucky Education Association president from Paducah, announced that she "was glad to be associated with hard-headed teachers" willing to fight for their program, "no bones about it."[17]

The KEA revised its program, calling for a larger pay hike than House Democrats had recently passed and for enactment of a controversial professional negotiations bill. Teachers, led by younger, more militant voices, made good on their threat to strike. Prospects for success were diminished, though, as a substantial portion of the $18 million unreserved funding was siphoned off for sales tax exemptions on prescription drugs and prosthetics, and legislators were cool to the KEA's requests for a cigarette tax increase. A number of western Kentucky lawmakers at least voiced sympathy for the teachers' cause, but others did not, including Representative Lloyd Clapp from Wingo, who surmised, "I see no promise of new money for teachers." Approximately 60 percent of teachers from 193 school districts, representing 24,000 teachers, participated in the strike. The work stoppage was widespread, but teachers in Murray, Calloway, and Carlisle schools in the Jackson Purchase continued to teach through the strike. Local school boards responded, led by the McCracken County School Board, by obtaining injunctions that ordered teachers to return to their classrooms. This action had a dampening effect elsewhere, and teachers throughout western Kentucky ended their work stoppage, followed shortly thereafter by the KEA's announcement that it would be ending the strike statewide. The KEA's ambitious legislative program failed to win passage, and classroom teachers had to accept the disappointing pay hikes approved by the House before the strike.[18]

An overarching topic of conversation during the 1970 session was the approaching Democratic gubernatorial primary and the possible candidacies of former governor Bert Combs and Lieutenant Governor Wendell Ford. There ensued a "war of nerves" as the two men, well acquainted from Ford's time as an administrative aide on Combs's gubernatorial staff, along with J. R. Miller, the party chair and Ford's closest political ally, engaged in a series of conversations with hopes that a primary battle could be avoided. Criticisms within the party, voiced publicly during the 1970 session by Mayfield senator Carroll Hubbard, that Ford had failed to provide the leadership needed and that his support came primarily from western Kentucky worked against him as the candidate who could defeat whoever Republicans would put up for governor in 1971. Combs, with his name recognition, seemed to many the stronger candidate. However, J. R. Miller commissioned a professional poll that convinced Ford that he stood a good chance of winning a primary against the former governor. Ford subsequently announced his candidacy in early May 1970, followed by Combs shortly thereafter. Happy Chandler also declared his intention to run as an independent in the general election.[19]

The contest turned bitter quickly when Julian Carroll upstaged Ford by announcing his plans to run for lieutenant governor with Combs days before Ford announced. Carroll was expected to balance geographically the ticket for the eastern Kentuckian Combs, but Miller, who had until this point been close to Carroll yet now was committed to Ford's candidacy, felt betrayed by Carroll to the point that the two men nearly came to blows. The relationship between Ford and Carroll was already tenuous; Miller later recalled that he was forced to intercede on several occasions "to keep these fellows from cutting each other's throats." Many considered Ford the underdog, but he ultimately won the primary by nearly 43,000 votes, carrying all but two congressional districts in the eastern part of the state, where Combs expected to be the strongest. A number of factors contributed to Ford's win, such as his long years of hard work, the superior organization put together by Miller and campaign chair Walter Huddleston, the positive impression the more youthful and personable Ford made on television, and voter uncertainty as to why Combs would give up his lifetime seat on the federal bench with its better salary. Inroads that Ford and Miller had made in urban areas of Kentucky in the past paid off now with wins in Jefferson County and northern Kentucky. Miller, who had resigned as Democratic Party chair after Ford entered the race, made effective use of his rural-electric-cooperative network, and Ford counted on his contacts statewide with members of the Jaycees (US Junior Chamber) as their fomer national president. Al Smith, then the publisher of the *Russellville News-Democrat*, observed that despite Ford's loss of Logan County to a political organization built by Tom Rhea and Doc Beauchamp, the youthful energy of Ford's Jaycees cut the loss to a mere 200 votes. One of them commented: "When the Courthouse boys began to fuss with us over our ads in the paper, we knew we were getting under their skin, and were bearing down on 'em." In the end, Ford hurt Combs in the closing weeks of the campaign by convincing voters that by supporting the KEA legislative program in the coming session, Combs was pledged to a substantial tax increase beyond the revenues that the coal severance tax, which both candidates supported, would bring. Ford did well in western Kentucky, beating his opponent by nearly 31,000 votes, losing, in addition to Logan County, Calloway, Christian, Livingston, and Trigg Counties, where longtime Clements faction "kingmaker" Smith Broadbent still carried considerable influence, by only small margins. Combs's strategy to cut Ford's advantage in the region by slating with Julian Carroll failed even in his home McCracken County. Ford ran well ahead of Combs in the First Congressional District, suggesting that, unlike the case of Breathitt and Waterfield, Ford's general election prospects were not dependent on Carroll.[20]

Julian Carroll became part of the general election Democratic slate after upsetting Attorney General John Breckinridge. Despite persistent tensions between the Carroll and the Ford camps, Kentucky Democrats united for the fall campaign against GOP candidate Tom Emberton, a public-services commissioner in the Nunn administration, who had an easy primary victory. Ford capitalized on the sluggish national economy under GOP president Richard Nixon. Emberton ran a lackluster campaign until scoring some political points on Ford for holding a meeting with mine operators in Virginia, but he failed to build on whatever momentum he gained as a result of the debate, leaving Nunn the task of trying to incite voters to vote for his party's candidate. Happy Chandler was crushed in western Kentucky, winning less than 3,000 votes in the running as a third-party candidate First Congressional District in his final gubernatorial race. Wendell Ford, the man from Owensboro's "Yellow Creek," won by a comfortable 60,000-vote margin—approximately 45,000 of which were from western Kentucky, where Emberton carried only traditionally GOP Crittenden, Butler, and Ohio Counties—to become the first governor from Daviess County. Julian Carroll was also swept into the lieutenant governor's office in what was a major victory for Kentucky democracy at all levels, but it was the Gibraltar of Kentucky Democracy that was once again at the center of state politics in the commonwealth. For the third time since 1955, western Kentucky Democrats held the governor and lieutenant governor posts.[21]

Ford promised to run state government on sound business principles. In his inaugural address in December 1971 and his state of the commonwealth address in 1972, he told listeners: "The attitude of my administration will be one where there is no patience for waste—waste of time, talent, energy, and resources"; "good government is good politics," and "good business is good politics." Landis Jones, compiler of Ford's speeches, saw in Ford's political philosophy "a conservative, no-nonsense belief in free enterprise, hard work, and the 'old ideals that made this country great.'" Upon taking office, Ford trimmed more than 1,000 state workers from the Highway Department, cancelled $5.6 million in personal-service contracts, and delegated to J. R. Miller and the Democratic Party the task of hiring the 5,000 state patronage workers. In his message to the General Assembly, he asked for the authority to reorganize state government so that each agency would be evaluated by its service to the people, and if it could not demonstrate a valued service, it would be abolished.[22]

Any thought that four years with a Republican in the governor's mansion would have ushered in "legislative independence" was quickly laid to rest as Ford, with considerable assistance from J. R. Miller, adopted a "hands on" approach in organizing the General Assembly. Of course, Julian Carroll as lieutenant governor presided over the Senate, where William Sullivan returned for a third term as president pro tempore and Tom Garrett for his second tour of duty as Democratic caucus chair. They were joined by Speaker pro tempore Billy Ray Paxton from Central City as the lone western Kentuckian in the House leadership. In addition to the legislative leaders, J. R. Miller played an active and somewhat controversial role in the General Assembly behind the scenes.[23]

Wendell Ford had reason to consider his first legislative session extremely satisfying. Despite Lieutenant Governor Carroll's repeated declarations of independence from the governor, he did little to undercut Ford. His decision to delay legislative redistricting to the end of the session helped keep at bay potential maverick lawmakers, such as Carroll Hubbard, who feared that Ford, who had little regard for the Mayfield senator, might punish him in redrawing his district. In fact, Ford's accomplishments were many, including the removal of the sales tax on groceries, a hike in the gasoline tax, and passage of a severance tax on coal to help replace some of the lost revenue from the grocery tax exemption. The severance tax—feverishly opposed by Muhlenberg County newspaper editor Larry Stone, who accused Ford and local representative Billy Ray Paxton of "murder" for killing the coal industry—had frustrated past governors. Its passage this time was made easier by Frankfort's effort to support the industry's position on potentially very costly miner disability benefits and by the sense, as one lawmaker later indicated, that mining would benefit in Frankfort once severance tax revenues became part of the state revenue pie. One of Ford's programs, easy to overlook, cleaned up election abuses by forcing voters to re-register in order to avoid "graveyard voting," in which the names of deceased voters and those no longer residing in counties were kept on voter rolls so that party bosses in some counties, notably Logan County, could manipulate election returns.[24]

Ford and J. R. Miller's leadership of the Kentucky Democratic Party was rewarded later in the year by the victory of Walter "Dee" Huddleston, Ford's campaign chair in his recent gubernatorial campaign and Senate majority floor leader from Elizabethtown, over former Republican governor Louie B. Nunn for the open US Senate seat created by the retirement of Republican John Sherman Cooper. This marked the first time since 1956 that Kentucky elected a Democrat for the US Senate. Huddleston made effective use of Nunn's nickel to encourage voter distrust. Although the election was relatively close, it was nevertheless noteworthy that Huddleston overcame the reelection landslide of GOP president Richard M. Nixon's over liberal Democrat George McGovern. Nixon, who had trailed Humphrey in western Kentucky four years earlier, now swept the First Congressional District by approximately 36,000 votes, but Huddleston won his Senate race there by 28,000. Liberal Democratic presidential campaigns from this point forward were unlikely to prevail in the Gibraltar of Kentucky Democracy.[25]

Ford's performance in the General Assembly's regular session in 1974 was also impressive, especially considering that Kentucky governors were still limited to one term at the time. Ford's election success in 1971 was followed by additional Democratic gains in the legislature. State financial coffers were in good shape in some part due to federal revenue sharing and greater demand for Kentucky coal due to the 1973 oil embargo imposed by Middle Eastern oil countries and related to the Israeli–Arab conflict. He was surrounded by a seasoned legislative leadership with a strong western Kentucky contingent as Julian Carroll, William Sullivan, and Billy Ray Paxton returned to the positions they had held in 1972 and as Paducahan Tom Garrett replaced Huddleston as Senate majority leader. A large gap in Ford's leadership team came with the departure of J. R. Miller, who was caught up in a federal probe that alleged he had taken kickbacks on state contracts, which forced him to resign as party chair.[26]

Ford's budget faced little opposition in the 1974 session. The major challenge Ford faced in the session arose when mountain lawmakers disrupted what had been a smooth session by attempting to direct a significant portion of coal severance revenues to coal-producing counties, including those in western Kentucky. Ford's legislative team was caught unawares by an amendment on the House floor that would have given the coal counties $43 million, half of the severance taxes in the Ford budget. After a spirited debate, the amendment was first approved, but it was then quickly reversed by administration forces, creating significant displeasure among the amendment's supporters, which they directed at the governor. Ford recognized this development as a threat to his plans to run for the US Senate and reached a consensus with coal county lawmakers based on the mountain caucus' plan to award coal counties a share of coal severance revenues above those projected in the state budget based on the value of their coal production. Coal severance was a welcome shot in the arm to many western Kentucky coal counties; Muhlenberg County, at that time the largest coal-producing county in the nation, was awarded approximately $867,000, and the $401,000 that Hopkins County received was slightly less than one-fourth of its entire budget. The money came through the state Coal-Producing County Development Fund, which was used over the years for a variety of economic-development projects, such as industrial parks, which the coal counties jealously guarded against intrusions from other regions. In the end, western Kentucky lawmakers were generally satisfied by Ford's support for important local projects, such as $3 million for a new vo-tech campus adjacent to Paducah Community College to replace the West Kentucky Vocational School, the underfunded black school established during Happy Chandler's first administration, and $1.6 million for a new Owensboro vo-tech school.[27]

For months, there had been great conjecture over whom the Democrats would run in the US Senate race against first-term GOP incumbent Marlow Cook in 1974. Some thought Ned Breathitt had the inside track, but eventually the choices were reduced to Wendell Ford and Julian Carroll. The two had never forged a warm working relationship, and J. R. Miller and Ford were not eager to anoint the lieutenant governor as Ford's successor in the governor's mansion. When Ford pressed Carroll to run for the Senate, Carroll told national Democratic Party leaders that there would be no incentive for the governor to support a Carroll candidacy, but Carroll would have strong reasons to support Ford in a Senate race because Carroll would then have an almost unassailable advantage in the 1975 governor's race in 1975. Carroll won the day, and Ford announced his candidacy for the Senate seat immediately after the 1974 legislative session.[28]

The Senate campaign proved to be a one-sided affair as Ford defeated Cook by a wide margin. Back in Owensboro after announcing, Ford made it clear that he intended to attack his opponent for his record of supporting Nixon at a time when the president's popularity was low because of the Watergate scandal. In addition, Ford sensed that Cook had failed to maintain a strong relationship with voters back home. In the primary, notable for young Carroll Hubbard's defeat of incumbent

Democratic congressman Frank Stubblefield for the First Congressional District, Ford rolled over his primary opponent. At the August Fancy Farm Picnic (that year for the first time, the political speeches were not held in the shade of the oak tree, which had been struck by lightning a week before the picnic), Ford charged that his opponent may have represented Washington in Kentucky, but Ford would "represent Kentucky in Washington." Ford lampooned Cook by holding a loaf of bread and saying that with the doubling of the federal gasoline tax, "this loaf of bread made with American wheat costs more in Paducah than the same loaf of bread costs in Communist Moscow." Both men attempted to tar the other with his party's political scandals, but the Watergate scandal and President Gerald Ford's controversial pardon of Nixon in the middle of the campaign had a more telling impact on Cook than the scandal associated with J. R. Miller on Ford. Party unity and organization undergirded the Ford campaign. Julian Carroll, out of self-interest, told an enthusiastic Paducah crowd days before the election that his name was on the ballot—"it is spelled F-O-R-D." Ford followed, taking off on Carroll's speaking style that one political reporter likened to a "fundamentalist preacher in the heat of a revival service" and joking that "I just go around and take up the collection." Ford defeated Cook by more than 70,000 votes statewide and trounced the incumbent in western Kentucky by a two-to-one margin, giving him more than half of his victory margin. Julian Carroll became, at long last, the first governor from the Jackson Purchase on December 28, 1974, as Senator Cook left office early to give Ford an important advantage in senatorial seniority.[29]

Ford's initial hesitation to run for the Senate did not predict a long Washington career, but he held onto his Senate seat until he retired, after four terms, in 1999. Several times over that period, he considered returning to the governor's mansion. However, his influence in Washington increased when he became majority whip in 1990. His political career was closely tied to efforts aimed at sustaining several legacy components of the western Kentucky economy, which were in decline in the last quarter of the twentieth century. Ford, who was a heavy smoker, believed that tobacco use was good for the Kentucky economy; in a speech to the tobacco exporters in 1980, he, perhaps humorously, told his audience to "smoke all you can and drink all you can because that helps our economy." As lieutenant governor in the late 1960s, he had supported a half-penny tax increase per pack of cigarettes to fund tobacco research at the University of Kentucky, which raised more than $3 million annually. At the annual meeting of the Burley and Dark Tobacco Association in 1973, Ford touted his efforts in development of the "reference cigarette," which he considered a step toward the creation of a "safe cigarette" so that "someday it will be possible to produce a cigarette that will not be labeled 'dangerous to your health.'" The quest proved futile despite the significant federal funding that Ford helped direct to the University of Kentucky for safe-cigarette research, which US surgeon general C. Everett Koop criticized during a speech in Lexington in 1990 by stating emphatically that "there has never been and never will be a safe cigarette."[30]

In western Kentucky, not only was tobacco grown for the cigarette market, but the dark tobacco was grown widely in the Jackson Purchase for chewing and dipping. Ford should have also told audiences to chew and dip all the tobacco they could because the region, especially the Jackson Purchase and Todd, Christian, Trigg, Simpson, Logan, Hopkins, Caldwell, Lyon, Livingston Counties, were part of the Black Patch, where dark tobacco (which was one-third of the cash value of Kentucky's tobacco crop in 2015) was grown and processed for "smokeless tobacco products."[31]

The health warnings against dark tobacco came later than those directed at other varieties of tobacco, including burley, used for producing cigarettes. A spokesperson for the Western Dark-Fired Tobacco Growers' Association saw much to praise about the crop in 1968, with its brisk foreign exports making up for a decade of disappointing sales as domestic cigarette makers looked to produce milder cigarettes and thus turned away from using dark tobacco. But by the mid-1980s research made a connection between chewing tobacco and oral cancer that brought dark tobacco, by that time a $40 million crop annually involving 20,000 farmers in western Kentucky, under the scrutiny of federal regulators. In 1986, the federal government imposed a tax of twenty-four cents per pound on manufacturers for snuff and a tax of eight cents per pound for chewing tobacco. Murray's Will Clark, head of the Western Dark-Fired Tobacco Growers' Association complained that this punitive tax "may have legislated some farmers out of business." The tax was followed in 1987 by quotas from the US Department of Agriculture that reduced dark-fired tobacco sales by 40 percent and air-cured tobacco sales by 30 percent, a move that Senator Ford criticized as an attempt to use a "meat ax" to solve problems associated with dark tobacco. The industry escaped its most serious threat during President Bill Clinton's administration when those working to develop his expansive health-care program floated the idea of draconian tax increases of $12.86 per pound for snuff and $4.14 per pound for chewing tobacco. This proposal brought a determined response from western Kentucky dark-tobacco growers, who went to Washington with the message that the tax would kill sales on snuff and chewing tobacco. By 1994, industry lobbyists welcomed a new, GOP-controlled Congress that would be more receptive to the perspective of tobacco growers, in contrast to the "neo-prohibitionists" responsible for the attack on the tobacco industry.[32]

By the turn of the century, as Ann Ferrell notes in *Burley: Kentucky Tobacco in a New Century* (2013), tobacco was losing its preeminent status in Kentucky's agriculture, becoming increasingly a "stigmatized crop." Although tobacco remained an important part of the western Kentucky agriculture scene, other crops such as corn, soybeans, and wheat increased in importance. The region was becoming the state's center of poultry, hog, and pig production, not simply for consumption by farm families as in the past but in large-scale, commercial operations that demanded significant cash investment (for example, an estimated $100,000 for each building holding 30,000 chickens), which often came from corporations that contracted for the commodity. These facilities, raising concerns over stench and pollution in a state with few industry regulations, added tensions between neighbors in rural areas, such as those that developed in Hickman County over proposed large-scale hog farms in the 1990s.[33]

Ford also fought to save the coal industry in Kentucky through what proved a disappointing quest for "clean coal technology" at a time when the environmental battle to reduce dependence on fossil fuels and the effects from acid rain was gearing up. In this contest, western Kentucky, with its high-sulfur coal, was especially vulnerable. The pessimism that settled over the Western Kentucky Coal Field was voiced in 1980 by J. A. Frost, a spokesman for the Western Coal Operators Association, who said that "if we can hold our own—or show a slight improvement—we'll be lucky." Even more pessimistically, Tommy Gaston, director of the regional chapter of the UMWA in Madisonville, said that prospects for improved production several years distant did not offset the fact that "people [miners] can starve to death in that length of time."[34]

Long-term prosperity of the coal industry at the time counted on enactment of reasonable federal clean-air regulations and implementation of steps to lower the amount of sulfur content in western Kentucky coal. These steps included use of expensive "scrubbers" for coal-fired plants after the coal is burned and development of new synthetic-coal techniques to convert the mineral to a cleaner-burning form of energy. Scrubbing coal used existing but costly technology. The TVA invested more than $1 billion on scrubbing technology in Kentucky, including an estimated $350 million (in addition to $150 million for coal-washing facilities) for scrubbers at the Paradise Steam Plant in Muhlenberg County to settle a lawsuit against it in the late 1970s. The 440-megawatt D. B. Wilson plant, constructed by Big Rivers Corporation in the early 1980s near Matanzas, a small Ohio County community west of Hartford, included scrubbers costing more than $150 million for use in the burning of 1.5 million tons of western Kentucky coal annually.[35]

Wendell Ford was an advocate for development of synthetic coal starting when as governor he pumped more than $50 million into research on liquefaction and gasification of coal. Once in the US Senate, he continued those efforts, eventually announcing plans for a demonstration public–private synthetic-coal fuel facility to be located near Newman, northwest of Owensboro in Daviess County. The cost of the facility, scheduled to be completed in 1982 with a workforce of 2,000, grew from $500 million to $4.5 billion in the commercialization stage. Enthusiasm for the project was high in the region in the project's early days, when a spokesman for the Western Kentucky Coal Operators Association confidently predicted that the question was not whether there was a future for synthetic-coal facilities in the region but rather when "we'll have them." Synthetic coal was a good fit for the mood in Washington following the energy volatility caused by the oil boycott initiated by the Arab oil-producing states, but it ran into difficulties during the Ronald Reagan years in the president's eagerness to eliminate questionable projects. Senator Wendell Ford managed to keep funding for synthetic coal in Reagan's first budget despite a determined floor fight mounted against it by Senator William Proxmire from Wisconsin. In the end, the push for synthetic coal collapsed, and despite years of research and planning, the private-sector interests behind the Newman site closed shop in 1984.[36]

The 1980s were a difficult time for mining in the Western Kentucky Coal Field. Mining employment was halved from 10,535 to 5,586; Muhlenberg and Ohio Counties lost approximately 2,000 mining jobs each. With the accompanying job losses to mine-service businesses and retail establishments, the unemployment rate jumped from approximately 3 percent to more than 10 percent in mining counties. The impact on the UMWA in the region was dramatic as its active membership was reduced from a high of more than 9,000 to 2,300 and the number of union mines was reduced from 75 to 22. The closing of the large River Queen surface mine in Muhlenberg County reduced the number of mines operated by the Peabody Coal Company from eleven in 1986 to five in 1991. Union miners dissatisfied with the direction their union was headed took over the local district office in December 1989 by defeating the candidate chosen by the former local union president. This action would not stop the long slump in the area mines, though, and the precipitate loss in union mines that the area would experience in coming years. Bad news for the UMWA continued. A major effort to unionize Pyro mines, the largest nonunion operator in the Western Kentucky Coal Field with more than 900 miners—including those at the William Station mine near Wheatcroft in Webster County, where 10 miners were killed in September 1989 due to operator negligence—was defeated in December 1990 by a close vote. Joe Holland, the regional UMWA president, charged that the company's campaign against unionization was marked by "fear and intimidation." Competition from cheaper, cleaner natural gas in later years drove TVA to convert its mammoth coal-fired Paradise Steam Plant in Muhlenberg County to natural gas. By 2015, there would not be one union mine in the Western Kentucky Coal Field.[37]

When Wendell Ford resigned as governor in late December 1974 to take his US Senate seat, Julian Carroll became the first governor from the far western Jackson Purchase. With five months to the primary,

Carroll organized a campaign to win the office at the polls, an achievement that had evaded Alben Barkley, Harry Lee Waterfield three times, and Henry Ward. Carroll's father was a tenant farmer and later a mechanic from Maxon Junction (later known as West Paducah), which had only a post office and one store when Carroll was a child. His interest in politics was whetted in 1949 when he was elected governor at Boys State, an event that brought high school students from across Kentucky to participate in a mock legislature. Carroll's father later reported that young Julian, after sitting in the real governor's chair, vowed, "I'll come back sometime and sit here in this chair for four years." Carroll stayed near home for his first two years of college at Paducah Junior College before transferring to the University of Kentucky for his bachelor's and law degrees. After a stint in the service as a military attorney, Carroll returned to Paducah to begin his law practice. He gained public recognition for his lead role in bringing public power to the city in 1960. That propelled him into the Kentucky House in 1961, where he served two terms as Speaker during the Nunn administration.[38]

Carroll was fortunate in many regards as he prepared for what was almost a certain campaign for a full term as governor. His independence from Ford the past three years had allowed him to sidestep thorny matters the former governor had faced, but there were some potential pitfalls related to promises Ford had made. They included the sale of Ben Hawes Park and golf course in Owensboro to the state as a state park. Included in a package of projects for his hometown, this matter was announced days before Ford left office. Ford had discussed the park with Carroll, though, who followed through with the plans early in 1975.[39]

Carroll called on Bill Cox, the Madisonville one-term House member whose legislative career was cut short after he voted for Nunn's nickel, to take charge of his primary campaign. Despite the advantages Carroll derived from his incumbency, some Democrats considered running against him. John Y. Brown Jr., the wealthy son of the longtime politician John J. Brown Sr., a native of Union County, briefly considered entering the race before deciding instead to take a position in the Carroll administration. Carroll defeated his principal opponent, Jefferson County judge Todd Hollenbach, in the Democratic primary, which he carried in a landslide fueled by a more than 50,000-vote bulge in the First Congressional District. He exclaimed, "I wanted to pull a lot of votes from back home just to show the rest of the state how powerful the Democrats are from Western Kentucky." Carroll ran unslated; Thelma Stovall, who had held a series of statewide offices, won the Democratic race for lieutenant governor in a crowded field, although she ran third in western Kentucky, which favored native son William Sullivan from Henderson. Sullivan had strong regional backing from Harry Lee Waterfield, Ned Breathitt, and J. R. Miller but finished third in the primary overall.[40]

The fall campaign opened with the traditional Fancy Farm Picnic, a picnic long remembered for when former extreme segregationist George Wallace, an expected candidate in the presidential campaign in 1976, was interrupted by a loud pop from a photographer's flash, which startled the candidate and reminded the crowd that he had been crippled by an assassin's bullet several years earlier. Carroll's GOP challenger, Robert Gable, a central Kentucky coal operator and tourism cabinet secretary during the Nunn administration, attacked the governor for failing to take a stand on the major issues during the campaign. Carroll drew approval from the audience when he linked Gable, who "came to Kentucky to manage the fortune of his family," to the eastern elites whom Wallace had just attacked. The campaign was a particularly negative affair in which Gable was a definite underdog. He did himself no favor during the televised debate before the November election by ignoring debate rules and ringing a "truth bell" each time Gable felt Carroll misled listeners. This ploy did not enhance his image as a potential governor, nor did his strident antibusing stance on desegregation of Jefferson County schools win over voters. For his part, Carroll continued to attack his opponent's profile as a wealthy non-Kentuckian out of touch with the local voters' experience. He also hit his opponent hard for failing to account for $100,000 in campaign funds from the Nixon campaign in 1968. Carroll ended his canvass with the traditional "Barkley tour" of the First Congressional District, accompanied by Senator Wendell Ford, Congressman Carroll Hubbard, and most of the Democratic ticket. He won the First District by 60,000 votes, taking even traditionally Republican Crittenden and Ohio Counties (although not Butler County) on the way to a landslide that approached 180,000 votes. Carroll's popularity helped the entire Democratic ticket, including Thelma Stovall, the first woman elected as lieutenant governor, and George

Atkins, the young mayor from Hopkinsville who was elected state auditor, which gave western Kentucky its second constitutional officer.[41]

Support for "legislative independence"—championed during the 1940s when Harry Lee Waterfield and Earle Clements worked to create the Legislative Research Commission, a professional staff organization capable of supporting lawmakers in their policy development and oversight of state government—was gradually taking shape. Carroll had staked his claim to legislative independence as Speaker during the Nunn administration with the legislative reforms in 1968 that created a parallel committee structure in both chambers based on a jurisdictional basis that reduced the powers of the governor and legislative leadership and encouraged meetings when the General Assembly was not in session. These reforms had taken place during a Republican administration, but Governor Wendell Ford had demonstrated little interest in legislative independence. Governor Carroll's actions in the weeks after the November election in 1975 confused lawmakers because he seemed to take a hands-off approach on legislative leadership races, even as some of his closest political allies, notably Sonny Hunt, the Democratic Party chair, were active in trying to determine the outcome of those races. Before the presession Democratic Party meeting at Kentucky Dam Village, where legislative leaders would be decided, several western Kentucky House members were clearly upset that Carroll's choice for House Speaker remained up in the air. One member exploded off the record, "I cannot believe it! I cannot believe the way this thing has been handled!" By the end of the presession conference, observers, such as Don Mills, communications director for Governor Breathitt from Hickman County and now the editor of the *Lexington Herald*, concluded that "all that talk about an 'independent' legislature is just so much talk" because lawmakers had demonstrated that selected legislators were like "sheep" who waited until "the 'word' came down" from the governor. When the word did come down, western Kentuckians held a strong position in the legislative leadership, with Wingo's Lloyd Clapp as House Speaker pro tempore, Paducahan Tom Garrett back for a second term as Senate majority leader, and Senator Pat McCuiston from Pembroke taking the newly created post of assistant president pro tempore.[42]

Those who still had hopes that the political winds favored legislative independence saw them crushed early in the session with the sound defeat of the alternative legislative budget prepared by the Legislative Research Commission under the direction of Representative Joe Clarke, chair of the House Appropriations and Revenue Committee, and with the disciplining of several members who supported Clarke (including Steve Beshear, an aspiring young Democratic House member from Lexington who had grown up in Dawson Springs in Hopkins County and would become governor in the twenty-first century). Governor Carroll preferred the approach of Owensboran Delbert Murphy, the Senate budget chair, who believed "it is not proper for the legislature to draft its own budget bill." By the end of the session, a disappointed Clarke characterized the General Assembly as "acquiescent." Carroll's "hands-on" management of legislative affairs was not restricted to the budget. To assist him, Bill Cox was brought onto the governor's staff as the legislative liaison shortly after the start of the legislative session and was one of the most influential of the governor's inner circle in all aspects of legislative affairs in the 1976 session. Carroll was meticulous in letting lawmakers, some of whom called him "Emperor Julian," know his positions on legislation. One eastern Kentucky senator colorfully captured the level of legislative control exerted by the Carroll team: "My gawd, a cockroach couldn't crawl across the Senate floor without an OK from the governor stamped on his back."[43]

The 1976 session was generally a success for the Carroll administration. One issue of great interest to western Kentucky that illustrated the governor's political skills was his call for changes in the coal severance tax. Carroll brokered amendments that gave coal counties considerable control over their portion of severance revenues, which were set to expire in July 1976 and had become a "political hot potato" that would need to be addressed before Carroll's budget could be passed. For the first month of the session, he kept the coal counties in suspense when he presented a budget in late February that was absent any provisions for the county allocations of severance revenues. Reaction from western Kentucky coal county politicians was quick, although more low key than the reaction from their colleagues in the mountain caucus. Area lawmakers felt pressure from local officials, who were insistent that the county allocations needed to be continued. The *Madisonville Messenger* exhorted that "the coal producing counties of Kentucky deserve [them] and should have [them]," and McLean County judge Wilbur T. Lee identified the critical need for improvements on the coal haul roads: "We need all the money we can get to repair the roads damaged by hauling coal over them." Eugene Doss, the Central City House member whose district included part of McLean County as well as Muhlenberg County, the largest beneficiary of the severance funds in the region, said of feedback from his district that "the people back home feel if we can't get the severance tax back we should fight the governor tooth and toenail and take the consequences." After intense negotiations, Carroll convinced lawmakers to raise the severance tax a half-penny and to give the state more control of severance taxes earmarked for coal counties so that they would be used more directly for economic development and road improvements. More road money for western Kentucky was directed to repairs on the coal haul roads. Outside of coal country, Louisville received assurances for completion of the Jefferson Expressway, and moneys were provided to fund the state's area-development districts. Coal operators, although not overjoyed by the severance tax increase, received significant help from the state with escalating workers' compensation claims. Doss, after reviewing the plan's impact on Muhlenberg County, asked, "How do you think a man who is getting $4,819,000 is going to react?" In the end, Carroll said, "I could have written [the bill] myself and just submitted it for passage," but "I let all sides have input and we came up with a satisfactory law."[44]

Western Kentuckians played a pivotal role in a controversial judicial-reform plan approved by voters in November 1975. Reformers, frustrated by the repeated failures to get voters to approve a constitutional convention to revise the existing state constitution of 1891, now concentrated on a sweeping revision of the court system. Under the existing system, the local police courts and justice-of-the-peace courts of western Kentucky, often presided over by nonattorneys and subsisting through traffic and other fines, had earned a bad reputation for the presence of speed traps eager to waylay travelers, such as those that existed on US 41 between Henderson and Hopkinsville at Hanson and Crofton. The complaints reached the American Automobile Association, which presented them to Governor Combs in the early 1960s, and he interceded in the matter.[45]

In 1974, during the Ford administration, with its emphasis on government reform, the Kentucky Citizens for Judicial Improvement sponsored a series of meetings that culminated with the drafting of a thorough revision of the judiciary in the commonwealth vs constitution. The reforms called for a unified judiciary, under a newly created Supreme Court. The existing police and county courts were to be eliminated in favor of state district and circuit courts and a new fourteen-judge court of Appeals to hear routine lower court appeals. The amendment was supported by the new chief justice of the Kentucky Court of Appeals, Earl T. Osborne from Benton, and by Governor Ford. With a federal grant, the group paid for an opinion poll, which convinced reformers to abandon support for a system in which judges would be appointed through a judicial-selection process, which risked defeat at the polls. The reform had strong backing from John Palmore, a Henderson justice on the Kentucky Court of Appeals who was instrumental in recruiting important Kentucky political figures, notably former lieutenant governor Wilson Wyatt, whose contributions were critical in the campaign to pass the reform at the polls. Nobody was more involved in seeing the reform become law than Morton Holbrook, a brilliant Harvard Law graduate and Owensboro attorney close to Wendell Ford, who drew the task of drafting the proposed legislation and would coordinate the activities of the various groups supporting the amendment after it passed the legislature.[46]

Two western Kentucky lawmakers were closely involved in the amendment's rocky passage during the 1974 session. Henderson's William Sullivan, Senate president pro tempore, was its author in the Senate. Court reform's progress through the General Assembly went smoothly enough until it was snagged in the House Elections and Constitutional Amendments Committee, chaired by Wingo Democrat Lloyd Clapp, who held it hostage to gather support for his own measure to rescind Kentucky's ratification of the Equal Rights Amendment (ERA). He believed, as the session neared adjournment, that he had an understanding that both measures would be approved, but after he provided the critical final vote needed for the passage of the court bill, which he did not particularly support, the committee adjourned without taking up the ERA measure. In the heat of the moment, Clapp succeeded in returning the court bill to committee.

Tempers soon cooled, and both bills were released to the floor, where the ERA rescission measure failed, and the court bill passed easily.[47]

Before voters had their say on the judicial amendment, there was considerable debate about it. There was anticipated opposition from local judges, many of whom were not attorneys and whose courts were to be eliminated. County judges, whose major duties were executive in nature, opposed the measure. Democratic candidate Julian Carroll and Republican candidate Robert Gable placed the issue outside the governor's race by jointly endorsing the reform. In western Kentucky, the two sides made their views public. In Logan County, Adairville city judge Arthur R. Blick, whose position was held by many city judges, opposed the reform, denying that justice was poorly served by nonattorneys close to the public and that "as the Courts, the Legislatures, the Executive Offices of our government are taken away from the people they govern, those in power tend to lose touch with the reality of the society they govern." County judges Mike Miller from Marshall County, Joe M. James from Simpson County, C. B. Embry from Ohio County, and James Fallin from Hancock toed the opposition line drawn by the Kentucky Association of County Judges. Fallin charged that taxpayers would be expected to pick up the tab for the courts currently funded by fines. Embry criticized reformers for failing to consult with county judges, who would have pinpointed the real judicial problems, which he said lay with the bottleneck at the Court of Appeals, and for ignoring the resulting revenue losses that cities and counties would incur under the new system.[48]

The reformers were active in their support of the measure in western Kentucky. William H. Gant, commonwealth attorney from Daviess County, told a local Lions Club gathering that the present system, with local trials held too often in meat markets or barbershops, degraded the state's justice administration and was driven by the demand for cash, which turned the judicial system into "cash register justice." John Palmore made several appearances to talk to lawyers in Bowling Green and Paducah about the efficiencies that passage of the proposition would render. Morton Holbrook, in addition to coordinating the reform campaign, also emphasized efficiency in an October opinion piece for the *Owensboro Messenger-Inquirer.* Attorneys from the First District Bar Association covering Ballard, Fulton, Hickman, and Carlisle Counties announced their support for the reform.[49]

As election day approached, reformers obtained polling data to suggest that passage seemed likely in urban areas. Opponents counted on a strong rural vote against court reform to overcome the urban vote. However, reformers eked out a narrow win by more than 1,700 votes in western Kentucky, perhaps aided by a popular amendment creating a homestead tax exemption for senior citizens and as the more urban McCracken, Christian, Henderson, Daviess, and Warren Counties, along with Calloway, Lyon, Muhlenberg, Ohio, Trigg, and Union Counties in the region, voted in favor of the reform.[50]

The 1960s ushered in new voices and new issues that would have a major repercussions at the turn of the century on western Kentucky politics; the first of these was the ERA, with very important impacts at the state and regional levels. The Kentucky General Assembly ratified the ERA, the nineteenth state to do so, at the urging of Governor Wendell Ford in a summer special session in 1972. The text of the ERA was rather simple in that it was meant to prevent the abridgement of rights on the basis of gender in laws passed by national and state governments, but opponents objected that federal courts would interpret it in ways that they would find objectionable. They gathered at the capitol voicing concerns that the ERA was contrary to the Bible and Communist inspired. In the House, two western Kentucky lawmakers, Ralph Graves from Bardwell and Nicholas Kafoglis from Bowling Green, were among the strongest voices in favor of the amendment. Graves, the chair of the House committee that considered the ERA, focused his debate on how the amendment would bring about gender equality under the law and how "it doesn't say men and women will use the same public toilets or end up in foxholes together." Along the same line, Kafoglis stated that "it won't change social relationships between men and women." Although the provision ultimately passed 56–31, it had to survive an immediate motion, supported by a number of western Kentucky lawmakers, that it be sent back to committee, but that motion failed 41–50. The Senate was deadlocked when the measure came up on the special session's final day, but Lieutenant Governor Carroll broke a tie vote on a motion to recommit the measure to committee (the motion would have failed in any case), and it was clear the ERA would pass despite western Kentuckians Carroll Hubbard, Delbert Murphy, and Ken Gibson voting with the opposition in a 20–18 vote.[51]

The historian Nancy Baker casts light on the efforts by anti-ERA forces to reverse the vote of 1972 in the regular sessions of the General Assembly in 1974, 1976, and 1978. Nationally, *rescission,* the term used to describe the reversal of state legislatures on the ERA, was the work of Phyllis Schlafly's organization STOP (Stop Taking Our Privileges) ERA. The organization had its first measure of success when Nebraska voted for rescission in 1973. A rescission movement soon developed in the commonwealth, with considerable strength in western Kentucky. However, as Baker suggests, the rescission effort in the commonwealth owed more to grassroots organizing in Kentucky than to the influence of Schlafly and STOP ERA. Much of the opposition's leadership and grassroots support came from western Kentucky, where it was centered in Mayfield in Graves County and Owensboro. Barbara Pagan of Owensboro, the head of Concerned Women of Kentucky, and Margaret Perkins of Mayfield joined hands with STOP ERA supporters from northern Kentucky to enlist others to lobby the General Assembly for rescission.[52]

Conservative Kentucky voters already had been aroused by what they perceived as an ultraliberal bent in the US Supreme Court under Chief Justice Earl Warren, including two rulings limiting prayer in school. They feared that the ERA, when subjected to "judge-made law," would threaten women's existing legal protections and would result, as Baker lists, in "radical change, including shoring up abortion rights; subjecting women to the military draft and combat; allowing husbands to shirk their bread-winning duties to their families; permitting women to disobey their husbands; establishing unisex restrooms; and defending homosexuals' right to marry, parent children, and teach in school." Local leaders made use of church directories to recruit women to the rescission movement. At a joint legislative hearing in July 1975, 600 advocates from both sides were present, divided evenly between the pro–ERA and anti-ERA forces. Also attending were Schlafly, opposing the ERA, and Lieutenant Governor Thelma Stovall and Katherine Peden, the former Democratic US Senate candidate from Hopkinsville, supporting the ERA. The rescission advocates were easily identified by their pink outfits, which came to be standard dress among them; one legislative staffer commented that he "had never seen so much pink polyester in my life." With anti-ERA Representative Lloyd Clapp, whose district was a hotbed for rescission, in the chair of the Legislative Committee on Elections and Constitutional Amendments, committee rules were changed to accommodate Schlafly, causing Peden, who referred to the anti-ERA national leader as "the trespasser from Illinois," to object that out-of-stater Schlafly was given extra time to speak during the two-hour hearing in which those asking to be recognized were limited to five minutes. Western Kentucky's influence in the anti-ERA contingent was clearly expressed, and several speakers from the region offered searing attacks that connected the ERA to rights for homosexual.[53]

When the rescission legislation came up in the 1976 session, western Kentucky lawmakers—Representatives Lloyd Clapp and Ward "Butch" Burnette from Fulton and Senators Richard Weisenberger from Mayfield and William Sullivan from Henderson, the former president pro tempore who had voted for the ERA in 1972—were in the forefront of the rescission effort. They scored a major success by passing a rescission measure authored by Democrats Burnette, Kenneth Imes of Murray, and Johnny Boatwright from McCracken County with a 57–40 margin, but the measure's prospects in the Senate were bleak because the Senate committee to which it was assigned had a pro-ERA majority. Instead, Sullivan, as the session's conclusion loomed, shucked an unrelated House resolution and inserted instead a provision that would allow voters to determine the fate of ERA at the polls. This questionable maneuver was approved by the Senate, but its future would be determined by the House, which required a majority vote to suspend rules before the resolution could pass. The earlier House vote gave rescission forces reason for optimism. But as time ran out in the session, the vote to suspend rules fell two votes short of the necessary majority.[54]

For the pink ladies, the 1978 session proved that the third time is the charm, even though the battle once more took the entire session. Momentum and organization were on the side of the rescission forces, which also found allies among those lobbying Frankfort in opposition to abortion, which had been made legal by the Supreme Court's *Roe v. Wade* (410 US 113) decision in 1973. The anti-ERA leadership first had to weather a storm resulting from a release sent to lawmakers in mid-February containing objectionable drawings of lesbians reportedly obtained from a recent national ERA meeting, which should have been withheld under normal legislative checks. Leaders of the pink ladies initially said that the material was the work of their opposition aimed at discrediting the rescissionists. However, when the House appointed a committee, with Paducah representative Dolly McNutt as chair, to investigate the matter, the committee traced the source to an anti-ERA leader from northern Kentucky. But the incident did not deter the anti-ERA supporters from inserting lesbianism and abortion into the ERA debate; a Mayfield supporter of rescission was censured for her comments along these lines to a school group visiting the House chamber. Nevertheless, rescission forces were determined to meet all challenges. When Pat McCuiston, a Pembroke senator, failed to vote with the anti-ERA supporters (which he had in the past), western Kentucky women, believing that Governor Carroll had influenced McCuiston, button-holed the senator and warned him that there would be political conse-quences if he did not support them. They also warned Carroll that they would work against his candidate in the 1979 gubernatorial race if he worked to defeat the rescission effort.[55]

Lieutenant Governor Thelma Stovall was still determined to do all that she could to defeat rescission. As in the previous session, the rescis-sion measure was bottled up in a committee controlled by pro-ERA senators. Several efforts to discharge the measure failed by close floor votes, and the Senate once more, led by Richard Weisenberger from Mayfield, shucked an unrelated House resolution to put the rescission language in it. Stovall ruled against this gamut several times but was overruled 19–17 before the measure was approved 23–15, with Tom Garrett from Paducah the lone western Kentucky senator opposed. The last hurdle was the Kentucky House, where approval was required on the Senate action. This time, the anti-ERA lawmakers were in the sad-dle. For reasons that remain unclear, pro-ERA Speaker Bill Kenton, who after the vote termed it a "tragedy," turned his gavel over to anti-ERA Speaker pro tempore Lloyd Clapp during three hours of heated debate before a gallery packed with women on both sides of the issue. As in the Senate, western Kentucky House members—with the excep-tion of Dolly McNutt, who said after the vote that "the commonwealth of Kentucky sends forth the word that the commonwealth of Kentucky no longer considers its women equal"—voted with the majority for a convincing 61–28 vote in favor of rescission, making Kentucky one of five states that have rescinded ratification of the ERA. Barbara Pagan, the Owensboro rescission leader, later recalled how she and others saw in the RESCISSION movement a moment in time that awakened them to a host of other issues that needed to be addressed, so "we've continued and will continue, until our last breath."[56]

The consensus story of legislative independence in Kentucky assigns too much weight to the role of Governor John Y. Brown Jr. after his election in 1979. His relative indifference to legislative organization, so this story goes, included taking a hands-off approach to organizing the General Assembly in the 1980 regular session and allowing lawmakers a great deal of autonomy in their proceedings, but this story is overly simplistic and ignores events during Governor Carroll's term, when legislative independence was kept alive principally by a small group of senators who came to be known as the "Black Sheep Squadron." In fact, legislators effectively won legislative independence over the course of the 1979 special session, which they were then able to sustain as a result of Brown's handling of legislative affairs once in office.[57]

The state legislative races in 1977 left Democrats with strong majorities, and the demand for legislative independence, fed by Governor Carroll's high degree of control over the work of the General Assembly, increased in 1978. House Speaker Bill Kenton won legislative approval for the "Kenton Amendment," which, after voters approved it in November 1979, moved legislative elections to even years so that lawmakers would run separately from governors and provided for brief organizational sessions, which then permitted interim committees to meet the remainder of the year before regular sessions. The *Owensboro Messenger-Inquirer* urged voters to approve the change in order to "give the legislature more control over the state budget and over the governor." There was no vigorous campaign for the amendment, but voters did approve it, along with another amendment allowing the General Assembly to place as many as four constitutional questions on general election ballots. Voters in eleven western Kentucky voters disapproved of the amendment, but it won in the region by nearly 7,000 votes as it passed easily statewide. The Kenton Amendment put a stop to the traditional presession conference at Kentucky Dam Village State Resort Park, which was, along with the Fancy Farm Picnic, one of two important events that brought politicians and lobbyists from all parts of the commonwealth to western Kentucky.[58]

By late 1978, Governor Carroll's political standing was weakened by allegations of overspending on personal-services contracts in state government, seemingly confirmed by state auditor George Atkins from Hopkinsville, who had his eye on the gubernatorial race in 1979. Lieutenant Governor Thelma Stovall, already committed to running for governor, had gained politically in many circles for her stand in favor of the ERA and demonstrated a considerable degree of independence from the governor during the 1978 session by voicing her support for legislation to limit taxes. In the legislature, after more than a dozen senators, behind John Berry's leadership, challenged Carroll for two leadership positions, including Pembroke senator Pat McCuiston's post as assistant president pro tempore, and others called for improved office space, more legislative staff, and a shared responsibility for setting revenue estimates, the governor declared at the presession meeting at Kentucky Dam Village that legislative independence had to be earned, which in his mind it had not. Supporters for independence had limited tangible success during the 1978 regular session, but the Black Sheep Squadron in the Senate, united in their support for legislative independence, gained in support throughout the year and was ready to play a major role in the December special session called by Stovall to enact tax cuts, perhaps hoping that lightning would strike once more, just as Happy Chandler's special session helped propel him into the governor's mansion in 1935.[59]

Governor Carroll, who by this time was known to be under FBI investigation, considered her action irresponsible, refused to take control of matters and created considerable confusion within the executive branch during the session's course. The Black Sheep Squadron's numbers had expanded to a majority of Senate Democrats, including western Kentuckians William Sullivan, Richard Weisenberger, and Ken Gibson. To negate the influence of Governor Carroll during the session, the Black Sheep Squadron members, working with Senate president pro tempore Joe Prather, a disgruntled gubernatorial candidate who resented Carroll's support of Terry McBrayer's gubernatorial bid, agreed to use the "committee of the whole," essentially the full Senate, with Senator Berry as chair, to develop legislation. On the other side, the House Democratic leadership created a policy committee to make recommendations to the Democratic caucus. Confusion reigned as lawmakers were now left to their own devices. Several Paducah-area lawmakers, including Senate majority leader Tom

Garrett, were eager simply to adjourn after the first week of confusion. Nevertheless, the experience gained during the special session with legislative independence, marked by the passage of a bill putting a lid on local property tax increases proved valuable and it established the legislative independence principle going forward.[60]

Governor Carroll's term in office represented the high-water mark of western Kentucky influence in twentieth-century commonwealth politics as he was the last of the seven governors from the Gibraltar of Kentucky Democracy since 1931. Carroll's tenure ended in scandal involving FBI probes into corrupt activities in his administration, conviction of his former Democratic Party state chairman, and Carroll invoking his Fifth Amendment protection against self-incrimination before a federal grand jury in June 1982. Terry McBrayer, well known to western Kentuckians for his industrial recruitment efforts as commerce secretary during the Carroll administration, ran as Carroll's gubernatorial candidate in the Democratic primary in 1979, only to finish a disappointing third. It was a difficult primary race for western Kentucky candidates statewide, as state auditor George Atkins of Hopkinsville and Ralph Ed Graves of Bardwell withdrew from the gubernatorial campaign in support of eventual winner John Y. Brown Jr. Carroll Hubbard, the First District congressman from Mayfield, finished a distant fourth, but he hurt McBrayer's chances in western Kentucky by winning Ballard, Carlisle, Fulton, Graves, Hickman, and Marshall Counties. Down the stretch, Governor Carroll singled out Hubbard for criticism during the campaign: "I've not heard the first remark yet by Carroll Hubbard about how he is going to make things better."[61]

Madisonville's Bill Cox, Carroll's campaign manager in 1975 and top aide in the legislative session of 1976 and once thought to be the frontrunner for the post of lieutenant governor, faltered at the finish line as allegations made against him by one of his opponents linked him to the political scandal in the governor's office and the presence of Benton native Richard Lewis on the ballot took crucial votes from Cox in western Kentucky—both of which were too much to overcome. While Cox sued his accuser for slander, Martha Layne Collins edged him out by a slim 5,000 votes. He polled strong in western Kentucky, where Collins took away wins only in Ballard, Daviess, Graves, Hancock, Logan, and

Union Counties. Bright spots for western Kentucky politicians who later won in the general election were Crittenden County's Alben Barkley II, grandson of the legendary late US senator and vice president from Paducah, who parlayed name recognition to win his race for agriculture commissioner, and Steve Beshear, the Dawson Spring native who was the Democratic Party's nominee for attorney general.[62]

The ultimate victor in the gubernatorial primary and general elections of 1979 was John Y. Brown Jr., the flashy Kentucky Fried Chicken millionaire son of the veteran Democratic campaigner from Sturgis in Union County. Brown and his wife, former Miss America Phyllis George, took the state by storm in a dazzling eight-week campaign to win the nomination with 28 percent of the vote. In the general election, he turned aside personal attacks by his GOP opponent, former governor Louie B. Nunn, to win in a landslide, with a strong showing in western Kentucky, and carried the rest of the Democratic statewide slate with him, including Barkley and Beshear. Hopkins County Democratic Party chair Eddie Ballard sensed that many voters remembered Nunn's broken tax promises from the gubernatorial race of 1967 and disliked his negative race against Brown. Brown's election ushered in what the longtime Kentucky political observer Al Smith calls "the era of rich amateurs," which also included governors Wallace Wilkinson, Brereton Jones, and Paul Patton, who could dispense with the traditional reliance on the courthouse rings and instead used large campaign chests and media blitzes that helped the Democrats hold on to the governor's mansion until 2003.[63]

In 1980, Kentucky Democrats faced a difficult test in the presidential election featuring incumbent Jimmy Carter and conservative former film star and two-term governor of California Ronald Reagan. Carter, with young Dale Sights from Robards, a small community in Henderson County, as his campaign manager, had won Kentucky in 1976 by approximately 84,000 votes, a majority of them coming from western Kentucky, against President Gerald Ford, who had carried the legacy of the Watergate scandal and Nixon pardon. However, Carter's prospects for a second term were hurt by (1) the shape of the national economy, staggered by the Arab oil producers' boycott of the United States, which the historian William E. Leuchtenburg writes resulted in "double-digit inflation, mounting unemployment, a greatly increased tax burden, and a decline in real wages"; and (2) public criticism of Carter's handling of the hostage crisis in Iran. Kentuckians responded to Reagan's promise of "Morning in America" with its mixture of optimism and conservatism. Dale Sights, Carter's Kentucky liaison, returned as campaign chair in the reelection campaign but was virtually the only sign of the president's campaign in Logan County, where he barely won. Reagan's Kentucky campaign chair, Lawrence "Larry" Forgy, who was raised Republican in the northern Logan community of Lewisburg and with Governor Nunn's administration had entered Kentucky politics as a young man, called Reagan's national landslide in the Electoral College, including a narrow victory in Kentucky, "a mandate, a positive response to what this man has been saying throughout the country." Reagan's performance in the Jackson Purchase, which he lost by slightly less than 18,000 votes, was a "Reagan victory" compared to the drubbing President Ford took in 1976. The McCracken County Republican campaign chair, Mark Whitlow, suggested that "more Democrats in McCracken County and all of western Kentucky are realizing that Republican candidates and the Republican platform more closely represent their own ideals and philosophy." Carter still won a majority of the region's counties, with the exception of traditionally Republican Crittenden, Butler, and Ohio Counties as well as Warren and Christian Counties, but Reagan cut his opponent's margins in other counties, such as Graves County in the Jackson Purchase, where Carter's margins went from 5,700 in 1976 to less than 500 in 1980, and he only squeaked by in Daviess County.[64]

The "Reagan Democrats" who aided Reagan in 1980 stayed with him in his huge landslide win in the state in 1984 against liberal Democrat Walter Mondale, whose chances of winning in the commonwealth, according to Senator Wendell Ford, were hurt by supporting a tax increase. Larry Forgy, back to manage Reagan's Kentucky campaign, told the audience at the Fancy Farm Picnic that the president was with them on hot-button moral issues such as school prayer, abortion, and homosexuality. Knowing that potential Republican voters remained registered Democrats, he echoed Reagan's explanation for why he changed party years earlier: "I'm not asking you to leave your party. Your party has left you." Reagan's overall performance in western Kentucky was impressive as he surged to a 43,000-vote majority, losing only Ballard and Marshall Counties in the Jackson Purchase, along with Lyon, Livingston,

Union, Webster, and Muhlenberg farther east. In taking the Gibraltar of Kentucky Democracy, Reagan won statewide by a landslide exceeding 280,000 votes.[65]

His landslide helped carry Jefferson County judge-executive Mitch McConnell's upset of two-term incumbent US senator Democrat Walter Huddleston by fewer than 5,000 votes statewide. Though the Gibraltar of Kentucky Democracy failed the Democratic Party in the presidential race, Huddleston took it by more than 43,000 votes, losing there in only traditionally Republican Crittenden, Butler, and Ohio Counties, but McConnell demonstrated some strength by taking urban Christian and Warren Counties as well as Wendell Ford's home Daviess County. He was a beneficiary of voters' increasing dissatisfaction with what they perceived as the Democratic Party's liberal stance on abortion, homosexuality, guns, and prayer in schools, issues associated with the Moral Majority, the political arm of the evangelical Christians. The latter's strong voice in the South resonated with western Kentucky voters, who were, McConnell thought, "closer to the national Republican Party than [to] the national Democratic Party" and "ripe" for his message. Senator McConnell would take much credit later, possibly too much, for GOP gains in the region. Certainly, Ronald Reagan deserves his share of the credit in paving the way for additional Republican victories in the next decade.[66]

Both political parties now had to fight in western Kentucky for votes. Democrats continued to dominate in gubernatorial and state legislative races. In a region where many voters held conservative religious convictions, Republicans increasingly appealed to voters on social issues such as abortion and homosexuality as well as support for gun rights. Democratic politicians, many of whom disagreed with the national Democratic Party's liberal stance on these issues, struggled against the surging number of western Kentucky voters who came to believe that it was not possible to be a Christian and a Democrat.

In the 1983 Democratic gubernatorial primary, western Kentucky split its vote, with Grady Stumbo coming away with the most votes. The statewide winner, Martha Layne Collins finished third in western Kentucky, winning only Fulton, Calloway, and Hickman Counties, but the region rallied behind her in November, with the exception of Butler County, against GOP candidate Jim Bunning, a former Major League pitcher. Voters also approved Dawson Springs's Steve Beshear for lieutenant governor. In 1987, western Kentucky voters bet on Wallace Wilkinson as the winning ticket, and he catapulted over two more seasoned western Kentucky politicians, Steve Beshear and former governor Julian Carroll, by proposing a state lottery. Carroll's plummeting status among Kentucky Democrats after 1975, when he had won 118 counties and lost only 2, was demonstrated clearly when his only wins in this race came from McCracken and Ballard Counties. Wilkinson easily defeated Republican John Harper, who had won his party's nomination after frontrunner Lawrence Forgy from Logan County withdrew in January. Wilkinson's coattails carried Fulton state representative Butch Burnette to victory as agriculture commissioner.[67]

In federal contests, US senator Wendell Ford from Owensboro won easily in his four Senate races before retiring in 1999. After Reagan thumped the Democrats in western Kentucky in 1984, they improved their performance in 1988 by splitting the vote in the presidential race pitting Vice President George H. W. Bush against Michael Dukakis from Massachusetts. The two men split the regional vote as Dukakis took, with the exception of Calloway, the far western counties. The Bush campaign made an effective attack on his liberal Democratic opponent by using archly conservative issues. Televangelist and fundamentalist preacher Pat Robertson, who had contested Bush in earlier GOP primaries that year, held campaign rallies for him in Bowling Green, Owensboro, and Paducah during a September swing through the region, telling audiences Bush would put God back in public schools and protect individuals' Second Amendment rights, whereas a Dukakis win would create a liberal judiciary that would approve same-sex marriages and child adoption for gays. Both campaigns' vice presidential nominees made late campaign stops in Owensboro, demonstrating that the region was an important battleground for both parties. During a late campaign stop in Owensboro that drew as many as 3,000 enthusiastic Democrats, the relatively conservative Democrat US senator Lloyd Bentsen from Texas, better suited than the liberal Dukakis to speak to western Kentucky audiences (he made an earlier stop as the featured speaker at the Fancy Farm Picnic), ripped into GOP efforts to scare conservative Democrats and independents into voting for Bush by means of pro-gun-control television spots. He was followed there by Dan Quayle, the Republican vice presidential candidate, who amplified the gun-control charges against Dukakis by claiming that

Dukakis was for government confiscation of firearms. Bush, despite losing fourteen western Kentucky counties, won the region by nearly 14,000 votes. US senator Wendell Ford, a much more moderate Democrat, concluded in his reaction to Dukakis's poor showing in Kentucky that "if we're that far out of the mainstream, we're going to have to pull it back in and try to make some adjustments."[68]

Mitch McConnell followed up Bush's triumph two years later with his reelection to a second term in the US Senate over Harvey Sloane, a two-term Louisville mayor with statewide name recognition after running credible losing gubernatorial primary races in 1979 and 1983. With six years to build a relationship with voters in western Kentucky, McConnell, who had lost the region by 43,000 votes in 1980 despite Reagan's landslide, in 1990 won the Gibraltar of Kentucky Democracy by 900 votes, picking up thirteen counties there (not Senator Wendell Ford's home Daviess County). His win in McCracken County was attributed to concerns over the uranium-enrichment facility's future and McConnell's close relationship to President Bush.[69]

A pattern was starting to settle in as the much larger Democratic voter-registration superiority in the region failed to assure Democratic wins in high-profile races, such as for president and US senator, but Democrats still dominated in congressional, state legislative, and local partisan races as the Republican candidates frequently lacked money or political experience. GOP emphasis on conservative "wedge issues," such as abortion and gun rights, was effective in western Kentucky, but for all the GOP's demonstrated strength on the top-of-ticket national races, it remained in western Kentucky uncompetitive on down-ballot races for the US House of Representatives and the Kentucky General Assembly. Between 1984 and 1990, Willard C. "Woody" Allen, veteran state representative from Morgantown representing GOP-leaning counties on the eastern border of the region, and James C. "Jimmy" Brown, a one-term Kentucky House member from Muhlenberg County elected in 1986, were the only Republican legislators from western Kentucky (several others who lived outside western Kentucky had parts of it in their districts).[70]

The turn of the century provided significant challenges to tobacco farmers and coal miners. The unease with which many area communities faced the future is clearly demonstrated by *Louisville Courier-Journal* reporters for the "Our Towns" series associated with the Kentucky bicentennial of 1992. The accounts salute the region's small-town heritage, but a striking number of western Kentuckians interviewed for the series voiced a strong sense of alienation from Frankfort and Washington, DC. In the towns of Fulton and Hickman (pop. 2,336 and 2,442, respectively, in 2000), located in Fulton County in the extreme southwestern tip of Kentucky, residents complained that their area was treated as a "step child," hanging "on the edge of the state," and needed "someone to jerk us back in" and that "people in places like Louisville think that Western Kentucky ends at Bowling Green." One local said that since the Mengel Box factory fire in 1942, Hickman had "gone from worse to worser." The mayor of Morganfield, home city of former governor Earle Clements, complained that "most everything has gone to the Golden Triangle," and "the west part of Kentucky has always been the last to get anything." For minority groups in western Kentucky, the belief that they had not made substantial gains in having their voices heard in local affairs or in obtaining a fair share in local employment opportunities was also plain. A young black man from Hopkinsville believed that the new industry coming to that city was unlikely to improve his situation: "For a person of my color, do you think I could walk in there and get a job?" Looking back at the racial strife that took place during school desegregation in parts of the Western Kentucky Coal Field, a local black leader in Morganfield complained that little had changed and that "there's a lot of subtle racism that exists from the city officials on down." This view comports with Jack Glazier's look at race relations in Hopkinsville in 2015, which he concludes ranks behind only Louisville as the most segregated city in Kentucky.[71]

Persistent concerns in many parts of western Kentucky from the 1950s on were the absence of jobs and decades of population loss (as depicted in Map 3), especially in the Mississippi River counties of the Jackson Purchase, which had lost as much as half their populations. Upriver from Hickman near the confluence of the Ohio and Mississippi Rivers in the small Ballard County town of Wickliffe, its 781 residents were excited by the arrival of the Westvaco paper mill (not so much the odor that came with it) in the late 1960s, with its nearly 700 good-paying jobs and $1 billion investment in the local economy by the

DEMOGRAPHIC CHANGES IN WESTERN KENTUCKY
1930-2010

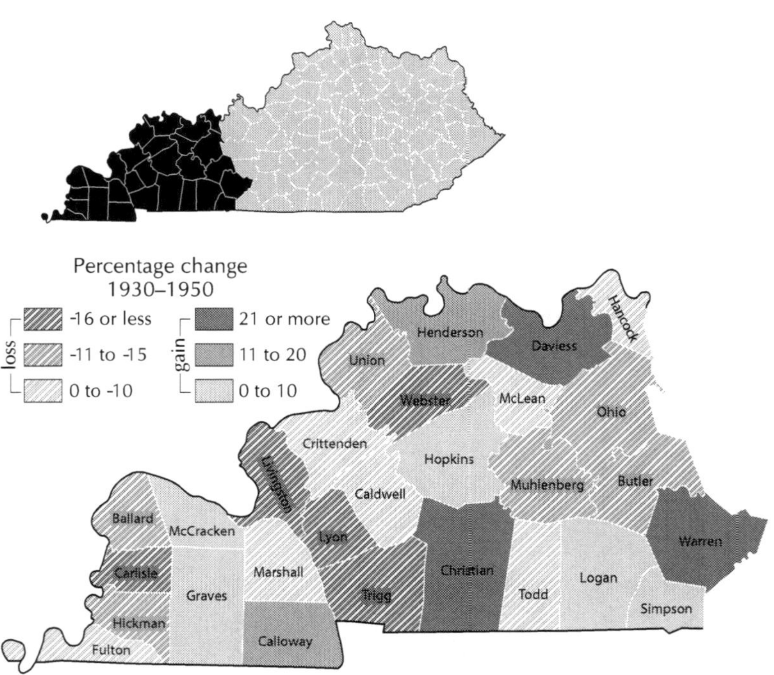

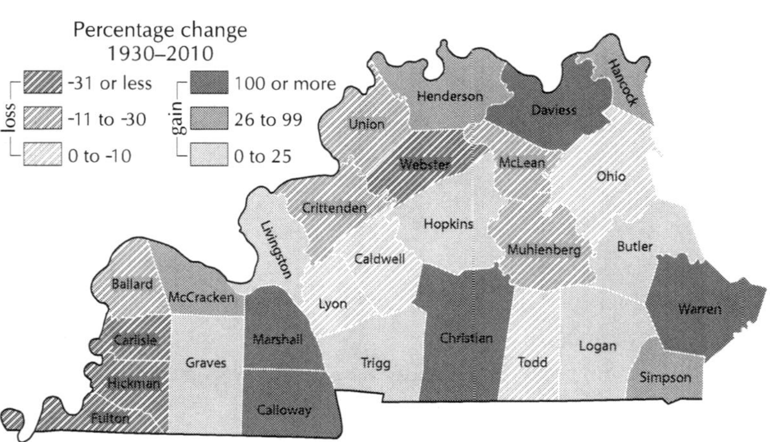

Population changes of western Kentucky counties, 1930–2010. *Source:* Maps created by Dick Gilbreath based on US Census data collected by George G. Humphreys.

early 1990s. Nevertheless, jobs remained hard to find, and the town and county continued to lose population. As one local resident explained, "Around here, you work for the river, Wesvaco [renamed Verso, closed in 2016, and reopened in 2019 as Phoenix Paper Wickliffe, a subsidiary of a China-based paper and pulp firm], farm or go somewhere else."[72]

Other communities in the Jackson Purchase had reason to fear their futures were bleak. This was certainly the case with Fulton and Mayfield in the Jackson Purchase. The city of Fulton had once been a prosperous community during the heyday of the railroads, when it was a hub for the Illinois Central, with a local workforce of approximately 500 handling thirty passenger trains and more than 3,000 freight cars daily. Before refrigerated cars, bananas were shipped to Fulton, where they were received and shipped all over the country. (Fulton has been since 1963 the home of the Banana Festival and its one-ton banana pudding.) But the railroad tracks were being removed (Fulton remains the one Amtrak station for passengers traveling the City of New Orleans train), and railroad employment dwindled to fewer than twenty jobs by 2015. The town struggled to make up the job loss because each of the remaining few industries employed fewer than 200 workers. One returning resident, after retiring from the military, said it was as if "Mayberry had turned into broken-up windows and shattered glass." Industry looking to locate in Fulton were attracted instead by Tennessee, which lacked a state income tax and had a right-to-work law; however, Tennessee's high sales tax encouraged retail to locate in Fulton rather than in South Fulton across the state line. As in the case of many western Kentuckians willing to find work wherever the opportunity presented itself, locals worked in the large tire factories in Union City, Tennessee, and in Mayfield. The downtown retail sector struggled with the arrival of Walmart, and access to good roads encouraged shoppers to take advantage of the retail box stores and shopping malls located nearby.[73]

The larger Jackson Purchase city of Mayfield (pop. 10,228 in 2000) suffered large job losses when its legacy clothing factories and the General Tire factory closed. At one point, Mayfield had more than 3,500 employed at the three clothing factories, including the large Merit clothing plant, which at its height employed 2,000 under the direction of Jackson Purchase Democratic boss William F. Foster. By the 1990s, the clothing factories had either closed, as in the case of the Merit plant in 1980, or passed into new out-of-state ownership, with a workforce of less than 500. Mayfield's downtown retailers, like those in many western Kentucky towns, struggled to compete with Walmart and the nearby Kentucky Oaks Mall, which opened in Paducah in 1982. The town's economy suffered further as General Tire, the Jackson Purchase's largest employer in 1990 with as many as 2,400 mostly union employees, began its long decline to 1,600 workers in 1993 due to a slackening demand for the radial passenger tires produced there. Continental Tire reopened the plant in 1997 with less than 1,000 workers before finally closing in 2007. Longtime county judge-executive Tony Smith grimly offered that "this is the biggest challenge this county has faced since I've been in this office." With all the plant closings, Graves County's largest employer going forward was the Pilgrim's Pride chicken-processing plant with its 1,200 employees.[74]

The region's rivers still played an important role in its life. The construction of Kentucky Dam in 1944 and of Barkley Dam later, which impounded the Tennessee and Cumberland Rivers, respectively, and provided year-around navigational channels for the large river barges that navigated the Ohio and Mississippi Rivers, led to the development of a chemical industry at Calvert City (pop. 2,723 in 2000). The community, which drew workers from Paducah and other surrounding cities and towns in western Kentucky, had four plants, each with at least 400 workers, by the early 1990s. The opening of the massive Tennessee-Tombigbee Waterway in 1985 cut the distance to ship to the Gulf of Mexico by 400 miles by connecting the Tennessee River with the Gulf of Mexico in Mobile. Up the Ohio River, near the eastern border of the region, Hancock County joined Marshall County as industrial areas with per capita incomes higher than the state average. As the coal fields of western Kentucky started to decline, Hancock County's leaders took aggressive steps in the early 1960s to recruit outside industry, especially aluminum plants with generous financial partnerships and low energy costs through Big Rivers Electric Corporation. Lewisport (pop. 1,628 in 2000) caught national attention for its daring issuance of $50 million in industrial revenue bonds to recruit Harvey Aluminum; the success in that venture led to the location of National-Southwire Aluminum near Hawesville (pop. 961 in 2000). This put Hancock County on the national map when the story appeared in the *Wall Street Journal*. The county judge-executive Danny Boling bragged to the *Courier-Journal* that "we have a total population of 7,864, and we have over 3,000 industrial jobs here." The Hancock County example invited imitation by Morgantown (pop. 2,545 in 2000) in Butler County, which, with the downturn in mining, had experienced a population exodus so extensive that the county newspaper editor said that while growing up in Gary, Indiana, "I hardly knew anyone who wasn't from Butler County." To turn things around, the city built the state's first speculative building in 1962, which helped lure Morgantown Plastics. A second, larger building was constructed, which Sumitomo Electric Wiring System, with its workforce of 1,000, occupied before closing in 2002.[75]

Western Kentucky's larger cities fared better overall at the end of the twentieth century. The "Our Towns" profile in the *Louisville Courier-Journal* portrayed Owensboro (at that time the state's third-largest city with a population of 54,312) as a city emerging from "a depression, economic and psychological." The city had weathered a number of significant disappointments, starting with the unrealized dream of clean-coal technology attached to the Newman project. In addition, the General Electric plant (formerly Ken-Rad), which had at one time employed more than 6,000 workers, fell on hard times as it failed to make the transition from its old-age vacuum-tube technology to the transistor; employment fell to 1,200 by 1975 and then to 400 in 1987 before the plant closed in 2010. Western Kentucky Gas president Earl Fischer, an Owensboro native, said of the recent hard times, "Thank God the Ohio Valley kept going with the aluminum industry [in Hancock County] and kept Owensboro from going backwards." The job loss was to an extent mitigated by new industry, including Ragu foods, Texas Gas, Pinkerton Tobacco, Green River Steel, and W. R. Grace.[76]

The Owensboro "renaissance," as Mayor David Adkisson termed it at a Henderson Rotary Club meeting in July 1989, had its roots in the expansive road projects of the late 1960s, encouraged by Lieutenant Governor Wendell Ford, which erased the city's long grievance that it had been passed over in Frankfort for construction of modern superhighways. Nevertheless, civic leaders recognized that Owensboro needed to turn things around by (1) launching the "Shine on Owensboro" campaign in late 1987 to instill local civic pride; (2) employing the campaign in local industrial recruitment efforts, especially with an audience of 700 gathered for the annual Owensboro-Daviess County Chamber of Commerce dinner; and

(3) bringing renowned urban expert and columnist Neal Peirce, funded by a local foundation established by newspaper publisher Lawrence Hager, to solicit his findings on Owensboro and ideas for the city's revitalization, which he presented in a series of five articles in the *Owensboro Messenger-Inquirer* in 1991. The "Shine on Owensboro" project claimed significant successes in downtown improvements, not the least of which were the $9 million RiverPark Center, which provided a fitting venue for the local symphony; establishment of the state's first new community college since 1968; approval of a new Ohio River bridge east of the city that would link the Green River Parkway (later renamed the Natcher Parkway before becoming currently I-165) to I-64 in Indiana as well as the Western Kentucky Turnpike and I-65 at Bowling Green; and the recruitment of Scott Paper with an anticipated 500 new jobs in 1990. Terry Woodward, whom Peirce called "Owensboro's extraordinary entrepreneur," created an empire through WaxWorks in the downtown area, with its sales of music and videos increasing from $200,000 in 1949 to $172 million in 1990. The one major setback was the failed proposed city–county merger effort, turned down by voters in 1990 in part because of, as Peirce said afterward, political cleavages in the county between the Campbell Club—a "crusty old-boy network" that met at a high-end private dining building on Frederica Street modeled after the prestigious Louisville Pendennis Club—and a rising new group, Leadership Owensboro. In the merger movement, its proponents failed to include rural, minority, and female perspectives. Peirce noted in 1991 there was only one woman in the forty-seven elected offices in Daviess County.[77]

Bowling Green (pop. 50,663 in 2000) was undergoing rapid expansion with a nearly one-third growth spurt in the 1990s that would enable it to shoot past Paducah (pop. 25,565) and Owensboro (pop. 54,312) as the largest city in the region and third largest in Kentucky by the 2010 census. It benefited from its location on the I-65 corridor between Louisville and Nashville and from the intellectual capital provided by Western Kentucky University. The city was rapidly becoming an important home to a diversified economy anchored by a number of large employers, such as the Huish Detergents, Fruit of the Loom, and General Motors Corvette plants, each of which employed considerably more than 500 workers. Bowling Green, which along with Owensboro is in the Second Congressional District, increasingly sees itself not as part of western Kentucky but as the hub of south-central Kentucky. The Owensboro regional campus of Western Kentucky University, for example, is the university's only such campus in western Kentucky (others are in Elizabethtown, Glasgow, and Somerset); and Bowling Green Technical College changed its name in 2012 to Southcentral Kentucky Community and Technical College. Murray State University has filled the regional campus needs with locations in Hopkinsville, Henderson, Madisonville, and Paducah.[78]

Of all western Kentucky cities, Paducah has struggled most, certainly in terms of population, which declined from more than 47,000 in the 1950s, when it was the state's fourth-largest city, to 25,565 in 1990, seventh largest, trailing Owensboro, Bowling Green, and Hopkinsville. Symbolic of the city's decline was the fate of the Illinois Central Railroad workshops, which once employed as many as 2,000 but was reduced to a workforce of less than 30 when three regional businessmen purchased the workshop, track, and rolling stock of the Illinois Central Gulf for $56 million in 1986. Under the new ownership, employment approached 700 in 1988 (but then was down to less than 200 employed by VMI Paducahbilt in 2019). Governor Carroll had attempted to give his home city a boost by pushing through road projects to finish I-24 through Paducah and the downtown Paducah access route and by providing approximately $4 million for the downtown convention center.[79]

The city soon experienced a significant blow connected with the uranium-enrichment plant, which had held such promise when originally announced during the Korean War. The historian John E. L. Robertson notes that the plant, with the tens of thousands of jobs it created for construction and 1,800 jobs for operations, had left a legacy of labor unrest during construction that "helped perpetuate the image of Paducah as a poor risk for new investment." Ultimately, that concern paled as serious allegations were made in a series of *Washington Post* investigative articles in 1999 regarding serious efforts to obscure the plant's deleterious health consequences to workers and long-term environmental damage to the community. The plant went through a painful decline before closing in 2013, leaving the federal Department of Energy with cleanup responsibilities.[80]

Legislative independence and the end of western Kentuckians' hold on the governor's mansion diminished, at least at first, the region's influence in the Democratic legislative leadership. At the prelegislative conference at Kentucky Dam Village Resort in 1979, the region suffered a series of setbacks that, when the smoke cleared, left it shut out of Democratic leadership positions. In the Senate, the death of Senator Tom Garrett of Paducah in February opened the majority leader position, which Delbert Murphy from Owensboro filled. However, Murphy lost that post in the 1980 regular session, and Pat McCuiston from Hopkinsville decided not to run for assistant majority leader. Western Kentuckians were also defeated in the House when Speaker Bill Kenton defeated challenger Don Blandford from Owensboro; Lloyd Clapp, after considering a challenge to Kenton, lost his race for another term as Speaker pro tempore; and Hopkinsville's Ramsey Morris lost a close contest for majority leader. Ironically, the only leadership position for a western Kentuckian went to Woodrow "Woody" Allen from Morgantown in Butler County who was elected House minority whip.[81]

Two years later, in 1981, western Kentucky lawmakers bounced back as David Thomason of Henderson won his race for House Speaker pro tempore, Delbert Murphy narrowly won the Senate assistant president pro tempore race, and Helen Garrett, the widow of former senator Tom Garrett from Paducah, became the first woman elected to a major legislative leadership post in Kentucky by becoming majority whip. Speaker Bill Kenton's death shortly before the final presession meeting at Kentucky Dam Village opened up that position for Majority Leader Bobby Richardson. An opportunity to add to the region's influence in the General Assembly was missed when Madisonville's William T. "Bill" Brinkley, after waging an aggressive campaign in a crowded field for Richardson's former post, lost it after two other candidates withdrew from the race and threw their support to Jim LeMaster.[82]

Western Kentucky's return as a major force in Frankfort rose with Don Blandford's election to the House Democratic leadership. He was not deterred by losing to Bobby Richardson in the 1979 Speaker's race. He defeated incumbent David Thomason despite support from the House Democratic leadership in a close race for the speaker pro tempore position during the 1983 organizational session. Blandford's backers were intent on sending a strong message to Speaker Bobby Richardson regarding dissatisfaction in the ranks for being too close to the Brown administration and not attentive enough to the concerns of his caucus.[83]

In many ways, Blandford, with the backing of two others on the five-member Democratic leadership team, was in a very strong position if he wished to challenge Speaker Bobby Richardson on matters in the 1984 session. In fact, Blandford played an obstructionist role in the debate on Governor Martha Layne Collins's $324 million education package, which she withdrew near the session's end as she realized the House votes were not there. When the package was first announced, Blandford said, "I'm sick about it," forecast that there were not more than thirty-five votes for it in the House, and concluded, "I just don't see any sentiment for a tax increase."[84]

There was wide speculation through the primary and general election campaigns in 1984 on the possibility of a Speaker's race, with both Blandford and Richardson boasting that they had the votes to win. Blandford counted on support from western Kentucky, much of Jefferson County, and coal counties in eastern Kentucky. He wanted to open up matters for the rank and file in the House and said that as Speaker he would put "the jelly on the bottom shelf where the little man can reach it." He enlisted the support of the "Young Turks," a small, tight-knit group of young pro-education lawmakers from Kentucky's Golden Triangle who wanted a bigger voice in educational policy than they had been given by Richardson, and Blandford promised them the opportunity to play an active role in shaping the House's response to an expected new education package that Governor Collins was almost certainly going to propose. Former governors Julian Carroll, Bert Combs, and John Y. Brown Jr. supported Richardson, but when Blandford prevailed in a 42–31 vote, the new Speaker crowed: "I busted 'em." The six-foot-five farmer and former Kroger union butcher from Philpot became the first Speaker from Daviess County.[85]

Despite Reagan's landslide victory in Kentucky in the general election of 1984, Democrats had strong majorities of 77–23 in the Kentucky House of Representatives and 28–10 in the Senate. Governor Collins shook off the defeat of her education program and carefully prepared a new plan that tied education more closely to economic development. Now, with the Collins administration working closely with the Young Turks, Speaker Blandford was a more willing partner. Having a broad consensus of educators and business leaders to support her program, the governor called a special session for early July 1985 to consider education reforms costing

$287.7 million, most of it to come from new business taxes. Former governors Chandler, Wetherby, Breathitt, Nunn, and Carroll were present as Collins presented her program to the General Assembly. Blandford urged that the reforms should be considered as "expeditiously as possible" but time still allowed for all those who wanted input to have their chance. The session was relatively short (in part because the legislative chambers were not air-conditioned) and orderly, with strong bipartisan votes for the education-reform plan but not for the financing of it, which received only one Republican House vote.[86]

In the spirit of legislative independence, Blandford took a leading role in persuading Collins to include on the special-session agenda a five-cent hike in the motor fuel tax. Although the hike was supported by county judge-executives and the highway lobby, it took a significant beating in the House on a 36–60 vote, but its defeat did not take away from the positive evaluation of the new Speaker's overall leadership. A *Paducah Sun* writer praised Blandford team's handling of the matter, which was consistent with the spirit of legislative independence in that no gubernatorial arm twisting or punishment was meted out to lawmakers who voted against the tax. In the Speaker's post mortem for the tax hike, he noted, "They made the choice to defeat the bill and that is their right." Patience paid dividends for Blandford in the 1986 session when the motor fuels tax hike was approved. After the House passed the bill 62–38, members applauded Blandford in recognition that this was the first time in memory that the General Assembly had passed a tax increase not initiated by the governor.[87]

Working with the Owensboro Citizens Committee on Higher Education, chaired by newspaper publisher Lawrence Hager, Blandford played a major role during these years in resolving the long-standing demand for a public college in Owensboro. He secured a $375,000 appropriation during the 1984 session to establish a broad set of classes through nearby Henderson Community College at several public-school sites for the fall 1984 semester. Student enrollment was sufficiently strong to support a study undertaken by the Legislative Research Commission on expanding a community college presence in Owensboro. The report presented a number of options, two of which would maintain an administrative link to Henderson Community College either by establishing Owensboro as an extended campus or one of two campuses administered by a separate board of trustees. A third, preferred by Owensboro leaders, including Blandford, called for the creation of a separate Owensboro Community College. When enrollment exceeded expectations, Governor Collins rewarded Blandford and the Owensboro area by including in her 1986 budget $12.5 million for the construction of a free-standing Owensboro Community College, the fifth and last western Kentucky community college in the University of Kentucky Community Colleges System and the first in the state since the creation of Madisonville Community College in 1968.[88]

Western Kentucky's representatives and senators sought to organize themselves to pursue regional policies that would benefit their constituents. This strategy had been used several times in the past, as when Senator Robert Humphreys had invited area legislators in the 1930s to meet in Mayfield; when Henry Ward had considerable success in soliciting his regional colleagues to unite on specific initiatives to push for the removal of tolls on bridges, and in fighting for the development of Kentucky Lake and against private-power utilities; when Fulton state representative Butch Burnette had more recently urged creation of a western Kentucky legislative caucus. The regional agenda became reality when Senator Helen Garrett of Paducah organized the Western Kentucky Legislative Caucus's first meeting, attended by twenty-one legislators from districts west of I-65, at Kentucky Dam Village in June 1986. There was considerable enthusiasm for the organization, which Bowling Green's Jody Richards thought would "in a positive way try to affect legislation that would enhance the position of western Kentucky." The meeting also drew US senator Wendell Ford, former governor Julian Carroll, and Governor Collins, along with a number of her cabinet secretaries. Aspiring GOP gubernatorial candidate Larry Forgy also encouraged the caucus's work as a step in the right direction that could lift the "malaise" that he now sensed in western Kentucky by taking advantage of its highway system, natural resources, and excellent workforce to form a "golden diamond" bounded by Bowling Green, Owensboro, Paducah, and Hopkinsville.[89]

The caucus's top priority coming out of the organizational meeting was the development of a "superhighway" along the US 68/Highway 80 corridor linking Bowling Green to Wickliffe on the Mississippi River through Hopkinsville, Cadiz, Murray, and Mayfield. Senator Pat

McCuiston from Christian County urged that this project should be the caucus's top priority because "that one thing would mean more for the area for economic development, education, and tourism." The initial plan called for the road to be added to the parkway system for speedy construction, financed by bonds that would be paid off by tolls, but this plan fell through. At a follow-up caucus meeting in late September at Lake Barkley State Resort Park, lawmakers endorsed an alternative plan calling for an "east–west highway link" from Bowling Green to Wickliffe that would require the construction of a four-lane highway from I-65 in Bowling Green to I-24 near Cadiz and another four-lane road following US 60 from Paducah to the Ohio River bridge at Wickliffe. An additional road project, asking for a four-lane reconstruction of US 60 between Henderson and Paducah, was approved at a caucus meeting in Henderson in December.[90]

Western Kentucky lawmakers also reaped dividends in the Democratic organizational session in January 1987, which followed a weekend of hunting in Ballard County, with Jody Richard's one-vote upset of an incumbent for House Democratic caucus chair. Richards, who had backed Richardson against Blandford and was replaced as Education Committee chair by one of the Young Turks, gave great credit to the new western Kentucky caucus, most of whose members (but not Blandford) voted for him: "In a close election every vote counts . . . so the vote of the [Western Kentucky] caucus was very important." Along with another term for incumbents Blandford as House Speaker and Helen Garrett as Senate Democratic caucus chair, western Kentucky lawmakers now stood to recoup some of the power it had lost in 1982 when Speaker Richardson's leadership punished Paducahan Dolly McNutt and J. R. Gray from Benton by removing them as committee chairs. Gray was restored as chair of the Labor and Industry Committee, and Senators Pat McCuiston and Greg Higdon from Fancy Farm were named chairs of the Banking and Insurance Committee and the Agriculture and Natural Resources Committee, respectively. Willard "Woody" Allen, the extremely conservative House member from Morgantown who had served four terms as minority whip, was elected minority leader in a hard-fought race.[91]

During a fall special legislative session, the Western Kentucky Legislative Caucus played a significant role in final negotiations on a workers' compensation bill. However, area lawmakers were somewhat frustrated when new Democratic governor Wallace Wilkinson, who had outpolled John Y. Brown Jr. in western Kentucky, rejected their pleas for help on the road-construction program they presented. They did enjoy a win by overcoming Don Blandford's opposition to a $5.3 million health-occupations building in Paducah to be shared by Paducah Community College and West Kentucky Vocational-Technical School. Working with a tight budget, Blandford initially bucked a Senate-sponsored plan with four construction projects, but Albert Jones from Paducah confronted the Speaker: "If we didn't get that building, all that we would get in far-western Kentucky was a roof over the lodge at Lake Barkley State Resort."[92]

The Wallace Wilkinson years were difficult ones for Kentucky lawmakers. His gubernatorial campaign victory owed a great deal to his support of the state lottery, and many considered it to be a virtual popular mandate, but Speaker Blandford, House author of the legislation during the 1988 legislative session, initially demonstrated little enthusiasm for it. His leadership team delayed taking up legislation to put the issue, which had never made it out of the House over the past decade, on the November ballot for voters to consider. When doubts arose over whether it could pass the House State Government Committee, chaired by Ramsey Morris from Hopkinsville, Blandford and Wilkinson, with assistance from the pro-lottery Right of Choice Committee, held rallies in Madisonville, Henderson, Greenville, and Hawesville in Hancock County to put pressure on undecided committee members to get the bill out of the committee and to obtain pledges from sixty House members needed for a constitutional amendment. This effort, resisted vigorously by Louis Johnson, also from Owensboro, split the western Kentucky delegation, but Blandford prevailed by a 63–35 vote. The November vote followed a vigorous campaign on both sides, but the lottery forces overwhelmed their opponents in advertising spending. The fundamentalist religious influence in western Kentucky and other areas of the state was insufficient to defeat the lottery question; pro-lottery views prevailed in religiously conservative western Kentucky, losing only in Caldwell, Crittenden, Butler, Simpson, Todd, and Logan Counties.[93]

The constitutional amendment gave the General Assembly the power to enact a lottery. Though enabling legislation was passed in a special session called in late November 1988, it did not address how the state's lottery proceeds should be spent. Wilkinson requested the money be spent on early childhood education, senior citizens programs, as well as a one-time bonus for Vietnam War veterans. Many legislators were by this time focused on the bombshell ruling from the Kentucky Supreme Court in June that year on a case brought by the Council for Better Education. The council, representing a number of school districts, including four independent and eight western Kentucky school districts, had filed suit to force the state to address school-funding inequities. The court's ruling found the entire K–12 public-school system unconstitutional for its failure to provide children in the commonwealth an "efficient education." Lawmakers now faced the gargantuan task of reconstructing the public-school funding and governance issues before the 1990–1991 school year.[94]

By the end of the special session, a very large rift between legislative leaders and Governor Wilkinson had developed over the cost of the educational reforms being considered. The governor, who had campaigned on no new taxes, took the bit by pushing for an immediate special session after the court ruling was rendered and touted his plan for rewarding schools for academic performance, but Speaker Blandford and Senate president pro tempore John "Eck" Rose found that Wilkinson's plan did not fulfill what the Supreme Court mandated. Blandford called Wilkinson's plan for a quick special session "ludicrous" and stated, "I think we're going to have to go back to the drawing board and start all over." Rose and Blandford won that round by delaying education reform to the 1990 regular session.[95]

The session got off on a sour note when Governor Wilkinson aired television ads in late January charging that lawmakers intended to "grab" lottery funds for deposit in the general fund rather than to earmark them for the purposes he had promised. When it became known that legislators leaned toward a sales tax rate hike rather than toward removing the exemptions in the tax that the governor favored, his political consultant, James Carville, indicated that they had blundered by giving the governor an additional line of attack in the ad campaign. However, Carville also went on to defame legislators, especially Blandford, in a remark to *Courier-Journal* reporter Al Cross that incensed legislators. Wilkinson attempted to apologize for Carville's indiscretions, but the apology did not deter former House Speaker Bobby Richardson's from comparing Carville to Rasputin, the corrupt adviser to the Russian czar Nicholas II. Speaker Blandford followed the same line in suggesting on television that "I don't think that Wallace Wilkinson breathes that Carville doesn't tell him what to do." Carville, who soon would become a highly visible adviser in Bill Clinton's successful 1992 presidential campaign, wisely left Frankfort, but the snafu undoubtedly cost the governor good will in his effort to persuade lawmakers to approve a constitutional question that would allow governors, including Wilkinson himself, more than one term.[96]

Tensions in Frankfort remained high as the governor repeatedly threatened to veto any legislation that included a hike in the sales tax, but he ultimately conceded to a penny increase when the legislature gave him $600 million road and $100 million economic-development bond issues. The Kentucky Education Reform Act (KERA) of 1990 had a profound impact on so many aspects of western Kentucky's public-school operations, not the least of which was in their governance. Prior to the passage of this act, school board members and school superintendents exercised tremendous influence over hiring and firing of public-school personnel. Because the school board was the largest employer in many counties, this influence carried over to local politics, where board members' and superintendents' power rivaled that of state lawmakers and county elected officials. This was illustrated by the case of James "Baby" Deweese in Graves County over his thirty-year tenure. At the time of Deweese's death in 1989, one Graves County local told a *Paducah Sun* reporter that "if you wanted anything done [in Graves County], all you had to do was call Baby, and it was taken care of." KERA, as Kentucky education historian William Ellis notes, significantly reduced the "nepotism and old-fashioned cronyism" that had given Deweese his influence.[97]

The bond issues were wonderful news for the Western Kentucky Legislative Caucus because they included $200 million to widen US 68/Highway 80 from Cadiz to Bowling Green, $19.4 million to widen US 60 from I-24 to Barkley Airport, $5 million for downtown cleanup in Paducah, more than $40 million for a 550-bed medium-security prison in Central City, a new learning center at Madisonville Community College, a $10 million athletic arena at Murray State University, and funding for the Institute for Economic Development at Western Kentucky

University and for the Kentucky Advanced Technology Center in Bowling Green. Owensboro received a significant share, including money for two buildings at Owensboro Community College and a parking garage at River Park Center.[98]

One of the big questions arising from the $1.3 billion KERA was whether voters would punish its supporters in the 1990 election. The answer was a mixed one as a small number of lawmakers from both parties who voted for the bill lost their seats, and the Democratic majorities were reduced by three in the House, although the party still held a commanding 68–32 majority, and by three in the Senate for a 27–11 majority. The biggest upset in western Kentucky was that of Helen Garrett, a member of the Senate Democratic leadership since 1982, who was defeated by Paducah city commissioner Bob Leeper in the Democratic primary. The other primary loser from the region was Senator John Hall from Henderson, beaten by former senator Henry Lackey in one of the state's most bitter primaries. The tax increase played a significant role in their races, and both Garrett and Hall would soon play important roles in one of major Kentucky political scandals of the century.[99]

The election of Brereton Jones as governor in November 1991 offered the legislature an opportunity to put aside the strife that had prevailed during the Wilkinson years. Speaker Blandford said hopefully that "it's got to be better" and that there would not be the "turmoil, tension, and anxiety that has been prevalent in the past four years." Shortly after the election, Jones and legislative leaders agreed to a December special session to take up the issue of legislative and congressional reapportionment, which had been made more difficult by the reduction of Kentucky's congressional districts from seven to six. In western Kentucky, the redrawing of its two congressional districts was conditioned by the insistence of US senator Wendell Ford and Speaker Blandford, both from Daviess County, as well as of Second District congressman William Natcher, who had held the seat since 1953, that Daviess County would remain part of the Second District. Because of Natcher's seniority on the US House Appropriations Committee, county boosters viewed remaining in that district essential to securing federal funding for a bridge over the Ohio River at nearby Maceo as a link from the Green River Parkway to I-64 in Indiana. Veteran state senator Pat McCuiston from Christian County opposed the plan that was passed, which retained Daviess County in Natcher's district and extended the First Congressional District eastern edge along the Tennessee state line by adding Republican-leaning Adair, Russell, Clinton, and Cumberland Counties. The First District now stretched approximately 250 miles from west to east. Eastern Kentucky took the brunt of the pain when lawmakers formed a single congressional district from the existing two there. Owensboro succeeded in its bridge efforts, to which Natcher's name was attached, but that success came at a substantial political price that would soon come due.[100]

With the November election behind him, in which the House Democratic majority was cut by a mere three seats despite the KERA tax increase, Blandford was rewarded with a fourth term as Speaker by acclamation in the January 1991 organizational session. He could not envision then that events were under way that would lead to his downfall. A political scandal, later referred to as "BOPTROT," drawing its name from the Business Organizations and Professions (BOP) Committee of the General Assembly and the horse-racing tracks (TROT), which is where the scandal began and were overseen by the committee. BOPTROT had very significant western Kentucky connections, starting with two small Henderson tracks' struggle to survive and their ability to conduct the intertrack wagering essential to their financial viability: the thoroughbred-racing Ellis Park and the harness-racing Riverside Downs. Of the two, Riverside Downs was most at risk to fail unless state laws and regulations could be changed in its favor. Senator Helen Garrett, the majority whip from Paducah, who was hoping to launch a lobbying career, had suggested in September 1990 (while still a lawmaker, after she lost her primary race in May) that the Riverside Downs owner could secure the wagering provisions that would save his track by investing $100,000 in her lobbying efforts. The owner immediately contacted the FBI, and BOPTROT was off and running. By using electronic-surveillance methods and planting an undercover man posing as a potential track investor, the FBI soon caught a number of additional political figures, including John Hall, another recently defeated senator from Henderson, in the scandal's web. The undercover man gained Hall's confidence, and the former senator was soon caught offering bribes to a number of his former colleagues for their assistance in helping Riverside Downs. Before BOPTROT was over, it ensnared numerous legislators, lobbyists, track insiders, and a nephew of Governor Wilkinson.[101]

The top catch was Blandford, who was accused, among a number of counts, of taking several $500 bribes from a longtime House member and close friend. After the indictment was handed down in November 1992, Blandford maintained that the money he accepted was a gift from a friend and announced his intent to run for a fifth term as Speaker. In western Kentucky, several newspapers issued editorials urging Blandford to step down. The *Paducah Sun* called failure to do so an act of "above-it-all arrogance" and pleaded for an act of "statesmanship" that "was sorely needed in Kentucky at the moment." This perspective was widely shared by House members in the Western Kentucky Legislative Caucus. Most vocal were Richard Lewis from Benton, Charles Geveden from Wickliffe, and Rex Smith from Paducah, who stated that "if Blandford continues to serve as speaker, it will cast a dark shadow over the entire General Assembly." With the fall-off in his support apparent, Blandford withdrew from the Speaker's race and ultimately was forced to leave office following his conviction in a federal trial for allegedly accepting $1,500 in bribes. He drew the harshest of the sentences of all those sentenced, with significant cash penalties and more than five years of incarceration. In contrast, Helen Garrett and John Hall were forced to pay smaller fines, and their prison sentences were reduced to probation. Years later, former Republican House member and congresswoman Anne Northrup from Louisville paid tribute to Blandford's leadership accomplishments in a conversation with *Courier-Journal* reporter Al Cross. While noting that Blandford was not as comfortable on the public stage as his predecessor Bobby Richardson, she added: "I can see a lot of leaders who would have been better if they had had some of his qualities, including toughness, straightforwardness and dependability."[102]

Even as the BOPTROT scandal unfolded, a second spectacular political scandal shook western Kentucky politics when the public learned of First District congressman Carroll Hubbard's part in the "rubbergate" affair of the US Congress. "Rubbergate" involved widespread financial misdeeds connected to a congressional financial institution that resulted in as many as seventy-seven congressmen losing office due to resignations or lost elections. Hubbard, a Mayfield Democrat who had represented his western Kentucky constituents since he had upset Frank Stubblefield in 1974, was the subject of in-depth reporting by the *Louisville Courier-Journal* that appeared in May 1992 detailing how Hubbard, as a senior member of the House Banking Committee and chair of one its subcommittees, had helped shield the savings-and-loan industry, which provided him with fees for speaking engagements and substantial campaign contributions. These reports, coming weeks before the May primary, and the news that Hubbard's wife, Carol Brown Hubbard, was running in an eastern Kentucky congressional district primary with strong financial backing through her husband's contacts in the savings-and-loan industry enabled Tom Barlow, a former congressional lobbyist from Paducah with no experience in elective office, to upset Hubbard in the First District congressional primary by less than 3,000 votes. Hubbard's loss was fueled by his poor performance in the Jackson Purchase, where he carried only Fulton County. His disappointment was compounded by his wife's defeat and his conviction in 1994 for obstruction of justice and campaign-related offenses. Barlow, perhaps riding on the political coat tails of Bill Clinton and Wendell Ford, took the general election by a comfortable margin, although he polled poorly in those eastern counties in southern Kentucky that had been added to the First District in recent redistricting plans.[103]

Setting aside the political scandals, 1992 was a promising year for western Kentucky Democrats. They had turned out loud and energized at the Fancy Farm Picnic, where Tennessee US senator Al Gore, running for vice president with the Arkansas governor Bill Clinton ticket, spoke. Governor Brereton Jones sent a charge through his party's faithful with the message that the Democratic Party was returning to its mainstream roots and that "there is no way the people of Kentucky can turn their back on Bill Clinton and Al Gore." Senator Mitch McConnell, however, noted that although Democratic vice presidential candidates' appearance at Fancy Farm had become quite a tradition, "in November, Republicans carry Kentucky." The Clinton–Gore team was considered a slight favorite in Kentucky given their southern origins, a hard-hitting message that contrasted favorably with President George H. W. Bush's broken "read my lips" no-tax pledge, and the slow American economy. Both presidential candidates made election-eve visits to the Bluegrass state. Bush appeared in Louisville, but Clinton, on the advice of Wendell Ford and

Brereton Jones, chose to make a campaign stop at Barkley Airport in Paducah on a final campaign swing the night before the election to shore up support from Kentucky, Indiana, Illinois, Missouri, Tennessee, and Arkansas. It was the first visit to Paducah by a presidential nominee since John F. Kennedy in 1960. Clinton won in Kentucky, the first Democratic win since Jimmy Carter in 1976. His 30,000-vote margin in western Kentucky, where Bush carried only traditionally Republican Butler County and Christian and Warren Counties, was approximately half of his overall victory margin statewide.[104]

Democratic fortunes in the Gibraltar of Kentucky Democracy, which had in the past several decades shown to be weakening, started a precipitous decline in the 1994 election cycle with a chain of events that started with the death of the eighty-four-year-old William Natcher, a forty-year veteran Second District congressman from Bowling Green, in late March 1994. The conservative Natcher, US House Appropriations Committee chair since June 1992, had built a solid reputation based on his low-key approach to campaigning, boasting that he had never accepted a campaign contribution and casting a record 18,401 consecutive votes in the House, a streak that ended only with the illness that caused his death. His hold on his district had been nearly impregnable, but that district, which took in considerable Republican territory from the redistricting in 1991, would likely be competitive whenever he left office. In the special election to fill the unexpired portion of Natcher's term, Democrats had several viable candidates interested in the race, including young David Adkisson, the mayor of Owensboro who had the support of Senator Wendell Ford, and former state Senate president pro tempore Joe Prather from Hardin County. Prather had the backing of Governor Jones and quickly secured the support of Democrat county leaders in the congressional district to face political newcomer Ron Lewis. Lewis was one of two GOP candidates who had filed to replace Natcher before Natcher's death and offered voters the opportunity to pick someone who was not a career politician. After Lewis got the nomination, party leaders worried he would not be able to raise enough money to defeat Prather in the May general election. Senator Mitch McConnell at this point stepped in to provide the behind-the-scenes organizational leadership needed to help

Lewis in a campaign that McConnell felt was winnable. Al Cross, the political reporter for the *Courier-Journal,* noted afterward that the secrecy McConnell employed was a "political pick off play masterminded by an old Little League pitcher." Using his influence, McConnell obtained funds for a poll that determined that despite the predominance of registered Democrats, the percentage of voters in Kentucky who considered themselves Republicans was only slightly less than those claiming to be Democrats. The poll suggested that Lewis, with sufficient funding for political advertising, could turn the election into a referendum on President Clinton, whose popularity was sagging due to his support for gays in the military and for higher cigarette taxes to fund his proposed health-care reform. McConnell convinced Republican funding sources to quietly direct $180,000 to the Lewis campaign and put experienced GOP campaign strategists in charge of the campaign. The region was flooded with political ads that made Prather morph into President Clinton, underscoring the theme that "if you love Bill Clinton, you'll love Joe Prather." The National Rifle Association chipped in with a direct mailing to voters in the district suggesting that the moderate Prather was for gun control, and the Christian Coalition put voter guides in evangelical churches designed to make the Democrat look bad on divisive social issues. Prather, who adopted a conservative campaign-financing model that precluded money from political action committees and out-of-state contributors, was caught off guard. Lewis won with 55 percent of the vote, taking almost all counties in the district, with the exception of four counties with strong Catholic voters.[105]

Could the winning strategy in Lewis's race be replicated in the First Congressional District, especially after the media attention it had been given? Tom Barlow, the first-term incumbent who had surprised many by his two-to-one victory margin in the 1992 general election, said, "The strategy they used to win the special election in the 2nd District won't work down here," given his record against the North American Free Trade Act and gun control as well as his pro-life stance. In fact, however, it did work: former Democratic state representative Ed Whitfield from Hopkinsville, who changed his party registration just before filing and was accused of not living in the district, narrowly defeated Tom Barlow in the November general election.[106]

In this race, Senator McConnell once again took a very active role in mapping out campaign strategy and helping to raise money. The Christian Coalition's voter guides distributed the Sunday before the election stated that Barlow opposed voluntary school prayer, and the National Rifle Association, which had supported Barlow before the primary, now downgraded him for voting on the US House floor to allow legislation that banned the purchasing of assault weapons. Media coverage of Carroll Hubbard's criminal trial at the end of the campaign soured Barlow for local voters, who were caught up in the anti-incumbency mood that prevailed across the country at the time. A *Newsday* reporter covering the last days of the race suggested that voters in western Kentucky were in an anti-incumbent mood, which did not bode well for Barlow. One person in Paducah explained that she wondered why she voted: "If they are not crooked when they go in, they are when they come out."[107]

The election returns stunned Barlow; he had not sensed when the campaign turned to his opponent's favor, but he was unable to match the large sums coming from Republican campaign committees, political action committees, and outside groups such as the Christian Coalition. Whitfield showed strength in western Kentucky by carrying Christian (his home county), Hopkins, Trigg, Todd, and Simpson Counties. Barlow could have survived those losses, but Whitfield's solid majorities in the eastern counties along the Tennessee border gave him a 2,400-vote win. Both the First and Second Congressional Districts now had their first GOP representatives since the Civil War. From that point forward, the Republican Party has held the two western Kentucky districts so strongly that it has been more than twenty years since Democrats have been able to run competitively in them. The Gibraltar of Kentucky Democracy was no more.[108]

An Owensboro reporter likened voter anger in western Kentucky in 1994 to that of Howard Beal, the "mad prophet of the airwaves" in the classic movie *Network* (Sidney Lumet, 1976) who urges all who listen to him to open their windows and shout, "I'm mad as hell, and I'm not going to take it anymore!" That anger, which Republicans tapped to win the two congressional seats, also enabled it to make significant inroads in western Kentucky state legislative races. Republicans represented a solid block of legislative districts on the eastern edge of western Kentucky. Mark Treesh added to their numbers by replacing Don Blandford in a special election and holding that seat in rural Daviess County for the next two terms Western Kentucky provided-three of the eight additional Seats Republicans picked up from the 1996 election cycle, including Brian Crall also in Daviess County, Sheldon Baugh in Logan and Todd counties, and Kathy Hogancamp whose district covered Crittenden, Livingston, and part of McCracken Counties.[109]

For the next decade, the two parties competed in western Kentucky, as in the 1995 gubernatorial campaign and the 1996 presidential race. Larry Forgy from Logan County, seeking to become the first Republican governor since William S. Taylor from Morgantown had been forced from office after the assassination of William Goebel in 1900, waged a competitive losing race against Paul Patton. Many believed that the election was Forgy's to win, but strategic misplays such as too closely embracing a pro-life position on the abortion question cost him heavily in Louisville, and allegations of vote buying, particularly in eastern Kentucky but also in Christian County, were later raised. Failure to campaign in western Kentucky in the closing days of the election may have cost Forgy in areas such as Muhlenberg County, adjacent to his home Logan County, where Patton won nearly two-thirds of the votes. The vote from organized labor, which saw in a Forgy administration a threat to pass a right-to-work measure, and the black vote in McCracken, Henderson, and Christian Counties went heavily to the Democrat. Years later, Forgy added to the aforementioned explanations for his defeat US senator Mitch McConnell's lack of support. The two men had their differences, especially on public financing of campaigns. McConnell, who has fought vigorously against publicly financed campaigns and for few restrictions on private contributions, stated that with the public-financing rules in place at the time "we lost the race because you can't run statewide in Kentucky with your hands behind your back." Looking ahead, McConnell may have projected a Forgy win as an obstacle in maintaining his control of the Republican organizational apparatus, which was established in 1993 when Marshall County native Terry Carmack, who was head of the Bush–Quayle campaign in Kentucky in 1988 and McConnell's political director in his 1990 Senate race, was installed as the party's executive director.[110]

Patton's victory margin included a 15,000-vote win in western Kentucky, where he campaigned vigorously during the two weeks before the election and was rewarded by limiting Forgy wins to Calloway, Crittenden, Logan, Todd, Warren, Ohio, and Butler Counties. Marshall County judge-executive and Patton campaign cochair Mike Miller exclaimed at his candidate's watch party in reaction to efforts to interject religion into the race: "We rejected tonight the tactics of a party that says if you are not a Republican, you are not a Christian. . . . I want to introduce the next Christian governor of Kentucky, Paul Patton."[111]

President Clinton brushed aside the Kentucky GOP victories in 1994, achieved at his expense, to win Kentucky for a second time, although losing Christian, Daviess, Warren, Crittenden, Butler, Ohio, and Todd Counties in western Kentucky to Kansas Republican Bob Dole. Voters in the region followed a national trend in splitting their tickets to cast their votes for Republican US senator Mitch McConnell, who won a third term. Steve Beshear, the Democratic candidate from Dawson Springs, won fifteen counties in western Kentucky, but McConnell picked up the most votes by winning McCracken, Christian, Daviess, and Warren Counties. In Warren, he won by a two-to-one margin. Voters in the region again split in the 1998 US Senate race to replace retiring Wendell Ford. The race pitted very conservative Baseball Hall of Fame congressman Jim Bunning from northern Kentucky against moderate former University of Kentucky basketball player Scotty Baesler. Bunning won by less than 7,000 votes. Baesler outperformed Bunning in western Kentucky in winning twenty-three counties in the region, but the 15,000-vote bulge there was too small to give the Democrat the victory.[112]

Democratic fortunes in western Kentucky continued to decline into the new century. Echoes of the past sounded from the former Gibraltar of Kentucky Democracy helped native son Steve Beshear in 2007 in his thumping of incumbent governor Ernie Fletcher, whose administration had been wracked by corruption allegations. Beshear prevailed in all but Butler County, outpolling Fletcher by 40,000 votes in the region. Beshear easily defeated the Kentucky Senate president David Williams for a second term. At the federal level, Republicans have a solid hold in western Kentucky from the White House to Congress. George W. Bush soundly defeated Al Gore in Kentucky in the presidential race of 2000, losing only Fulton, Ballard, Henderson, and Muhlenberg Counties in western Kentucky. Barack Obama won two presidential terms, but he polled poorly in western Kentucky. Donald Trump attracted enthusiastic support in the region in his two presidential campaigns. The times when Democratic presidential candidates visited western Kentucky, especially in general campaigns, appears to have ended as it has become one of the reddest (most Republican) areas in a red state.[113]

Republicans picked up state legislative seats, despite Bowling Green Democrat representative Jody Richards's long hold on the House speakership from 1995 to 2009, and many county offices. Richards rewarded his western Kentucky Democratic colleagues with committee chairs, which helped them in their reelection bids and gave the region additional influence in Frankfort. There is a sense of poetic justice that the end of Democratic control in the General Assembly was achieved when Paducahan Democratic senator Bob Leeper, who defeated Helen Garrett in 1990, changed party affiliation in the fall of 1999 to give Republicans control of the state Senate for the first time in history. The Kentucky House followed with the "Trump Tsunami" in 2016, sweeping away most of the remaining Democrat lawmakers from western Kentucky (Patti Minter of Bowling Green was the only Democrat in the legislature from the former Gibraltar of Kentucky Democracy following the elections in 2020). Veteran House member Brent Yonts from Muhlenberg County chalked up his loss to straight Republican Party voting for Trump: "No way I could win with that happening."[114]

In an insightful article published before the Fancy Farm Picnic in 1998, Al Smith, whose study of western Kentucky politics began in the 1950s when he arrived in Russellville as editor of the local newspaper, offered a number of useful observations about the region's place in Kentucky life and politics. Although western Kentuckians had for more than a century felt themselves isolated and overlooked by decision makers in Frankfort, western Kentucky, as the Gibraltar of Kentucky Democracy since the New Deal, had delivered large Democratic majorities, for which it was richly rewarded with governorships and more than its share of state legislative leaders and US senators. With those positions also came public roads, state parks, and state institutions. Smith noted that was no longer the case at the turn of the twenty-first century, however. He in large part placed the blame for the demise of involvement in political parties in the region on the advent of television, symbolized by Governor John Y. Brown Jr.'s campaign in 1979, which bypassed the county courthouse rings, and his administration, and tended to neglect Democratic county parties. As Bill Cox, the former state legislator, political adviser in Governor Julian Carroll's administration, and later mayor of Madisonville, put it so well, "West Kentucky sort of loss its vision and became so sectional, four or five little pockets of provincialism."[115]

Making effective use of divisive social issues, and influenced daily by messaging from conservative talk radio and cable news, the GOP now has a solid lock on area voters. But in contrast to the experience of Democrats after the New Deal, western Kentucky has yet to reap the harvest for this switch to the Republican Party from Frankfort or Washington. There is no current great Republican western Kentucky political leader comparable to Democrats Alben Barkley, Happy Chandler, Earle Clements, Ned Breathitt, or Wendell Ford. In the case of Kentucky's junior US senator, Rand Paul from Bowling Green, who grew up in Texas and is the son of former libertarian congressman Ron Paul, he was elected in 2010 to replace Jim Bunning, but because he has no deep roots in western Kentucky, his interests have been focused on national matters as a representative of the very conservative Tea Party movement. The First Congressional District, which shifted eastward in 1994 in electing Ed Whitfield, is now represented by James Comer from Tompkinsville, nearly two hundred miles east of Paducah. Second Congressional District congressman Brett Guthrie, a Republican from Bowling Green first elected in 2008 after Ron Lewis dropped out at the end of the filing period and Senator McConnell tapped him for the position, is western Kentucky's voice in the Congress representing a district lying mostly in the south-central part of the commonwealth. It remains to be seen if the leadership void that presently exists can be filled so that western Kentucky can move forward in addressing the very serious challenges of revitalizing the economy, most notably in the Western Kentucky Coal Field, where the mining industry has collapsed, and creating opportunities to discourage the further emigration of young people.

Notes

Preface

1. Berry Craig, *Kentucky Confederates: Secession, Civil War, and the Jackson Purchase* (Lexington: University Press of Kentucky, 2014).

2. James C. Klotter and Craig Thompson Friend, *A New History of Kentucky*, 2nd ed. (Lexington: University Press of Kentucky, 2018), 261–62; George G. Humphreys, *A Century to Remember: A Historical Perspective on the Oklahoma House of Representatives* (Oklahoma City: Oklahoma House of Representatives, 2000).

1. Western Kentucky: A Geographical, Economic, and Historical Introduction

1. Jesse Stuart, *My World* (Lexington: University Press of Kentucky, 1975), 22; Robert M. Ireland, *The Little Kingdoms: The Counties of Kentucky* (Lexington: University Press of Kentucky, 1979); Penny M. Miller, *Kentucky Politics and Government: Do We Stand United?* (Lincoln: University of Nebraska Press, 1994), 40; James C. Klotter, "Clio in the Commonwealth: The Status of Kentucky History," *Register of the Kentucky Historical Society* 80, no. 1 (Winter 1982): 86; "Charting the Path of Twentieth-Century Kentucky: Current Courses and Future Directions," *Register of the Kentucky Historical Society* 113, nos. 2–3 (Spring–Summer 2015): 182; Robert S. Weise, "Socially Relevant History: Appalachian Kentucky in the Twentieth Century," *Register of the Kentucky Historical Society* 113, nos. 2–3 (Spring–Summer 2015): 321–55; Thomas Kiffmeyer and Robert S. Weise, "Introduction: Building a History of

Twentieth-Century Kentucky," *Register of the Kentucky Historical Society* 113, nos. 2–3 (Spring–Summer 2015): 163–69.

2. E. Merton Coulter, *The Civil War and Readjustment in Kentucky* (Gloucester, MA: Peter Smith, 1926), 439; Berry Craig, *Kentucky Confederates: Secession, Civil War, and the Jackson Purchase* (Lexington: University Press of Kentucky, 2014); Al Cross and David Cross, "Republican Redoubt: The Politics of Kentucky's Upper Cumberlands," in *People of the Upper Cumberland: Achievements and Contradictions,* ed. Michael E. Birdwell and W. Calvin Dickinson (Knoxville: University of Tennessee Press, 2015), 86; Anne E. Marshall, *Creating a Confederate Kentucky: The Lost Cause and Civil War Memory in a Border State* (Chapel Hill: University of North Carolina Press, 2013), 4; Patricia Anne Hoskins, "'The Old First Is with the South': The Civil War, Reconstruction, and Memory in the Jackson Purchase Region of Kentucky," PhD diss., Auburn University, 2008, 3; Maryjean Wall, *How Kentucky Became Southern: A Tale of Outlaws, Horse Thieves, Gamblers, and Breeders* (Lexington: University Press of Kentucky, 2012).

3. Ann K. Ferrell, *Burley: Kentucky Tobacco in a New Century* (Lexington: University Press of Kentucky, 2013); Tracy Campbell, *The Politics of Despair: Power and Resistance in the Tobacco Wars* (Lexington: University Press of Kentucky, 1993); Christopher Waldrep, *Night Riders: Defending Community in the Black Patch* (Durham, NC: Duke University Press, 1993); Suzanne Marshall, *Violence in the Black Patch of Kentucky and Tennessee* (Columbia: University of Missouri Press, 1994); Bill Cunningham, *On Bended Knees: The Night Rider Story* (Kuttawa, KY: McClanahan, 1983); Bobbie Smith Bryant, *Farming in the Black Patch* (Morley, MO: Acclaim Press, 2015).

4. Richard Ulack, "Kentucky: Its Setting," in *Atlas of Kentucky,* ed. Richard Ulack, Karl Raitz, and Gyula Pauer (Lexington: University Press of Kentucky, 1998), 6–7; Joseph R. Schwendeman, *Geography of Kentucky,* 5th ed. (Lexington: Kentucky Images, 1974); Thomas D. Clark, *A History of Kentucky* (Lexington, KY: John Bradford Press, 1960), 1–7; *Agrarian Kentucky* (Lexington: University Press of Kentucky, 1977); William E. Ellis, *A History of Education in Kentucky* (Lexington: University Press of Kentucky, 2011), 327; Miller, *Kentucky Politics and Government,* 62.

5. Clark, *A History of Kentucky,* 1–7; Miller, *Kentucky Politics and Government,* 60–67; James C. Klotter and Freda C. Klotter, *A Concise History of Kentucky* (Lexington: University Press of Kentucky, 2008), 44–52; "Kentucky's Policy Regions," in *Atlas of Kentucky,* ed. Ulack, Raitz, and Pauer, 282; Mike Cherry, interviewed by the author, November 30, 2010, Kentucky Legislature Oral History Project, Louie B. Nunn Center for Oral History, University of Kentucky, Lexington; John H. Fenton, *Politics in the Border States: A Study of the Patterns of Political Organization, and Political Change, Common to the Border States—Maryland, West Virginia, Kentucky, and Missouri* (New Orleans: Hauser

Press, 1959); *Western Kentucky,* a regional roadmap (Vancouver: GM Johnson Maps, 2012).

6. "Farm Characteristics," in *Atlas of Kentucky,* ed. Ulack, Raitz, and Pauer, 156–57.

7. W. F. Axton, *Tobacco and Kentucky* (Lexington: University Press of Kentucky, 1995), 49, 64, 77, 133; Bryant, *Farming in the Black Patch,* 66.

8. US Bureau of the Census, *U.S Census of Agriculture, 1925, vol. 2, part 2: The Southern States: Kentucky* (Washington, DC: US Department of Commerce, 1932), 657–69, at agcensus.mannlib.cornell.edu; Virginia Jewell, *Lick Skillet and Other Tales of Hickman County* (Union City, TN: Lanzer, 1986), 186–87 (interview of Edna Humphreys).

9. James C. Klotter and Craig Thompson Friend, *A New History of Kentucky,* 2nd ed. (Lexington: University Press of Kentucky, 2018), 217.

10. Clark, *Agrarian Kentucky,* viii; James C. Klotter, *Kentucky: Portrait in Paradox, 1900–1950* (Frankfort: Kentucky Historical Society, 1996), 21; "Horse Traders," *Owensboro Messenger,* March 12, 1898. Unless otherwise indicated, all newspapers cited in the notes are Kentucky newspapers.

11. "Turbulent Mississippi Makes a Venice of Hickman," *Paducah News-Democrat,* April 19, 1927; "Hickman," *Louisville Courier-Journal,* March 30, 1992.

12. Klotter, *Kentucky,* 105; Suzanne M. Hall, "Working the Black Patch: Tobacco Farming Traditions, 1890–1930," *Register of the Kentucky Historical Society* 89, no. 3 (Summer 1991): 276.

13. Albert B. Chandler, *Heroes, Plain Folks, and Skunks: The Life and Times of Happy Chandler* (Chicago: Bonus Books, 1989), 9; Bobby Ann Mason, *Clear Springs: A Memoir* (New York: Random House, 1999), ix, 57.

14. Melanie Beals Goan, *Simple Justice: Kentucky Women Fight for the Vote* (Lexington: University Press of Kentucky, 2020), 31, 111–13; "Miss Susan B. Anthony," *Hopkinsville South Kentuckian,* October 28, 1879; "Mrs. Franceway's Interesting Address," *Madisonville Hustler,* September 20, 1907.

15. Kentucky Woman Suffrage Project, n.d., at https://networks.h-network.org/kywomanssuffrage; Goan, *Simple Justice,* 142, 151, 162, 186.

16. Lee A. Dew and Aloma W. Dew, *Owensboro: The City on the Yellow Banks* (Bowling Green, KY: Riverdell, 1988), 127–30; Goan, *Simple Justice,* 155; "Suffragettes March through City Streets," *Owensboro Daily Messenger,* November 8, 1914.

17. "Overwhelming Vote Given in Both Houses," *Lexington Herald,* January 7, 1920.

18. Klotter and Friend, *A New History of Kentucky,* 80; "Peter Cartwright," *Russellville News-Democrat,* November 29, 1934; John Boles, *Religion in Antebellum Kentucky* (Lexington: University Press of Kentucky, 1976), 30.

19. John Boles, *The Great Revival: Beginnings of the Bible Belt* (Lexington: University Press of Kentucky, 1996), 60–61; Alan Bearman, "'The South Carolina

of Kentucky': Religion and Secession in the Jackson Purchase," *Filson Club Historical Quarterly* 76 (October 2002): 495–521; Craig, *Kentucky Confederates,* 25–27; Nancy E. Baker, "Integrating Women into Modern Kentucky History: The Equal Rights Amendment Debate (1972–1978) as a Case Study," *Register of the Kentucky Historical Society* 113, nos. 2–3 (Spring–Summer 2015): 477–507; George G. Humphreys, "Western Kentucky in the Twentieth Century: From the End of Isolation to the Collapse of the 'Gibraltar of Democracy,'" *Register of the Kentucky Historical Society* 113, nos. 2–3 (Spring–Summer 2015): 380–81.

20. Hughie G. Lawson, "Geographical Origins of White Migrants to Trigg and Calloway Counties in the Ante-Bellum Period," *Filson Club Historical Quarterly* 57 (October 1983): 286; Hoskins, "'The Old First Is with the South'"; Craig, *Kentucky Confederates,* 20–22; Helen Bartter Crocker, "A War Divides Green River Country," *Register of the Kentucky Historical Society* 70, no. 4 (October 1972): 295–311; Otto Rothbert, *A History of Muhlenberg County* (Louisville, KY: John P. Morton, 1913), 252–53.

21. Jasper Berry Shannon and Ruth McQuown, *Presidential Politics in Kentucky, 1824–1948: A Compilation of Election Statistics and an Analysis of Political Behavior* (Lexington: Bureau of Government Research, University of Kentucky, 1950), 32–36; Hoskins, "'The Old First Is with the South,'" 75; Craig, *Kentucky Confederates,* 36–37.

22. Craig, *Kentucky Confederates,* 71–92, 156–59, 293, 330.

23. Marshall, *Creating a Confederate Kentucky,* 181–82, 204–25; "Jefferson Davis Obelisk to Pass into Kentucky's Devoted Keeping," *Paducah News-Democrat,* June 7, 1924; Patrick Lewis, draft of "Jefferson Davis State Historic Site Interpretive Background Document," April 2018, Kentucky Historical Society, Frankfort; "Blue Gray Park Given to State," *Danville Daily Messenger,* September 2, 1929; "Blue and Gray State Park Is in Todd County," *Paducah Sun-Democrat,* May 5, 1935.

24. Klotter and Friend, *A New History of Kentucky,* 195; Hoskins, "'The Old First Is with the South,'" 244–81; George C. Wright, *Racial Violence in Kentucky, 1865–1945: Lynchings, Mob Rule, and "Legal Lynchings"* (Baton Rouge: Louisiana State University Press, 1980), 16, 71.

25. Richard D. Parker, "The Black Patch Tobacco War's Effects on African Americans and Women," *Jackson Purchase Historical Society Journal* 45 (2019): 14–23; Bill Cunningham to the author, email, April 5, 2021; Cunningham, *On Bended Knees,* 143; Wright, *Racial Violence in Kentucky,* 123–24; Melinda Meador, "The Truth Is Not Always Black or White: Facts and Fictions Surrounding the David Walker Lynchings," *Jackson Purchase Historical Society Journal* 47 (2020): 23–40; James W. Loewen, *Sundown Towns: A Hidden Dimension of American Racism* (New York: Touchstone Press, 2005), 141; Luther Adams, "My Old Kentucky Home: Black History in the Bluegrass State," *Register of the Kentucky Historical Society* 113, nos. 2–3 (Spring–Summer 2015): 413–15; US

Bureau of the Census, *U.S Census of Agriculture, 1910, vol. 2, part 2: The Southern States: Kentucky* (*Washington, DC: US Department of Commerce, 1913*), *67–74; US Bureau of the Census, United States Census of Agriculture, 1950, Kentucky, 622–34, Census of Agriculture Historical Archive, Albert R. Mann Library, Cornell University, Ithaca, NY, at* agcensus.mannlib.cornell.edu.

26. Bill Cunningham, *A Distant Light: Kentucky's Journey toward Racial Justice* (Kuttawa, KY: McClanahan, 2005), 44–207; Christopher Waldrep, "The Impact of Race on Law in Kentucky: A Research Note," *Register of the Kentucky Historical Society* 90, no. 2 (Spring 1992): 165–82.

27. Adams, "My Old Kentucky Home," 413–15; US Bureau of the Census, *U.S Census of Agriculture, 1910, vol. 2, part 2: The Southern States: Kentucky, 67–74; US Bureau of the Census, United States Census of Agriculture, 1950, Kentucky, 622–34, Census of Agriculture Historical Archive, Albert R. Mann Library, Cornell University, Ithaca, NY, at* agcensus.mannlib.cornell.edu; Wright, *Racial Violence in Kentucky,* 141–43.

28. Wright, *Racial Violence in Kentucky,* 123–24, 135–28; "Negroes Taken to Jail at Mayfield," *Paducah Evening Sun,* December 19, 1918; Gerald L. Smith, *A Black Educator in the Segregated South: Kentucky's Rufus B. Atwood* (Lexington: University Press of Kentucky, 1994), xx; Jack Glazier, *Been Coming through Some Hard Times: Race, History, and Memory in Western Kentucky* (Knoxville: University of Tennessee Press, 2012), 140.

29. Alice Allison Dunnigan, *A Black Woman's Experience—from Schoolhouse to White House* (Philadelphia: Dorrance, 1974); Carol Crowe Carraco, "Dunnigan, Alice Allison," in *The Kentucky African American Encyclopedia,* ed. Gerald L. Smith, Karen Cotton McDaniel, and John A. Hardin (Lexington: University Press of Kentucky, 2015), 414; Donald A. Ritchie, *Reporting from Washington: The History of the Washington Press Carps* (New York: Oxford University Press, 2005), 38–45; Glazier, *Been Coming through Some Hard Times,* 219; Kathleen A. Hauke, *Ted Poston: Pioneer American Journalist* (Athens: University of Georgia Press, 1998); "Taking Another Look at Influential Women in Kentucky: Gloria Jean Watkins (bell hooks)," Kentucky Women in the Civil Rights Era, University of Kentucky, Lexington, at http://www.kywcrh.org/archives/tag/bell-hooks.

30. Shannon and McQuown, *Presidential Politics in Kentucky,* 41–44; Irvin S. Cobb, *Those Times and These* (New York: George H. Doran, 1917), 309; Lon Carter Barton, "Gibraltar of Democracy," in *The Kentucky Encyclopedia,* ed. John E. Kleber (Lexington: University Press of Kentucky, 1992), 373.

31. "Foreword," *Paducah Sun-Democrat,* January 17, 1922; "Welcome Brothers," *Paducah Evening Sun,* May 26, 1923; "George H. Goodman, 85, Dies," *Paducah Sun-Democratm* September 23, 1961; "Urey Woodson Served as *Owensboro Messenger* Publisher 48 Years," *Owensboro Messenger,* June 22, 1934; "Newsman, Civic Leader Lawrence Hager, Sr. Dies," *Owensboro Messenger-Inquirer,* December 26, 1982; Al Smith, *Wordsmith: My Life in Journalism*

(Louisville, KY: Clark Legacies, 2011); Laura A. Clemmons, "Paxton Media Group Extends Its Influence Far beyond Its Western Kentucky Base," Fall 2005, Institute for Rural Journalism, University of Kentucky, at www.uky.edu/CommInfoStudies/IRJCI/reports/Clemmons.htm; "Paxton Media Group Purchases *The Messenger*," *Madisonville Messenger*, August 1, 1995.

32. James C. Klotter, *William Goebel: The Politics of Wrath* (Lexington: University Press of Kentucky, 1977); James C. Klotter, "William S. Taylor," in *Kentucky Governors*, updated ed., ed. Lowell Harrison (Lexington: University Press of Kentucky, 2004), 131–36.

33. David Howarth, with others, "Natural Environment," in *Atlas of Kentucky*, ed. Ulack, Raitz, and Pauer, 22; Hambleton Tapp and James C. Klotter, *Kentucky: Decades of Discord, 1865–1900*, (Frankfort: Kentucky Historical Society, 1977), 299–306; Rothbert, *History of Muhlenberg County*, 368–79.

34. *Preliminary Map of Kentucky Prepared by the Kentucky Geological Survey for the Kentucky Railroad Commissioners, 1891*, Library of Congress, Washington, DC, at www.loc.gov/item/98688487; Roy Carson, "Coal Industry in Kentucky," *Filson Club Historical Quarterly* 40 (January 1966): 32–34; James Duane Bolin, "'An Air of Tenseness': Labor Strife and Tragedy in Kentucky's Western Coal Field, 1888–1939," *Filson Club Historical Quarterly* 73 (January 1999): 6; "The City of Earlington, KY," *Madisonville Messenger*, June 24, 1967; Richard L. Massamore, *Dawson Springs: A Bridge to the Past* (Evansville, IN: Evansville Bindery, 1995), 86; "Three Major League Teams in Kentucky," *Paducah News-Democrat*, March 15, 1915.

35. "The Exchange," *Owensboro Messenger*, June 11, 1880; "Owensboro's Telephone Connections," *Owensboro Messenger and Examiner*, December 20, 1882; Dew and Dew, *Owensboro*, 99; Alben W. Barkley, *That Reminds Me—* (New York: Doubleday, 1954), 55; Jewell, *Lick Skillet*, 64–65; *US Bureau of the Census, United States Census of Agriculture, 1954, Kentucky*, 102–11, Census of Agriculture Historical Archive, Albert R. Mann Library, Cornell University, Ithaca, NY, at agcensus.mannlib.cornell.edu.

36. "Ledgers Launch Initiative," *Owensboro Messenger-Inquirer*, May 13, 1984; "The Illinois Central Shops and Industrial Expansion Edition," *Paducah News-Democrat*, September 29, 1927; "Illinois Central Shops Here among Greatest in America," *Paducah News-Democrat*, September 29, 1927; "Illinois Central's Plans and Activities Here Described in Rotary Luncheon," *Paducah Sun-Democrat*, March 27, 1930; "Mayfield Woolen Mills Is Giant of the World," *Paducah Evening Sun*, July 26, 1927; "Rebound from Plant Loss Predicted," *Paducah Sun*, June 15, 1980; City of Hickman Register of National Historic Places Application, US Department of Interior, April 17, 1990, at https://npgallery.nps.gov/NRHP/GetAsset/NRHP/64500231_text.

37. Helen Bartter Crocker, *The Green River of Kentucky* (Lexington: University Press of Kentucky, 1976), 1–70; "Wharf Blaze Damage Near $75,000," *Bowling Green Park City News*, July 27, 1931.

38. "The Fight on Again," *Owensboro Messenger,* July 25, 1896; "Purchase Complete," *Paducah Sun,* April 30, 1897; "For Free Roads," *Owensboro Messenger,* August 14, 1897; "To Forfeit Charters," *Owensboro Daily Messenger,* March 19, 1899; "The Gravel Roads," *Owensboro Daily Messenger,* March 24, 1899; "80 Per Cent," *Hopkinsville Kentuckian,* April 24, 1900; "Toll Gates Going," *Owensboro Messenger,* April 11, 1903; Tapp and Klotter, *Kentucky,* 404–8.

39. Ireland, *Little Kingdoms,* 120; Barkley, *That Reminds Me,* 45.

40. "Great Good Roads Convention," *Hopkinsville Kentuckian,* June 28, 1901; "Great Success," *Hopkinsville Kentuckian,* July 12, 1901; "Organized," *Louisville Courier-Journal,* July 12, 1901; "Thousands Attend," *Owensboro Inquirer,* July 19, 1901.

41. "To Vote for Better Roads," *Madisonville Semi-weekly Hustler,* October 15, 1909; "Vote for Good Roads," *Paducah News-Democrat,* October 31, 1909; "Vote 'Yes' on the Good Roads Amendment," *Owensboro Messenger,* November 2, 1909; "Majority for Highways Amendment," *Paducah News-Democrat,* November 23, 1909; "Fiscal Court Is Given the Power to Issue Bonds," *Owensboro Daily Messenger,* June 23, 1915.

42. "'Evil Communications Corrupts Good Manners': Kentucky Has at Last Harkened to the Proverb and in the Lincoln and Jackson Way, Jeff Davis Way and Better Roads Generally, Holds Out Glad Hand Generally," *Louisville Courier-Journal,* February 4, 1912; "Jackson Way in Three Years," *Louisville Courier-Journal,* September 25, 1915; "What Is Wrong with Highway?," *Louisville Courier-Journal,* November 7, 1920; "Two Millions to Be Spent on Roads," *Owensboro Messenger,* March 15, 1915.

43. "Paducahans at Memphis Peacemakers," *Paducah News-Democrat,* February 18, 1916; "Weille's Is 100 Years Old," *Paducah Sun-Democrat,* October 16, 1960; "Road Conditions during Winter," *Louisville Courier-Journal,* December 31, 1922; "Bee Line Follows the Dixie Flyer," *Evansville Press,* November 5, 1915; "Driving on the Dixie Bee Line," *Madisonville Messenger,* November 30, 1926; "Highway Body Travels Bee Line to Meet," *Madisonville Messenger,* December 12, 1926.

44. "'The Detour State,'" *Louisville Courier-Journal,* February 24, 1923; "Why Detour Kentucky?," *Paducah News-Democrat,* October 6, 1928; "War Declared on Detour State," *Owensboro Messenger-Inquirer,* April 27, 1930.

45. "Concrete Surfacing Is Urged by Good Roads Association," *Owensboro Messenger,* June 11, 1930; "Rudy as Head of Bridge Committee Makes Dream Real," *Paducah News-Democrat,* May 6, 1929; "Vehicular Bridge to Span Ohio River at Paducah," *Paducah News-Democrat,* September 29, 1917.

46. "Bridges Mean Progress," *Paducah News-Democrat,* July 15, 1928.

47. "Seventeen Spans Instate Included in Contract," *Owensboro Messenger,* January 9, 1930; "Muhlenberg to Speed Up Work on Its Highways," *Owensboro Messenger and Inquirer,* August 2, 1931.

48. "Western State Hospital Marks Its First Century," *Louisville Courier-Journal,* September 27, 1954; "Care, Efficiency, and Humane Spirit Marks Management Western Ky. Hospital," *Paducah News-Democrat,* September 28, 1919; Tapp and Klotter, *Kentucky,* 177–82; Nancy Disher Baird, *Luke Pryor Blackburn: Physician, Governor, Reformer* (Lexington: University Press of Kentucky, 1979), 44–49, 105–6; Bill Cunningham, *Castle: The Story of a Kentucky Prison* (Kuttawa, KY: McClanahan, 1995), 16, 23; "15,000 Are Expected at Dawson Springs," *Owensboro Messenger,* February 22, 1922; "Hospital Day Set for May 12," *Madisonville Hustler,* May 7, 1926.

49. James K. Libbey, *Alben Barkley: A Career in Politics* (Lexington: University Press of Kentucky, 2016), 29; Ellis, *A History of Education in Kentucky,* 120–22.

50. Lowell H. Harrison, *Western Kentucky University* (Lexington: University Press of Kentucky, 1987), 15–60; "Normal Act Is Upheld by Judge Hurst," *Louisville Courier-Journal,* January 12, 1923; William Ray Mofield, "Rainey T. Wells: His Role in the Establishment of Murray State University," *Jackson Purchase Historical Society Journal* 19 (1991): 6–8; John Wesley Carr, *Recollections of Murray State College: An Adventure in Education in Old Kentucky, 1918–1952* (Murray, KY: Murray State University, 1998), 9–17, 87.

51. Alicestyne Turley-Adams, *Rosenwald Schools in Kentucky* (Lexington: Kentucky Heritage Council, 1997), 8–9, 25–29; "There's an Air of Sadness as Rosenwald School Closes," *Madisonville Messenger,* May 17, 1966

52. "Western Kentucky Negro School Bill Passed in Senate," *Paducah Evening Sun,* March 8, 1918; "Dedicate Girls Dormitory at Negro College Today," *Paducah Sun-Democrat,* September 15, 1929; Janette M. Blythe, *Upward Stride: A Pictorial History of West Kentucky Community & Technical College* (Virginia Beach, VA: Donning, 2008), 18–23.

2. The New Deal and Western Kentucky

1. "Laffoon Given a Huge Ovation in Frankfort," *Madisonville Messenger,* December 8, 1931; "125 Travel on Special Train," *Madisonville Messenger,* December 8, 1931.

2. John Ed Pearce, *Divide and Dissent: Kentucky Politics, 1930–1963* (Lexington: University of Kentucky Press, 1987), 32; Vernon Gipson, *Ruby Laffoon: Governor of Kentucky, 1931–1935* (Hartford, KY: McDowell, 1978), 21–61; Bill Cox, interviewed by the author, September 14, 2011, Kentucky Legislature Oral History Project, Louis B. Nunn Center for Oral History, University of Kentucky, Lexington.

3. "This Is Not News," *Owensboro Messenger,* October 22, 1931; "Woes of Country Blamed on Country's Political Chiefs," *Paducah Sun-Democrat,* October 30, 1931; "To You—West Kentucky," *Paducah Sun-Democrat,* November 1,

1931; "Editorial in Which We Preach Sectionalism," *Madisonville Daily Messenger,* November 2, 1931.

4. Malcolm E. Jewell, *Kentucky Votes,* vol. 2: *Gubernatorial Primary and General Elections, 1923–1959* (Lexington: University Press of Kentucky, 1963), 12–13.

5. Pearce, *Divide and Dissent,* 33; James C. Klotter, *Kentucky: Portrait in Paradox, 1900–1950* (Lexington: University Press of Kentucky, 1996), 297.

6. George T. Blakey, *Hard Times & New Deal in Kentucky, 1929–1945* (Lexington: University Press of Kentucky, 1986), 8; US Bureau of the Census, *U. S. Census of Agriculture, 1930,* vol. 2, part 2: *The Southern States: Kentucky* (Washington, DC: US Department of Commerce, 1932), at agcensus.mannlib. cornell.edu; Klotter, *Kentucky,* 245; "West Kentucky Counties Suffer from Dry Siege," *Paducah Sun-Democrat,* August 15, 1930; "Tobacco Sales Suspended until Monday," *Owensboro Inquirer,* December 2, 1931; "Farmers Stop Weed Sales," *Madisonville Messenger,* December 1, 1931.

7. Lee A. Dew and Aloma W. Dew, *Owensboro: The City on the Yellow Banks* (Bowling Green, KY: Riverdell, 1988), 90–92, 142–47; "Business Is Good in This Section Despite Depression," *Owensboro Messenger-Inquirer,* October 12, 1930; "C. of C. Report Tells Why Owensboro Is One of 15 Optimistic Cities of U.S.," *Owensboro Messenger-Inquirer,* October 26, 1930; "Bradshaw Takes Own Life," *Paducah Sun-Democrat,* January 7, 1930; "City National Bank Closes; Others Declared Sound," *Paducah Sun-Democrat,* October 28, 1931; "Utterback Drowns in Lake," *Paducah Sun-Democrat,* October 30, 1931; Tim Meador, Kentucky Department of Financial Institutions, to the author, email, November 29, 2010; "National Bank of Kentucky Closes Doors," *Paducah Sun-Democrat,* November 17, 1930; "State Banking Situation Takes Brighter Aspect," *Owensboro Messenger,* August 26, 1931; "Nab Jones in Rumor Case," *Madisonville Messenger,* November 22, 1930.

8. "Unemployed of City to March Monday Night," *Paducah Sun-Democrat,* November 16, 1930; James P. Johnson, "Theories of Labor Union Development and the United Mine Workers, 1932–1933," *Register of the Kentucky Historical Society* 70, no. 2 (April 1975): 156; "Red Cross to Assist Miners," *Madisonville Messenger,* December 2, 1931; "Free Lunches for Needy Kids in Muhlenberg," *Owensboro Inquirer,* December 8, 1931; "Plan to Help County Needed Drafted Here," *Madisonville Messenger,* December 11, 1931; "Hail the Governor!," *Madisonville Messenger,* December 8, 1931; "Opportune," *Paducah Sun-Democrat,* December 18, 1931.

9. "Sales Tax Is Planned for State," *Louisville Courier-Journal,* January 16, 1932; "Democrats in House Ban Tax Caucus," *Louisville Courier-Journal,* February 18, 1932; "General Sales Tax Is Urged by Gov. Laffoon," *Paducah Sun-Democrat,* February 23, 1932; "Gov. Laffoon Recommends Slash in Sales Tax Measure," *Paducah Sun-Democrat,* February 26, 1932; "Sales Tax Bill Foes Plan

Fight," *Louisville Courier-Journal,* February 26, 1932; "House Passes Cent Sales Tax 64–31," *Owensboro Messenger-Inquirer,* February 28, 1932.

10. "Merchants Told Their Pleas Will Be Given Consideration," *Paducah Sun-Democrat,* March 4, 1932; "Retailers Are Opposing Sales Tax Proposal," *Madisonville Hustler,* March 1, 1932; "Merchants to Join Protest against Levy," *Madisonville Messenger,* March 2, 1932; "Owensboro Represented," *Owensboro Inquirer,* March 3, 1931; "Thousands Protest against Sales Tax," *Louisville Courier-Journal,* March 5, 1932; "State House Is Damaged by 'Visitors,'" *Paducah Sun-Democrat,* March 4, 1932.

11. "Revenue Bills Die as House Adjourns," *Louisville Courier-Journal,* March 16, 1932; "Laffoon Says He Will Cut," *Louisville Courier-Journal,* March 18, 1932.

12. "Senator Barkley Urges Resubmission Plank," *Paducah Sun-Democrat,* June 18, 1932; "Barkley Boomed for Vice President," *New York Times,* June 28, 1932; "Spontaneous Confusion," *Time,* July 4, 1932; "Down to Business," *Paducah Sun-Democrat,* June 29, 1932; James K. Libbey, *Alben Barkley: A Life in Politics* (Lexington: University Press of Kentucky, 2016), 160–63 (including quote from Will Rogers).

13. "180,000 Lead Forecast for Democrats," *Louisville Courier-Journal,* November 11, 1932; Kentucky State Board of Elections, election returns for 1932, CD requested by the author, November 2011; Earle C. Clements, interviewed by James W. Hammack, November 17, 1976, Jackson Purchase Oral History Project, Pogue Library, Murray State University, Murray, KY.

14. David M. Kennedy, *Freedom from Fear: The American People in Depression and War, 1929–1935* (New York: Oxford University Press, 1999), 102–33; "Time for Calm, Clear Thinking," *Owensboro Messenger,* March 2, 1933; "Banks of Kentucky Reopen Today," *Owensboro Messenger,* March 3, 1933; "Purchase Bankers Disregard Governor's Action; Their Banks Operating as Usual," *Paducah Sun-Democrat,* March 1, 1933; "West Kentucky Banks Continue Usual Business," *Paducah Sun-Democrat,* March 2, 1933.

15. "A Man Speaks Out," *Paducah Sun-Democrat,* March 13, 1933; "Return of Confidence Noted as Bank Deposits Mount," *Owensboro Messenger,* March 15, 1933; "First-Owensboro Gains $64,000 in Deposits Friday," *Owensboro Messenger,* March 18, 1933.

16. "McCracken County to Send 97 Jobless Men to Federal Conservation Corps," *Paducah Sun-Democrat,* April 13, 1933; "Erosion Camp at Benton Worth Millions to Area," *Paducah Sun-Democrat,* September 22, 1933; "An Attack on Idleness," *Paducah Sun-Democrat,* March 30, 1933.

17. Connie M. Huddleston, *Kentucky's Civilian Conservation Corps* (Charleston, SC: History Press, 2009), 37, 80, 121–23; "Camp Owen Now Begins to Wear Permanent Garb," *Owensboro Messenger,* October 6, 1935.

18. "Columbus Park Move Launched," *Paducah Sun-Democrat,* July 7, 1929; "Seen While Roaming," *Paducah Sun-Democrat,* March 28, 1934; "Governor Will Be Present at Park Ceremony," *Paducah Sun-Democrat,* June 28, 1935; "New Columbus–Belmont Park Has Historical Setting," *Paducah Sun-Democrat,* October 13, 1935; Blakey, *Hard Times & New Deal,* 78; Huddleston, *Kentucky's Civilian Conservation Corps,* 35, 73.

19. "Her Dream of Memorial Comes True," *Louisville Courier-Journal,* June 19, 1938; John Palmore, *From the Panama Canal to Elkhorn Creek* (Louisville, KY: Butler Books, 2006), 84–85; Mark Kellen, interviewed by the author, James B. Audubon State Park, March 17, 2011, West Kentucky Politics Project, Nunn Center; "Kentucky State Parks," *Owensboro Messenger-Inquirer,* June 2, 1935; "Wild Life Sanctuary near Henderson to Become Nest Station for Birds," *Owensboro Messenger-Inquirer,* August 30, 1937; "Trees, Birds, and Relics in an Audubon Museum," *Louisville Courier-Journal,* July 2, 1938.

20. Blakey, *Hard Times & New Deal,* 21–22; "Kentucky as a Mendicant," *Louisville Courier-Journal,* July 23, 1932; "Gatton Directs State Relief," *Louisville Courier-Journal,* October 5, 1932; "Relief of 50,000 Families Granted by State's Group," *Paducah Sun-Democrat,* December 7, 1932; "825,993 People Given Help by Relief Group," *Paducah Sun-Democrat,* August 14, 1933; "Relief Group Is Watching Action," *Owensboro Messenger,* August 20, 1933.

21. "Two More CWA Projects Give 253 Men Work," *Paducah Sun-Democrat,* December 5, 1933; Joseph E. Brent, "The Civil Works Administration in Western Kentucky: Work Relief's Dress Rehearsal under Fire," *Filson Club Historical Quarterly* 67 (July 1993): 259–76.

22. List of New Deal courthouse projects at https://exploreuk.uky.edu/cat alog/?q=courthouse&f%5Bsource_s%5D%5B%5D=Goodman-Paxton+Photo graphic+Collection%2C; Dew and Dew, *Owensboro,* 159; "Dedication Plans Ready," *Owensboro Messenger-Inquirer,* July 28, 1940; Blakey, *Hard Times & New Deal,* 75–76.

23. Blakey, *Hard Times & New Deal,* 21–22; "State Asks for $15,000,000 Loan from U.S.," *Paducah Sun-Democrat,* July 22, 1932; "$3,000,000 Aid Needed in State," *Louisville Courier-Journal,* July 31, 1932.

24. "Legislature Control Big Issue Today," *Bowling Green Park City Daily News,* August 5, 1933; "Issues Confused; in Many Races; Contests Bitter," *Owensboro Messenger-Inquirer,* August 6, 1933; "Special Session Is Being Urged," *Owensboro Inquirer,* July 24, 1933; "Action Imperative," *Owensboro Messenger,* August 16, 1933; "Muhlenberg Jobless Leave in Trucks for Frankfort," *Madisonville Messenger,* September 15, 1933; "House Again Turns Down Gross Tax Bill," *Paducah Sun-Democrat,* September 23, 1933; "Move to Appeal to Solons under Way," *Madisonville Messenger,* September 16, 1933; "Laffoon Hears Jobless' Plea," *Louisville Courier-Journal,* September 17, 1933; "Food

Demanded by 300 Jobless at Central City," *Owensboro Messenger,* September 28, 1933; "Tell Laffoon 'Only God Knows What Will Happen.'" *Owensboro Messenger,* September 28, 1933.

25. Blakey, *Hard Times & New Deal,* 49–50; "Gov. Laffoon Denies Threat of Boycott," *Owensboro Inquirer,* August 23, 1933; "House Votes Consumers, Beer, and Whisky Taxes," *Louisville Courier-Journal,* September 22, 1933.

26. "Senator Franklin Debates for Relief Measure Killed by Senate 24–13," *Madisonville Messenger,* September 23, 1933; "Senate Kills Consumers' Tax by 23–13 Vote," *Louisville Courier-Journal,* September 23, 1933.

27. "State Relief Set-Up Ready," *Louisville Courier-Journal,* September 28, 1933; "State's Relief Burden in Federal Lap," *Paducah Sun-Democrat,* November 6, 1933; "Relief Work in Kentucky Turned Over to U. S. Group," *Owensboro Messenger,* November 7, 1933; Blakey, *Hard Times & New Deal,* 51–52.

28. William E. Ellis, "Ruby Laffoon (1931–1935)," in *Kentucky's Governors,* updated ed., ed. Lowell Harrison (Lexington: University Press of Kentucky, 2004), 166; "Laffoon Dominates Party Caucus Sessions," *Owensboro Messenger-Inquirer,* January 2, 1934; "Laffoon Man Is Senate Leader," *Louisville Courier-Journal,* January 2, 1934; "'Brain Trust' of Laffoon Listed," *Louisville Courier-Journal,* April 15, 1934.

29. "Chandler Is Stripped," *Louisville Courier-Journal,* January 3, 1934; "Chandler Stripped of His Power," *Owensboro Messenger,* January 3, 1934; "Seen While Roaming," *Paducah Sun-Democrat,* January 4, 1934.

30. James C. Klotter and John W. Muir, "Boss Ben Johnson, the Highway Commission, and Kentucky Politics, 1927–1937," *Register of the Kentucky Historical Society* 84, no. 1 (Winter 1986): 40–43; "Tom Rhea Elected Chairman of Highway Commission," *Owensboro Messenger-Inquirer,* January 8, 1935; "Ben Johnson Ousted as Chairman of Highway Commission," *Owensboro Messenger-Inquirer,* January 8, 1935; "Representatives of District United," *Paducah Sun-Democrat,* November 28, 1933; Pearce, *Divide and Dissent,* 33.

31. "Raising Revenues to Be Left with Legislature," *Owensboro Messenger,* January 3, 1934.

32. "Committee to Ask 3 Percent Levy on Sales," *Paducah Sun-Democrat,* April 9, 1934; "Sales Tax War Waged in Other Parts of the State," *Paducah Sun-Democrat,* April 13, 1934; "Proposed Tax on Retail Sales Soundly Flailed in Meeting at Woman's Club," *Paducah Sun-Democrat,* April 13, 1934.

33. "Report Made on Finances in Kentucky," *Louisville Courier-Journal,* April 2, 1934; "Laffoon Machine Says It Has Pledges Enough to Put Over All Policies," *Paducah Sun-Democrat,* April 8, 1934; "Administration Pleased with KEA Tax Resolutions," *Owensboro Messenger-Inquirer,* April 22, 1934; "Both Sides Are Entrenched for Sales Tax Fight," *Paducah Sun-Democrat,* May 18, 1934; "Farmers Plan Capitol Trip," *Madisonville Messenger,* May 19, 1934; "Thousands Visit State Capitol to Urge Sales Tax," *Owensboro Messenger,* May

21, 1934; "Thousands Hit Frankfort," *Madisonville Messenger,* May 21, 1934; "Immense Crowd Invades Capital Urging Sales Tax," *Owensboro Inquirer,* May 22, 1934.

34. "Receipts Tax Beaten, 66 to 32," *Louisville Courier-Journal,* May 23, 1934; "House Deadlock on Revenue Bill Continues as Move in Senate to Adjourn Hits Snag," *Owensboro Messenger,* May 24, 1934; "Administration to Continue Sales Tax Drive," *Owensboro Inquirer,* May 30, 1934; "Compromise Tax Opinions Vary Widely," *Louisville Courier-Journal,* May 24, 1934.

35. "Sales Tax Bill Is Passed," *Owensboro Messenger,* May 9, 1934; "House Passes Receipts Tax Bill," *Louisville Courier-Journal,* June 8, 1934; "KY House Passes Sales Tax on Third Attempt," *Paducah Sun-Democrat,* June 8, 1934.

36. "Gross Receipts Tax Made Law," *Louisville Courier-Journal,* June 16, 1934; "Kentucky State Senate Passes Sales Tax by 20–16," *Owensboro Inquirer,* June 15, 1934.

37. "Within Year, Laffoon Rises from Self-Styled Figurehead to Possessor of Unlimited Power," *Madisonville Messenger,* December 22, 1934; "G. H. Goodman Given Command of State Relief," *Paducah Sun-Democrat,* October 29, 1934; "Excellent Selection," *Owensboro Messenger-Inquirer,* October 31, 1934; Gipson, *Ruby Laffoon,* 130–33.

38. "Over $57,000,000 Given to State under Roosevelt Relief," *Owensboro Inquirer,* March 18, 1936.

39. Blakey, *Hard Times & New Deal,* 30–35; "Special Section to Be Set Up to Aid Home Owners," *Paducah Sun-Democrat,* January 4, 1934; "Merchants and Manufacturers Exposition Ends," *Owensboro Messenger-Inquirer,* June 21, 1936.

40. "Sign-Up for Tax Exempt Cotton Opens in State," *Paducah Sun-Democrat,* August 1, 1933; "Last of Cotton Payments Received," *Paducah Sun-Democrat,* November 26, 1933; "More Than 3,000 Corn–Hog Contracts Signed in District," *Paducah Sun-Democrat,* May 3, 1935; Blakey, *Hard Times & New Deal,* 106–7, 116.

41. "Corn–Hog Pact Signing Closes," *Owensboro Inquirer,* May 1, 1934; "Hogs to Slaughter," *Paducah Sun-Democrat,* September 3, 1933; Blakey, *Hard Times & New Deal,* 108–16.

42. "Local Tobacco Prospects Are Good," *Paducah Sun-Democrat,* October 19, 1934; George T. Blakey, "The New Deal and Rural Kentucky," *Register of the Kentucky Historical Society* 84, no. 2 (Spring 1986): 156–60.

43. Blakey, *Hard Times & New Deal,* 142.

44. "The Blue Eagle," *Owensboro Messenger-Inquirer,* July 30, 1933; "NRA Parade Sets Record Here; over 5 Miles Long," *Owensboro Messenger-Inquirer,* September 1, 1933; "Plant of Ken-Rad Joins Ranks of NRA Blue Eagle," *Owensboro Messenger-Inquirer,* August 17, 1933; "Paducah Army of Blue Eagle Ready to Drive," *Paducah Sun-Democrat,* September 12, 1933; "The Sign of the

Times," *Bowling Green Park City Daily News,* September 12, 1933; "50 Merchants Fix Hours of Opening Here," *Madisonville Hustler,* August 4, 1933; "Mayfield News," *Paducah Sun-Democrat,* August 30, 1933.

45. "Group Declares Blue Eagle Has Delayed Recovery," *Owensboro Inquirer,* April 19, 1935; Blakey, *Hard Times & New Deal,* 148–55.

46. James Duane Bolin, "An 'Air of Tenseness': Labor Strife and Tragedy in Kentucky's Western Coal Field, 1888–1939," *Filson Club Historical Quarterly* 73 (January 1999): 3–33; Johnson, "Theories of Labor Union Development and the United Mine Workers, 1932–1933," 150–70.

47. "Kentucky Mining," n.d., GenDisasters, at https://gendisasters.com/mainlist/kentucky/mining; Bobby Anderson, *Coal: Memories of a Coal Miner's Son* (Goodlettsville, TN: self-published, 2013), 133–40; "Lewis Demands $5-Day," *Madisonville Messenger,* August 10, 1933; "To the Public," *Madisonville Messenger,* September 13, 1933.

48. "U. M. W. A. Seeks District Wage Meeting Here," *Madisonville Messenger,* July 22, 1933; "U. M. W. A. Mass Meets Resumed in District 23," *Madisonville Messenger,* September 6, 1933; "Hart and Sixth Vein Men Walk Out on Strike," *Madisonville Messenger,* August 17, 1933; "Labor Board Prober Will Visit Field," *Madisonville Messenger,* August 25, 1933; "Many Hurt in Pit Clashes," *Madisonville Messenger,* September 30, 1933; "Union Leader Free on Bond," *Madisonville Messenger,* October 6, 1933; "Board Airs Pit Charges," *Madisonville Messenger,* October 12, 1933.

49. Johnson, "Theories of Labor Union Development and the United Mine Workers, 1932–1933," 158–59, 165; "Discuss Coal Wage Edict," *Madisonville Messenger,* April 2, 1934; "Suit on Wage Scale to Get Hearing Tuesday," *Madisonville Messenger,* April 4, 1934; "Operators Waiting on Coal Code Hearing," *Owensboro Messenger-Inquirer,* April 4, 1934; "Coal Miners Idle in This District," *Owensboro Messenger-Inquirer,* April 25, 1934; "Dawson Grants Pit Writ," *Madisonville Messenger,* May 2, 1934; "Injunction for Kentucky Mines Seen," *Louisville-Courier-Journal,* May 2, 1934; "Reopening Forecast for Mines in State," *Louisville Courier-Journal,* May 3, 1934; "Mines Operated by Company Union Opens," *Owensboro Messenger-Inquirer,* May 4, 1934; "I.M.U Ratifies New Contract at Madisonville," *Owensboro Messenger-Inquirer,* May 6, 1934; "Number of Coal Mines in Area Are Reopened," *Owensboro Messenger-Inquirer,* May 12, 1934; "Muhlenberg Pits to Open on $4 Scale," *Madisonville Messenger,* May 10, 1934; "8 Muhlenberg Pits Working," *Madisonville Messenger,* May 11, 1934.

50. "West Kentucky Instructed to Drop Contract," *Madisonville Messenger,* February 28, 1938; "Labor Board Orders EMBA Be Dissolved," *Paducah Sun-Democrat,* December 5, 1938; "Details of Ruling against Firms Listed by NLRB," *Madisonville Messenger,* February 27, 1939; "Kentucky Mines Are Idled," *Owensboro Messenger,* May 5, 1939; "Outlying U. M. W. A. Districts

Told to Sign 2-Year Pacts with Operators," *Madisonville Messenger,* May 11, 1939; "Whistles Call 6,000 Back in West Kentucky," *Owensboro Messenger-Inquirer,* May 12, 1939; "West Kentucky Miners Vote No on UMW Representation," *Madisonville Messenger,* November 27, 1941.

51. "1st District Counties for Primary Race," *Louisville Courier-Journal,* January 15, 1935 (quoting *Hickman Courier* and *Hopkinsville New Era*); "Jackson Purchase in Favor of Primary," *Louisville Courier-Journal,* January 17, 1935; "Democratic Voting on Primary," *Louisville Courier-Journal,* January 23, 1935; "Talking Too Soon," *Owensboro Messenger-Inquirer,* February 3, 1935; "Editorial Comment on Democratic Convention," *Paducah Sun-Democrat,* February 4, 1935.

52. Albert B. Chandler, *Heroes, Plain Folks, and Skunks: The Life and Times of Happy Chandler* (Chicago: Bonus Books, 1989), 102–3; "Ward Would Favor State Primary," *Paducah Sun-Democrat,* February 6, 1935.

53. "Laffoon Favors Runoff Primary," *Owensboro Messenger,* February 13, 1935; Gipson, *Ruby Laffoon,* 145–47.

54. "Thom Rhea's Legacy Nearly Forgotten," *Russellville News-Democrat & Leader,* November 11, 1997.

55. Chandler, *Heroes,* 77, 95; Stephen D. Boyd, "The Campaign Speaking of A. B. Chandler," *Register of the Kentucky Historical Society* 79, no. 3 (Summer 1981): 228–30, 233, 268–69.

56. Jewell, *Gubernatorial Primary and General Elections, 1923–1959,* 14–17; "Thomas S. Rhea for Governor," *Paducah Sun-Democrat,* September 3, 1935; "Beckham and the Women Voters," *Paducah Sun-Democrat,* September 4, 1935; "Last Chance for Democrats," *Paducah Sun-Democrat,* September 6, 1935; "Billy Klair Said It," *Madisonville Messenger,* August 22, 1935.

57. Gipson, *Ruby Laffoon,* 161; "Final Pleas Are Voiced by Rival Candidates," *Louisville Courier-Journal,* November 5, 1935; Jewell, *Gubernatorial Primary and General Elections, 1923–1959,* 24–25.

58. "Ferguson's Board Ripped by Happy," *Paducah Sun-Democrat,* January 7, 1935; "Utility Board and Logan Feel Governor's Axe," *Paducah Sun-Democrat,* December 19, 1935; "Chandler Stirs Up Hornet's Nest over Cherry," *Owensboro Messenger,* August 29, 1937. See also Lowell H. Harrison, *Western Kentucky University* (Lexington: University Press of Kentucky, 1987), 108–9.

59. "Caucus Selects Kirtley to Be House Speaker," *Louisville Courier-Journal,* January 7, 1936.

60. "Chandler Plans Repeal Bill with Emergency Lines," *Owensboro Messenger,* January 3, 1936; "M'Lean County Again Honored in State Politics," *Owensboro Messenger-Inquirer,* January 5, 1936; "Regular Session of Legislature to End Feb. 15," *Owensboro Inquirer,* January 8, 1936; "Sales Tax Repealers Pass in Both Chambers," *Louisville Courier-Journal,* January 11, 1936; "One Feeble 'Nay,'" *Owensboro Messenger-Inquirer,* January 12, 1936; "Sales Tax Is Dead," *Madisonville Messenger,* January 16, 1936.

61. "Convict Labor Optional with County Officials," *Owensboro Inquirer*, February 18, 1936; "Convicts Have Different Slants on Road Working," *Owensboro Inquirer*, February 19, 1936; "Use of Convicts for Road Work Will Be Limited," *Owensboro Inquirer*, February 20, 1936; "Drought Stricken Farmers to Get Chance at Jobs," *Owensboro Inquirer*, July 9, 1936.

62. "Reorganization Bill Draws Fire at State Capital," *Owensboro Messenger*, February 25, 1936; "Seen While Roaming," *Paducah Sun-Democrat*, March 4, 1936; "House Passes Reorganization Bill," *Owensboro Messenger*, March 5, 1934; "Chandler Bill Re-passed with Items Stricken," *Paducah Sun-Democrat*, March 8, 1936; Charles P. Roland, "Albert Benjamin Chandler (1935–1939, 1955–1959)," in *Kentucky's Governors*, ed. Harrison, 171; Klotter, *Kentucky*, 309, emphasis in original.

63. "State Budget Calls for More Than $23,000,000," *Owensboro Inquirer*, March 17, 1936; "Chandler Asks Legislature to Pass Budget Bill," *Owensboro Inquirer*, March 17, 1936; "Total Amount of Revenue Not Yet Divulged," *Owensboro Inquirer*, March 19, 1936; "House Recommits Administration's Budget," *Owensboro Inquirer*, March 20, 1936; "Definite Break in Chandler's Office," *Owensboro Inquirer*, March 21, 1936; "Opposition to Ben Johnson and Talbott Growing," *Owensboro Inquirer*, March 23, 1936; "'Happy' Ready for Budget Showdown Now," *Paducah Sun-Democrat*, March 23, 1936; "Seen While Roaming," *Paducah Sun-Democrat*, March 24, 1936; "What's News," *Paducah Sun-Democrat*, March 24, 1936; "Seven Aides of State Fair Fired," *Owensboro Messenger-Inquirer*, March 24, 1936; "Ouster Order to Be Ignored," *Owensboro Inquirer*, March 25, 1936; "Administration's Budget Bill Passes House 94–3," *Owensboro Inquirer*, March 26, 1936.

64. "$7,000,000 in Rum Levy for State Asked," *Louisville Courier-Journal*, March 31, 1936; "Attack Seen on Motor Sales Tax," *Owensboro Inquirer*, April 6, 1936; "Chandler Gives His Tax Program to Democrats," *Owensboro Inquirer*, April 7, 1936; "Leaf Products Tax Bill Introduced in House," *Louisville Courier-Journal*, April 10, 1936; "Cardwell Calls Leaf Growers Meet Here," *Madisonville Messenger*, April 11, 1936; "Proposed Sales Tax on Tobacco Is Condemned," *Owensboro Messenger-Inquirer*, April 12, 1936; "Meeting in Henderson," *Madisonville Messenger*, April 13, 1936; "Legislators to Confer Tonight," *Louisville Courier-Journal*, April 13, 1936; "Farmers Ready to Fight Tax," *Paducah Sun-Democrat*, April 14, 1936; "Thousands at Stormy Session of Legislature," *Owensboro Inquirer*, April 15, 1936; "Doubt Revival of Weed Levy in This Session," *Paducah Sun-Democrat*, April 16, 1936; "Chandler Appeals for Support of Tax Bill," *Louisville Courier-Journal*, April 21, 1936; "From the State Capitol," *Louisville Courier-Journal*, April 26, 1936; "$12,000,000 Tax Legislation for State Complete," *Louisville Courier-Journal*, May 10, 1936.

65. Blakey, *Hard Times & New Deal*, 180–82; Pearce, *Divide and Dissent*, 42.

66. Kennedy, *Freedom from Fear*, 246–48; "WPA Setup Explained," *Madisonville Messenger*, July 8, 1935; "K. E. R. A. Program in State Faces Brief Delay," *Owensboro Inquirer*, July 11, 1935; "KERA Force in State Will Be Cut Down Half," *Madisonville Messenger*, July 15, 1935; "$1,120,395 Granted for WPA Projects," *Paducah Sun-Democrat*, August 13, 1935; "First WPA Job Starts Monday," *Madisonville Messenger*, August 19, 1935; "$50,000 for State Projects Ok'd by WPA," *Paducah Sun-Democrat*, December 2, 1935; Blakey, *Hard Times & New Deal*, 59–76.

67. Kennedy, *Freedom from Fear*, 253; "$2,014,656 W. P. A. Warrant Sent Kentucky," *Louisville Courier-Journal*, October 24, 1935; "Goodman Insists on Honest Work," *Paducah Sun-Democrat*, February 16, 1936; "Roads Gets Share of WPA Money in Kentucky," *Paducah Sun-Democrat*, February 18, 1936; "Many Children Given Clothing," *Madisonville Messenger*, February 13, 1936; "WPA Sewing Center Invites Public to Examine Products," *Paducah Sun-Democrat*, March 12, 1936.

68. Dew and Dew, *Owensboro*, 156–57; "West Kentucky Sums Approved," *Madisonville Messenger*, October 24, 1935; "Completion Seen for Colored Park Here in 6 Months," *Paducah Sun-Democrat*, January 2, 1938; "Paducah and the Purchase," *Paducah Sun-Democrat*, July 26, 1936; Blakey, *Hard Times & New Deal*, 59–60.

69. Roger Biles, *The South and the New Deal* (Lexington: University Press of Kentucky, 1994), 157; "U. S. to Acquire Big State Tract to Form Refuges," *Paducah Sun-Democrat*, December 6, 1936; "Coalins Forest Is Established," *Madisonville Daily Messenger*, November 11, 1935; "A Fresh Start for Land and Men," *Louisville Courier-Journal*, June 14, 1936; "Moonshiner Paradise Lost," *Louisville Courier-Journal*, March 21, 1936; "A Million-Dollar Playground for Outsiders, Work and Fertile Farms for the Natives," *Louisville Courier-Journal Sunday Magazine*, February 2, 1938; Blakey, *Hard Times & New Deal*, 126–27.

70. "New Homes for Old Land (and $1,000,000)," *Louisville Courier-Journal*, October 24, 1937; "Ex-tenants Top Average Farm Earnings," *Louisville Courier-Journal*, July 22, 1940; C. A. Baldwin Homestead National Registration of Historic Places Application, February 3, 2015, National Park Service, US Department of the Interior, at https://heritage.ky.gov/historic-places/national-register/Property%20Listings/Christian_CABaldwinFarmstead.pdf; Blakey, *Hard Times & New Deal*, 129–30.

71. Bobbie Faust, "George Luther Draffen," *Jackson Purchase Historical Society Journal* 37 (2010): 30; "Tennessee River Project Is Watched by City," *Paducah Sun-Democrat*, August 18, 1928.

72. Neal R. Peirce, *The Border South States: People, Politics, and Power in the Five States of the Border South* (New York: Norton, 1975), 362; "West Kentucky and Tennessee to Support Dam," *Paducah Sun-Democrat*, December 20, 1933;

"Aurora Dam Body Elects T. O. Turner," *Paducah Sun-Democrat,* December 28, 1933; "Construction of Aurora Dam Will Be Early Project," *Paducah Sun-Democrat,* December 17, 1933; "The Aurora Dam, What It Means," *Paducah Sun-Democrat,* December 24, 1933.

73. "Aurora Dam Is Menace to Mines Operator Says," *Paducah Sun-Democrat,* July 5, 1934; "West Kentucky Has Been 'Dam-Minded,'" *Paducah Sun-Democrat,* August 8, 1934; "Gregory Says Aurora Dam Is Now Certainty," *Paducah Sun-Democrat,* October 16, 1934; "Aurora Pledged by Roosevelt," *Paducah Sun-Democrat,* November 19, 1934; "40,000 Will Ask Start on Aurora Dam," *Paducah Sun-Democrat,* November 28, 1934; "Delegation Asks Quick Start Be Made on Aurora Dam," *Paducah Sun-Democrat,* May 28, 1935; Bill Cunningham, *Flames in the Wind: An Inspiring Collection of Stories about Courageous West Kentuckians* (Princeton, KY: McClanahan, 1997), 253–67; Blakey, "The New Deal and Rural Kentucky, 1933–1941," 179–80.

74. D. Clayton Brown, *Electricity for Rural America: The Fight for the REA* (Westport, CT: Greenwood Press, 1980), ix–xvi; Blakey, *Hard Times & New Deal,* 139.

75. David Dick, *Let There Be Light: The Story of Rural Electrification in Kentucky* (North Middletown, KY: Plum Lick, 2008), 1; "Association Being Formed in State to Secure Rural Electrification," *Owensboro Messenger-Inquirer,* May 23, 1937; "850 Are Members of Cooperative," *Owensboro Messenger,* September 26, 1937; "Two More REA Extensions Will Be Energized," *Paducah Sun-Democrat,* October 24, 1938; "Ready to Start Calloway and Graves Line," *Paducah Sun-Democrat,* December 30, 1938; "Dream of 3 Years Realized as Current Flows to Rural Homes," *Paducah Sun-Democrat,* April 17, 1938; "REA Work in Fulton, Hickman Starts Soon," *Paducah Sun-Democrat,* May 13, 1938; Blakey, *Hard Times & New Deal,* 140; Thomas Clark, "Lighting the Soul of Kentucky," *Kentucky Living,* July 1998, 20–23.

76. "47 Other States Vote for Roosevelt and His Program," *Owensboro Messenger,* June 16, 1934; "*Literary Digest'*s Poll Reflects Anti–New Deal Sentiment," *Paducah Sun-Democrat,* December 1, 1935; "23 States Voting against New Deal," *Owensboro Messenger,* December 22, 1935; "City Favors the New Deal," *Madisonville Messenger,* January 27, 1936; "Danville Votes for the New Deal in the *Digest* Poll," *Danville Advocate,* January 27, 1936.

77. "Barkley Blasts Landon, Sounds Democrats' War Cry," *Paducah Sun-Democrat,* June 24, 1936; "We Are Proud of Barkley," *Paducah Sun-Democrat,* June 25, 1936.

78. "Cary Re-elected to Congress by 30,913 Majority," *Owensboro Messenger,* November 5, 1936; "County Casts Greatest Demo Vote in District," *Paducah Sun-Democrat,* November 6, 1936; "Glover H. Cary Dies," *Owensboro Inquirer,* December 6, 1936.

79. A. Scott Berg, *Wilson* (New York: Putnam, 2013), 263; Calvin P. Jones, "Kentucky's Irascible Conservative: Supreme Court Justice James C. McReynolds," *Filson Club Historical Quarterly* 57 (January 1983): 24; "Judiciary: Alone," *Time*, December 4, 1939; Ian Millhiser, *Injustices: The Supreme Court's History of Comforting the Comfortable and Afflicting the Afflicted* (New York: Nation Books, 2015), 77–78; "McReynolds Nears 78, Still Going Strong on High Court," *Birmingham (AL) News-Age-Herald*, January 28, 1940; Jeff Shesol, *Supreme Power: Franklin Roosevelt vs. the Supreme Court* (New York: Norton, 2010), 6.

3. From the Ohio River Great Flood to the Atomic Age

1. "Rescue Workers Move Families from Point; River at 35.3 Feet," *Louisville Courier-Journal*, January 20, 1937; Richard B. Davis, "From Despair to Hope: The Story of Paducah's 1937 'Super Flood' from the Accounts of Those Who Survived," *Jackson Purchase Historical Society Journal* 43 (2016): 24; John E. L. Robertson with Ann Robertson, *Paducah, Kentucky: A History* (Charleston SC: History Press, 2016), 16; "Ohio Coming Up, but No Flood Is Likely," *Paducah Sun-Democrat*, January 15, 1937; "Story of Paducah's Record Flood in 1937," *Paducah Sun-Democrat*, March 7, 1937; "Troubled Waters, the Great Flood of 1937," *Owensboro Messenger-Inquirer*, January 26, 1987; David Welky, *The Thousand-Year Flood: The Ohio–Mississippi Disaster of 1937* (Chicago: University of Chicago Press, 2011).

2. "Ohio River Passes Flood Stage, Crest Due Tuesday," *Owensboro Messenger-Inquirer*, January 17, 1937; "High Water Causes Highway 60 to Close," *Owensboro Messenger*, January 19, 1937; "Crest of Flood May Reach All-Time Record," *Owensboro Messenger*, January 20, 1937; "Torrential Rains Cause Increasing Hazards from Floods," *Owensboro Messenger*, January 21, 1937; "New Flood Record Seen for Area," *Owensboro Messenger*, January 22, 1937; "Every Main Road to Owensboro May Be Closed," *Owensboro Messenger*, January 22, 1937; "Owensboro Isolated as Ohio River Passes High Mark of 1913 Flood," *Owensboro Messenger*, January 19, 1937; "8 in Henderson County Family Are Feared Lost," *Owensboro Messenger*, January 23, 1937; "Hopkins Soldier on Rescue Duty Loses His Life," *Owensboro Messenger*, January 24, 1937; "Some Aspects of the Flood," *Paducah Sun-Democrat*, October 25, 1937.

3. "Evacuation of Stranded People about Complete," *Owensboro Messenger*, January 27, 1937.

4. "60 Billion Tons of Water Moving toward Paducah," *Owensboro Messenger*, January 29, 1937; "High Water Situation in Paducah District," *Paducah Sun-Democrat*, January 21, 1937; "Complete Evacuation Order," *Paducah Sun-Democrat*, January 30, 1937; "Murray Receives 3,000 Refugees," *Paducah*

Sun-Democrat, January 30, 1937; "Fulton Is Caring for 1,200 Now," *Paducah Sun-Democrat*, January 31, 1937.

5. Welky, *The Thousand-Year Flood*, 100–104; "Civil Rule of Flood Relief Work Here Is Decided," *Paducah Sun-Democrat*, February 1, 1937; "Story of Paducah's Record Flood in 1937," *Paducah Sun-Democrat*, March 7, 1937; "Warren Middleton Tells How Amateur Radio Set Served Flood-Swamped City," *Paducah Sun-Democrat*, February 18, 1937; "Coast Guard Fleet Winds Up Gallant Task at Paducah," *Paducah Sun-Democrat*, February 18, 1937.

6. Robertson, *Paducah, Kentucky*, 74–75; "Find Sisters Drowned in Dwelling," *Paducah Sun-Democrat*, March 24, 1937.

7. Joseph Alsop and Turner Catledge, *The 168 Days* (New York: Doubleday, Doran, 1938), 35–36; Jeff Shesol, *Supreme Power: Roosevelt v. the Supreme Court* (New York: Norton, 2012), 295.

8. "Logan to Back Roosevelt in Court Proposal," *Paducah Sun-Democrat*, March 2, 1937.

9. Shesol, *Supreme Power*, 405–9; William E. Leuchtenberg, "Charles Evans Hughes: The Center Holds," *North Carolina Law Review* 83, no. 5 (June 2005): 1187–2003.

10. Donald A. Ritchie, "Alben W. Barkley: The President's Man," in *First among Equals: Outstanding Senate Leaders of the Twentieth Century*, ed. Richard A. Baker and Roger H. Davidson (Washington, DC: Congressional Quarterly Press, 1991), 127–28; James K. Libbey, *Alben Barkley: A Career in Politics* (Lexington: University Press of Kentucky, 2016), 187–90; Polly Ann Davis, "Alben W. Barkley: Senate Majority Leader and Vice President," PhD diss., University of Kentucky, 1963, 22–28; William E. Leuchtenburg, "FDR's Court-Packing Plan: A Second Life, a Second Death," *Duke Law Review* 34, nos. 1–2 (1985): 684; Alben W. Barkley, *That Reminds Me*—(New York: Doubleday, 1954), 154.

11. Libbey, *Alben Barkley*, 184; Barkley, *That Reminds Me*, 152; "Ickes, Barkley Urge Approval of FDR Court Proposals," *Owensboro Messenger*, April 11, 1937; "Roosevelt Court Change Will Win, Barkley Says," *Owensboro Inquirer*, April 13, 1937; David M. Kennedy, *Freedom from Fear: The American People in Depression and War, 1929–1935* (New York: Oxford University Press, 1999), 334–36; Roger Biles, *The South and the New Deal* (Lexington: University Press of Kentucky, 1994), 141–45.

12. "Flood Wall Member Will Go to Capital," *Paducah Sun-Democrat*, March 2, 1937; "Fate of Flood Wall Is in Balance," *Paducah Sun-Democrat*, March 7, 1937; "Barkley Promises Aid in Flood Plan," *Paducah Sun-Democrat*, March 14, 1937; "The Truth on Dams," *Louisville Courier-Journal*, January 8, 1938.

13. "See Victory in City's Fight to Get Flood Wall," *Paducah Sun-Democrat*, August 15, 1937; "Barkley Keeps His Word," *Paducah Sun-Democrat*, August 15, 1937; "Senate Passes Flood Measure as Amended by House, Goes

to FR," *Paducah Sun-Democrat*, August 20, 1937; "The Flood Wall Issue Is Made Clear," *Paducah Sun-Democrat*, August 22, 1937; "Ask Bond Issue for Flood Wall," *Paducah Sun-Democrat*, September 22, 1937; "Flood Wall Is Called Vital If City Is to Grow," *Paducah Sun-Democrat*, October 12, 1937; "Why the Manufacturers and Wholesalers Favor the Floodwall Bond Issue," *Paducah Sun-Democrat*, October 17, 1937; "$200,000 Bond Issue for Wall Right-of-Way Given Approval," *Paducah Sun-Democrat*, November 3, 1937; "City to Decline Wall Keys When Offered Friday," *Paducah Sun-Democrat*, July 14, 1949; "$40,000–$50,000 Bill to Operate, Maintain Floodwall Foreseen by City Manager Moffett," *Paducah Sun-Democrat*, June 15, 1949; "Cold Weather Adds to Woes in Flooded Areas," *Paducah Sun-Democrat*, January 19, 1950.

14. "Building of 3 New Locks for Valley Is Requested," *Paducah Sun-Democrat*, March 30, 1936; B. Anthony Gannon, "Vision or Obsession? Arthur E. Morgan and the Superdam," *Register of the Kentucky Historical Society* 97, no. 1 (Winter 1999): 45–82; B. Anthony Gannon, "The Photo Finish: Political Victory and the TVA Presence in Kentucky," part 1, *Jackson Purchase Historical Society Journal* 30 (2003): 1.

15. B. Anthony Gannon, "The Photo Finish: Political Victory and the TVA Presence in Kentucky," part 2, *Jackson Purchase Historical Society Journal* 31 (2004): 5–9; "The Best of News," *Paducah Sun-Democrat*, April 26, 1938; "House Votes Gilbertsville Dam Money," *Louisville Courier-Journal*, April 26, 1938.

16. "House Votes Tentatively to Halt Dam," *Paducah Sun-Democrat*, February 8, 1939; "Solons Receive LTVA Appeal to Restore Cut," *Paducah Sun-Democrat*, February 15, 1939; "Text of Washburn's Letter to May Released for Publication," *Paducah Sun-Democrat*, February 21, 1939; "House Approves Gilbertsville Fund," *Paducah Sun-Democrat*, March 1, 1939.

17. "Kentucky Dam Was Started in 1938; TVA Project Affected Most of West KY," *Mayfield Messenger*, December, 27, 1969; "Power Being Produced at Kentucky Dam," *Paducah Sun-Democrat*, September 11, 1944.

18. "Chandler Boasts Nominee for Congress in Second 'Will Be the Fellow I Want,'" *Owensboro Messenger-Inquirer*, January 17, 1937; "Hubert Meredith Chandler's 'Man' Defeated 8 to 7," *Owensboro Messenger*, February 2, 1937; "Hubert Meredith Succeeds Vincent," *Owensboro Messenger*, March 13, 1937.

19. "The Highways and Bridges," *Paducah Sun-Democrat*, April 15, 1936; "Rambles," *Owensboro Messenger-Inquirer*, April 30, 1936.

20. "Effort to Free Bridges of Toll Started by Paducahans," *Paducah Sun-Democrat*, February 21, 1936; "Paducah Joined in Fight to Set Toll Bridges Free," *Paducah Sun-Democrat*, March 22, 1936; "Johnson Backs Effort to Free All Toll Bridges," *Paducah Sun-Democrat*, March 18, 1936; "Seen While Roaming," *Paducah Sun-Democrat*, May 17, 1936; "Kentucky Hopes for Free Bridges

Despite Bond Debt," *Paducah Sun-Democrat,* May 17, 1936; "Paducahans on Trip in Interest of Free Spans in State," *Paducah Sun-Democrat,* October 7, 1938; "Ward Finishes State Campaign for Free Spans," *Paducah Sun-Democrat,* December 12, 1937; "Chandler Talks against Drive for Free Spans," *Paducah Sun-Democrat,* December 10, 1937; "Seen While Roaming," *Paducah Sun-Democrat,* January 6, 1938; "Chandler Offers 10-Point Program," *Paducah Sun-Democrat,* January 4, 1937; "Seen While Roaming," *Paducah Sun-Democrat,* January 12, 1938; "Legislative Plans Drafted by State Farm Federation," *Paducah Sun-Democrat,* January 13, 1938.

21. "50% Cut in Bridge Tolls Won't Hold Up Bond Payments," *Paducah Sun-Democrat,* January 14, 1938; "State Promises Bridge Toll Study," *Paducah Sun-Democrat,* March 1, 1938; "What of Other Bridges?," *Paducah Sun-Democrat,* March 27, 1938; "Goodwill Tours," *Paducah Sun-Democrat,* July 15, 1938; "Rain Fails to Dampen West Ky. Day Spirit," *Paducah Sun-Democrat,* August 30, 1938; "Paducah to Be Host for Meet," *Owensboro Messenger,* August 27, 1938; "Ramblings," *Paducah Sun-Democrat,* August 27, 1938; "Toward Free Bridges," *Paducah Sun-Democrat,* January 19, 1939; "John Young Brown and Keen Johnson Picnics," *Paducah Sun-Democrat,* July 9, 1939; "Thousands at Eggner's Ferry Marking Freeing of Toll Bridges," *Paducah Sun-Democrat,* August 26, 1945; "Regional Authorities Patterned after TVA Urged by Truman in Speech Dedicating Kentucky Dam," *Paducah Sun-Democrat,* October 10, 1945; "The Next Stage of the Job," *Paducah Sun-Democrat,* October 11, 1945.

22. Charles F. Faber, "West Kentucky Community and Technical College," in *The Kentucky African American Encyclopedia,* ed. Gerald L. Smith, Karen Cotton McDaniel, and John A. Hardin (Lexington: University Press of Kentucky, 2015), 525; "Seen While Roaming," *Paducah Sun-Democrat,* March 19, 1936; "Seen While Roaming," *Paducah Sun-Democrat,* March 25, 1936.

23. Joshua D. Farrington, "Anderson, Dennis Henry," in *The Kentucky African American Encyclopedia,* ed. Smith, McDaniel, and Hardin, 20–21; John A. Hardin, *Fifty Years of Segregation: Black Higher Education in Kentucky* (Lexington: University Press of Kentucky, 1997), 30, 53–56; John A. Hardin, *Onward and Upward: A Centennial History of Kentucky State University, 1886–1986* (Frankfort: Kentucky State University, 1987), 38; "Move to Keep Colored School Here Is Started," *Paducah Sun-Democrat,* December 15, 1937; "W. K. I. C. Deserves Support," *Paducah Sun-Democrat,* December 17, 1937; "The Attitude of Colored People," *Paducah Sun-Democrat,* December 22, 1937; "Negroes Oppose Merger of Two Colleges," *Louisville Courier-Journal,* January 3, 1937; "Chandler Has Plan to Establish New Industrial Center at WKIC," *Paducah Sun-Democrat,* January 11, 1938; "Seen While Roaming," *Paducah Sun-Democrat,* January 13, 1937; "Dr. D. H. Anderson Funeral, Monument Fund Started," *Paducah Sun-Democrat,* October 7, 1952; Wilma Fletcher Cotton, interviewed by William Peyton, July 2, 1979, Jackson Purchase Oral History

Project—Schools and Education, Pogue Library, Murray State University, Murray, KY; Bettie Coulter Cox, interviewed by Mary Bates, September 13, 1979, Jackson Purchase Oral History Project—Schools and Education, Pogue Library; John Paul Hill, "A. B. 'Happy' Chandler and the Politics of Civil Rights," PhD diss., University of Georgia, 2009, 45–47; Janette M. Blythe, *Upward Stride: A Pictorial History of West Kentucky Community & Technical College* (Virginia Beach, VA: Donning, 2008), 35–37.

24. John Ed Pearce, *Divide and Dissent: Kentucky Politics, 1930–1963* (Lexington: University of Kentucky Press, 1987), 41; "Chandler Says Barkley Dinner Is Taking On Political Tone," *Louisville Courier-Journal,* January 17, 1938; "5 Senators Plan to Honor Barkley Here," *Louisville Courier-Journal,* January 19, 1938; "Roosevelt Is Sending McIntyre as Emissary to Barkley Dinner," *Louisville Courier-Journal,* January 22, 1938; "Chandler Says Johnson Can Handle His Job," *Louisville Courier-Journal,* January 23, 1938; Hill, "A. B. 'Happy' Chandler and the Politics of Civil Rights," 45–50.

25. Pearce, *Divide and Dissent,* 41; "Pension Raise Promised by Chandler," *Owensboro Inquirer,* July 21, 1938; "Chandler Says Barkley Thinks He Is Too Big," *Paducah Sun-Democrat,* August 4, 1938.

26. "Senate Needs Barkley," *Louisville Courier-Journal,* July 9, 1938; "President Is Greeted Here by Great Crowd," *Bowling Green Park City Daily News,* July 10, 1938; "President's Train Makes Stop Here," *Russellville News-Democrat,* July 14, 1938; Hill, "A. B. 'Happy' Chandler and the Politics of Civil Rights," 48–53.

27. Thomas L. Stokes, *Chip Off My Shoulder* (Princeton, NJ: Princeton University Press, 1940), 535; "Thomas Lunsford Stokes of Scripps-Howard Newspaper Alliance," 1939 Prize Winner in Reporting, Pulitzer Prizes, at https://www.pulitzer.org/winners/thomas-lunsford-stokes; "Barkley–Chandler Backers Fight at Alliance Meeting," *Paducah Sun-Democrat,* July 12, 1938; Davis, "Alben W. Barkley," 60–67; "Roosevelt Endorses Proposal to Extend Hatch Act," *Baltimore Sun,* March 6, 1940.

28. George W. Robinson, "The Making of a Kentucky Senator: Alben W. Barkley and the Gubernatorial Primary of 1923," *Filson Club Historical Quarterly* 42 (April 1966): 130; "Chandler Says Illness Won't Stop Campaign," *Louisville Courier-Journal,* July 23, 1938; Albert B. Chandler, *Heroes, Plain Folks, and Skunks: The Life and Times of Happy Chandler* (Chicago: Bonus Books, 1989), 208–9; Barkley, *That Reminds Me,* 164.

29. "Barkley Brings Campaign to First District," *Paducah Sun-Democrat,* July 3, 1938; "Pension Raise Promised Aged by Gov. Chandler," *Owensboro Inquirer,* July 21, 1938; "Barkley Claims Chandler Pawn of Wall Street," *Paducah Sun-Democrat,* July 22, 1938; "Chandler Used Pension Cash on Budget—Barkley," *Paducah Sun-Democrat,* August 1, 1938; "Barkley Asserts Never Bought

a Vote in Career," *Paducah Sun-Democrat,* August 4, 1938; "Gov. Chandler at Bowling Green," *Owensboro Messenger-Inquirer,* August 4, 1938.

30. Walter L. Hixson, "The 1938 Kentucky Senate Election: Alben W. Barkley, 'Happy' Chandler, and the New Deal," *Register of the Kentucky Historical Register* 80, no. 3 (Summer 1982): 328; "Pressure upon College Gang Swept Warren," *Madisonville Messenger,* August 10, 1938; "Mayfield News," *Paducah Sun-Democrat,* July 3, 1938; Kentucky Board of Elections, election returns for 1936, CD requested by the author, November 2011.

31. "From the State Capitol," *Louisville Courier-Journal,* November 27, 1938; "From the State Capitol," *Louisville Courier-Journal,* February 5, 1939; "From the State Capitol," *Louisville Courier-Journal,* February 26, 1939; "State Editors Believe Johnson Can Beat Brown," *Owensboro Messenger,* February 5, 1939.

32. "Johnson Raps C. I. O. as Run by John L. Lewis," *Owensboro Messenger,* July 5, 1939; "Don't Vote to Establish Communism," *Paducah Sun-Democrat,* July 19, 1939; "Keen Johnson in West Kentucky," *Owensboro Messenger,* July 30, 1939; "Brown Talks Free Bridge Plan," *Paducah Sun-Democrat,* July 23, 1939; "John Y. Brown Independence Day Speaker at Barbecue of Woodmen at Chautauqua Park," *Owensboro Messenger,* July 25, 1939.

33. Malcolm E. Jewell, *Kentucky Votes,* vol. 2: *Gubernatorial and Primary Elections, 1923–1959* (Lexington: University Press of Kentucky, 1963), 20–21.

34. Frederic D. Ogden, "Keen Johnson," in *Kentucky's Governors,* updated ed., ed. Lowell Harrison (Lexington: University Press of Kentucky, 2004), 177–79; James C. Klotter, *Kentucky: Portrait in Paradox, 1900–1950* (Frankfort: Kentucky Historical Society, 1996), 318; Elizabeth M. Fraas, "Keen Johnson: Newspaperman and Governor," PhD diss., University of Kentucky, 1984, 199.

35. Richard E. Holl, *Committed to Victory: The Kentucky Home Front during World War II* (Lexington: University Press of Kentucky, 2015), 145; Ogden, "Keen Johnson," in *Kentucky's Governors,* ed. Harrison, 178; Klotter, *Kentucky,* 318.

36. "The Ward Bill Must Pass," *Paducah Sun-Democrat,* March 5, 1940; "Ramblings," *Paducah Sun-Democrat,* December 23, 1940; "Conference on TVA Power Is Called for February 24," *Paducah Sun-Democrat,* February 16, 1941; "League to Campaign for TVA Power in State Formed at District-Wide Meeting at Murray," *Paducah Sun-Democrat,* February 25, 1941; "Johnson Tells Ward He'll Aid TVA Program," *Paducah Sun-Democrat,* February 27, 1941.

37. "40 Delegates from 9 Purchase Towns Urge TVA Enabling Law, Oppose State's Control," *Paducah Sun-Democrat,* January 13, 1942; "West Kentucky Has a Case," *Paducah Sun-Democrat,* January 14, 1942.

38. "Ward and Dickson Come to Front in Legislature Opening Tuesday," *Louisville Courier-Journal,* January 4, 1942; "2 Verbal Clashes Mark Hearing on T. V. A. Bill," *Louisville Courier-Journal,* February 4, 1942; "Ward Says K. U.

Tried to Shape T. V. A. Measure," *Louisville Courier-Journal,* February 5, 1942; "Governor Hits Kirtley's Stand," *Louisville Courier-Journal,* February 7, 1942; "Ward Asserts Johnson Back of TVA Bill," *Paducah Sun-Democrat,* February 5, 1942; "Kirtley Made One Correct Statement on TVA—Johnson," *Paducah Sun-Democrat,* February 6, 1942.

39. Keen Johnson, "Tennessee Valley Authority Bill," February 11, 1942, in *The Public Papers of Keen Johnson, 1939–1943,* ed. Frederic D. Ogden (Lexington: University Press of Kentucky, 1982), 67–68; "Kirtley Quits as Johnson Asks T. V. A. Bill Passage," *Louisville Courier-Journal,* February 12, 1942; "TVA Enabling Bill Approved by House 85 to 10," *Owensboro Messenger,* February 18, 1942; "Stormy Debate Precedes Vote on Ward Bill," *Paducah Sun-Democrat,* February 19, 1942.

40. "Bowling Green to Seek Tie-In for Local TVA Power," *Paducah Sun-Democrat,* March 18, 1942; "Mayfield Council Approves Purchase of Power Plant," *Paducah Sun-Democrat,* April 16, 1942; "Electric Deal Is Completed," *Owensboro Messenger-Inquirer,* April 15, 1942; "Murray Electric Plant Reports $117,000 in Surplus, Rate Cuts," *Paducah Sun-Democrat,* June 11, 1944; "City of Clinton Seeking Facts on TVA Power," *Paducah Sun-Democrat,* August 25, 1944; "Ballard Towns Wonder About Getting Power," *Paducah Sun-Democrat,* August 27, 1944; "Ramblings," *Paducah Sun-Democrat,* September 5, 1944; Ernest W. Peterson Jr., TVA general manager of Kentucky relations, to author, email, May 16, 2021; "T. V. A. Ripper Bill Wins First Test Vote in Senate," *Louisville Courier-Journal,* February 5, 1946; "T. V. A. Official Warns against 'Ripper,'" *Louisville Courier-Journal,* February 7, 1946; "Senate Passes Bill to Amend T. V. A. Act, 24–14," *Louisville Courier-Journal,* February 8, 1946; "Ward Reveals Effort to Buy Vote in House for Anti-T. V. A. Bill," *Louisville Courier-Journal,* February 22, 1946; "House Kills Moss Bill," *Paducah Sun-Democrat,* February 27, 1946; "House Mutilates, Then Kills Anti-T. V. A. Bill by 60–31," *Louisville Courier-Journal,* February 28, 1946.

41. "Initial Move in Redistricting Problem Made," *Paducah Sun-Democrat,* March 5, 1942; "Redistributing to Hit Counties in Second District," *Owensboro Messenger,* March 8, 1942; "Ramblings," *Paducah Sun-Democrat,* March 31, 1942.

42. "Another Special Assembly Special Session May Be Called," *Paducah Sun-Democrat,* March 27, 1942; "Johnson Urges Assembly to Redistrict State," *Paducah Sun-Democrat,* March 30, 1942; "Redistricting of State to Begin at Special Session," *Louisville Courier-Journal,* March 5, 1942; "Here's How Senate and House Districts Vary," *Louisville Courier-Journal,* March 16, 1942; "'Judge' Johnson Has Given a One-Sided Jury," *Louisville Courier-Journal,* March 16, 1942; "House Rebels, Tabling Bill to Redistrict," *Louisville Courier-Journal,* March 26, 1942; "House Passes Redistricting Bill, 54–41," *Louisville Courier-Journal,* April 2, 1942; Kentucky Legislative Research Commission,

Kentucky General Assembly Membership, 1900–2005, 2 vols. (Frankfort, KY: Legislative Research Commission, 2005), 1:273–83, 2:299, at https://legislature. ky.gov/LRC/Publications/Pages/Informational-Bulletins.aspx?View=Out%20 0f%20Print&Title=OutOfPrint&Col=Number&Search=175.

43. Holl, *Committed to Victory,* 86, 88.

44. "Owensboro Firm Will Make Buoys," *Owensboro Inquirer,* October 26, 1941; "Ken-Rad Products in the Forefront of Battle," *Owensboro Inquiry,* June 4, 1942; "Glenmore Will Make Alcohol," *Owensboro Inquirer,* January 16, 1942; "Mayfield Firm Gets Second Army Order," *Paducah Sun-Democrat,* January 23, 1942; Lee A. Dew and Aloma W. Dew, *Owensboro: The City on the Yellow Banks* (Bowling Green, KY: Riverdell, 1988), 161.

45. "Henderson Gets Advance Thrill over Big Plant," *Owensboro Messenger,* February 16, 1941; "Plans for Future Activities in District Are Made by Council," *Paducah Sun-Democrat,* July 31, 1942; "$30,000,000 Arms Plant to Be Made in M'Cracken County," *Paducah Sun-Democrat,* February 27, 1942; "When Blockbusters Go Boom-Boom, West Kentucky Plants Score Again," *Louisville Courier-Journal,* July 5, 1943; "Job Outlook Here Appears Favorable for Some Time; War Contract Cancellation Felt Sharply in Graves County," *Paducah Sun-Democrat,* August 19, 1945; Joseph E. Brent and Maria Campbell Brent, "History of the National Fireworks Shell Loading Plant at Viola, Kentucky," *Jackson Purchase Historical Society Journal* 43 (2016): 90–122; "Deal Completed for Ohio River Ordnance Works," *Owensboro Messenger,* May 5, 1950.

46. "Coast Guard Training Station to Be Located Here," *Owensboro Messenger,* March 5, 1942; "Armored Division at Camp Activated," *Clarksville Leaf-Chronicle,* September 15, 1942; John O'Brien, *A History of Fort Campbell* (Charleston, SC: History Press, 2014), 34–39, 67; "Army to Triple Size of Camp at Morganfield," *Owensboro Messenger,* April 5, 1942; "Morganfield Returns to Normal with Excess Population Gone," *Owensboro Messenger,* August 11, 1946.

47. Holl, *Committed to Victory,* 7, 307; O'Brien, *A History of Fort Campbell,* 101–8; "20,000 Men Slated for Camp Breckinridge," *Madisonville Messenger,* July 22, 1948; "Army Orders Reopening of Breckinridge Sept. 1," *Louisville Courier-Journal,* July 25, 1950; "Camp Breckinridge," US Army Corps of Engineers, n.d., at https://www.lrl.usace.army.mil/Missions/Environmental/Camp-Breckinridge/; "Breckinridge Gets New Face," *Owensboro Messenger-Inquirer,* April 25, 1965.

48. Holl, *Committed to Victory,* 68–69; "Ken-Rad Plant Employees Vote Union by 382," *Owensboro Inquirer,* August 14, 1942; "Women Engineers, Machinists Are Doing Good Job of Men's Work, Ken-Rad Official Says," *Owensboro Messenger,* November 11, 1942; "Ken-Rad War Work Hampered Somewhat as 105 Girls Quit," *Owensboro Messenger,* February 5, 1943;

"Addressed to Ken-Rad Workers," *Owensboro Messenger,* February 5, 1943; "Ken-Rad and Union Views in Conflict," *Owensboro Inquirer,* January 26, 1944; "FDR Orders Army to Take Over Ken-Rad Plants Here," *Owensboro Inquirer,* April 14, 1944; "Ken-Rad Files Suit to Prevent Army from Paying W. L. B. Scale," *Louisville Courier-Journal,* April 16, 1944; "Army Moves Out of Ken-Rad Plant," *Owensboro Messenger,* May 26, 1944.

49. Holl, *Committed to Victory,* 70–74; "Coalmen Reject Lewis's Demand," *Madisonville Daily Messenger,* March 12, 1943; "Lewis Assails Intelligence Agents; Charges Miners Being Intimidated," *Madisonville Messenger,* April 2, 1943; "Miners Await Cue from Lewis," *Madisonville Messenger,* April 30, 1943; "FDR Orders Mines Run!," *Madisonville Messenger,* May 1, 1943.

50. "Eyes of the World on U. S. Coal Mining Crisis," *Owensboro Messenger-Inquirer,* May 1, 1943; "Progressive Mine Workers Protest UMW Resolutions," *Madisonville Messenger,* May 19, 1943; "48-Hour Week, Meaning $9 More for Miners," *Madisonville Messenger,* August 17, 1943; "PMW Quits Mine Field, Announced," *Madisonville Messenger,* September 16, 1943; "Miner Contracts Will Be Signed," *Madisonville Messenger,* December 21, 1943.

51. Jewell, *Gubernatorial and Primary Elections, 1923–1959,* 28–29; "The Republican Sweep Is Traced to Sources," *Paducah Sun-Democrat,* November 5, 1943; "The Wages of Johnson's Achievement Was Defeat," *Louisville Courier-Journal,* December 5, 1943; "Says Meredith Bolted the Party," *Owensboro Messenger,* October 28, 1943; "Hubert Meredith Comes Out for Both Willkie and Parks," *Louisville Courier-Journal,* October 24, 1944; Klotter, *Kentucky,* 322–23.

52. "'Anti' Victory Showed How Wind Blew," *Louisville Courier-Journal,* December 26, 1943; Harry Lee Waterfield, interviewed by John Kleber, May 7, 1984, Lawrence W. Wetherby Oral History Project, Louie B. Nunn Center for Oral History, University of Kentucky, Lexington; Harry Lee Waterfield Jr., interviewed by the author, March 7, 2011, West Kentucky Politics Oral History Project, Nunn Center; "Ramblings," *Paducah Sun-Democrat,* December 21, 1943.

53. Earle C. Clements, interviewed by Forrest C. Pogue and James Hammack, January 24, 1975, Jackson Purchase Oral History Project, Pogue Library; "Tuggle 'Ripper' Bill Laid to Donaldson," *Louisville Courier-Journal,* January 5, 1944; Thomas S. Syvertsen, "Earle Chester Clements and the Democratic Party, 1920–1950," PhD diss., University of Kentucky, 1982, 92.

54. "The Hard Facts That Face Kentucky If the Income Tax Is Repealed, *Louisville Courier-Journal,* January 2, 1944; "State's Outgo Will Beat Income If Willis Keeps His Promises," *Louisville Courier-Journal,* January 2, 1944; "Signs Grow That Willis Must Keep Income Tax but Not His Pledge," *Louisville Courier-Journal,* January 9, 1944; "Willis Asks General Assembly to Retain State Income Tax Until Revenues Are Revived," *Louisville Courier-Journal,* January 11,

1944; "Frank Approach," *Madisonville Messenger,* January 11, 1944; "Editorial and Current Comment," *Owensboro Inquirer,* January 18, 1944; "Campaign Pledges Should Be Sacred Things," *Paducah Sun-Democrat,* January 14, 1944.

55. Klotter, *Kentucky,* 324; "Democratic Control of the Kentucky Legislature Is Expected," *Louisville Courier-Journal,* January 6, 1946; "Willis Asks for Repeal of Personal Income Tax," *Louisville Courier-Journal,* January 9, 1946; "Income Tax Repeal Dealt Death Blow," *Louisville Courier-Journal,* January 25, 1946; "House Votes to Keep State Income Tax, Blocks Chance for Repeal at 1946 Session," *Paducah-Sun Democrat,* January 25, 1946; "The Income-Tax Fiasco Signaled the End of the Republican Ascent," *Louisville Courier-Journal,* January 27, 1946.

56. "Public Rights Will Never Be Safe from Danger," *Paducah Sun-Democrat,* March 17, 1944; "House Defeated Moss Anti-TVA Bill in 1944, but Situation Is Different This Year," *Paducah Sun-Democrat,* February 10, 1946; "Ramblings," *Paducah Sun-Democrat,* February 11, 1946; "Effective Help against the Moss Bill," *Paducah Sun-Democrat,* February 18, 1946; "A Direct Effect on Rural People," *Paducah Sun-Democrat,* February 19, 1946; "Moss Bill to Destroy TVA Enabling Act and Appropriations Measure Will Probably Be Determined during Present Week," *Paducah Sun-Democrat,* February 24, 1946; "Ward and Moss Clash at Probe of Utility Bill," *Paducah Sun-Democrat,* February 26, 1946; "House Kills Moss Bill," *Paducah Sun-Democrat,* February 27, 1946; "Moss Bill Defeated," *Paducah Sun-Democrat,* February 28, 1946; "Paducah Votes to Acquire KU," *Paducah Sun-Democrat,* November 9, 1960.

57. Barkley, *That Reminds Me,* 186–87; "Kentucky Editors Overboard in Support of FDR Again," *Louisville Courier-Journal,* October 20, 1940; Libbey, *Alben Barkley,* 211–13; "Roosevelt Carries First District by 36,645 Votes," *Paducah Sun-Democrat,* November 7, 1940.

58. Barkley, *That Reminds Me,* 170.

59. Barkley, *That Reminds Me,* 169–79; Davis, "Alben W. Barkley," 141–55; George W. Robinson, "Alben Barkley and the 1944 Tax Veto," *Register of the Kentucky Historical Society* 67, no. 3 (July 1969): 197–210; Ritchie, "Alben W. Barkley," 144–49.

60. Barkley, *That Reminds Me,* 176–77; "Senator Barkley's Action Meets with Our Approval," *Paducah Sun-Democrat,* February 24, 1944; "The Barkley–Roosevelt Dispute," *Owensboro Inquirer,* February 25, 1944; "Revolt Builds a Barkley Bandwagon," *New York Daily News,* February 25, 1944.

61. Ritchie, "Alben W. Barkley," 147–48; Barkley, *That Reminds Me,* 181–83, 190; Libbey, *Alben Barkley,* 231.

62. "68,000 Lead in Kentucky for Roosevelt," *Paducah Sun-Democrat,* November 8, 1944; "Vote by Counties," *Lexington Herald,* November 8, 1944; "FDR, Barkley, and Clements Carry County," *Owensboro Messenger-Inquirer,* November 8, 1944.

63. Syvertsen, "Earle Chester Clements," 236–37; Harry Lee Waterfield, interviewed by John Kleber, May 7, 1984, Lawrence W. Wetherby Oral History Project, Nunn Center; Edward Allen Farris, interviewed by the author, March 7, 2011, West Kentucky Politics Project, Nunn Center; Edward Allen Farris, interviewed by Terry L. Birdwhistell, February 17, 1977, Earle C. Clements Oral History Project, Nunn Center; Earle C. Clements, interviewed by James W. Hammack, January 24, 1975, Jackson Purchase Oral History Project, Pogue Library.

64. "Clements Backs More Pay for Teachers, Public Electricity," *Paducah Sun-Democrat*, March 23, 1947; Syvertsen, "Earle Chester Clements," 236; "Waterfield Charges Clements' Fundamental Views Different," *Paducah Sun-Democrat*, July 3, 1947; "Clements Ruled by Utilities, Opponent Says," *Louisville Courier-Journal*, July 29, 1947; "Candidates Please Note," *Paducah Sun-Democrat*, July 15, 1947; "Waterfield, Clements Both Claim Victories in Addresses at Annual Fancy Farm Picnic," *Paducah Sun-Democrat*, July 31, 1947.

65. Jewell, *Gubernatorial and Primary Elections, 1923–1959*, 30–31; "Clinton Publisher's Margin Climbs in 1st District to 17,836," *Paducah Sun-Democrat*, August 4, 1947.

66. "Leaders Pledge Support to Victors in Primary," *Louisville Courier-Journal*, August 6, 1947; "Democrats Open Drive for November Victory as Clements Says GOP Is 'Divided and Prostrate,'" *Paducah Sun-Democrat*, September 28, 1947; "Clements Opens West Kentucky Campaign at Rally in Murray; Waterfield Explains Absence," *Paducah Sun-Democrat*, October 5, 1947; "Clements and Waterfield Meet at Airport Here," *Paducah Sun-Democrat*, October 17, 1947; "Clements Predicts Big 1st District Majority," *Madisonville Messenger*, October 18, 1947; "1st District Dissension Denied by Democrats," *Louisville Courier-Journal*, October 24, 1947; "Large Crowd Hears Clements Make One of Final Pre-election Speeches Here," *Owensboro Inquirer*, November 3, 1947; Syvertsen, "Earle Chester Clements," 309–10, 313–14.

67. Klotter, *Kentucky*, 331; "Morton Raps C. I. O. Backing of Clements," *Louisville Courier-Journal*, October 4, 1947; Syvertsen, "Earle Chester Clements," 309–10; "Earle Clements Majority Climbs to 91,617 Votes," *Owensboro Messenger*, November 6, 1947; Jewell, *Gubernatorial and Primary Elections, 1923–1959*, 34–35; "Nominees Are Unopposed for Congressional Posts," *Bowling Green Park City Daily News*, March 8, 1948; Al Smith, *Wordsmith: My Life in Journalism* (Louisville, KY: Clark Legacies, 2011), 187.

68. Pearce, *Divide and Dissent*, 151–52; Farris, interviewed by Birdwhistell, February 17, 1977; Farris, interviewed by the author, March 7, 2011.

69. "School-Fund Equalization Gains Wide Victory Margin," *Louisville Courier-Journal*, November 9, 1949; "Add Your Own Comment," *Paducah Sun-Democrat*, November 10, 1949; Pearce, *Divide and Dissent*, 50–51; "District

Votes against Pay Increase," *Paducah Sun-Democrat*, November 10, 1949; "Constitutional Convention Should Be Possible Now," *Louisville Courier-Journal*, November 13, 1949.

70. "Kentucky Legislature Has a Distinct Obligation," *Paducah Sun-Democrat*, January 6, 1948; "Clements Asks Record 111-Million Outlay for Coming Two Years," *Louisville Courier-Journal*, January 13, 1948; "House O. K. on Budget due Today," *Louisville Courier-Journal*, January 14, 1948; "House Passes Peak Budget 94–0, without Any Debate," *Louisville Courier-Journal*, January 15, 1948; "Judge Stewart in Capitol on Special Mission for Governor," *Paducah Sun-Democrat*, January 11, 1948; "Clements Exercising Complete Control over General Assembly," *Paducah Sun-Democrat*, January 18, 1948; "Clements Asks 7-Cent Gasoline Tax in Kentucky," *Paducah Sun-Democrat*, February 3, 1948; "7 Cents Gallon State Gas Tax Urged," *Owensboro Messenger*, February 4, 1948; "Clements Asks 8 Million in Gasoline-Tax Boost to Improve Rural Roads," *Louisville Courier-Journal*, February 3, 1948; "House Votes 81–14 to Boost Gas Tax," *Louisville Courier-Journal*, February 5, 1948; "Bill Increasing Gas Tax by 2 Cents Becomes Law," *Louisville Courier-Journal*, February 7, 1948; "'Doc' Beauchamp Qualified for Post," *Owensboro Messenger-Inquirer*, September 29, 1948; "Rural-Road Chief Emerson Beauchamp Is a Small Chap in a Very Big Spot," *Louisville Courier-Journal*, December 16, 1948; "Kentucky Goes into 1950 on Better Roads," *Louisville Courier-Journal*, January 3, 1950; "Clements Says He Has Always Favored Farm Legislation," *Owensboro Messenger*, October 5, 1950.

71. "Kentucky Lake Ass'n Formed at Mayfield Meeting," *Paducah Sun-Democrat*, November 23, 1944; "Big Things Are Planned for Kentucky Lake Park," *Louisville Courier-Journal*, January 4, 1948; "Paducahans Confer with State Officials," *Paducah Sun-Democrat*, February 13, 1948; "Cooperation Is Appreciated," *Paducah Sun-Democrat*, February 17, 1948; "Ramblings," *Paducah Sun-Democrat*, February 27, 1948; "Clements Favorable to TVA Village Purchase," *Paducah Sun-Democrat*, March 4, 1948; Syvertsen, "Earle Chester Clements," 388–89.

72. "Henry Ward New Head of State Conservation Dept.," *Paducah Sun-Democrat*, March 31, 1948; "Ward Appointed to State Post," *Lexington Herald*, April 1, 1948; "Ramblings," *Paducah Sun-Democrat*, April 2, 1948.

73. "State Parks to Get $600,000 for Improvements," *Paducah Sun-Democrat*, January 12, 1949; "Reporters Notebook," *Paducah Sun-Democrat*, January 4, 1950; "This Looks Like a Crucial Year for the State's Parks," *Louisville Courier-Journal*, February 26, 1950; "Henry Ward Will Take Flair for Conservation to New Washington Job," *Louisville Courier-Journal*, November 27, 1955.

74. William E. Ellis, *A History of Education in Kentucky* (Lexington: University Press of Kentucky, 2011), 276; "The K. E. A. Says Clements 'Promised'

$34 Million, so a Fight Is Brewing," *Louisville Courier-Journal,* January 1, 1950; "Enabling Acts for Assessment Reforms Due," *Louisville Courier-Journal,* February 20, 1949; "Clements Is Handed Setbacks in House as General Assembly Convenes for Special Session," *Louisville Courier-Journal,* March 2, 1949; "School Aid Is Key to Clements' Program," *Louisville Courier-Journal,* March 6, 1949; "If Assembly Wants to Fight, Clements Has Weapons," *Louisville Courier-Journal,* March 6, 1949.

75. "Assessment-Reform Bills Are Lambasted by Murray Democrat," *Louisville Courier-Journal,* March 10, 1949; "House Okehs Clements' 4 Tax Measures," *Paducah Sun-Democrat,* March 25, 1949; "Crucial Test Set for Bills in Legislature," *Louisville Courier-Journal,* March 25, 1949; "2 Legislators Resign in Row over Debate Limit as House Approves Assessment Bills," *Louisville Courier-Journal,* March 26, 1949.

76. Don Flatt, *Footsteps across the Commonwealth: A Tribute to Adron and Mignon Doran* (Morehead, KY: Morehead State University, 1976), 1–6; Christopher Beckham, "'A Man Unsatisfied by Little Things': The Life and Times of Graves County Native Adron Doran," *Jackson Purchase Historical Society Journal* 43 (2016): 68–76; "Adron Doran, Graves Educator and Politician, to Head K.E.A.," *Paducah Sun-Democrat,* April 12, 1946.

77. Adron Doran, interviewed by Jeffrey Suchanek, April 18, 1991, Kentucky Legislative Oral History Project, Nunn Center.

78. "Teachers Ask More School Money, Sales Tax," *Paducah Sun-Democrat,* October 15, 1950; "K. E. A. Asks 13-Million Rise in Common-School Fund," *Louisville Courier-Journal,* November 22, 1949; "Teachers Propose Increase in Taxes; May Go on Strike to Put Pressure on Clements," *Louisville Courier-Journal,* January 13, 1950; "Five Young, Principled Men Lead Assembly's Democrats," *Louisville Courier-Journal,* January 29, 1950.

79. "Clements Asks Record Budget of $131,635,390 for 2 Years," *Louisville Courier-Journal,* January 10, 1950; "K. E. A. President Hits 'Repudiation,'" *Louisville Courier-Journal,* January 10, 1950; "School Officials Meet Today to Talk Means of Tax Increase," *Paducah Sun-Democrat,* January 12, 1950; "Anti-Clements Forces Hold Up Budget Action after Battle in House," *Louisville Courier-Journal,* January 12, 1950; "Teachers Propose Increase in Taxes," *Louisville Courier-Journal,* January 13, 1950; "House Passes Record Budget of 131 Million," *Louisville Courier-Journal,* January 14, 1950.

80. "The School Fund Fight Ignores Schools," *Paducah Sun-Democrat,* January 16, 1950; "Clements Suggests KEA Work for Tax Hike at Local Level," *Paducah Sun-Democrat,* January 19, 1950; "Madisonville to Up Assessments for Schools," *Paducah Sun-Democrat,* January 24, 1950; "District Teachers' Meetings Back K.E.A.," *Louisville Courier-Journal,* January 22, 1950; "House Takes Pay Bill from Committee, Adjourns during Try to Bring Out School Fund Measure," *Paducah Sun-Democrat,* February 8, 1950.

81. "School-Aid-Bill Vote Averted in House by Adjournment," *Louisville Courier-Journal,* February 8, 1950; "K. E. A. Is Defeated in House Action," *Louisville Courier-Journal,* February 9, 1950; "Attempt to Bring Out School Aid Bill Is Defeated 72–18," *Paducah Sun-Democrat,* February 9, 1950.

82. "Clements Reported Feeling 'Abused' by Teachers Marching on Capitol," *Louisville Courier-Journal,* February 15, 1950; "KEA Calls District Meets to Name Group for Lobbying," *Paducah Sun-Democrat,* February 16, 1950; "Carlisle Teachers Would Support School 'Recess,'" *Paducah Sun-Democrat,* February 17, 1950; "Teachers 'Misrepresented' by KEA Leaders, Clements Says; Chambers Answers Charges," *Paducah Sun-Democrat,* February 17, 1950; "Chambers Says He Would Quit If Funds Assured," *Paducah Sun-Democrat,* February 19, 1950; "K. E. A. Leader Chambers Is Known as a Man Who Always Keeps His Word," *Louisville Courier-Journal,* March 12, 1950; "Will the Teachers' Revolt against the K. E. A. Hierarchy Succeed?," *Louisville Courier-Journal,* February 19, 1950; "Teachers Vote to Hold Firm Front at Frankfort," *Louisville Courier-Journal,* March 1, 1950; "More Pressure for School Money Set This Week," *Paducah Sun-Democrat,* March 5, 1950; "Calmer Voices in the School-Money Row Urge a Study of the Tax Structure," *Louisville Courier-Journal,* March 5, 1950; "Clements Recommends Increasing State Salaries," *Owensboro Messenger-Inquirer,* March 7, 1950.

83. "Democrats of State Refuse to Join Southern Revolt," *Louisville Courier-Journal,* March 16, 1948; "Rufus B. Atwood," KET Distinguished Kentuckian Series, 1976, at https://ket.org/program/distinguished-kentuckian/rufus-b-atwood/; Pearce, *Divide and Dissent,* 151; Herman L. Donovan, *Keeping the University Free and Growing* (Lexington: University Press of Kentucky, 1959), 97–98; Ellis, *A History of Education in Kentucky,* 349.

84. "House Votes Amendment to Day Law, 50–16," *Louisville Courier-Journal,* March 17, 1950; Ellis, *A History of Education in Kentucky,* 350–51; John E.L. Robertson with Ann E. Robertson, *Paducah, Kentucky: A History* (Charleston, SC: History Press, 2014), 116–17.

85. "Cherokee Park on Kentucky Lake for the Colored," *Paducah Sun-Democrat,* August 27, 1950; Gerald L. Smith, "Cherokee State Park," in *The Kentucky African American Encyclopedia,* ed. Smith, McDaniel, and Hardin, 98.

86. Alonzo L. Hamby, *Man of the People: A Life of Harry S. Truman* (New York: Oxford University Press, 1995), 439; David McCullough, *Truman* (New York: Simon and Schuster, 1992), 608; "Wah, Wah, Wah—Mr. Truman Spanks the Press," *Paducah Sun-Democrat,* June 18, 1948; Irwin Ross, *The Loneliest Campaign: The Truman Victory of 1948* (New York: New American Library, 1968), 96.

87. Barkley, *That Reminds Me,* 200; Ross, *The Loneliest Campaign,* 117–18; E. Neal Claussen, "Alben Barkley's Rhetorical Victory in 1948," *Southern Speech Communication Journal* 45, no. 1 (Fall 1979): 87.

88. Barkley, *That Reminds Me,* 198–202; Davis, *Alben W. Barkley,* 256; "Barkley Is Chosen after Brief Flurry," *New York Times,* July 15, 1948.

89. Barkley, *That Reminds Me,* 203; "Paducah Will Welcome an Honored Son," *Paducah Sun-Democrat,* July 17, 1948.

90. Hamby, *Man of the People,* 459; Zachary Karabell, *The Last Campaign: How Harry Truman Won the 1948 Election* (New York: Knopf, 2000), 199, 258; Jules Abels, *Out of the Jaws of Victory* (New York: Holt, 1959), 174–76.

91. Libbey, *Alben Barkley,* 253; Karabell, *The Last Campaign,* 258; David Petrusza, *1948: Harry Truman's Improbable Victory and the Year That Transformed America's Role in the World* (New York: Union Square Press, 2011), 360.

92. "Senator Barkley Comes Home," *Paducah Sun-Democrat,* October 31, 1948; "First District Gives Truman and Barkley 35,316 Margin," *Paducah Sun-Democrat,* November 4, 1948; "Second District Gives Democrats Big Majority," *Owensboro Messenger,* November 3, 1948.

93. "Clements Predicts He Will Carry 8 Districts; Dawson Attacks Governor's REA Record," *Paducah Sun-Democrat,* October 26, 1950; "Clements Speaks at Mayfield; Introduced by Waterfield," *Paducah Sun-Democrat,* November 1, 1950; "The Qualifications of Earle C. Clements," *Paducah Sun-Democrat,* November 2, 1950; "Clements' Record Proves His Worth," *Owensboro Messenger,* November 5, 1950; "Clements Wins in District by 18,965 Margin," *Paducah Sun-Democrat,* November 8, 1950; "Clements and Dawson Split Victory Here," *Owensboro Messenger-Inquirer,* November 8, 1950.

94. "Atomic Plant Would Take up to 5,000 Acres," *Paducah Sun-Democrat,* December 8, 1950; "A-Plant Assured for Paducah," *Paducah Sun-Democrat,* December 15, 1950; "Details of A-Bomb Facility near Paducah Are Revealed," *Louisville Courier-Journal,* December 16, 1950.

95. Bobbie Ann Mason, "Fallout: Paducah's Secret Nuclear Disaster," *New Yorker,* January 10, 2000; Welky, *The Thousand-Year Flood,* 287; James K. Libbey to author, email, October 5, 2015; "Why Barkley Is So Much with Us," *Paducah Sun,* April 30, 2006; "Lone Oak Ceremony Remembers Barkley," *Paducah Sun,* May 1, 2006.

96. John E. L. Robertson, *Paducah: Frontier to the Atomic Age* (Charleston, SC: Arcadia, 2002), 103.

4. Happy Days and the Last Hurrah of State Democratic Party Factionalism

1. Harry W. Schacter, *Kentucky on the March* (New York: Harper, 1949), 4, 49–55; "The Committee and Kentucky Progress," *Paducah Sun-Democrat,* June 29, 1948; "Committee for Kentucky Nears End of Its Work," *Owensboro Messenger,* February 4, 1950; "The Committee's Service," *Paducah Sun-Democrat,* January 30, 1950; James C. Klotter, *Kentucky: Portrait in Paradox, 1900–1950* (Frankfort: Kentucky Historical Society, 1996), 337–39.

2. US Census Bureau, *Census of Population: 1950*, vol. 1, no. 17 (Washington DC: US Department of Commerce, 1952), 7–8; "Purchase Loses 8,100 People in 1950 Census," *Paducah Sun-Democrat*, June 29, 1950; US Department of Commerce, Agriculture Division, *U. S. Census of Agriculture, 1954*, vol. 1, no. 19: *Counties and Economic Areas: Kentucky*, (Washington, DC: US Department of Commerce, 1956), at agcensus.mannlib.cornell.edu; "Madrid Bend Is Strange, Isolated Peninsula Formed by Queer Flow of the Mississippi," *Paducah Sun-Democrat*, October 14, 1951; "Huge Farms Make Up the Fabulous Delta," *Paducah Sun-Democrat*, October 2, 1952; "RTA, Answer to Old Plea," *Paducah Sun-Democrat*, July 18, 1951; "West Kentucky Phone Co-op Ready to Ask PSC Approval," *Paducah Sun-Democrat*, November 11, 1951; "Russellville Firm Granted $743,000 REA Loans," *Owensboro Messenger-Inquirer*, July 28, 1955.

3. "The Demise of an Industry Deals Blow to a Way of Life," *Owensboro Messenger*, March 18, 1951; "Flames Destroy Mengel Company Plant at Hickman," *Paducah Sun-Democrat*, October 18, 1942; Agriculture and Industrial Development Board of Kentucky and Kentucky Chamber of Commerce, *Kentucky Industrial Directory, 1955–56* (N.p.: n.p., n.d.); "Paducah Atomic Plant Force to Hit 22,000 in Two Months," *Paducah Sun-Democrat*, April 23, 1952.

4. "Congressional Delegations of Three States Sent Short Route Resolutions," *Owensboro Messenger-Inquirer*, December 6, 1931; "Tri-state Road Meeting Is Held," *Owensboro Messenger-Inquirer*, April 30, 1933; "Expect Owensboro Bridge to Pay Self Free in Eight Years," *Owensboro Inquirer*, November 11, 1940; "Group Urges Completion of Highway 75," *Owensboro Messenger*, October 16, 1952; "Highway 75 to Get Federal Marking after Long Fight," *Owensboro Messenger*, July 12, 1953; "Harding Elected President of U. S. 431 Association," *Owensboro Messenger*, January 17, 1954.

5. Swift & Staley, *The Story of the Paducah Gaseous Diffusion Plant: Megawatts to Megatons to Megawatts* (Paducah, KY: Paducah Sun, 2013), 22–45; "Biggest Single Load of Power in the World to Be Used in A-Plant," *Paducah Sun-Democrat*, January 5, 1951.

6. Swift & Staley, *The Story of the Paducah Gaseous Diffusion Plant*, 123–25; "Strike Blame at Paducah Spread Widely," *Louisville Courier-Journal*, June 12, 1953; "'143 Strikers' Slow Atomic Plant Work," *Paducah Sun-Democrat*, June 11, 1953.

7. "Expanded Online Kentucky Coal Facts," n.d., at http://www.coaleducation.org/Ky_Coal_Facts/; "Mine Offers to Negotiate with U.M.W.," *Louisville Courier-Journal*, November 10, 1953; "Eaton Puts Fortune in Coal Future," *Madisonville Messenger*, June 6, 1953; "Organized by the Wall Street Route," *Madisonville Messenger*, December 19, 1953; "C-J's Writer Missed the Main Point," *Madisonville Messenger*, December 28, 1953; "The Strange Romance between John L. Lewis and Cyrus Eaton," *Harper's Magazine*,

December 1961; "UMW Guilty of Conspiracy," *Nashville Tennessean,* May 20, 1961.

8. Eileen Michelle Hagerman, "Water, Workers, and Wealth: How 'Mr. Peabody's' Coal Barge Stripped Kentucky's Green River Valley," *Register of the Kentucky Historical Society* 115, no. 2 (Spring 2017): 183–88, 208; "James R. Hines, 92, Founder of BG River Towing Firm Dies," *Bowling Green Park City Daily News,* September 25, 1995; "Flood Control Resolution Is Called Green River Valley League's First Positive Step," *Owensboro Messenger,* April 29, 1952; "Opening of Green River to Modern Commerce Seen," *Owensboro Messenger,* September 21, 1952.

9. "Report Gives Only Minor Encouragement to Green River Improvement," *Bowling Green Park City Daily News,* February 19, 1953; "Ike Seeks New Locks on Green," *Madisonville Messenger,* January 22, 1954; "Ky. Lawmakers Push Green River Plans," *Owensboro Messenger,* April 29, 1955; "It's Time We Awoke to Our Opportunity," *Bowling Green Park City Daily News,* August 31, 1955.

10. "Expanded Online Kentucky Coal Facts"; Roy Carson, "Coal Industry in Kentucky," *Filson Club Historical Quarterly* 40 (January 1966): 37–41; "Peabody's Huge Shovel Starts Work This Week," *Madisonville Messenger,* August 29, 1962; "New Plant to Boost West State Economy," *Madisonville Messenger,* October 2, 1959; "State's Largest Mine to Deliver Coal to T.V.A.," *Madisonville Messenger,* October 2, 1959; "Muhlenberg County to Get $100 Million T. V. A. Plant," *Louisville Courier-Journal,* October 2, 1959.

11. James K. Libbey, *Alben Barkley: A Career in Politics* (Lexington: University Press of Kentucky, 2016), 259–60, 265–90; Alben W. Barkley, *That Reminds Me*—(New York: Doubleday, 1954), 223–32; Alonzo L. Hamby, *Man of the People: A Life of Harry S. Truman* (New York: Oxford University Press, 1995), 600–601; "Democrats Look for New Party Leader; Stevenson, Barkley Draw Support," *Paducah Sun-Democrat,* March 31, 1952; "Barkley Keeps Mum on 1952 Plans," *Paducah Sun-Democrat,* May 18, 1952; "Veep's Decision to Run Cheered by Supporters," *Paducah Sun-Democrat,* May 30, 1952; "Barkley's Hat in the Ring," *Paducah Sun-Democrat,* July 8, 1952.

12. Harry S. Truman memorandum to his files, July 6, 1952, Harry S. Truman Papers, President's Secretary's Files, Harry S. Truman Library, Independence, MO; Donald Ritchie, "Alben W. Barkley: The President's Man," in *First Among Equals: Outstanding Senate Leaders of the Twentieth Century,* ed. Richard A. Baker and Roger H. Davidson (Washington, DC: Congressional Quarterly Press, 1991), 155; Libbey, *Alben Barkley,* 266–68; Barkley, *That Reminds Me,* 229–32.

13. "Labor Leaders Tell Barkley He's Too Old," *Paducah Sun-Democrat,* July 21, 1952; "Barkley Withdraws from Race," *Paducah Sun-Democrat,* July 22, 1952; Barkley, *That Reminds Me,* 236–42, 248; Libbey, *Alben Barkley,* 268–70;

"Convention Gives Barkley Great Ovation," *Paducah Sun-Democrat,* July 24, 1952; John Barlow Martin, *Adlai Stevenson of Illinois: The Life of Adlai E. Stevenson* (New York: Doubleday, 1976), 595.

14. "Top State Democrats 'Draft' Veep," *Louisville Courier-Journal,* March 13, 1954; "Barkley Lashes GOP on Whirl Wind Tour," *Paducah Sun-Democrat,* November 1, 1954; "District Margin 35,260," *Paducah Sun-Democrat,* November 3, 1954; Libbey, *Alben Barkley,* 274–75.

15. "Alben Barkley Is Dead," *Paducah Sun-Democrat,* May 1, 1956; "Candidates, Ex-President, Many Other Dignitaries Pay Tribute to Barkley," *Paducah Sun-Democrat,* May 3, 1956; "End of an Era," *Paducah Sun-Democrat,* May 6, 1956; Libbey, *Alben Barkley,* 276–77.

16. Albert B. Chandler, *Heroes, Plain Folks, and Skunks: The Life and Times of Happy Chandler* (Chicago: Bonus Books, 1989), 247; "Political Observers Expect Underwood to Get Senate Seat," *Paducah Sun-Democrat,* March 15, 1951; "Tom Underwood, the New Senator, Is Aware He Faces Hard Contests, but Isn't Scared," *Louisville Courier-Journal,* March 18, 1951; "Belief Grows That Chandler Has Decided Not to Run," *Louisville Courier-Journal,* April 28, 1951.

17. Christopher Beckham, "'A Man Unsatisfied by Little Things': The Life and Times of Graves County Native Adron Doran," *Jackson Purchase Historical Society Journal* 43 (2016): 68–76; Adron Doran, interviewed by Jeff Suhanek, April 18, 1991, Kentucky Legislative Oral History, Louie B. Nunn Center for Oral History, University of Kentucky, Lexington; "From Bill Powell's Notebook," *Paducah Sun-Democrat,* December 17, 1951.

18. John E. Kleber, "Lawrence W. Wetherby," in *Kentucky Governors,* updated ed., ed. Lowell H. Harrison (Lexington: University Press of Kentucky, 2004), 193; John Ed Pearce, *Divide and Dissent: Kentucky Politics, 1930–1963* (Lexington: University Press of Kentucky, 1987), 54; Lowell H. Harrison and James C. Klotter, *A New History of Kentucky* (Lexington: University Press of Kentucky, 1997), 402; "Redistricting Bill Sent to Governor," *Louisville Courier-Journal,* March 1, 1952; "Legislature in Review," *Louisville Courier-Journal,* March 23, 1952.

19. Pearce, *Divide and Dissent,* 61.

20. "The Selection," in *Bert Combs the Politician: An Oral History,* ed. George W. Robinson (Lexington: University Press of Kentucky, 1991), 33–34; Pearce, *Divide and Dissent,* 60–61.

21. "Foster Will Support Chandler in Race," *Paducah Sun-Democrat,* February 13, 1955; "Chandler Quite 'Happy' at Foster's Support," *Louisville Courier-Journal,* February 15, 1955; "Waterfield and Chandler May Team Up," *Louisville Courier-Journal,* March 20, 1951; "Waterfield Files, Allies Himself with Chandler," *Paducah Sun-Democrat,* March 20, 1955; "Waterfield Files as Running Mate of A. B. Chandler," *Louisville Courier-Journal,* March 20, 1955; "Chandler

Glad Waterfield Running Mate," *Louisville Courier-Journal*, March 21, 1955; "Wetherby Contradicts Waterfield," *Louisville Courier-Journal*, March 22, 1955; "Princeton Man to Head Campaign of Demo Candidate Bert Combs," *Paducah Sun-Democrat*, March 23, 1955; "Headquarters Here Are Nerve Centers for Chandler and Combs," *Louisville Courier-Journal*, July 24, 1955.

22. Pearce, *Divide and Dissent*, 63–64; "The Campaigner," "Shelbyville," and "Chandler v. Combs," in *Bert Combs*, ed. Robinson, 39–57; Chandler, *Heroes*, 248–49; "The Sales Tax Issue and the Gubernatorial Primary," *Paducah Sun-Democrat*, August 9, 1955.

23. "Chandler First Gubernatorial Candidate in 32 Years to Open Campaign in Owensboro," *Owensboro Messenger-Inquirer*, May 14, 1955; "Chandler Rips Wetherby Regime," *Owensboro Messenger-Inquirer*, May 15, 1955; "Chandler Speaks at Eddyville," *Paducah Sun-Democrat*, July 13, 1955; "Combs Forces Jubilant over Barkley Move," *Paducah Sun-Democrat*, July 15, 1955; "Add Your Own Comment," *Paducah Sun-Democrat*, July 17, 1955; "Chandler, Combs Will Stump West," *Paducah Sun-Democrat*, August 1, 1955; "Huge Crowd Hears Combs and Chandler," *Paducah Sun-Democrat*, August 4, 1955.

24. "Chandler v. Combs," in *Bert Combs*, ed. Robinson, 54; "Combs Carries First District by 1,667 Votes," *Paducah Sun-Democrat*, August 9, 1955; Malcolm E. Jewell, *Kentucky Votes*, vol. 2: *Gubernatorial and Primary Elections, 1923–1959* (Lexington: University of Kentucky Press, 1963), 42–43, 46–47; "Kentucky Demos Call for Unity," *Paducah Sun-Democrat*, August 30, 1955; "Democrats Bury Hatchets at Rally," *Louisville Courier-Journal*, September 25, 1955; "Chandler Denies He Plans Revenge against Opponents," *Paducah Sun-Democrat*, October 27, 1955; "Barkley, Chandler, and Waterfield Plan Tour," *Paducah Sun-Democrat*, October 28, 1955; "'Dead' Four Years Ago, Waterfield Now Eyes Governorship in 1959," *Louisville Courier-Journal*, November 20, 1955.

25. John Paul Hill, "A. B. 'Happy' Chandler and the Politics of Civil Rights," PhD diss., University of Georgia, 2009, 155–88; Charles P. Roland, "Happy Chandler," *Register of the Kentucky Historical Society* 85, no. 2 (Spring 1987): 159; James C. Klotter and Craig Thompson Friend, *A New History of Kentucky*, 2nd ed. (Lexington: University Press of Kentucky, 2018), 391; Chandler, *Heroes*, 252–54; Pearce, *Divide and Dissent*, 66–67.

26. "Shape of Taxes to Come," *Paducah Sun-Democrat*, February 17, 1956; "Budget Measure Due Senate's Vote Friday," *Paducah Sun-Democrat*, April 5, 1956; "House Approves Happy's Income Tax Bill," *Paducah Sun-Democrat*, April 18, 1956; "Senate Passes Income Tax Bill after Hot Debate," *Paducah Sun-Democrat*, April 20, 1956; "Senate Passes Income-Tax Raises by 21–15," *Louisville Courier-Journal*, April 21, 1956.

27. "New Chandler Attack Hinted on Clements by Advancing Primary Balloting to Spring," *Louisville Courier-Journal*, February 7, 1956; "Clements'

Opener Assails Chandler," *Louisville Courier-Journal*, April 18, 1956; "Chandler Names Humphreys U. S. Senator until November," *Paducah Sun-Democrat*, June 22, 1956; "Democrats Name Wetherby for Senate Run by 35–0 Vote," *Louisville Courier-Journal*, June 20, 1956; "Senator Grace Says 'Enemies' Will Be Fired," *Paducah Sun Democrat*, June 27, 1956; "Waterfield Says Workers Owe Loyalty," *Paducah Sun-Democrat*, June 27, 1956; "Battle for Control of Democratic Party in State Opens Today," *Louisville Courier-Journal*, June 30, 1956; "Chandler Forces Seize Party Control," *Paducah Sun-Democrat*, July 1, 1956.

28. "Chandler Runs Convention and Becomes a 'Favorite Son,'" *Louisville Courier-Journal*, July 4, 1956; "Chandler Plans Midwest Tour," *Paducah Sun-Democrat*, July 11, 1956; "Chandler Still Confident after Washington Trip," *Louisville Courier-Journal*, July 15, 1956; "Chandler Swats Twice at Adlai," *Louisville Courier-Journal*, August 15, 1956; "Happy Chandler Is Placed in Nomination by Leary," *Paducah Sun-Democrat*, August 17, 1956; "Chandler Gets 36½ Votes from 7 States," *Louisville Courier-Journal*, August 17, 1956; "Chandler Says He'd Do It Differently 'Next Time,'" *Paducah Sun-Democrat*, August 20, 1956; "Kentucky Wallaceites Not so Happy about Happy," *Madisonville Messenger*, September 7, 1968; "Chandler–Wallace Split Leaves an Older Union," *Louisville Courier-Journal*, September 11, 1968; "Chandler Hints Wallace Ruled by a 'Mr. Big,'" *Louisville Courier-Journal*, September 18, 1968.

29. "Chandler for Democrats, 'Every Durn One of Them!,'" *Louisville Courier-Journal*, August 30, 1956; "Chandler Leaders Stage Sit-Down Strike to Swing Victory to Ike," *Louisville Courier-Journal*, October 13, 1956; "Leary Joins Clements in 2nd District Tour," *Owensboro Messenger-Inquirer*, November 4, 1956; "Democrats Win Big Margins in District," *Paducah Sun-Democrat*, November 7, 1956; "Eisenhower Tops Slate Here with Vote of 11,501," *Owensboro Messenger-Inquirer*, November 7, 1956; "Morton Wins Only Two Districts," *Louisville Courier-Journal*, November 9, 1956.

30. "Senate Vote Benefits Bill, Rebuffs Ike," *Louisville Courier-Journal*, July 18, 1956; Robert A. Caro, *Master of the Senate*, vol. 2: *The Years of Lyndon Johnson* (New York: Knopf, 2002), 680–82; Rowland Evans and Robert D. Novak, *Lyndon B. Johnson: The Exercise of Power, a Political Biography* (New York: New American Library, 1966), 159; Robert G. Baker, interviewed by Tracy Campbell, October 19, 2009, Earle C. Clements Oral History Project, Nunn Center; Robert G. Baker, interviewed by Donald Ritchie, 2009, published in Todd S. Purdum, "Sex in the Senate: Bobby Baker's Salacious Secret History of Capitol Hill," *Politico Magazine*, November 19, 2013; Earle C. Clements, interviewed by Michael L. Gillette, December 26, 1977, Lyndon B. Johnson Presidential Library, Austin, TX; "Chandler Leaders Stage Sit-Down Strike to Swing Victory to Ike," *Louisville Courier-Journal*, October 13, 1956;

Edward A. Farris, interviewed by Terry Birdwhistell, February 2, 1977, Earle C. Clements Oral History Project, Nunn Center; Edward A. Farris, interviewed by the author, March 2, 2011, West Kentucky Politics Project, Nunn Center; "The Winner: A. B. Chandler," *Louisville Courier-Journal,* November 11, 1956.

31. David L. Wolford, "Resistance on the Border: School Desegregation in Western Kentucky, 1954–1964," *Ohio Valley History Quarterly* 4 (Summer 2004): 51–53; "Negroes Demand Speedy Integration," *Madisonville Messenger,* July 14, 1956; "Will Our National Guardsmen Stay in Sturgis Until School Ends in May?," *Madisonville Messenger,* September 7, 1956; "It Was a Mistake, Maybe, to Separate Our State from the Old Dominion," *Madisonville Messenger,* September 24, 1956.

32. Wolford, "Resistance on the Border," 41–62; Hill, "A. B. 'Happy' Chandler and the Politics of Civil Rights," 10, 129–34, 149, 159–75; Chandler, *Heroes,* 257; John M. Trowbridge, *Sturgis and Clay: Showdown for Desegregation in Kentucky Education* (Frankfort: Kentucky Department of Military Affairs, 2006); Catherine Fosl and Tracy E. K'Meyer, *Freedom on the Border: An Oral History of the Civil Rights Movement in Kentucky* (Lexington: University Press of Kentucky, 2009), 65.

33. Chandler, *Heroes,* 226; Hill, "A. B. 'Happy' Chandler and the Politics of Civil Rights," 159–80; Trowbridge, *Sturgis and Clay;* Bonnie J. Burns, "The Sturgis Incident—Desegregation of Public Schools in Union County, Kentucky," MA thesis, Murray State University, 1969, 65; "Mass Meeting at Morganfield; Suggest Removal of Governor," *Sturgis News,* September 11, 1956, "Late, Lame . . . and Insulting," *Sturgis News,* September 20, 1956; "Crowd of 500 Block Way of Nine Negro Students Endeavoring to Enter in the Local All-White School," *Sturgis News,* September 6, 1956; Kentucky Office of Attorney General, Opinion 38,945, September 13, 1956.

34. Hill, "A. B. 'Happy' Chandler and the Politics of Civil Rights," 179–80; "Hopkins, Union, Webster Schools Ordered to Admit Negroes in Fall," *Louisville Courier-Journal,* February 9, 1957; "Integration under Way in Most West Kentucky Schools," *Louisville Courier-Journal,* September 2, 1956; Wolford, "Resistance on the Border"; James W. Miller, *Integration: The Lincoln Institute, Basketball, and a Vanished Tradition* (Lexington: University Press of Kentucky, 2017); "Community Will Lose Its High School," *Owensboro Messenger-Inquirer,* January 19, 1964; "In My Opinion," *Madisonville Messenger,* March 26, 1966.

35. William E. Ellis, *A History of Education in Kentucky* (Lexington: University Press of Kentucky, 2011), 351–52; Lowell H. Harrison, *Western Kentucky University* (Lexington: University Press of Kentucky, 1987), 145–46; "Murray State Honors Honors Holland as First Black Student at School," 65th Anniversary of Desegregation, n.d., https://murraystate.edu/campus/

diversity/desegregation/index.aspx; "Toppers Rip Cats 107–83 in First Meeting," *Bowling Green Park City Daily News*, March 19, 1971; "Western Honors Its 'Champs,'" *Louisville Courier-Journal*, March 20, 1971; belle hooks, *Bone Black: Memories of Girlhood* (New York: Holt, 1996), 154–55; Vivian Caldwell, interviewed by Hannah O'Daniel, November 13, 1980, Education and Desegregation Project, Pogue Library, Murray State University, Murray, KY; Jack Glazier, *Been Coming through Some Hard Times: Race, History, and Memory in Western Kentucky* (Knoxville: University of Tennessee Press, 2012), 192–93.

36. Bobbie Ann Mason, *Clear Springs: A Memoir* (New York: Random House, 1999), 83.

37. Thomas D. Clark, "Country Stores," in *The Kentucky Encyclopedia*, ed. John E. Kleber (Lexington: University Press of Kentucky, 1992), 232; Klotter and Friend, *A New History of Kentucky*, 216; "Country Stores Not What, or Where, They Used to Be," *Madisonville Messenger*, June 3, 1987; "Old Country Store Part of Dying Breed," *Madisonville Messenger*, February 2, 1983; "Country Store Hangs In as Community Hangout," *Paducah Sun*, November 19, 1986; "Our Town . . . Old-Timer Recalls—and Yearns," *Louisville Courier-Journal*, April 6, 1984.

38. Ellis, *A History of Education in Kentucky*, 151; "Ramblings," *Paducah Sun-Democrat*, May 23, 1947; "Marion High to Hold Last Graduation Rites," *Paducah Sun-Democrat*, May 16, 1957.

39. "Hearing on Ballard High School Case Is Postponed until April Term," *Paducah Sun-Democrat*, February 1, 1950; "Trigg School Board, Pinched by Loss of Land to U.S., Embarks on Expansion Plan," *Paducah Sun-Democrat*, September 3, 1950; "Columbus Purchases 51-Year-Old School for $2,500," *Paducah Sun-Democrat*, March 26, 1978; "Former State Board Chairman, Rev. Brown, Dies of Heart Attack," *Russellville News-Democrat*, August 7, 1980; "How Todd Met Its School Challenge," *Russellville News-Democrat*, December 12, 1963; "Logan County Sees Change Adding Up to Bigger Things," *Louisville Courier-Journal*, November 24, 1982; "Warren County Schools Consolidation Is Voted," *Louisville Courier-Journal*, March 22, 1967; "Graves School Board Looks for More Funds," *Paducah Sun-Democrat*, April 15, 1979; "Graves Takes Bid for Central High," *Paducah Sun*, June 17, 1983.

40. "Hike Will Make 69.3 Tax Rate Here," *Madisonville Messenger*, August 10, 1966; "Central City School Consolidation Urged," *Owensboro Messenger-Inquirer*, June 10, 1983; "Long Battle Led to School Merger Vote," *Owensboro Messenger-Inquirer*, February 25, 1984; "Faculty, Students Say Farewell to Drakesboro Elementary," *Owensboro Messenger-Inquirer*, May 19, 2005.

41. "First Region's Tournament History Explored," *Paducah Sun-Democrat*, March 7, 1973; "Cuba High School Will Become History," *Paducah Sun-Democrat*, March 13, 1977; Marianne Walker, *The Graves County Boys: A Tale of Kentucky Basketball, Perseverance, and the Unlikely Championship of the Cuba*

Cubs (Lexington: University Press of Kentucky, 2013); "School Sees Top Ratings with Instant-Replay Screen," *Louisville Courier-Journal*, March 21, 1986; "When Buzzer Sounds, Jacket History Ends," *Madisonville Messenger*, February 28, 1975; "County Had Many Top Athletes in 20th Century," *Madisonville Messenger*, January 1, 2000; "Tradition Runs Deep for Players, Coaches at Central City High," *Owensboro Messenger-Inquirer*, February 18, 1990; "Girls Basketball Made Its Mark in Muhlenberg," *Owensboro Messenger-Inquirer*, February 19, 1980.

42. "Second Clerk Named to Court of Appeals as Issue Deadlocks," *Louisville Courier-Journal*, January 18, 1957; "It's Chandler vs. the Court of Appeals," *Louisville Courier-Journal*, January 27, 1957; "Auditor Backs Chandler in Pay Dispute," *Paducah Sun-Democrat*, March 6, 1971; "Political Novice Stages a Miracle," *Louisville Courier-Journal*, May 30, 1957; "A Political Miracle Is Miss Owens," *Louisville Courier-Journal*, November 11, 1957; Pearce, *Divide and Dissent*, 71.

43. "Chandlerites Move for State Senate Control, but Clements Faction Hasn't Shown Its Hand," *Louisville Courier-Journal*, March 3, 1957; "Anti-Chandler Forces Win All but Two Districts," *Paducah Sun-Democrat*, May 30, 1957; "Candidates Primed to Run in Tuesday's Local Primary," *Owensboro Messenger-Inquirer*, May 26, 1957; "Chandler Suffered Some Hard Knocks in Primary but Voters Gave Him Friendly Assembly, It Seems," *Owensboro Messenger-Inquirer*, June 9, 1957; Lon Carter Barton, interviewed by Jeff Suchanek, February 21, 1991, Kentucky Legislature Oral History Project, Nunn Center; "Voters Reject Chandler's Efforts to Purge Critics in State Senate and House," *Louisville Courier-Journal*, May 30, 1957; "Richmond Wins to Increase Chandler's Power in Senate," *Paducah Sun-Democrat*, November 7, 1957.

44. "Freeman Says He'll Not 'Bow Down' to Governor Chandler," *Paducah Sun-Democrat*, November 9, 1957; "Chandler's Power in Assembly Due Decision Tuesday," *Paducah Sun-Democrat*, November 3, 1957; "Chandler's Pick Beaten for Top Senate Position in Rare Secret Ballot," *Louisville Courier-Journal*, January 7, 1958; "Will 'Ingrates' and Hard-Core Foes Break Chandler?," *Louisville Courier-Journal*, January 12, 1958; "Happy Erred at Least Once," *Owensboro Messenger-Inquirer*, March 9, 1958.

45. "House Revolts against Happy," *Paducah Sun-Democrat*, January 17, 1958; "Rebel House Bans Moving Health Office to Frankfort," *Louisville Courier-Journal*, January 17, 1958; "Battle-Torn Budget Faces Senate," *Madisonville Messenger*, January 17, 1958; "Thursday Wasn't Governor's Day," *Owensboro Messenger-Inquirer*, January 18, 1958; "Compromise Budget Passes Senate, Goes Back to House for Concurrence," *Louisville Courier-Journal*, February 7, 1958.

46. "Chandler Forces Seek Budget Compromise," *Louisville Courier-Journal*, January 30, 1958; "Compromise Budget Passes, 24 to 5," *Louisville Courier-Journal*, February 7, 1958; "Republicans Helped Governor Win

Victory," *Owensboro Messenger-Inquirer,* February 9, 1958; "Punishing Louisville," *Paducah Sun-Democrat,* February 17, 1958.

47. "3 Defeats Damage Chandler's Prestige," *Louisville Courier-Journal,* May 29, 1958; Al Smith, *Wordsmith: My Life in Journalism* (Louisville, KY: Pied Type Press, 2011), 171–72; Al Smith, interviewed by the author, October 25, 2010, West Kentucky Politics Project, Nunn Center; "Happy Says Gregory to Ask Recount," *Paducah Sun-Democrat,* May 29, 1958; "FBI Takes No Action in Logan Probe," *Paducah Sun-Democrat,* June 5, 1958; "Deweese Named as Vote Conspirator," *Paducah Sun-Democrat,* June 22, 1958; "Osborne Cites 'Forgeries' in Logan," *Paducah Sun-Democrat,* June 24, 1958; "Stubblefield Wins Election," *Paducah Sun-Democrat,* September 19, 1958.

48. "3 West Kentuckians 'Contenders' for Governor's Office in 1959," *Paducah Sun-Democrat,* March 13, 1958; "'Rebels' Doubt That Wyatt Could Win," *Louisville Courier-Journal,* April 13, 1958; "Rumsey Taylor, 1955 Aide to Combs, Supports Wyatt," *Louisville Courier-Journal,* July 20, 1958; "Wyatt Teams Up with Combs," *Paducah Sun-Democrat,* January 21, 1959.

49. "Chandler Says He Would Like to See Thomas Fired as Game Warden," *Louisville Courier-Journal,* December 18, 1958; Pearce, *Divide and Dissent,* 91–94; "The Team You Can Trust," in *Bert Combs,* ed. Robinson, 85–86.

50. "Waterfield Concedes, Pledges Support," *Paducah Sun-Democrat,* May 28, 1959; Jewell, *Gubernatorial Primary and General Elections, 1923–1959,* 48–51; "Happy Threatens to 'Clean 'Em Out' in 1963," *Paducah Sun-Democrat,* May 29, 1959; "Nine Incumbents in House, Senate Lose in Election," *Owensboro Messenger-Inquirer,* May 27, 1959; "Combs Reverses 1955 Loss to Win Big Victory Here," *Madisonville Messenger,* May 27, 1959; "Chandler Wasn't Invited to Rally," *Paducah Sun-Democrat,* October 23, 1959; "A Vote for John Robsion Is a Vote for Happy Chandler," *Paducah Sun-Democrat,* October 23, 1959; "Combs and Slate Win in Landslide," *Louisville Courier-Journal,* November 4, 1959; Pearce, *Divide and Dissent,* 96–97.

51. "Combs and Slate Win in Landslide,"; "Wyatt Vote Sets Record in Kentucky," *Paducah Sun-Democrat,* November 20, 1959; "Clements Named Roads Commissioner," *Paducah Sun-Democrat,* December 9, 1959; "Clements Quits $22,500 Position," *Paducah Sun-Democrat,* December 10, 1959; "Governor Abolishes Chandler Merit System," *Louisville Courier-Journal,* December 10, 1959; "Clements Already Has Fine Record as Builder of Roads," *Paducah Sun-Democrat,* December 12, 1959; Pearce, *Divide and Dissent,* 107–8; "The Truck Deal," in *Bert Combs,* ed. Robinson, 126–27.

52. "Kentucky General Assembly Adjourns," *Paducah Sun-Democrat,* March 22, 1958; Pearce, *Divide and Dissent,* 111–12; "The Sales Tax," in *Bert Combs,* ed. Robinson, 101–5.

53. "Bonus and Tax Bills Run into Opposition in Both Chambers," *Louisville Courier-Journal,* January 22, 1960; "Sales Tax Measure Approved by House,"

Paducah Sun-Democrat, January 29, 1960; "28-to-8 Senate Vote Sends Sales Tax Bill to Combs," *Louisville Courier-Journal,* February 4, 1960.

54. "Budget of Billion 'to Lift State,'" *Louisville Courier-Journal,* February 18, 1960; "House Votes Billion Dollar State Budget," *Louisville Courier-Journal,* March 1, 1960; "The Merit System," *Bert Combs,* ed. Robinson, 106–10; Pearce, *Divide and Dissent,* 120; "Merit Bill Gets House Okey, 86–7," *Paducah Sun-Democrat,* February 24, 1960.

55. "Combs Praises Record of 1960 Session," *Paducah Sun-Democrat,* March 2, 1960; "State to Rent 34 Trucks from New Louisville Firm for $425 a Month Apiece," *Louisville Courier-Journal,* April 13, 1960; "Combs Delays Truck Lease Deal," *Louisville Courier-Journal,* April 19, 1960; "Combs Will Select Clements Successor within Two Weeks," *Louisville Courier-Journal,* August 19, 1960; Pearce, *Divide and Dissent,* 135–39; "Ward New Commissioner of Highways," *Paducah Sun-Democrat,* August 26, 1960.

56. "Clements–Chandler Alliance Nothing New," *Louisville Courier-Journal,* September 18, 1960; "Logan Assails Combs, Wyatt on Truck Deal," *Louisville Courier-Journal,* February 22, 1962; "Clements Says Truck Deal Interested Combs, Wyatt," *Louisville Courier-Journal,* February 27, 1962; "Raney Bribe Charge Held True," *Louisville Courier-Journal,* March 15, 1962; "Infighting Kept Senate in a Perpetual Turmoil," *Louisville Courier-Journal,* March 18, 1962; "Combs Lauds General Assembly Work; Criticizes 'Political Wrecking Crew,'" *Madisonville Messenger,* March 18, 1962; "G. O. P. Selects West Kentuckian," *Louisville Courier-Journal,* January 2, 1962; Pearce, *Divide and Dissent,* 191–95; "The Truck Deal," in *Bert Combs,* ed. Robinson, 121–36.

57. "Kennedy Cuffs GOP in Speech Here," *Paducah Sun-Democrat,* October 9, 1960; "Kennedy Says Perilous Times Demand Democratic Leadership," *Bowling Green Park City Daily News,* October 9, 1960; "District Edge May Hit 16,000," *Paducah Sun-Democrat,* November 9, 1960; "Kentucky Vote on Big Races," *Louisville Courier-Journal,* November 10, 1960; "Explanations Numerous on Defeat of Revision," *Louisville Courier-Journal,* November 10, 1960; "The Truck Deal," in *Bert Combs,* ed. Robinson, 133–34.

58. Pearce, *Divide and Dissent,* 180; "Weakening the Sales Tax Would Weaken Kentucky," *Paducah Sun-Democrat,* May 22, 1961; "Kentucky Sales Tax Faces First Political Test in Tuesday Primary," *Paducah Sun-Democrat,* May 21, 1961; "Combs-Backed Senate Hopefuls Win at Least 6 of 13 Contests," *Louisville Courier-Journal,* May 24, 1961; "Combs Claims Legislative Majority," *Paducah Sun-Democrat,* May 24, 1961; "Where Was the People's Revolt against Combs and the Tax?," *Louisville Courier-Journal,* May 25, 1961; "Combs' Allies Beat Foes of Sales Tax in Assembly Races," *Louisville Courier-Journal,* May 25, 1961; "Louise G. Kirtley Is Seeking Election to State Legislature," *Owensboro Messenger-Inquirer,* March 19, 1961.

59. John S. Palmore, *An Opinionated Career: Memoirs of a Kentucky Judge* (Georgetown: Kentucky River Press, 2003), 69–72; John Palmore, interviewed by the author, October 15, 2010, West Kentucky Politics Project, Nunn Center; "Ned Breathitt Has Climbed High in a Short Career," *Paducah Sun-Democrat,* February 4, 1962; "Breathitt Enters Governor's Race," *Bowling Green Park City Daily News,* May 2, 1962; Edward T. "Ned" Breathitt, interviewed by Terry Birdwhistell, July 27, 1994, Edward T. "Ned" Breathitt Jr. Oral History Project, Nunn Center; "Election Campaigns," in *Bert Combs,* Robinson, ed. 137–42; Pearce, *Divide and Dissent,* 199.

60. "Turn to Happy Is Strange Role for Taylor," *Paducah Sun-Democrat,* January 25, 1963; "Chandler Camp Split on Morgan," *Louisville Courier-Journal,* September 25, 1962; "Waterfield Is Praised by Chandler," *Louisville Courier-Journal,* November 24, 1962; "Ward Won't Seek No. 2 State Post," *Louisville Courier-Journal,* December 4, 1962; "Waterfield Backs Chandler," *Louisville Courier-Journal,* May 2, 1962; "Breathitt Campaign Emphasizes Youth," *Paducah Sun-Democrat,* December 9, 1962; "Overflow Crowd Hears Breathitt at County Organization Rally," *Dawson Springs Progress,* January 17, 1963; Edward T. "Ned" Breathitt, interviewed by James Hammack, March 15, 1994, People and Politics Collection, Pogue Library.

61. "Breathitt Raps His Foe in All Day Tour Here," *Paducah Sun-Democrat,* April 16, 1963; "T. V. Probe Requested by Walters," *Louisville Courier-Journal,* May 1, 1962; "U. S. Says WHAS Violated Rules," *Louisville Courier-Journal,* May 23, 1963; Chandler, *Heroes,* 268–69.

62. Kentucky State Board of Elections, election returns for 1963, CD requested by the author, October 5, 2011; "Chandler Plays Golf, Delaying Statement," *Hopkinsville New Era,* May 29, 1963; Pearce, *Divide and Dissent,* 215–16; "Newcomer Carries 6 Districts," *Paducah Sun-Democrat,* May 29, 1963; "Exit on Cue," *Louisville Courier-Journal,* May 29, 1963; "Young Governor Must Build on Old Foundations," *Louisville Courier-Journal,* June 2, 1963; "Dry-Eyed Good-Byes," *Louisville Courier-Journal,* June 1, 1963; "Still in Politics, Chandler Says," *Louisville Courier-Journal,* June 12, 1963.

63. Edward T. "Ned" Breathitt Jr., interviewed by James Hammack, May 24–25, 1994, People and Politics Collection, Pogue Library; "Edward T. "Ned" Breathitt, interviewed by James C. Klotter, February 6, 1993, Edward T. "Ned" Breathitt Oral History Project, Nunn Center; "Nunn Assailed by Breathitt," *Louisville Courier-Journal,* September 22, 1963.

64. "Combs Hits Blow at Citizen's Basic Right to Control His Property," *Madisonville Messenger,* June 26, 1963; "Reaction Mixed in Paducah," *Paducah Sun-Democrat,* June 27, 1963; "State's Republicans Short on Issues," *Paducah Sun-Democrat,* July 5, 1963; "Nunn vs. Combs and Robert Kennedy," *Paducah Sun-Democrat,* July 10, 1963; "Breathitt–Nunn Engage in One Hour Debate," *Louisville Courier-Journal,* September 28, 1963; "Not Pledging Aid, Chandler

Asserts," *Louisville Courier-Journal,* October 3, 1963; "Nunn Democrats Would Punish West Kentucky," *Paducah Sun-Democrat,* October 16, 1963; "Editors Predict Breathitt by Margin of 22–1," *Paducah Sun-Democrat,* October 24, 1963; "Democrats See Large Area Edge," *Paducah Sun-Democrat,* November 4, 1963; Edward T. "Ned" Breathitt, interviewed by Tracy Campbell, June 22, 1994, Edward F. Prichard Jr. Project, Nunn Center; Robinson, notes, in *Bert Combs,* 220; Edward T. "Ned" Breathitt, interviewed by Terry Birdwhistell, February 6, 1997, Edward T. "Ned" Breathitt Oral History Project, Nunn Center; "Oral Interview on Governor Breathitt on Civil Rights," interview by Betsy Brinson and Kenneth H. Wilkins," *Register of the Kentucky Historical Society* 99, no. 1 (Winter 2001): 23–24.

65. Kentucky State Board of Elections, election returns for 1963, CD requested by author, October 5, 2011; "First District 'Saves the Day' for Breathitt," *Paducah Sun-Democrat,* November 6, 1963; "Unity Is Breathitt Aim," *Paducah Sun-Democrat,* November 7, 1963; "Proclaiming Lasting Unity, Breathitt Calls Bolt Feeble," *Louisville Courier-Journal,* November 7, 1963; "Scare May Unify Democrats," *Louisville Courier-Journal,* November 7, 1963; Harry Lee Waterfield Jr., interviewed by the author, March 7, 2011, West Kentucky Politics Project, Nunn Center; Breathitt, interviewed by Birdwhistell, February 6, 1997.

66. "Before Another Summer," *Nashville Tennessean,* June 23, 1950; "Way Open for Authorization of Dam," *Paducah Sun-Democrat,* November 9, 1951; "Authorization of Cumberland High Dam Asked by Association," *Paducah Sun-Democrat,* January 1, 1953; "Gregory Is a Big Man in the Lower Cumberland Dam Plan," *Paducah Sun-Democrat,* March 20, 1956; "Cumberland Dam Is Far Out of Dream Stage," *Paducah Sun-Democrat,* July 5, 1955; "Attention Shifts to Cumberland as Work of Harnessing Tennessee Nears Completion," *Nashville Tennessean,* August 14, 1955; "Cumberland Valley Group to Push Construction of Dam," *Nashville Tennessean,* August 16, 1955; "Resolution by Clements Was a Key Measure," *Paducah Sun-Democrat,* August 6, 1966.

67. "Barkley Lake to Be Dedicated Saturday," *Madisonville Messenger,* August 15, 1966; "Breathitt Outlines Plans for Park on Barkley Lake," *Paducah Sun-Democrat,* October 8, 1964.

68. Pearce, *Divide and Dissent,* 69; "Toll Roads, Parks, and Tourism," in *Bert Combs,* ed. Robinson, 111–16; "Last Big Kentucky Link of I-65 Ready," *Louisville Courier-Journal,* November 14, 1968; "The 60's Brought Kentucky Progress amid Turmoil," *Louisville Courier-Journal,* January 4, 1970.

69. "Southern Route for Toll Road OKed," *Paducah Sun-Democrat,* March 14, 1961; "Legal Action against Toll Road Talked," *Paducah Sun-Democrat,* March 21, 1961; "Executives of Northwest Road Group Set Meeting," *Owensboro Messenger-Inquirer,* March 22, 1961; "Bids due on Western Turnpike Oct. 13," *Owensboro Messenger-Inquirer,* September 20, 1961; "Parkway Opens to West," *Louisville Courier-Journal,* September 24, 1963.

70. "New Talks Slated on Road Route," *Paducah Sun-Democrat*, January 30, 1961; "W. Kentucky Superhighway Route Talked," *Paducah Sun-Democrat*, March 9, 1961; "State for Tie-Up of I-24, Toll Road," *Paducah Sun-Democrat*, March 15, 1961; "Ward Says Old Proposal for I-24 Was Dead," *Paducah Sun-Democrat*, March 21, 1961; "I-K-T Group Plans Meet with Ward," *Paducah Sun-Democrat*, March 23, 1961; "Indiana Placed into I-24 Picture," *Paducah Sun-Democrat*, June 1, 1961; "I-24 Route Plan Will Be Told to Kennedy," *Paducah-Sun Democrat*, September 18, 1963; "Preliminary Work on I-24 Scheduled," *Paducah Sun-Democrat*, August 19, 1964; "At Last, an Unbroken I-24 from Here South," *Paducah Sun-Democrat*, May 22, 1980.

71. "Breathitt Favors Highway for West Kentucky Counties," *Paducah Sun-Democrat*, February 6, 1962; "Breathitt Pledges Parkway Dedication during His Term," *Paducah Sun-Democrat*, September 18, 1964; "Purchase Parkway Will Fill the Dream of a Lifetime," *Paducah Sun-Democrat*, October 11, 1964; "First Ground Is Broken for Purchase Parkway," *Paducah Sun-Democrat*, August 31, 1966; "State Highway Chief Dedicates Parkway," *Paducah Sun-Democrat*, March 28, 1969; "Toll Plan to 4-Lane US-41 All the Way," *Madisonville Messenger*, June 9, 1965.

72. "New Salesman for Kentucky," *Paducah Sun-Democrat*, December 16, 1963; "Gardner Nearly Certain to Be Key Legislator," *Owensboro Messenger-Inquirer*, December 17, 1963; "Selection of Gardner Holds Firm," *Owensboro Messenger-Inquirer*, December 18, 1963.

73. Richard Frymire, interviewed by author, September 3, 2010, Kentucky Legislature Oral History Collection, Nunn Center; Breathitt, interviewed by Birdwhistell, February 6, 1997; "Task Facing Legislature," *Paducah Sun-Democrat*, January 2, 1964; "Breathitt Must Lean upon Waterfield in Assembly," *Louisville Courier-Journal*, January 5, 1964.

74. "House Speaker Bones Up on Procedures after Errors," *Paducah Sun-Democrat*, January 21, 1964; "Budget Delayed until February for Possible New Cuts," *Louisville Courier-Journal*, January 5, 1964; "Breathitt Asks $1.4 Billion, but No Increases in Taxes," *Louisville Courier-Journal*, February 11, 1964; "House Defers Vote on Budget a Week," *Louisville Courier-Journal*, February 12, 1964; "Budget Goes to Breathitt after Changes," *Louisville Courier-Journal*, February 26, 1964.

75. "Waterfield Rift with Breathitt Comes to Light," *Paducah Sun-Democrat*, February 26, 1964; "Capitol Discord," *Louisville Courier-Journal*, February 28, 1964; "Watchdog Bill Called 'No Ripper,'" *Louisville Courier-Journal*, March 1, 1964; "Breathitt's School-Tax Beaten," *Louisville Courier-Journal*, March 20, 1964.

76. Kenneth E. Harrell, "Edward Thompson Breathitt Jr," in *Kentucky's Governors*, ed. Harrison, 202.

77. "Breathitt Presents State 6 Challenges," *Paducah Sun-Democrat*, January 8, 1964; Catherine Fosl and Tracy E. K'Meyer, *Freedom on the Border: An*

Oral History of the Civil Rights Movement in Kentucky (Lexington: University Press of Kentucky, 2009), 105–10; "Assembly's Action on Rights Unsure," *Paducah Sun-Democrat*, January 17, 1964; "Surprising Compliance with Bias Law Forecast at Civil Rights Meeting Here," *Paducah Sun-Democrat*, January 18, 1964; "Outlook for the Civil Rights Bill," *Paducah Sun-Democrat*, February 12, 1964; "2 Marches on Frankfort Are Two Too Many," *Madisonville Messenger*, February 21, 1964.

78. "Meeting Is Planned Here to Set Up Role in 'March,'" *Paducah Sun-Democrat*, February 20, 1964; "Local Group to Appear in Capital March," *Owensboro Messenger-Inquirer*, March 3, 1964; "Governor's Daughter Joins Rights March," *Paducah Sun-Democrat*, March 6, 1964.

79. "Civil Rights Leaders Meet with Gov. Breathitt Today," *Paducah Sun-Democrat*, March 6, 1964; "10,000 Brave Chill, March on Frankfort," *Louisville Courier-Journal*, March 6, 1964; "Lawmakers Little Affected by March," *Louisville Courier-Journal*, March 6, 1964; "Legislative Report," *Owensboro Messenger-Inquirer*, March 16, 1964; "House Balks in Face of Demonstrators," *Owensboro Messenger-Inquirer*, March 17, 1964.

80. "Breathitt Urges Action on Rights," *Louisville Courier-Journal*, March 13, 1964; "House Rules Unit Kills Rights Bill," *Louisville Courier-Journal*, March 13, 1964; "Ineptness, Political Cowardice Bury Civil Rights in Frankfort," *Louisville Courier-Journal*, March 14, 1964; "Breathitt Plea Fails to Win Majority for Special Session," *Louisville Courier-Journal*, July 21, 1964; "'Outside Interference' Blamed for Failure of Civil Rights Bill," *Paducah Sun-Democrat*, March 21, 1964; "Veteran Republican Claims Civil Rights Bill Chance Killed by Outside Pressure," *Owensboro Messenger-Inquirer*, March 21, 1964; "Breathitt Pledge Ends Long Fast," *Paducah Sun-Democrat*, March 21, 1964.

81. "Rights Law Urged by Mayors," *Louisville Courier-Journal*, May 16, 1966; "40 Mayors Back Civil Rights Bill," *Paducah Sun-Democrat*, May 16, 1964; "State Civil Rights Leaders Request an Emergency Meet with Governor," *Owensboro Messenger-Inquirer*, July 21, 1964; "GOP Charges Breathitt Insincere on Rights Bill," *Paducah Sun-Democrat*, July 21, 1964; "The State Public Accommodations Bill," *Paducah Sun-Democrat*, July 23, 1964.

82. "Breathitt Backs Miss Peden's Plan," *Paducah Sun-Democrat*, May 3, 1964; "State's Industry Program Jolted," *Paducah Sun-Democrat*, May 10, 1964; "Waterfield Hits Hiring of Fossett," *Paducah Sun-Democrat*, May 10, 1964; "Waterfield and Miss Peden Clash on Hiring Practices," *Paducah Sun-Democrat*, June 9, 1964; Breathitt, interviewed by Hammack, March 15, 1994; "Waterfield vs. Miss Peden," *Louisville Courier-Journal*, June 10, 1964; "Waterfield Is Fired over Economic Development Breach," *Paducah Sun-Democrat*, June 15, 1964; "The Retreat from Harmony at Frankfort," *Louisville Courier-Journal*, June 14, 1964; "Breathitt Turns Out Waterfield as Chief of Development," *Louisville Courier-Journal*, June 15, 1964.

83. "Breathitt, Waterfield Forces Agree on One Thing—Senate Fight Brewing," *Louisville Courier-Journal,* February 26, 1965; "Breathitt Confident on Voting," *Louisville Courier-Journal,* January 10, 1965; "Ten Senate Seats Key to Breathitt-Waterfield Collision," *Louisville Courier-Journal,* April 25, 1965; "Ford Squeaks by in One of Closest Votes," *Owensboro Messenger-Inquirer,* May 26, 1965; "There Is Glory for Both Senatorial Aspirants," *Owensboro Messenger-Inquirer,* May 26, 1965; "Ned's Allies Win in 7 of 10 Senate Races," *Madisonville Messenger,* May 26, 1965; Frymire, interviewed by the author, September 3, 2010; "Breathitt-Foe Gardner Falls by Slim Margin," *Louisville Courier-Journal,* May 27, 1965.

84. "Smith and Dr. Walker Oppose Waterfield's Rate Proposal," *Paducah Sun-Democrat,* August 20, 1965; "Administration Takes Dim View of Waterfield Plan," *Paducah Sun-Democrat,* August 21, 1965; "Breathitt and Waterfield Give Their Versions of Political Rift," *Paducah Sun-Democrat,* September 5, 1965; "Breathitt Asks Session to Freeze Tax Bills," *Louisville Courier-Journal,* August 24, 1965; "House Backs Breathitt Tax Plan 64–31 in Stormy Session," *Paducah Sun-Democrat,* September 3, 1965; "Breathitt Takes Control of Senate with the Help of Jefferson Republicans," *Louisville Courier-Journal,* September 3, 1965; "Senate 'Adjourns'—Breathitt Men Continue Session," *Louisville Courier-Journal,* September 10, 1965; "Breathitt Signs His Tax Bill into Law," *Paducah Sun-Democrat,* September 17, 1965; "Who's on First in Frankfort?," *Louisville Courier-Journal,* September 19, 1965; "Out of Senate Battleground, Breathitt Emerges as a Power," *Paducah Sun-Democrat,* September 19, 1965.

85. "$176-Million Bond Project Debated," *Owensboro Messenger-Inquirer,* October 26, 1965; "Bond Proposal Critics Flayed by Breathitt," *Paducah Sun-Democrat,* October 27, 1965; "Massive Majority Passes Bond Issue," *Paducah Sun-Democrat,* November 3, 1965; "Has Waterfield Taken His Third Strike?," *Paducah Sun-Democrat,* November 7, 1965.

86. "Breathitt Wins in First Test in Senate," *Paducah Sun-Democrat,* January 4, 1966; "Governor Has Control of Senate," *Paducah Sun-Democrat,* January 5, 1966; "Breathitt's Forces Win in Battle for Senate," *Owensboro Messenger-Inquirer,* January 4, 1966; "Waterfield's Bid to Control Senate Crushed," *Paducah Sun-Democrat,* January 5, 1966; "Breathitt Backers Clip Waterfield," *Louisville Courier-Journal,* January 5, 1966.

87. "Breathitt Offers $2 Billion Budget," *Louisville Courier-Journal,* January 5, 1966; "Breathitt: Make Possible Better Lives . . . for Our People," *Louisville Courier-Journal,* January 5, 1966.

88. "Rights Bill Far Stronger than Ill-Fated One of '64," *Louisville Courier-Journal,* January 2, 1966; "Rights Bill Endorsed by Vote of 76–12," *Paducah Sun-Democrat,* January 18, 1965; "Civil Rights Bill Readied for Passage as GOP Senators Causing Delay," *Louisville Courier-Journal,* January 21, 1966; "State Civil Rights Bill Approved by Senate, 36–1," *Louisville Courier-*

Journal, January 26, 1966; "100 Years—'a Moral Commitment' Is Kept," *Paducah Sun-Democrat*, January 28, 1966; "Rights Law a Beginning, Breathitt Says at Signing," *Louisville Courier-Journal*, January 28, 1966; "Kentucky Takes Honorable Step," *Paducah Sun-Democrat*, January 29, 1966; "Martin Luther King Praises Kentucky's Civil Rights Law," *Louisville Courier-Journal*, January 29, 1966; "Oh, Weep No More Today," *Atlanta Constitution*, February 2, 1966.

89. "Kentucky's Ravaged Land," *Louisville Courier-Journal*, January 5, 1964; "Strip-Mine Compact Pushed," *Louisville Courier-Journal*, November 5, 1965; "Pennsylvania's Doing It, so Can We, Breathitt," *Louisville Courier-Journal*, October 9, 1966; "Ruin Creeps Like Cancer," *Louisville Courier-Journal*, January 5, 1964; "West Kentucky Has an Ugly Face," *Louisville Courier-Journal*, January 5, 1964; "County Will Buy Own Mosquito Spray Plane," *Madisonville Messenger*, January 14, 1966; "Widow vs. Bulldozer—Has Mrs. Combs Beaten Strip Miners?," *Louisville Courier-Journal*, November 28, 1965.

90. "Tough Strip-Mine Bill Is Given Top Priority," *Louisville Courier-Journal*, January 5, 1966; "Legislators See Need for Strip-Mine Curbs," *Louisville Courier-Journal*, January 11, 1966.

91. "Governor to Seek Pollution, Strip Mine Controls," *Louisville Courier-Journal*, January 2, 1966; "Two Industries and the '66 Legislature," *Madisonville Messenger*, January 1, 1966; "Legislators Not Shown Real Fruits of Early Reclamations," *Madisonville Messenger*, January 11, 1966.

92. "Strip Mining Is Called Ruinous," *Louisville Courier-Journal*, January 19, 1966; "Caudill Urges Outlawing of East Kentucky Strip Mining," *Madisonville Messenger*, January 20, 1966; Edward T. Breathitt, "On the Cutting Edge—the Gadfly and the Strong Voice—Raising Hell," *Appalachian Heritage* 21, no. 2 (Spring 1993): 21–25.

93. "House Passes Ned's Strip Mining Bill," *Owensboro Messenger-Inquirer*, January 25, 1966; "Strip Mine Bill Passes," *Madisonville Messenger*, January 27, 1966; "Senate Votes Toughest Mine Law, 36–2," *Louisville Courier-Journal*, January 28, 1966.

94. Marc Landry, *The Politics of Environmental Reform: Controlling Kentucky Strip Mining* (Washington, DC: Resources for the Future, 1976); "Coal History," n.d., at www.coalindustry.org/ky_coal_facts/history_of_coal; Hagerman, "Water, Workers, and Wealth," 220.

95. "Remapping Bill to Be Offered Monday," *Paducah Sun-Democrat*, March 1, 1966; "Redistricting Bill Wins Senate Approval," *Paducah Sun-Democrat*, March 9, 1966; "Breathitt's Redistricting Plan Would Aid Cities," *Louisville Courier-Journal*, March 5, 1966.

96. "Unlike First Session, Second Was a Smashing Success for Breathitt," *Louisville Courier-Journal*, March 20, 1966; "The Political Struggles Looked Innocent," *Louisville Courier-Journal*, March 20, 1966; "The Breathitt Administration," *Paducah Sun-Democrat*, March 22, 1966; "Breathitt's Record Is

Good; Financial Record Doubtful," *Owensboro Messenger-Inquirer*, March 23, 1966.

97. Ellis, *A History of Education in Kentucky*, 378–79; "Murray State University Fall Enrollment," 1923–2020, at https://www.murraystate.edu/headermenu/administration/PresidentsOffice/institutional-effectiveness/OfficeOfInstitutionalResearch/Enrollment%20history_1923-present_2020511.pdf; "'Second Phase' of New Era Begins at Murray State," *Paducah Sun-Democrat*, August 13, 1957; Harrison, *Western Kentucky University*, 144–51, 175–76; Ellis, *A History of Education in Kentucky*, 366–78.

98. Ellis, *A History of Education in Kentucky*, 371–72; "Towns Told to Work for Colleges," *Louisville Courier-Journal*, February 11, 1962; "College Rites Set at Hopkinsville," *Louisville Courier-Journal*, September 9, 1965; "Pact Highlights Autonomy Effort of PJC Trustees," *Paducah Sun-Democrat*, May 17, 1967; Janette M. Blythe, *Upward Stride: A Pictorial History of West Kentucky Community & Technical College* (Virginia Beach, VA: Donning, 2008); Harrison, *Western Kentucky University*, 188.

99. George G. Humphreys, *The Quest for Excellence: Madisonville Community College, 1968–2009* (Madisonville, KY: Madisonville Community College, 2009), 1–15; Blythe, *Upward Stride*, 65–66; "Graduate Consortium Gets $300,000," *Owensboro Messenger-Inquirer*, July 25, 1974; Harrison, *Western Kentucky University*, 212–14; "WKU Sees Need for Owensboro Facility," *Owensboro Messenger-Inquirer*, November 27, 1987; "Building Ready for Occupancy," *Owensboro Messenger-Inquirer*, November 25, 2009.

100. "Madisonville May Make Bethel Bid," *Madisonville Messenger*, December 13, 1963; "Brescia Grows to Young Adulthood," *Owensboro Messenger-Inquirer*, January 4, 1970; "KWC Left Its 'Corn Field Days' and Found Its Growth in '60s," *Owensboro Messenger-Inquirer*, January 4, 1970; "Mid-Continent Celebrates Growth in Paducah," *Paducah Sun*, April 28, 2010; "Baptists Split on Area School," *Paducah Sun-Democrat*, November 20, 1988; "Little College Makes Its Horizon Expand," *Paducah Sun-Democrat*, March 20, 1998; "No Longer a 'Best Kept Secret,'" *Paducah Sun-Democrat*, August 31, 2001; "Questions Surround Mid-Continent Closing," *Paducah Sun*, June 30, 2014.

101. "Between-Rivers Bill Is Planned," *Paducah Sun-Democrat*, February 1, 1962; "'Area' Will Take 3 Towns, Highway 68 Improvements," *Paducah Sun-Democrat*, January 16, 1964.

102. "Opposition to TVA Plan Takes Shape," *Paducah Sun-Democrat*, February 17, 1964; Betty Jo Wallace, *Between the Rivers: History of the Land between the Lakes* (Clarksville, TN: Austin Peay State University, 1992), 207–47; Ronald A. Foresta, *The Land between the Lakes: A Geography of the Future* (Knoxville: University of Tennessee Press), 103–4.

103. John Egerton, *The Americanization of Dixie: The Southernization of America* (New York: Harper and Row, 1974), 58; David Nickell, "Between the

Rivers: A Socio-historical Account of Hegemony and Heritage," *Humanity & Society* 31, no. 2 (May–August 2007): 171–78; David Nickell, interviewed by the author, July 8, 2011, West Kentucky Politics Project, Nunn Center; Foresta, *The Land between the Lakes,* 3.

104. "The Breathitt Years," *Louisville Courier-Journal,* December 10, 1964; Edward T. Breathitt, "Industrial Appreciation Luncheon, September 22, 1967," in *The Public Papers of Governor Edward Breathitt, 1963–1967,* ed. Kenneth E. Harrell (Lexington: University Press of Kentucky, 1984), 119; Raymond Arsenault, "The End of the Long Hot Summer: The Air Conditioner and Southern Culture," *Journal of Southern History* 50, no. 4 (November 1984): 597–628.

105. Berry Craig, "Mayfield," in *Kentucky Encyclopedia,* ed. Kleber, 619–20; Lee A. Dew, "Hancock County," in *Kentucky Encyclopedia,* ed. Kleber, 401–2; "Program to Diversify Its Industry Helped Madisonville Win Award," *Louisville Courier-Journal,* March 16, 1972; "Emerson Electric to Build $2 Million Factory Here," *Russellville News-Democrat,* April 15, 1960; "The Tennessee Farm Boy Who Ran a Kentucky Town," *Russellville News-Democrat,* December 10, 1964; "2,600 Jobs Balance Agriculture with Industry," *Russellville News-Democrat,* September 2, 1965; "Elkton Getting Factory to Employ 100 Men," *Louisville Courier-Journal,* September 8, 1965.

106. David Dick, *Let There Be Light: The Story of Rural Electrification in Kentucky* (North Middleton, KY: Plum Lick, 2008), 5–14; "J. R. Miller: 'Mr. Power' of Kentucky's Democratic Party," *Louisville Courier-Journal,* July 30, 1972; "Big Rivers Electric: Ailing but Medicine Taking Effect," *Paducah Sun-Democrat,* May 8, 1978.

107. "Ward's Strength Would Complicate Move by Combs," *Paducah Sun-Democrat,* October 31, 1966; "Ward Can Win, according to Poll," *Paducah Sun-Democrat,* November 4, 1966; "Ward to Run for Governor with Breathitt Backing," *Paducah Sun-Democrat,* November 11, 1966; "Breathitt to Leave Race to Henry Ward," *Paducah Sun-Democrat,* December 8, 1966; Henry Ward, "Recollections of 45 Years in Government and Politics," 1974, Henry Ward Collection, Pogue Library, Murray State University, Murray, KY, 55–56; "Ward Is and Should Be Mr. Kentucky," *Louisville Courier-Journal,* October 15, 1967; "W. F. Foster—Civics and Political Leader Dies," *Paducah Sun-Democrat,* March 1, 1967; "Chandler Slams Fiscal Habits of Breathitt's Administration," *Owensboro Messenger-Inquirer,* March 21, 1967.

108. "A. B. Chandler Exuding Health, Claims Victory," *Owensboro Messenger-Inquirer,* April 13, 1967; "It's Been a Muted Campaign for Ward, a Veteran Battler," *Paducah Sun-Democrat,* May 14, 1967; "Chandler 'Mouthing Untruths,' Opponent Henry Ward Asserts," *Paducah Sun-Democrat,* May 18, 1967; "Happy Doesn't Improve with Age," *Paducah Sun-Democrat,* May 17, 1967; "Battle Royal Looms in Final Stages of Democratic Race," *Paducah Sun-Democrat,* May 18, 1967; "Ward's Showing Should Perk Up the Democrats,"

Paducah Sun-Democrat, May 21, 1967; "Ward Would Let People Settle Kentucky's Assessment Issue," *Paducah Sun-Democrat,* May 22, 1967; Ward, "Recollections," 51–54.

109. "Ward Coasts to Easy Win," *Paducah Sun-Democrat,* May 24, 1967; "Ward Carries District by 22, 598 Votes," *Paducah Sun-Democrat,* May 24, 1967; "How Democrats Voted for Governor," *Louisville Courier-Journal,* May 24, 1967.

110. "Nunn Opens Vote Campaign," *Paducah Sun-Democrat,* September 17, 1967; "Fight 1968 Fight Then, Says Ward," *Paducah Sun-Democrat,* October 12, 1967; "Chandler Says He Supports GOP's Nunn," *Louisville Courier-Journal,* October 20, 1967; "Chandler Swings His Support to Louie B. Nunn," *Paducah Sun-Democrat,* October 20, 1967; Chandler, *Heroes,* 270.

111. "Nunn Accuses Foe of Being 'Tax Man,'" *Paducah Sun-Democrat,* September 28, 1967; "Nunn Says War Is an Issue," *Louisville Courier-Journal,* October 21, 1967; "More Salable Personality Aided Nunn," *Louisville Courier-Journal,* November 8, 1967; "Allan Trout Looks at State's Past and Future," *Paducah Sun-Democrat,* December 10, 1967; Julius Rather, interviewed by the author, August 16, 2011, Manuscripts and Folklife Archives, Western Kentucky University, Bowling Green.

112. "Ward vs. Nunn: Anatomy of a Campaign," *Louisville Courier-Journal,* November 5, 1967; "Both Sides Predict Victory: Ward, 66,000; Nunn, 60,000," *Paducah Sun-Democrat,* November 6, 1967; "Key Purchase Counties Weak for Democrat," *Paducah Sun-Democrat,* November 8, 1967; "Warren County in Dem Column," *Bowling Green Park City Daily News,* November 8, 1967; "Ward's Margin Here Is Smallest in 24 Years," *Madisonville Messenger,* November 8, 1967.

113. "We Should Compliment Ford with a Large Majority," *Owensboro Messenger-Inquirer,* October 22, 1967; "Ford Majority in Daviess Exceeds 8,000," *Owensboro Messenger-Inquirer,* November 8, 1967; "Wendell Ford's Future Looks Bright," *Paducah Sun-Democrat,* November 9, 1967.

5. From Democratic Resurgence to the Collapse of the Gibraltar of Kentucky Democracy

1. James C. Klotter and Craig Thompson Friend, *A New Kentucky History,* 2nd ed. (Lexington: University Press of Kentucky, 2018), 399; "Chandler Possibly May Join Nunn," *Owensboro Messenger-Inquirer,* November 18, 1967; "Delbert Murphy Victorious in 8th District Senate Race," *Owensboro Messenger-Inquirer,* December 20, 1967.

2. "Pre-legislative Conference Expected to Provide a Few Leadership Clues," *Owensboro Messenger-Inquirer,* December 10, 1967; "Carroll and Morgan Picked for House Leadership Posts," *Paducah Sun-Democrat,* December

18, 1967; "GOP Appears Set; Demos Unsettled," *Owensboro Messenger-Inquirer,* December 18, 1967; "Ford Emerges Victorious in Senate Leadership Race," *Owensboro Messenger-Inquirer,* December 19, 1967; "1968 Legislature: GOP Is Set but Democrats Maneuver," *Louisville Courier-Journal,* December 16, 1967; "Democratic Leaders Try for Coalition," *Louisville Courier-Journal,* December 18, 1967; "Lawmakers Pick Leaders," *Louisville Courier-Journal,* December 19, 1967.

3. "Nunn's Budget Coming Feb. 15–22," *Louisville Courier-Journal,* January 27, 1968; "Budget Doesn't Meet Approval of Some Area Lawmakers," *Paducah Sun-Democrat,* February 14, 1968; "Carroll Indicates Demo Budget Plan May Be Introduced," *Owensboro Messenger-Inquirer,* February 19, 1968; "Tax Bills Offered by Nunn, Morgan Offered to Kentucky House," *Paducah Sun-Democrat,* February 19, 1968; "Ford Wants Tax Exemptions Before Aiding Nunn Program," *Louisville Courier-Journal,* February 21, 1968.

4. "House Kills Exemption, Votes Tax Bill," *Louisville Courier-Journal,* March 7, 1968; "Legislators Explain Nunn's Fiscal Arm Twisting," *Louisville Courier-Journal,* March 7, 1968; William Cox, interviewed by John Klee, May 21, 2008, Kentucky Legislature Oral History Project, Louie B. Nunn Center for Oral History, University of Kentucky, Lexington; William Cox, interviewed by the author, September 14, 2011, West Kentucky Politics Project, Nunn Center; Richard L. Frymire, interviewed by the author, September 3, 2010, West Kentucky Politics Project, Nunn Center; Lawrence E. "Larry" Forgy, interviewed by the author, January 15, 2011, West Kentucky Politics Project, Nunn Center; George G. Humphreys, *The Quest for Excellence: Madisonville Community College, 1968–2009* (Madisonville, KY: Madisonville Community College, 2009), 7–12.

5. "'People's Hearing' Called on Sales Tax Increase: Ford Rips Tactics," *Louisville Courier-Journal,* March 8, 1968; "Merchants See Customers Crossing Lines," *Owensboro Messenger-Inquirer,* March 8, 1968; "5% Sales Tax, $2.47 Billion Budget Passed," *Louisville Courier-Journal,* March 14, 1968; "State Sen. Carl Hadden Votes for Tax Increase; Cites Education Needs," *Franklin Favorite,* March 14, 1968; "Nearly All First District Senators Opposed Nunn's Tax," *Paducah Sun-Democrat,* March 14, 1968.

6. Catherine Fosl and Tracy E. K'Meyer, *Freedom on the Border: An Oral History of the Civil Rights Movement in Kentucky* (Lexington: University Press of Kentucky, 2009), 139–41; "Kentucky Senate Votes Open Housing Measure," *Louisville Courier-Journal,* March 13, 1968; "Kentucky Legislature Enacts Statewide Open Housing Bill," *Louisville Courier-Journal,* March 16, 1968.

7. "Owensboro–Daviess County Need Assurance They Will Get Roads," *Owensboro Messenger-Inquirer,* June 7, 1964; "Mayor's Hard Question Renews Our Demand for Better Roads," *Owensboro Messenger-Inquirer,* January 7, 1965; "Owensboro Group, Ward Discuss Roads," *Owensboro Messenger-Inquirer,*

January 8, 1965; "State's 4th Largest City Should Find Place on Map," *Owensboro Messenger-Inquirer*, May 2, 1965; "New Toll Road Plan Announced at Owensboro," *Louisville Courier-Journal*, August 13, 1966; "Highway Equality Dimming for Owensboro Trade Area," *Owensboro Messenger-Inquirer*, September 29, 1965.

8. "New Highway to Bowling Green Will Be Built, Henry Ward Vows," *Owensboro Messenger-Inquirer*, September 12, 1967; "Ward and Ford Offer Opportunity for Owensboro," *Owensboro Messenger-Inquirer*, November 1, 1967; "Catching-Up, Nunn Vows Highways in Mountains," *Owensboro Messenger-Inquirer*, November 2, 1967.

9. "Owensboro to Parkway Four Laner Reaffirmed," *Owensboro Messenger-Inquirer*, February 18, 1968; "Money Question Again Delays Owensboro Highway Decisions," *Owensboro Messenger-Inquirer*, June 9, 1868; "Ford Wants New Parkways Constructed," *Owensboro Messenger-Inquirer*, June 9, 1968; "Four New Toll Roads May Require $20 Million Yearly from Road Fund," *Owensboro Messenger-Inquirer*, June 18, 1968; "Campaign to Acquire New Highways Urged by Owensboro's WOMI Radio," *Owensboro Messenger-Inquirer*, June 19, 1968; "Four New Toll Roads Approved by 4–0 Vote," *Owensboro Messenger-Inquirer*, July 16, 1968; "Christmas Comes Early to Area," *Owensboro Messenger-Inquirer*, December 16, 1972; "4 Parkways Will Keep Tolls until about 2005," *Louisville Courier-Journal*, February 11, 1997.

10. Kentucky Legislative Research Commission, *Kentucky General Assembly Membership, 1900–2005*, 2 vols. (Frankfort, KY: Legislative Research Commission, 2005), 2:388–91, at www.e-archives.ky.gov/Pubs/LRC/infobull/1B175b.pdf; "This Year Four Kentucky Women Will Be in Legislature," *Louisville Courier-Journal*, January 8, 1950; "Mrs. J. T. Linton Asks for Office She Now Holds," *Russellville News-Democrat*, May 25, 1951; "Gardner, Kirtley, and Hale Win in State Contests," *Owensboro Messenger-Inquirer*, May 24, 1961; "Attorney Kirtley Was Admired for Her Professionalism," *Owensboro Messenger-Inquirer*, August 20, 1995.

11. Mimi O'Malley, *Remarkable Women: More Than Petticoats* (Guilford, CN: Morris Book, 2012), 123–33; "Katherine Peden Hopes to Stay in Limelight," *Louisville Courier-Journal*, August 16, 1967; "Breathitt Cites Industrial Boom during Last Four Years," *Paducah Sun-Democrat*, September 5, 1967; "Fantus Takes 'Fresh Look' at Western Kentucky Areas," *Paducah Sun-Democrat*, December 7, 1967.

12. "Katherine Peden May Run for Senate," *Paducah Sun-Democrat*, November 22, 1967; "Miss Peden Takes Slap at 'Doubting Thomases,'" *Louisville Courier-Journal*, March 17, 1968; "Miss Peden Throws Hat in the Ring," *Paducah Sun-Democrat*, January 16, 1968; "Breathitt Pledges Support to Peden," *Paducah Sun-Democrat*, March 1, 1968; "Ockerman Possible Senate Candidate," *Paducah Sun-Democrat*, March 5, 1968; "Breathitt Unlikely Candidate," *Paducah*

Sun-Democrat, March 6, 1968; "Miss Peden Is in Race to Stay," *Paducah Sun-Democrat,* March 7, 1968; "Carroll Enters Race for U. S. Senate," *Paducah Sun-Democrat,* March 31, 1968; "Peden Rally Attracts 300 Women," *Paducah Sun-Democrat,* May 17, 1968; "Politics Perk Up as Primary Nears," *Paducah Sun-Democrat,* May 19, 1967; "Peden, Cook Are Nominees," *Paducah Sun-Democrat,* May 29, 1967; "Durbin Loses by 16,921," *Paducah Sun-Democrat,* May 29, 1968; "Peden to Face Cook in Fall," *Louisville Courier-Journal,* May 29, 1968; "November Promises a Fascinating Race," *Paducah Sun-Democrat,* May 30, 1968.

13. "'Nunn' Sales Tax Boils Up as Major Issue at Fancy Farm," *Paducah Sun-Democrat,* August 4, 1968; "The Senatorial Race," *Paducah Sun-Democrat,* September 29, 1968; "Miss Peden Says Foe Failed in Enforcing Law and Order," *Paducah Sun-Democrat,* October 1, 1968.

14. "Humphrey Turns Back Wallace Bid in First," *Paducah Sun-Democrat,* November 6, 1968; "Nixon Gets State," *Hopkinsville New Era,* November 6, 1968; "Presidential Vote in Kentucky," *Louisville Courier-Journal,* November 7, 1968; "Vote in Senate Race," *Louisville Courier-Journal,* November 7, 1968; "Peden Concedes, Eyeing 1972," *Hopkinsville New Era,* November 7, 1968; "J. R. Miller Suddenly Emerges as Behind-the-Scenes Power," *Louisville Courier-Journal,* October 3, 1968; Katherine Graham Peden, interviewed by Joe B. Frantz, November 13, 1970, Lyndon Baines Johnson Presidential Library, Austin, TX.

15. "Miller Elected Party Chair," *Owensboro Messenger-Inquirer,* June 2, 1968; "Most Young Democrats Have Ideas but Support Party," *Owensboro Messenger-Inquirer,* August 14, 1968; "Don Mills Raps Nunn in Calloway," *Paducah Sun-Democrat,* November 19, 1969.

16. "2 Who Backed Nunn on Tax Are Defeated," *Louisville Courier-Journal,* May 28, 1969; "Area Voters to Decide Three Races for the Legislature," *Owensboro Messenger-Inquirer,* November 2, 1969; "Democrats Hold Majority in Legislature," *Louisville Courier-Journal,* November 5, 1969; "Miss Foust Wins Race for Auditor," *Paducah Sun-Democrat,* November 5, 1969; "Area Democrats Score House Sweep," *Paducah Sun-Democrat,* November 5, 1969; "White Defeats Ellis in Race for State Senate," *Bowling Green Park City Daily News,* November 5, 1969; "Democrats Show Mettle in Elections," *Owensboro Messenger-Inquirer,* November 6, 1969; "Democrats Seem Happier over Vote Than Governor," *Paducah Sun-Democrat,* November 7, 1969.

17. "Area Democrats Score House Sweep", *Paducah Sun-Democrat,* November 5, 1969; "Nunn's Budget: An $18 Million Tax Cut?," *Louisville Courier-Journal,* January 8, 1970; "Teachers Assail Nunn for Omitting Pay Hike," *Louisville Courier-Journal,* January 11, 1970; "KEA Strategy under Discussion," *Paducah Sun-Democrat,* January 12, 1971; "Kentucky Public Teachers and Public Opinion," *Paducah Sun-Democrat,* January 14, 1971; "State Democrats Earmark Items for Surplus Funds," *Louisville Courier-Journal,* January 15,

1970; "Teachers Determine Standing of Fight," *Paducah Sun-Democrat*, January 30, 1971; "Democrats Version of Budget Passes Senate, Goes to Nunn," *Louisville Courier-Journal*, February 12, 1970; "Budget to Become Law without Nunn's Blessing," *Louisville Courier-Journal*, February 24, 1970.

18. "Kentucky's Teachers Issue Stiff Salary Hike Demands," *Paducah Sun-Democrat*, February 3, 1970; "Teachers Vote to Start Strike Monday," *Louisville Courier-Journal*, February 19, 1970; "The Battle Lines—KEA vs. Legislators," *Louisville Courier-Journal*, February 23, 1970; "Strike Shuts 118 School Districts," *Louisville Courier-Journal*, February 24, 1970; "Prolonged Strike Expected in State," *Paducah Sun-Democrat*, February 24, 1970; "Other School Systems Watch Situation Here," *Paducah Sun-Democrat*, February 24, 1970; "Teacher Groups Vote Return to School," *Paducah Sun-Democrat*, February 26, 1970; "Teachers' Strike Handed a Legal Blow," *Louisville Courier-Journal*, February 26, 1970; "Teacher Strike Nearly Over?," *Louisville Courier-Journal*, February 28, 1970; "Work Stoppage Ends in All W. Kentucky School Systems," *Paducah Sun-Democrat*, March 3, 1970; "KEA Delegates Vote to End Teacher Strike," *Louisville Courier-Journal*, March 3, 1970; "'New Breed' of Teachers Fails to Win Top Legislative Goals," *Louisville Courier-Journal*, March 22, 1970.

19. "Man Who Isn't There Is Hot Frankfort Topic," *Louisville Courier-Journal*, February 9, 1970; "State Democratic Chairman Lashes Back at Sen. Hubbard," *Paducah Sun-Democrat*, March 11, 1970; "Ford Being Edged out of Governor Picture," *Paducah Sun-Democrat*, March 23, 1970; "Ford Makes It Official: He'll Run for Governor," *Owensboro Messenger-Inquirer*, May 10, 1970; "The 1971 Gubernatorial Primary," in *Bert Combs the Politician: An Oral History*, ed. George W. Robinson (Lexington: University Press of Kentucky, 1991), 188–94.

20. "Former Gov. Combs, Carroll Will Team Up in '71 Primary," *Paducah Sun-Democrat*, April 30, 1970; "Carroll Makes It Clear He's on Combs' Team," *Louisville Courier-Journal*, April 30, 1970; "This May Be a Crucial Week in Ford's Political Career," *Paducah Sun-Democrat*, May 4, 1970; "KEA's Legislative Program Cost Put at $75.9 Million," *Paducah Sun-Democrat*, May 8, 1971; "Ford Roundly Defeats Combs in Upset," *Owensboro Messenger-Inquirer*, May 26, 1971; "Ford Wins District by 18,786; Carroll's Margin Is 6,213," *Paducah Sun-Democrat*, May 26, 1971; "It's Ford vs. Emberton for Governor Next Fall," *Louisville Courier-Journal*, May 26, 1971; "For Ford, the Clue to Victory Was in the 'Urban Triangle,'" *Louisville Courier-Journal*, May 26, 1971; "Wendell Ford: Hard Work Makes a Gamble Pay Off," *Louisville Courier-Journal*, May 27, 1971; "Managers Showed Skill in Races—All Won Some," *Russellville News-Democrat*, May 27, 1971; Julian Carroll, interviewed by author, May 17, 2011, West Kentucky Politics Project, Nunn Center; Robinson, *Bert Combs*, 187–200.

21. "Ford Wins It!," *Owensboro Messenger-Inquirer,* November 3, 1971; "Ford and Carroll Carry 21 Counties in First District," *Paducah Sun-Democrat,* November 3, 1971; "Chandler Acknowledges He's Through with Politics," *Owensboro Messenger-Inquirer,* November 4, 1967; Kentucky State Board of Elections, election returns data for 1971, CD requested by the author, October 5, 2011.

22. Wendell H. Ford, "Inaugural Address" and "State of the Commonwealth Address, January 4, 1972," in *The Public Papers of Governor Wendell H. Ford, 1971–74,* ed. W. Landis Jones (Lexington: University Press of Kentucky, 1978), 7–10, 19 (including quote from Jones), 91; Landis Jones, "Wendell Hampton Ford," in *Kentucky's Governors,* updated ed., ed. Lowell Harrison (Lexington: University Press of Kentucky, 2004), 212; "Democratic Patronage Jobs to Be Handled Differently," *Louisville Courier-Journal,* December 10, 1971; "Patronage Limited to 5,000," *Paducah Sun-Democrat,* December 21, 1971; "An Experiment Well Worth Trying," *Paducah Sun-Democrat,* December 27, 1971.

23. "Race for Speaker of Kentucky House Stirs Pre-legislative Meeting Opening," *Paducah Sun-Democrat,* December 13, 1971; "Blume Elected Speaker by House Democrats," *Louisville Courier-Journal,* December 14, 1971; "The Ford Budget: Target of Brickbats and Bouquets," *Louisville Courier-Journal,* February 4, 1972; "One Phone Call Spelled Death for Mobile Home Bills," *Louisville Courier-Journal,* March 13, 1972; "Mobile-Home Bills Killed," *Louisville Courier-Journal,* March 9, 1972; "Industrial Loan Bill: Senate Approves Rate Hike," *Louisville Courier-Journal,* March 10, 1972; "Senate Passes Controversial Industrial Loan Bill, 19–14," *Paducah Sun-Democrat,* March 10, 1972; "Political Aspirations Began Surfacing during the Session," *Louisville Courier-Journal,* March 19, 1972.

24. Jones, "Wendell Hampton Ford," in *Kentucky's Governors,* ed. Harrison, 211–12; "Muhlenberg County Newspaper Slams Governor's Coal Severance Attack," *Owensboro Messenger-Inquirer,* March 11, 1972; "Workers' Compensation Bill Goes to Governor Ford," *Owensboro Messenger-Inquirer,* March 17, 1972; Billy Ray Paxton, interviewed by the author, October 20, 2010, Kentucky Legislature Oral History Project, Nunn Center; "Election Reform Bill Given New Life," *Louisville Courier-Journal,* March 16, 1972; "An Assembly of Contrasts," *Louisville Courier-Journal,* March 19, 1972; "Coal: Severance Tax Is Only Setback," *Louisville Courier-Journal,* March 19, 1972.

25. "Headache Strikes Nunn, Ending Huddleston Debate," *Louisville Courier-Journal,* August 6, 1972; "Huddleston Defeats Nunn for Senate," *Louisville Courier-Journal,* November 8, 1972; "Kentucky Voting by County," *Louisville Courier-Journal,* November 8, 1972; "Ticket-Splitting Stems a Strong Tide in Kentucky Races," *Louisville Courier-Journal,* November 18, 1972; "First

District Democrat 'Gibraltar' Goes for Nixon," *Paducah Sun-Democrat,* November 8, 1972; "Gibraltar Lead for Smith Shrinks to 6,078," *Paducah Evening Sun,* November 7, 1928; "Local Voters Split Tickets to Give Huddleston Aid," *Owensboro Messenger-Inquirer,* November 8, 1972.

26. Jones, "Wendell Hampton Ford," in *Kentucky's Governors,* ed. Harrison, 214; "J. R. Miller to Step Down as Party Chief," *Louisville Courier-Journal,* August 17, 1973; "Miller Resigns as State Dem. Chairman," *Owensboro Messenger-Inquirer,* October 23, 1973.

27. "The General Assembly: It Could Be Productive," *Louisville Courier-Journal,* January 13, 1974; "The Governor's Budget," *Louisville Courier-Journal,* January 23, 1974; "House Votes 1974–76 Budget Bill," *Louisville Courier-Journal,* March 6, 1974; "House Approves Gov. Ford's Recommended Budget," *Madisonville Messenger,* March 6, 1974; "Coal Counties Will Get Excess Severance Revenue," *Madisonville Messenger,* March 15, 1974; "Hopkins County Expected to Receive up to $500,000," *Madisonville Messenger,* July 26, 1974; "42 Counties Await Coal Severance-Tax Refunds," *Owensboro Messenger-Inquirer,* July 27, 1974; "County Will Receive $401,609 from Coal," *Madisonville Messenger,* August 2, 1974; Wendell H. Ford, "Industrial Coal Conference, April 25, 1974," and "Industry Appreciation Annual Luncheon, May 8, 1974," in *Public Papers of Governor Wendell H. Ford,* 432–35.

28. "Ford Suggests He Won't Be Candidate in '74," *Louisville Courier-Journal,* December 4, 1972; "Waves of Speculation in Kentucky Politics," *Louisville Courier-Journal,* October 21, 1973; "A Lasting Quarrel." *Louisville Courier-Journal,* November 4, 1973; Carroll, interviewed by the author, May 17, 2011; "Democrats Scent Victory with Ford and Carroll," *Paducah Sun-Democrat,* February 27, 1974; "What Sort of Deals Are Ford, Carroll Trying to Make?," *Russellville News-Democrat,* March 14, 1974; "Ford–Cook Race Takes Shape," *Louisville Courier-Journal,* March 22, 1974.

29. "Nixon Administration to Be an Issue in Senate Campaign," *Owensboro Messenger-Inquirer,* March 24, 1974; "State Sen. Carroll Hubbard Unseats Rep. Stubblefield," *Paducah Sun-Democrat,* May 29, 1974; Carroll Hubbard, interviewed by the author, November 11, 2011, Kentucky Legislature Oral History Project, Nunn Center; "Fancy Farm Picnic," *Paducah Sun-Democrat,* August 4, 1974; "Ford, Cook Open Senate Campaign with Verbal Blasts," *Paducah Sun-Democrat,* August 4, 1974; "Final Ford Campaign Stop Here Draws 1,800 Persons," *Paducah Sun-Democrat,* November 1, 1974; "Cook–Ford Senate Battle Tops Kentucky Scene," *Paducah Sun-Democrat,* November 3, 1974; "Gov. Ford's Margin Is 2–1 in District," *Paducah Sun-Democrat,* November 6, 1974; "Analysis: Party Unity, Popularity Help Ford," *Louisville Courier-Journal,* November 6, 1974; "Carroll Plans as He Nears Political Goal," *Louisville Courier-Journal,* November 7, 1974.

30. "'Safe Cigarettes' Could Save Kentucky's Tobacco Industry," *Dawson Springs Progress,* October 25, 1973; "UK Tobacco Money Could Be Cut," *Louisville Courier-Journal,* February 21, 1979; "Koop Attacks Tobacco on Its Home Turf," *Lexington Herald-Leader,* March 6, 1990.

31. "Unmatched: Miller, Froelich Differ on Anti-smoking Campaign," *Owensboro Messenger-Inquirer,* November 11, 1981; William Snell, "Tobacco Census for KY 2017," email to the author, July 29, 2020.

32. "'Black' Tobacco Reaches a New Golden Age," *Paducah Sun-Democrat,* January 22, 1969; "Smokeless Tobacco," *Paducah Sun,* July 2, 1986; "Dark Tobacco Groups Pool Efforts to Devise Long-Range Quota Strategy," *Paducah Sun,* March 13, 1987; "Health-Care Tax on Tobacco Will Fail, Growers Say," *Paducah Sun,* December 13, 1993; "Tobacco Growers Like GOP," *Paducah Sun,* November 18, 1994.

33. Ann K. Ferrell, *Burley: Kentucky Tobacco in a New Century* (Lexington: University Press of Kentucky, 2013), 9–11; Karl Raitz, "The Agricultural Landscape," in *Atlas of Kentucky,* ed. Richard Ulack, Karl Raitz, and Guyla Pauer (Lexington University Press of Kentucky, 1998), 155–74; "Hooked on Tobacco, Farm Full Options," *Lexington Herald-Leader,* September 16, 1994; "Scratching Out a Living: The Uncertainties of Chicken Farming," *Louisville Courier-Journal,* September 17–19, 1995; "West Kentuckians Fear State Can't Control Hog Farming," *Louisville Courier-Journal,* June 5, 1997; "Neighbors Remain Cross over Hog Farms," *Paducah Sun,* November 6, 2013.

34. "Better Times Predicted for Coal—but Not Soon," *Owensboro Messenger-Inquirer,* February 12, 1980.

35. "TVA Faces Decision on Pollution Suit," *Owensboro Messenger-Inquirer,* December 14, 1978; "Many Support Coming of New Plant," *Owensboro Messenger-Inquirer,* November 2, 1982.

36. Wendell H. Ford, "Energy Message, January 16, 1974," "Environmental Protection Agency Meeting, May 9, 1973," and "Madisonville State Government Day, July 30, 1974," in *Public Papers of Governor Wendell H. Ford,* 57–64, 334–35, 530–31; "Three Top Leaders Agree: America Turning to Coal for Energy Needs," *Russellville News-Democrat,* May 16, 1974; "Hopes High for Region's Coal," *Owensboro Messenger-Inquirer,* November 4, 1979; "Newman Construction to Begin This Summer," *Owensboro Messenger-Inquirer,* January 3, 1980; "Newman Aid Survives Test," *Owensboro Messenger-Inquirer,* October 28, 1981; "Pork Barrel Politics?," *Owensboro Messenger-Inquirer,* February 14, 1982; "ICRC Closing Office," *Owensboro Messenger-Inquirer,* June 22, 1984.

37. "'70s Boom Goes Bust in '80s," *Owensboro Messenger-Inquirer,* November 26, 1989; "District 23 Solid, Patterson Says," *Owensboro Messenger-Inquirer,* November 26, 1989; "Holland Picked District 23 President," *Madisonville Messenger,* December 13, 1989; "UMW Optimistic about Pyro Drive," *Madisonville*

Messenger, June 20, 1990; "Pyro Rejects Union," *Madisonville Messenger*, December 13, 1990; "Peabody Will Soon Have Only 5 Mines in State," *Madisonville Messenger*, June 12, 1991; "Paradise Fossil Plant Full Steam Ahead; New Construction to Begin 2013," *Owensboro Messenger-Inquirer*, September 6, 2011.

38. "Carroll Begins Planning as He Nears His Goal," *Louisville Courier-Journal*, November 7, 1974; "Julian Combs Takes Oath as 50th Governor," *Paducah Sun-Democrat*, December 29, 1974; "Carroll Inherits Many Problems," *Owensboro Messenger-Inquirer*, January 1, 1975; "Coal-Lit Union Fires Dying Out," *Paducah Sun*, September 6, 2015.

39. "Ford to Air State Park Plan," *Owensboro Messenger-Inquirer*, December 24, 1964; "Governor Ford Delivers 'Gifts' to Owensboro," *Owensboro Messenger-Inquirer*, December 25, 1964.

40. "Carroll Praises Brown," *Paducah Sun-Democrat*, December 16, 1974; "It's Carroll, Stovall for Democrats; Gable, Palmer-Ball for Republicans," *Louisville Courier-Journal*, May 28, 1975; "Carroll Wins Demo Nomination in Landslide," *Paducah Sun-Democrat*, May 28, 1975; "Three Political Newcomers Record Primary Victories," *Paducah Sun-Democrat*, May 28, 1975; "Carroll Wins in Democratic Sweep," *Louisville Courier-Journal*, November 5, 1975; "Thelma Stovall Wins Historic Victory," *Louisville Courier-Journal*, November 6, 1975.

41. "GOP Opponent Raps Carroll in Stumping at Fancy Farm," *Paducah Sun-Democrat*, August 3, 1975; "Gable Not Certain of Nixon Fund Use," *Owensboro Messenger-Inquirer*, October 20, 1975; "Carroll Ad May Be Controversial," *Owensboro Messenger-Inquirer*, October 20, 1975; "Rally Audience of 2,000 Hears Carroll at Heath," *Paducah Sun-Democrat*, November 2, 1975; "Carroll Records Landslide in District Voting Returns," *Paducah Sun-Democrat*, November 5, 1975.

42. Malcolm E. Jewell and Penny M. Miller, *The Kentucky Legislature: The Decades of Change* (Lexington: University Press of Kentucky, 1988), 100–104; "Carroll Gets 'Heat' on Speaker Issue," *Louisville Courier-Journal*, November 28, 1975; "Legislative Leaders to Be Carroll's Team," *Owensboro Messenger-Inquirer*, December 1, 1975; "Partnership Call Is Made by Governor," *Paducah Sun-Democrat*, December 2, 1975; "Garrett, Clapp Get Key Legislative Posts," *Paducah Sun-Democrat*, December 1, 1975; "The Same Old Story at Kentucky Dam Village," *Lexington Herald*, December 4, 1975; "Legislative Freedom: Who Wants It?," *Louisville Courier-Journal*, January 18, 1976; "The Governor's Legislative Hands," *Louisville Courier-Journal*, March 7, 1976.

43. "Our 'Independent' Legislature," *Louisville Courier-Journal*, December 3, 1975; "Murphy Agrees Critics of Panel 'Probably' Right," *Owensboro Messenger-Inquirer*, January 14, 1976; "The Record . . . The Governor Used Election 'Mandate,'" *Louisville Courier-Journal*, March 22, 1976; "The Gover-

nor's Great Legislative Session—and Why," *Louisville Courier-Journal,* March 21, 1976; "Rep. Clarke Has Final Kick in Ribs," *Owensboro Messenger-Inquirer,* March 23, 1976.

44. "Spirit of '76: State Lawmakers Ready to Tackle Wide Variety of Issues," *Madisonville Messenger,* January 3, 1976; "Deserve Coal Tax Funds," *Madisonville Messenger,* January 6, 1976; "Carroll Recommends End to Coal Tax Rebate . . . ," *Owensboro Messenger-Inquirer,* January 29, 1976; "Legislators Say All Not Lost in Tax Move," *Owensboro Messenger-Inquirer,* January 30, 1976; "Lawmaker Sits, Waits, Mulls Coal Tax Outcome," *Owensboro Messenger-Inquirer,* February 14, 1976; "Counties Convinced of Fund Sharing," *Owensboro Messenger-Inquirer,* February 8, 1976; "Coal County Representative Likes Tax Plan," *Owensboro Messenger-Inquirer,* February 29, 1976; "Coal Counties Prepare for New Rebate Rules," *Owensboro Messenger-Inquirer,* March 4, 1976; "But Carroll Says: Secret of Success in Golden Rule," *Owensboro Messenger-Inquirer,* March 21, 1976.

45. "Tourists Can Avoid Speed Traps in Kentucky," *Paducah Sun-Democrat,* December 6, 1957; "Important to Kentucky," *Paducah Sun-Democrat,* December 7, 1959; "Combs Promises to Correct Trap Abuse as Charged by AAA," *Owensboro Messenger-Inquirer,* June 2, 1962; "Hanson Rejects Speed-Trap Tag," *Louisville Courier-Journal,* June 21, 1962.

46. Pam Miller, *Kentucky Politics and Government: Do We Stand United?* (Lincoln: University of Nebraska Press, 1994), 150–57; Kurt X. Metzmeier, *United at Last: The Judicial Article and the Struggle to Reform Kentucky's Courts* (Frankfort: Kentucky Court of Justice, 2006); John S. Palmore, *An Opinionated Career: Memoirs of a Kentucky Judge* (Georgetown: Kentucky River Press, 2003), 51.

47. "Constitutional Amendment Proposed That Reforms Kentucky Courts," *Louisville Courier-Journal,* February 1, 1974; "In Committee: ERA Scrap Stalls Court Reform Amendment Bill," *Louisville Courier-Journal,* March 13, 1974; "House Panel Rescinds Judicial Reform Move," *Bowling Green Park City Daily News,* March 12, 1974.

48. "Carroll, Gable Agree on Court Reform," *Paducah Sun-Democrat,* October 2, 1975; "Local Judge Sees Problems," *Russellville News-Democrat,* October 6, 1975; "Judicial Change—Is It Needed or Not?," *Owensboro Messenger-Inquirer,* October 19, 1975; "Judicial Reform Here at Home," *Franklin Favorite,* October 23, 1975; "Judge Miller Talks on Judicial Reform," *Paducah Sun-Democrat,* October 24, 1975; "Court Changes: Judicial Reform or 'Deform,'" *Owensboro Messenger-Inquirer,* October 26, 1975.

49. "Gant Calls for Judicial Reforms to Eliminate 'Cash Register' Justice," *Owensboro Messenger-Inquirer,* May 22, 1974; "Speedier Justice," *Bowling Green Park City Daily News,* October 23, 1975; "Amendment Subject of Meet Here,"

Paducah Sun-Democrat, October 28, 1975; "Bar Group Endorses Amendment," *Paducah Sun-Democrat,* November 3, 1975.

50. "Poll Shows," *Madisonville Messenger,* October 27, 1975; "2 Constitutional Amendments Apparently Win Approval," *Louisville Courier-Journal,* November 5, 1975.

51. "Equal Rights Amendment for Women Draws Attack," *Bowling Green Park City Daily News,* June 12, 1972; "House Votes 56–31 to Ratify Equal Rights Act," *Louisville Courier-Journal,* June 13, 1972; "Kentucky Becomes the 19th to Ratify Equal-Rights-for-Women Amendment," *Louisville Courier-Journal,* June 16, 1974.

52. Nancy E. Baker, "Integrating Women into Modern Kentucky History: The Equal Rights Amendment (1972–78) as a Case Study," *Register of the Kentucky Historical Society* 113, nos. 2–3 (Spring–Summer 2015): 477–507, esp. 486–89; Nancy E. Baker, interviewed by Elizabeth Van Allen, April 16, 2011, Kentucky Historical Society, Frankfort.

53. Barbara Pagan, June Barnett, and Wanda Bradbury, interviewed by the author, April 11, 2012, West Kentucky Politics Project, Nunn Center; "Hundreds Hear ERA Arguments," *Madisonville Messenger,* July 8, 1975; "Latest Verbal Battle over ERA Ends Inconclusively," *Paducah Sun-Democrat,* July 8, 1975; Baker, "Integrating Women into Modern Kentucky History," 487.

54. "ERA Issue Shifts to State Senate," *Paducah Sun-Democrat,* February 19, 1976; "Anti-ERA Move Revitalized," *Paducah Sun-Democrat,* March 16, 1976; "ERA Foes Will Try New Tactics," *Louisville Courier-Journal,* March 16, 1976; "Anti-ERA Effort Dies," *Owensboro Messenger-Inquirer,* March 20, 1976; "ERA Rescission Measure Doesn't Make It," *Paducah Sun-Democrat,* March 20, 1976.

55. "Explicit Papers on Desks Cause Uproar in House," *Paducah Sun-Democrat,* February 10, 1978; "Filth from Women's Meet, Stop-ERA Says," *Paducah Sun-Democrat,* February 12, 1978; "Report: Porno Work Put Out by Anti-ERA," *Paducah Sun-Democrat,* March 9, 1978; "House Members Criticize Mayfield Women's Remarks," *Paducah Sun-Democrat,* March 15, 1978; Baker, "Integrating Women," 495–97; "Anti-ERA Vote Result of Women Doing House-Work and Senate-Work," *Louisville Courier-Journal,* March 8, 1978.

56. "State Senate Votes to Rescind ERA Approval," *Louisville Courier-Journal,* March 14, 1978; "State Senate Votes to Cancel ERA Approval," *Louisville Courier-Journal,* March 14, 1978; "ERA Rescission Okayed," *Owensboro Messenger-Inquirer,* March 17, 1978; Pagan, Barnett, and Bradberry, interviewed by the author, April 11, 2012.

57. Jewell and Miller, *The Kentucky Legislature,* 185; Miller, *Kentucky Politics and Government,* 101; Mary Kay Bonsteel Tachau and Bruce L. McClure, "John Y Brown Jr.," in *Kentucky's Governors,* ed. Harrison, 225.

58. "Kenton Planning to Offer Constitutional Amendment," *Lexington Herald,* January 9, 1978; "Constitutional Amendment No. 2 Deserves Your Support on Nov. 6," *Owensboro Messenger-Inquirer,* October 25, 1979; "County, City Races and Tax Issues in Western Kentucky," *Paducah Sun,* November 7, 1979; Kentucky State Board of Elections, "Kentucky Election Results, 1970–1979," https://elect.ky.gov/results/Pages//default/.aspx, "Hospitality's Sweet . . . as Pre-session Conference Goes, so Goes Lobbyists," *Louisville Courier-Journal,* November 23, 1981; "Prelegislative Conference Starts Saturday," *Owensboro Messenger-Inquirer,* November 27, 1981. The constitutional amendment moving the election of legislative leaders from these presession conferences passed in 1979, but the last presession conference was held in 1981. In 1983, the organization sessions started.

59. "Independence Must Be Earned, Legislators Told," *Louisville Courier-Journal,* December 4, 1977; "Routine Opening of Assembly Includes Votes for Leadership and 'Old Home Week' Mood," *Louisville Courier-Journal,* January 4, 1978; "House Votes to Seek Organizing Session between Sessions," *Louisville Courier-Journal,* March 8, 1978; "Carroll Raps Lawmakers for Lack of Interest in Key Legislative Issues," *Paducah Sun-Democrat,* December 4, 1978.

60. "Independent Senators Jockey for Control," *Louisville Courier-Journal,* December 10, 1978; "House Democrats Vote to Control Own Program," *Owensboro Messenger-Inquirer,* January 10, 1979; "Lawmakers Say Special Session Should Be Ended," *Paducah Sun-Democrat,* January 14, 1979; "State Legislature Should Come Home," *Paducah Sun-Democrat,* January 16, 1979; "Carroll, Stovall Evaluate Special Session," *Louisville Courier-Journal,* February 10, 1979; "Laying Down the Law: In a Session with Few Winners, at Least Legislators Took Command," *Louisville Courier-Journal,* February 20, 1979; Miller, *Kentucky Politics and Government,* 381–82; Jewell and Miller, *The Kentucky Legislature,* 231; Stuart Seely Sprague and Al Cross, "Julian Morton Carroll," in *Kentucky's Governors,* ed. Harrison, 219–20.

61. "Bell, Hunt Reportedly Clashed Often on Strip-Mining Policy," *Louisville Courier-Journal,* March 5, 1978; "Transcript Concerning Carroll Is Made Public," *Louisville Courier-Journal,* July 21, 1982; "Atkins, Seeing Defeat, Supports Brown," *Paducah Sun,* May 17, 1979; "McBrayer Wins Most Counties, but Brown Won Best," *Paducah Sun,* May 30, 1979; "Democratic Officials Say McBrayer Had a Really Big Problem: Julian," *Louisville Courier-Journal,* May 30, 1979; "Carroll Sees Problem If Hubbard Wins," *Paducah Sun,* May 1, 1979.

62. "Name Helps Barkley Effort," *Paducah Sun,* May 30, 1979; "What's in a Name? Alben Barkley Is Trustee of a Political Legacy," *Louisville Courier-Journal,* June 4, 1979; "Buses Roll for Second Trip," *Madisonville Messenger,* February 21, 1979; "Cox May Sue Opponent," *Madisonville Messenger,* May 3, 1979; "Cox Opens Records; Will Sue Vernon," *Madisonville Messenger,* May 14, 1979; Cox, interviewed by author, September 14, 2011; "Mrs. Collins

Credits Win to Big Turnout, Large Field," *Louisville Courier-Journal,* May 31, 1979; Kentucky State Board of Elections, "Primary and General Election Results, 1979," at https://elect.ky.gov/results/1973–1979.

63. "Stretch-Run Brown Blitz Pays Off," *Paducah Sun,* May 30, 1979; "Brown Played the Campaign with All the Skill of a Virtuoso," *Louisville Courier-Journal,* November 7, 1979; "Purchase Remains Democratic Strong in Brown Landslide," *Paducah Sun,* November 7, 1979; "Democrats Sweep into Top State Offices on Brown's Coattails," *Louisville Courier-Journal,* November 7, 1979; "'Little People' Credited," *Madisonville Messenger,* November 7, 1979; Al Smith, *Wordsmith: My Life in Journalism* (Louisville, KY: Clark Legacies, 2011), 395.

64. William E. Leuchtenburg, *The American President: From Teddy Roosevelt to Bill Clinton,* (New York: Oxford University Press, 2015), 573; "Dale Sights: Carter Man in Kentucky," *Louisville Courier-Journal,* May 10, 1976; "Carter's Loss Turns Dale Sights Eyes Back on His Future," *Louisville Courier-Journal,* November 13, 1980; "The Vote: Big Turnout, Carter Win Makes Logan an Exception," *Russellville News-Democrat,* November 6, 1980; "West Kentucky Loss Can Be Seen as a Victory," *Paducah Sun,* November 5, 1980; "Carter Squeaks by in Owensboro Region," *Owensboro Messenger-Inquirer,* November 5, 1980; "The Region," *Bowling Green Park City Daily News,* November 5, 1980; "Reagan Wins Kentucky; Ford Easily Re-elected," *Louisville Courier-Journal,* November 5, 1980; Kentucky State Board of Elections, "Kentucky Election Results, 1980–1989," at https://elect.ky.gov/results/1980–1989.

65. "Weather Mild, Politics Stormy," *Paducah Sun,* August 5, 1984; "Kentucky Sweep Seen as a Republican Revival," *Bowling Green Park City Daily News,* November 7, 1984; "Reagan Sweeps Kentucky by Nearly 300,000 Votes," *Louisville Courier-Journal,* November 7, 1984; "McConnell Sees Voter Maturity," *Owensboro Messenger-Inquirer,* November 16, 1984; Forgy, interviewed by the author, January 15, 2011; Kentucky State Board of Elections, "Kentucky Election Results, 1980–1989."

66. "McConnell Anticipates Moral Majority Support," *Owensboro Messenger-Inquirer,* August 21, 1984; "McConnell Claims Win in Tight Race," *Louisville Courier-Journal,* November 5, 1984; "McConnell Credits Reagan for Upset," *Owensboro Messenger-Inquirer,* November 8, 1984.

67. "Grady Stumbo's Western Strength Not Enough," *Paducah Sun,* May 25, 1983; "Jot 'Collins' in History Book," *Paducah Sun,* November 9, 1983; "District Support Came Just in Time," *Paducah Sun-Democrat,* May 27, 1987; "Julian M. Carroll: Once State's Most Powerful Governor, the Landslide Turned around This Time," *Paducah Sun,* May 27, 1987; "Burnette Completes Trip from Farm to Frankfort," *Paducah Sun,* November 4, 1987.

68. "Robertson Pledges Allegiance to Bush," *Owensboro Messenger-Inquirer,* October 12, 1988; "A Little Town Counts Big," *Paducah Sun,* August

7, 1988, "Bentsen Promises Crowd Another Upset," *Owensboro Messenger-Inquirer,* November 2, 1988; "Local Republicans Schooled for Today's Visit by Quayle," *Owensboro Messenger-Inquirer,* November 2, 1988; "Purchase Democrats Too Few to Win Conservative 'Gibraltar,'" *Paducah Sun,* November 9, 1988; "Kentucky Paves Way for Republicans," *Owensboro Messenger-Inquirer,* November 9, 1988; Kentucky State Board of Elections, "Kentucky Election Results, 1980–1989."

69. "GOP Nominee Woos Local Democrats," *Owensboro Messenger-Inquirer,* November 3, 1998; "No Voter Backlash for McConnell," *Paducah Sun-Democrat,* November 7, 1990; Kentucky State Board of Elections, "1990–1999 Primary and General Election Results," at https://elect.ky.gov/results/1990–1999.

70. Legislative Research Commission, *Kentucky General Assembly Members, 1900–2005,* vol. 2.

71. Louisville Courier-Journal, *Our Towns: Kentucky's Communities after 200 Years* (Louisville, KY: Courier-Journal Press, 1993); *Clark's Kentucky Almanac and Book of Facts, 2006* (Lexington, KY: Clark Group, 2006), 309–15 for population figures; "Fulton," *Louisville Courier-Journal,* January 11, 1993; "Hickman," *Louisville Courier-Journal,* March 30, 1992; "Morganfield," *Louisville Courier-Journal,* August 19, 1991; "Hopkinsville," *Louisville Courier-Journal,* May 11, 1992; Jack Glazier, *Been Coming through Some Hard Times: Race, History, and Memory in Western Kentucky* (Knoxville: University of Tennessee Press, 2012), 166–70.

72. "Wickliffe," *Louisville Courier-Journal,* April 19, 1993; "Verso Could Cost Ballard County $301 Million," *Paducah Sun,* April 24, 2016; "Phoenix Paper Celebrates Restart of Wickliffe Mill," *Paducah Sun,* June 1, 2019.

73. "Fulton," *Louisville Courier-Journal, January* 11, 1993; "Future of Fulton Remains to Be Seen," *Paducah Sun,* February 8, 2015.

74. "Merit Clothing Announces Plans to Close Operations," *Paducah Sun,* June 20, 1980; "Mayfield Clothing Manufacturer Says Expansion Will Add Many Jobs," *Owensboro Messenger-Inquirer,* June 24, 1985; "Mayfield Cringes at Plant's Prospects," *Paducah Sun,* December 11, 1993; "Job Losses Cut Deep," *Louisville Courier-Journal,* January 3, 2005; "Plant Shutdown Dries Up Oasis," *Owensboro Messenger-Inquirer,* January 4, 2005; "Small-Town Shop Blames Paducah Mall for Closing Business," *Owensboro Messenger-Inquirer,* January 25, 1987; "Continental to Buy Part of Tire Plant," *Paducah Sun,* July 15, 2008.

75. "Calvert City," *Louisville Courier-Journal,* October 12, 1992; "Long River Trip Ends, Begins at Dedication," *Paducah Sun,* May 27, 1985, "Hawesville," *Louisville Courier-Journal,* January 25, 1993; "Morgantown," *Louisville Courier-Journal,* June 24, 1991; "City Reels from Cuts," *Bowling Green Park City Daily News,* December 2, 2001.

76. "Owensboro," *Louisville Courier-Journal,* November 2, 1992; "GE in Owensboro Closes; 6,600 Once Worked There," *Owensboro Messenger-Inquirer,* October 30, 2010.

77. "Song, Art Part of New Pride Program," *Owensboro Messenger-Inquirer,* November 20, 1987; "A River Town Winds Its Way through History," *Owensboro Messenger-Inquirer,* May 8, 1988; "Exciting, Hectic Times for Downtown Owensboro, Inc.," *Owensboro Messenger-Inquirer,* May 8, 1988; "Owensboro Is Now Area's Community 'on the Move," *Owensboro Messenger-Inquirer,* July 9, 1989; "Fifty Years of WaxWorks," *Owensboro Messenger-Inquirer,* October 8, 1999; "The Peirce Report," *Owensboro Messenger-Inquirer,* September 29, 30, October 1, 2, 1991; "Owensboro's Campbell Club," *Owensboro Messenger-Inquirer,* September 3, 1995; "Campbell Club Closes Its Door," *Owensboro Messenger-Inquirer,* December 23, 2017.

78. For information on Bowling Green industries, see "Industry Appreciation Week," *Bowling Green Park City Daily News,* October 12, 1997; "Fruit of the Loom and New Industries Adding to Economy," *Bowling Green Park City Daily News,* May 9, 1993; "Owensboro Still Third-Largest City," *Owensboro Messenger-Inquirer,* March 21, 2001; Southcentral Kentucky Community and Technical College, "Our History," n.d., at https://southcentral.kctcs.edu/about/our-history.

79. "New Railroaders Dream of Revitalized Shops," *Paducah Sun,* February 25, 1986; "P&L Sales Promises More Growth," *Paducah Sun,* September 6, 1988; "VMV, P&L Plan Public Stock Sale," *Paducah Sun,* August 2, 1990; "Paducah," *Louisville Courier-Journal,* August 17, 1992; "Carroll Is Giving Final Push to Local Projects," *Paducah Sun,* November 27, 1979.

80. John E. L. Robertson, *Paducah, Kentucky: A History* (Charleston, SC: History Press, 2016), 107; "In Harm's Way, but in the Dark," *Washington (DC) Post,* August 8, 1999; Bobbie Ann Mason, "Fall Out," *New Yorker,* January 10, 2000; "Operator to Cease Enrichment of Uranium," *New York Times,* May 25, 2013; "Slide," *Paducah Sun,* May 28, 2015.

81. "Blandford Unopposed Tuesday, but Faces Big Vote," *Owensboro Messenger-Inquirer,* November 4, 1979; "Clapp and Kenton Square Off," *Paducah Sun,* November 8, 1979; "Carroll, J. R. Miller Reportedly Involved in Legislative Races," *Louisville Courier-Journal,* November 16, 1979; "Legislative Posts Up for Grabs," *Owensboro Messenger-Inquirer,* November 20, 1979; "Clapp Unseated as Speaker Pro Tempore," *Paducah Sun,* November 20, 1979.

82. "The End Draws Nigh for Lobbyists' Row," *Louisville Courier-Journal,* November 23, 1981; "Brinkley Appears Ahead in Majority Leader Race," *Louisville Courier-Journal,* November 28, 1981; "House Democrats Pick Jim LeMaster to Lead Them at Legislature," *Louisville Courier-Journal,* December 1, 1981; "Helen Garrett's Tune Is Merrier This Session," *Paducah Sun,* January 6, 1982.

83. "Local Legislators Seeking Legislative Positions," *Owensboro Messenger-Inquirer*, January 4, 1983; "Blandford, Murphy Win Leadership Posts," *Owensboro Messenger-Inquirer*, January 5, 1983; "The Gentleman from Philpot," *Owensboro Messenger-Inquirer*, February 12, 1983.

84. "Legislators Expect No School Action," *Owensboro Messenger-Inquirer*, January 10, 1984; "Mood Shifts on Education Reform," *Owensboro Messenger-Inquirer*, January 19, 1984; "Collins Says Her Plan Requires 'Courage to Do What's Right,'" *Louisville Courier-Journal*, January 27, 1984; "Collins' Budget Draws Varied Responses," *Owensboro Messenger-Inquirer*, January 27, 1984; "Collins' Plan for Education Reform Earns High Marks," *Louisville Courier-Journal*, January 28, 1984; "Collins' Tax Plan Faltering in House, Democratic Leaders Say," *Louisville Courier-Journal*, March 14, 1984; "House Support Lags for Collins Tax Plan," *Owensboro Messenger-Inquirer*, March 20, 1984; "Collins Attacks State House," *Owensboro Messenger-Inquirer*, March 22, 1984; "Blame Should Be Shared in Package's Demise," *Louisville Courier-Journal*, March 22, 1984; Jewell and Miller, *The Kentucky Legislature*, 185–86; Donald J. Blandford, interviewed by the author, October 12, 2011, Kentucky Legislature Oral History Project, Nunn Center.

85. "Speaker's Job May Create Heated Battle," *Louisville Courier-Journal*, July 1, 1984; "Blandford Confident in His Bid for Speaker," *Owensboro Messenger-Inquirer*, November 12, 1984; Blandford, interviewed by the author, October 12, 2011; "Blandford Wins Speaker's Chair in State House," *Owensboro Messenger-Inquirer*, January 9, 1985; "House Democrats Oust Richardson in Favor of Blandford," *Louisville Courier-Journal*, January 9, 1985; "Blandford Ousts Richardson as House Speaker," *Bowling Green Park City Daily News*, January 9, 1985; "Young Turks Change Leadership, Get More Powerful Roles," *Louisville Courier-Journal*, January 13, 1985.

86. William E. Ellis, *A History of Education in Kentucky* (Lexington: University Press of Kentucky, 2011), 331–33; "Tax, Prison, Youth Issues Join Education on Agenda," *Louisville Courier-Journal*, July 6, 1985; "Fairness Demands Improved Schools, Collins Contends," *Louisville Courier-Journal*, July 9, 1985; "Collins Says Approval of Education Package Bodes Well for State," *Louisville Courier-Journal*, July 20, 1985.

87. "Gas Tax Prospects Dim as Special Session Nears," *Louisville Courier-Journal*, July 4, 1985; "Leaders Find No Clear Picture of How the Gasoline Tax Will Fare," *Louisville Courier-Journal*, July 12, 1985; "House Crushes Proposal to Raise Fuel Tax 5 Cents," *Louisville Courier-Journal*, July 13, 1985; "Independence Day Dawns in Frankfort," *Paducah Sun*, July 21, 1986; "Outlook for Gas Tax Is Good, Two Leaders Say," *Louisville Courier-Journal*, March 7, 1986; "Clapp Feels Falling Gas Prices Will Aid Fuel Tax Hike," *Paducah Sun*, March 7, 1986; "Speedy Vote Moves Gas-Tax Bill from Committee to House Floor," *Louisville Courier-Journal*, March 11, 1986; "Measure to Increase Gasoline Tax

Appears Ready for Passage," *Louisville Courier-Journal,* March 18, 1986; "House Passes Gasoline Tax," *Owensboro Messenger-Inquirer,* March 19, 1986.

88. "College Courses Outlined," *Owensboro Messenger-Inquirer,* June 28, 1984; "New College's Financing Speculated," *Owensboro Messenger-Inquirer,* September 23, 1984; "College Quest in High Gear," *Owensboro Messenger-Inquirer,* November 6, 1985; "OCC Heartened by Speaker Election," *Owensboro Messenger-Inquirer,* January 10, 1985; "Gov. Collins Boosts Higher Education in Area," *Owensboro Messenger-Inquirer,* January 22, 1986; Donald J. Blandford, interviewed by John Klee, February 28, 2007, Kentucky Community Colleges Project, Nunn Center.

89. "Western Kentucky Legislators Plan Caucus," *Bowling Green Park City Daily News,* June 5, 1986; "Owensboro Lawmakers Unsure about Caucus," *Owensboro Messenger-Inquirer,* June 6, 1986; "Western Kentucky Lawmakers Flex Their Political Muscle," *Paducah Sun,* June 29, 1986; "Caucus Has Already Succeeded," *Paducah Sun,* July 1, 1986; "Fear of Being Ignored Spawns Western Kentucky Caucus," *Louisville Courier-Journal,* July 7, 1986; "Forgy Says West Kentucky Contains 'Golden Diamond' for Industrial Development," *Paducah Sun,* July 10, 1986.

90. "Lawmakers Seek New Area Road Links," *Paducah Sun,* September 28, 1986; "Area Lawmakers Unite in Push for Better Roads," *Paducah Sun,* December 7, 1986.

91. "Western Influence Swayed Caucus Victory—Richards," *Paducah Sun,* January 7, 1987; "Democrats in State House Elect New Caucus Chairman," *Louisville Courier-Journal,* January 7, 1987; "Area Regaining Its Proper Place," *Paducah Sun,* January 9, 1987; "Woody Allen Not a Minor Character in House Ranks," *Owensboro Messenger-Inquirer,* January 11, 1987; "Our Area Regains Political Voice," *Paducah Sun,* October 21, 1987.

92. "District Support Came Just in Time," *Paducah Sun,* May 27, 1987; "Health Building Wins Budget Fight," *Paducah Sun,* March 30, 1988.

93. "Anti-lottery Force Aims at House Undecideds," *Owensboro Messenger-Inquirer,* February 23, 1988; "Lottery Bill in Trouble, Legislator Says," *Owensboro Messenger-Inquirer,* March 3, 1988; "Blandford Confident about Lottery Vote," *Owensboro Messenger-Inquirer,* March 4, 1988; "House Sets Friday Vote on Lottery," *Owensboro Messenger-Inquirer,* March 10, 1988; "House Votes to Put Lottery on Ballot," *Owensboro Messenger-Inquirer,* March 12, 1988; "Lottery Opponents Will Focus on Laws Implementing Lottery," *Paducah Sun,* November 9, 1988; Kentucky State Board of Elections, "1980–1989 Primary and General Election Results," at https://elect.ky.gov/; "Lottery Spending Plans Rejected," *Lexington Herald-Leader,* November 29, 1988.

94. "Court: Start Over on Schools," *Paducah Sun-Democrat,* June 7, 1989; "Kentucky Schools Unconstitutional," *Owensboro Messenger-Inquirer,* June 9,

1989; Ellis, *A History of Education in Kentucky,* 402–4; Miller, *Kentucky Politics and Government,* 251–55.

95. "Lawmakers Back to Education Drawing Board," *Owensboro Messenger-Inquirer,* June 8, 1989.

96. "Governor Urged to Try Honey, Not Vinegar," *Louisville Courier-Journal,* January 26, 1990; "'Gutter' Talk by Wilkinson Aide Decried," *Paducah Sun,* January 26, 1990; "Wilkinson Apologizes for Aide's Obscene Remark," *Louisville Courier-Journal,* January 27, 1990; "James Carville's Kentucky Strategy Recalled," *Louisville Courier-Journal,* July 15, 2012.

97. "Tax Compromise Good for Paducah," *Paducah Sun,* March 10, 1990; "Desire to Improve the State Led to 'Historic Day,'" *Louisville Courier-Journal,* March 11, 1990; Ellis, *A History of Education in Kentucky,* 407.

98. "Tax Plan Compromise Bodes Well for BG Projects," *Bowling Green Park City Daily News,* March 11, 1990; "Ballard Predicts Package Passage," *Madisonville Messenger,* March 15, 1990; "Area Projects Still Intact," *Owensboro Messenger-Inquirer,* March 21, 1990; "House Head Counts Bode Well for Reform, Tax Vote," *Louisville Courier-Journal,* March 16, 1990; "Education Supporters Get Projects as Opponents Are Criticized," *Bowling Green Park City Daily News,* March 20, 1990.

99. "10 Incumbents Defeated in State's Primary Voting," *Paducah Sun,* May 30, 1990; "Lackey Wins in Taxpayers' Revolt," *Paducah Sun,* May 30, 1990; "Issues, Garrett Campaign Gave Field to Leeper," *Paducah Sun,* May 31, 1990.

100. "Blandford Expects Easier Session Next Month with Jones as Governor," *Owensboro Messenger-Inquirer,* November 9, 1991; "Natcher Wants Daviess in 2nd," *Owensboro Messenger-Inquirer,* December 11, 1991; "Remap Plan Merging Two E. Kentucky Seats Passes," *Louisville Courier-Journal,* December 19, 1991; "Redrawing the Political Map," *Paducah Sun,* December 13, 1991; "Districts Reshaped," *Madisonville Messenger,* December 19, 1991; "Natcher Honored for Bridge Effort," *Owensboro Messenger-Inquirer,* December 13, 1993; Miller, *Kentucky Politics and Government,* 185.

101. Miller, *Kentucky Politics and Government,* 325–28; Al Cross and Tom Loftus, "Lies, Bribes, and Videotape," *State Legislatures,* July 1, 1993, at www.thefreelibrary.com.

102. "Blandford Seeks House Chair Again," *Owensboro Messenger-Inquirer,* November 7, 1992; "Attorneys: He Wants to Clear His Name," *Owensboro Messenger-Inquirer,* November 13, 1992; "Blandford Quits Speaker Race," *Louisville Courier-Journal,* November 26, 1992; "Blandford Made the Right Decision," *Owensboro Messenger-Inquirer,* November 29, 1992; "Prosecutors Deliver Video Bombshell," *Owensboro Messenger-Inquirer,* April 24, 1993; "'I Know What a Bribe Is,'" *Owensboro Messenger-Inquirer,* May 2, 1993;

"BOPTROT Casualties," *Kentucky Post* (Covington), August 7, 1995; "Anatomy of a Scandal," *Louisville Courier-Journal,* July 30, 1995; "Former Speaker in Halfway House," *Owensboro Messenger-Inquirer,* January 13, 1998; "Prisoner 34391–032," *Owensboro Messenger-Inquirer,* December 12, 1993; Al Cross to author, email, May 23, 2021 (quotation from Northrup).

103. "Delayed Deposits Caused Overdrafts, Hubbard Says," *Louisville Courier-Journal,* April 11, 1992; "Hubbards Reaping S & L Help, Barlow Says," *Paducah Sun,* April 25, 1992; "Carroll Hubbard: A Friend of Special Interest," *Louisville Courier-Journal,* May 17–18, 1992; "Hubbard, Opponents View Impact of House Scandals Differently," *Owensboro Messenger-Inquirer,* May 22, 1992; "Barlow Roars to Victory," *Paducah Sun,* May 27, 1992; "S&L, Check Scandals Turn Voters against Hubbard," *Paducah Sun,* May 27, 1992; "Experts: Don't Take Voters for Granted," *Owensboro Messenger-Inquirer,* May 28, 1992; "Barlow: Debates Let Voters Hear the Issues," *Paducah Sun,* November 4, 1992; "Hubbard Sentenced to 3 Years in Prison," *Owensboro Messenger-Inquirer,* November 10, 1994.

104. "Farm Goers Go for Gore," *Paducah Sun,* August 2, 1992; "Democrats Return to the Fold at Fancy Farm," *Owensboro Messenger-Inquirer,* August 2, 1992; "Kentucky Remains Top Bush, Clinton Priority," *Owensboro Messenger-Inquirer,* September 14, 1992; "Clinton Recalls JFK Visit," *Paducah Sun,* November 2, 1992; "Crowd Roars for Hoarse Clinton," *Owensboro Messenger-Inquirer,* November 3, 1992; "Stumbo: Clinton's Paducah Trip Crucial," *Bowling Green Park City Daily News,* November 4, 1992; "Big Kentucky Turnout Boosts Clinton," *Paducah Sun,* November 4, 1992; "Clinton Sweeps to Victory, Ends 12 Years of GOP Rule," *Owensboro Messenger-Inquirer,* November 4, 1992; Kentucky State Board of Elections, "1990–1999 Primary and General Election Results."

105. John David Parker, interviewed by the author, May 10, 2012, West Kentucky Politics Project, Nunn Center; "'He Always Tried to Do It Right,'" *Owensboro Messenger-Inquirer,* March 31, 1994; "Battle over Successor Heating Up," *Owensboro Messenger-Inquirer,* March 31, 1994; "Meeting Joe Prather," *Owensboro Messenger-Inquirer,* April 10, 1994; "Meet Ron Lewis," *Owensboro Messenger-Inquirer,* April 17, 1994; "GOP Victor Made Clinton His Opponent," *Louisville Courier-Journal,* May 25, 1994; "McConnell Stealth Helped Pick Off Prather," *Louisville Courier-Journal,* May 25, 1994; "GOP Revels in Lewis Win, Claiming Blow to Clinton," *Louisville Courier-Journal,* May 26, 1994; Al Cross, "Coming on Strong Down the Stretch: Republican Leaves Democrats in the Dust in Kentucky's 2nd District in 1994," in *Campaigns & Elections: Contemporary Case Studies,* ed. Michael A. Bailey, Ronald A. Faucheux. Paul S. Herrnson, and Clyde Wilcox (Washington, DC: Congressional Quarterly, 2000), 112–17.

106. "It's Barlow vs. Whitfield in November," *Paducah Sun,* May 25, 1994; "Republican Wins Natcher's Seat," *Owensboro Messenger-Inquirer,* May 25, 1994.

107. "Political Spice," *Paducah Sun,* August 7, 1994; "Politicians Disgust Small-Town America," *Paducah Sun,* November 1, 1994, reprinting the *Newsday* article.

108. "Democrats Stayed Home," *Madisonville Messenger,* November 9, 1994; "Whitfield Makes GOP History," *Paducah Sun,* November 9, 1994; "Whitfield, Lewis Wins Spark GOP Jubilation," *Louisville Courier-Journal,* November 9, 1994; "Balance of Power Shifts as Whitfield, Lewis Win," *Louisville Courier-Journal,* November 9, 1994.

109. "Voters Show Just How Mad They've Become," *Owensboro Messenger-Inquirer,* November 9, 1994; "Hogancamp's Big Win Arouses Vigor," *Paducah Sun,* November 9, 1994; "GOP Gains in General Assembly," *Owensboro Messenger-Inquirer,* November 9, 1994.

110. "Patton, Morris Win Here," *Owensboro Messenger-Inquirer,* November 8, 1995; "Yielding to the Extreme," *Lexington Herald Leader,* November 9, 1995; "Voters Went for Patton in a Big Way," *Owensboro Messenger-Inquirer,* November 9, 1995; "Forgy Cites Union, Black Turnout for Loss," *Louisville Courier-Journal,* November 10, 1995; "Democrats' Push for Patton Questioned," *Louisville Courier-Journal,* March 30, 1996; Forgy, interviewed by the author, January 15, 2011; "Marshall Native Terry Carmack Heads State GOP," *Paducah Sun,* May 26, 1993; "Financing Law Beats Forgy: McConnell," *Paducah Sun,* November 12, 1995; Al Cross to the author, email, June 5, 2021.

111. "The Next Wave Is Forming," *Paducah Sun,* November 8, 1995.

112. "Clinton Wins Narrow Victory in Kentucky," *Louisville Courier-Journal,* November 6, 1996; "Clinton Has No Coattails Here," *Owensboro Messenger-Inquirer,* November 6, 1996; "Trips to Area Pay Off for McConnell," *Paducah Sun,* November 6, 1996; "Election Shows Voters Are Tired of Both Political Parties," *Paducah Sun,* November 8, 1998; Kentucky State Board of Elections, "1990–1999 Primary and General Election Results."

113. "A Bush Victory Was Never in Doubt," *Louisville Courier-Journal,* November 8, 2000; "Bush Rolls through the Bluegrass State," *Lexington Herald-Leader,* November 8, 2000; Kentucky State Board of Elections, "Election Results, 2000–2009 and 2010–2019," https://elect.ky.gov/.

114. "Leeper to Join Republican Party," *Paducah Sun,* August 22, 1999; "Major Changes After GOP Takes KY House," *Louisville Courier-Journal,* November 9, 2016; "GOP Takes House after 95 Years of Democratic Control," *Lexington Herald Leader,* November 8, 2016; Robert Joseph "Bob" Leeper, interviewed by the author, December 8, 2015, Kentucky Legislature Oral

History Project, Nunn Center; "Kentucky House Flips, but Watkins, Coursey Survive," *Paducah Sun,* November 9, 2016; "Bevin to Stumbo: 'Good Riddance,'" *Bowling Green Park City Daily News,* November 9, 2016; "Democrats Blame Losing Majority on 'Long Coattails' of Trump Landslide in State," *Lexington Herald-Leader,* November 10, 2016.

115. Al Smith, "Fancy Farm Picnic Masks Political Changes," *Louisville Courier-Journal,* July 26, 1998.

Index

Topics in Kentucky History

James C. Klotter, Series Editor

Books in the Series

The Family Legacy of Henry Clay: In the Shadow of a Kentucky Patriarch
Lindsey Apple

Kentucky and the Great War: World War I on the Home Front
David J. Bettez

Our Rightful Place: A History of Women at the University of Kentucky, 1880–1945
Terry L. Birdwhistell and Deirdre A. Scaggs

George Keats of Kentucky: A Life
Lawrence M. Crutcher

Enid Yandell: Kentucky's Pioneer Sculptor
Juilee Decker

A History of Education in Kentucky
William E. Ellis

Madeline McDowell Breckinridge and the Battle for a New South
Melba Porter Hay

Committed to Victory: The Kentucky Home Front During World War II
Richard E. Holl

The Fall of Kentucky's Rock: Western Kentucky Democratic Politics since the New Deal
George G. Humphreys

Alben Barkley: A Life in Politics
James K. Libbey

Henry Watterson and the New South: The Politics of Empire, Free Trade, and Globalization
Daniel S. Margolies

Murder and Madness: The Myth of the Kentucky Tragedy
Matthew G. Schoenbachler

How Kentucky Became Southern: A Tale of Outlaws, Horse Thieves, Gamblers, and Breeders
Maryjean Wall

Madam Belle: Sex, Money, and Influence in a Southern Brothel
Maryjean Wall